Death before Sentencing

Death before Sentencing

Ending Rampant Suicide, Overdoses, Brutality, and Malpractice in America's Jails

ANDREW R. KLEIN
WITH JESSICA L. KLEIN

ROWMAN & LITTLEFIELD
Lanham • Boulder • New York • London

Published by Rowman & Littlefield
An imprint of The Rowman & Littlefield Publishing Group, Inc.
4501 Forbes Boulevard, Suite 200, Lanham, Maryland 20706
www.rowman.com

86-90 Paul Street, London EC2A 4NE, United Kingdom

British Library Cataloguing in Publication Information Available

Library of Congress Cataloging-in-Publication Information Available

ISBN 9781538162279 (cloth : alk. paper) | ISBN 9781538162286 (epub)

∞™ The paper used in this publication meets the minimum requirements of American National Standard for Information Sciences—Permanence of Paper for Printed Library Materials, ANSI/NISO Z39.48-1992.

This book is dedicated to the thousands who have died in the nation's jails and the local reporters and editors who have kept the scandal of their deaths front and center in their publications' pages and newscasts.

Contents

Introduction

American Jails: Capital Punishment First, Trial Second

The COVID-19 pandemic laid bare how deadly the nation's more than 3,150 local, county, and municipal jails are for those incarcerated in them. Infection rates in jails have been three times higher and the death rate double than outside them.[1]

But America's jails have a history of killing inmates that begins well before the coronavirus's origin. Even before COVID-19, jails killed more people every year than were executed for capital crimes in state prisons. Most who die in jails have not been convicted of the crime for which they have been jailed. Deaths behind bars are a direct result of correctional facilities' policies combined with abysmal, mostly for-profit medical providers; largely absent administrators; and unchecked brutality by jail deputies.

And years before Minneapolis police murdered George Floyd, inmates' families were suing jails on behalf of relatives whose last words were also "I can't breathe."

Jails have largely escaped scrutiny for deaths in their facilities for several reasons. First, the nation's jails are local affairs. Even repeat jail deaths warrant no more than limited local coverage at most. Jails are mostly run by sheriffs, often the most powerful and largely untouchable political figure in a local community. In Kentucky, although county jails are not run by sheriffs, like sheriffs, jailers are elected in each of the state's 120 counties, including

41 counties that don't have jails! Less than a quarter are appointed by and responsible to county governments.

Second, until Big Pharma and complicit doctors helped bring drug addiction to the white middle class, the families of deceased jail inmates did not have the resources to sue or socioeconomic clout to be heard demanding jail accountability for loved ones' deaths.

And lastly, before police murders of black men changed default assumptions about official versions of in-custody deaths, many understood jail deaths as occurring from "natural causes," the verdict medical examiners and coroners erroneously employ to allow those responsible for the deaths to escape any accountability.

A quick search for "jail death" on Google News on June 8, 2020, brought up the following: 1) "Estate of jail inmate sues over 2016 drug overdose death," Madison.com, 7 hours ago; 2) "He was punched in the face at Santa Rita Jail. He died 10 days later. His family wants answers," Berkeleyside, yesterday: 3) "North Dakota BCI investigating death of jail inmate in Rolette County," KFYR-TV, yesterday; 4) "Inmate's death at Elmore County Jail under investigation," WSFA, yesterday; 5) "Investigation underway after inmate death at Boyd County jail," *Huntington Herald Dispatch*, yesterday; 6) "Another Jefferson Parish jail inmate died by suicide last year after left unobserved, suit says," NOLA.com, 2 hours ago; 7) "Coroner rules Gulf War veteran's death at Santa Rita Jail a homicide," KTVU San Francisco, yesterday; 8) "Amid nationwide protests, group renews call for 'justice' in Shawnee man's death [in Pottawatomie County jail]," *Enid News & Eagle*, yesterday; 9) "Man dies at hospital days after apparent suicide attempt in Davis County Jail," *Standard-Examiner*, yesterday; and 10) "Jamel Floyd suffered 'permanent' injuries from metal in jail food prior to death: lawsuit," *Brooklyn Paper*, 1 hour ago.

To understand how American jails have become death traps, first it is important to understand the difference between a jail (which also may be called a "detention center," "house of correction," "lockup," even a "prison") and a state or federal prison (which may also be called a "penitentiary" or "correctional or penal institution"). Although people tend to use the term "jail" liberally (and sloppily) to refer to all correctional facilities, jails and state and federal prisons are quite distinct from one another. The latter get most of the attention because of the people housed within them, but the former get most of those incarcerated.

It's also worth noting the difference between a "detainee," held before trial, and an "inmate," a person actually convicted of a crime after pleading guilty, not contesting the charges brought against him or her, or being found guilty after a trial before a jury or before a judge alone. Most persons held in jails are detainees.

1

Jails versus Prisons

Before COVID-19, there were approximately 2 million people behind bars in the United States. Of those, more than half—1.17 million—were in state prisons, and another 738,400 were in county and locally run jails. Another much smaller number, 179,200, were in federal prisons. If viewed on a pie chart, the largest slice would represent people in state prisons.[1]

However, the pie chart, and the numbers it reflects, would be greatly misleading. While these numbers are accurate, they obscure the fact that in any given year, the number of people who spend time in jails vastly outnumber those in state (and federal) prisons. To understand why, one must appreciate the fact that prisons and jails serve very different functions. State prisons hold people who have been found guilty or admitted to committing crimes, typically classified as felonies. These crimes range from murder and rape to robbery, burglary, drug trafficking, and aggravated assaults, or repeat misdemeanor convictions for which offenders have received enhanced sentences. The average prison time served by these offenders, as opposed to the time they were sentenced to, was a little more than two and a half years in 2016.[2]

By contrast, most people in the nation's county or municipal jails are presumptively innocent, having neither been convicted of nor pleaded guilty to the crimes for which they have been charged. They are mostly in jail because they cannot afford even modest cash bails required to ensure they return to court for their trial. Only slightly more than a third of people in jail have been

convicted or have pleaded guilty to anything, usually a misdemeanor. Misdemeanor crimes range from vandalism and disorderly conduct to simple drug
possession and drunk driving. In half of the states, the maximum sentence
for a misdemeanor is no more than a year. Only a handful of states allow for
longer misdemeanor sentences, including eighteen months in Colorado and
up to two and a half years in Massachusetts.

Because most people held in jails are pretrial "detainees," they are usually
not there very long. They get out as soon as they raise their bail, or they are
released by the court usually at either arraignment, when they are officially
charged with a crime, or after trial if they are not convicted or sentenced to
jail or prison. Detainees on average spend only a couple of weeks in jail. Like
overall incarceration rates, pretrial detention rates vary considerably, ranging
from 395 per 100,000 in St. Louis to only 71 per 100,000 in New York City;
330 in Baltimore, Maryland, to 118 in Boston, Massachusetts; 174 in Sioux
Falls, South Dakota, to 53 in Manchester, New Hampshire. The Prison Policy
Initiative, after examining these data, called the varying rates "inexplicable,"
pointing out that they do not correspond to local crimes or violent crime
rates. They do respond, however, to the key criminal justice actors in each
jurisdiction: sheriffs, prosecutors, defense attorneys, magistrates, and judges.[3]

What this means is that in a year, while the state prisons population
remains mostly static, housing two million inmates, ten million people pass
through county and local jails. If these annual correctional populations were
captured on a pie chart, the largest piece would be jail, exceeding the slice
allotted for the prison population by more than five times. In three weeks,
jails have contact with as many people as prisons do in an entire year.

As the following chart indicates, the number jailed on any particular day
throughout a state is dwarfed by the number jailed during the course of the
entire year.

State	Jail Population as of One Day (2018)	Jail Population for Entire Year (2018)
Montana	1,800	18,000
Utah	5,700	32,000
Massachusetts	9,900	70,000
Alabama	13,000	90,000
Michigan	17,000	163,000
Ohio	19,000	150,000
Illinois	23,000	173,000

State	Jail Population as of One Day (2018)	Jail Population for Entire Year (2018)
New York	27,000	267,000
Georgia	39,000	236,000
Florida	53,000	350,000
Texas	55,000	505,000
California	82,000	368,000

Source: Prison Policy Initiative, 2018, https://www.prisonpolicy.org/profiles/AL.html.

There is another major difference between state prisons and jails. While states may have multiple prison facilities, each is part of a unified prison system administered by a single state agency, typically under a commissioner of corrections accountable to the governor and funded by state taxpayers. The nation's jails, by contrast, are run by county or local authorities. As a result, even within the same state, there is little central accounting of jails. How they are run, and who is dying within them, isn't monitored by a single authority. Locally elected county sheriffs run about 80 percent of jails. Unlike governors, they are far down the political food chain, largely ignored by national and state politicians, as well as the media. Further, in most counties, being elected sheriff has become a political sinecure. While sheriffs may work hard, they typically don't have to sweat reelections.

Because most jails are part of sheriffs' offices, jail security staffers are often referred to as "deputies," as opposed to "correctional officers." Both may also be referred to as "guards," although this term no longer accurately reflects their role in contemporary corrections. Beginning in 1973, after introduction by the Federal Bureau of Prisons, jails began implementing "direct supervision" of inmates to reduce violence and vandalism prevalent in jail. Most deputies or officers now mingle with inmates, no longer separated by barriers where they acted as sentry "guards." Notwithstanding these distinctions, the terms "deputies," "correctional officers," "guards," as well as "jailers," are often used interchangeably.

There is little uniformity across jails within the same state, much less across states. In Massachusetts, for example, there are only fourteen county jails, each run by an elected sheriff. However, in fiscal year 2018, the most recent year for which complete expenditure figures are available, the Barnstable County Sheriff's Department spent more than $83,000 per detainee. That was more than double neighboring Bristol County, where the sheriff's department spent just shy of $40,000 per detainee. Franklin County spent $8,566 per detainee on health services, but just to the south in Hampshire County, health services expenditures were 40 percent lower, at $5,050 per detainee. Meanwhile, Suffolk County (mostly Boston) spent $8,371 and Middlesex County, the largest in the state, spent $5,140. The differences across agencies are even larger when comparing program services, a category that includes education, job training, counseling, and reentry support. On a per-detainee basis, Franklin County, at $5,468 per detainee, spent six and a half times more on program services than Essex County at $831. Barnstable County spent $4,609,

---

Dauphin County, Pennsylvania, Jail

In July 2020, the family of Trelle Thomas filed a $35 million wrongful death suit against the Harrisburg police and county jail after Thomas died of a heart attack in the county jail where he was booked. Arrested for drug trafficking, Thomas "was found in possession of crack cocaine inside his mouth" while seated in his car, according to the arresting officer. Thomas collapsed within an hour of being placed in a cell at the booking center. Only after he suffered cardiac arrest did officers at the booking center take him to the hospital where he died three days later, the cocaine's white powder still visible on his lips. According to the lawsuit, the officers violated the department's policy by not taking Thomas directly to the hospital after observing he had ingested the drug. Officials at the booking center also failed to send Thomas to the hospital—until after he fell to the floor, hitting his head. Thomas was the fifth person to die after getting booked in the Dauphin County jail since 2019. His twin sister, Sherelle Thomas, asked, "How many more, especially Black civilians, must die due to a wrongful death before reform and justice will be served?" The suit also charged that both the city and county failed to train or supervise their employees.

Sources: C. Vendel, "Family files $35M suit, claims Harrisburg police took overdosing man to jail, not hospital," *Real-Time News*, July 10, 2020, https://www.pennlive.com/news/2020/07/family-files-35m-suit-claims-harrisburg-police-took-overdosing-man-to-jail-not-hospital.html; C. Vendel, "Harrisburg police took man who swallowed crack to jail but he 'should have received urgent medical care': mayor," *Real-Time News*, January 17, 2020, https://www.pennlive.com/news/2020/01/harrisburg-police-took-man-who-swallowed-crack-to-jail-but-he-should-have-received-urgent-medical-care-mayor.html.

three times more than Bristol County. Not surprisingly, the few who pay any attention to county jails lament that allowing a different elected sheriff in each county to run them creates "justice by geography."[4]

Nearly every county in California operates at least one long-term facility, with more than 115 such facilities statewide and more than 79,000 beds collectively. In addition, many counties operate several types of jails, including court holding facilities, temporary holding facilities, as well as long-term facilities.[5]

BOOKING VERSUS NONBOOKING JAILS

After an arrest, the suspect must be "booked" or processed before being released. During booking, a police officer or deputy typically takes the criminal suspect's personal information; records information about the alleged crime; performs a criminal record search, including checking for outstanding warrants; fingerprints, photographs, and searches the suspect; confiscates any personal property, and places the suspect in a police station holding cell or local jail. The officer may perform a full body search, along with a health screening to see if the suspect needs immediate care or presents a health threat to others in the jail. After booking for a minor offense, the suspect may be released after signing a citation promising to appear in court to answer the charges at a certain date. Otherwise, the suspect will be held in a booking jail or police lockup until trial or posting bail. After the defendant's first appearance in court, generally for an arraignment (a formal reading of the defendant's criminal charges and assignment of counsel if they have no attorney), the defendant may then be transferred to another jail or released by the court.

Among jails, there are "booking" and "nonbooking" jails. The former includes people who have been arrested and taken directly to jail where they are processed for their first court appearance. The latter includes people who have been arrested but are not transported to jail until they are booked in a police lockup or alternative facility and then arraigned in court.

Where people are booked can also determine where they die.

POLICE LOCKUPS

Like county jails, police lockups may hold people until the court either releases them or orders them held in county or municipal jails. Oregon statute, for example, defines "lockup" as a facility for the temporary detention of arrested people held up to thirty-six hours, excluding holidays, Saturdays, and Sundays, though their time in lockup must not exceed ninety-six hours post-booking. This differs from what the statute calls a "local correction facility," which it defines as "a jail or prison for the reception and confinement of prisoners that is provided, maintained and operated by a county or city and holds people for more than 36 hours." Those operated by cities are generally referred to as "municipal jails."

In Massachusetts, once arrested, people are held in local police lockups maintained by each police department, usually in or next to the police station. They remain there unless released by a bail commissioner or until police transport them to court for arraignment. So if a person is arrested Friday afternoon and his or her paperwork is not completed before the lower criminal courts (called District Courts in Massachusetts) close for day, that person may be held until Monday morning when court opens (or Tuesday if Monday happens to be a holiday). However, many arrestees may be released before court convenes by a bail commissioner for a slight fee and/or cash bail or their promise to go to court when it next opens. Once at court, if a judge imposes a bail that they cannot raise or if held for preventive detention after a judge finds the defendants constitute a danger, the detainees will then be transported to a county jail.

But there is an exception, indicating again how varied the system can be even within the same state. In 2020, the Middlesex County sheriff, Peter Koutoujian, generously agreed to open his jail facility to arrestees before they went to court. Unlike the local police lockups, the county jail had the medical staff to provide care for the many arrestees withdrawing from drugs and alcohol.

Although people are not held in police lockups for very long, lockup staffs are still required to provide for the welfare of their residents just like jail staffs, only they must do so with far fewer resources. This means most police departments must rely on medical institutions in the community to provide health care when needed. But those institutions can only provide care if police bring detainees to them. In 2017, for example, Westland, Michigan, police arrested William Marshall for a driving violation and drug possession. He complained of a medical problem and went into convulsions at the jail. By the time he was taken to the hospital, he had died. According to the police complaint, during the traffic stop, Marshall swallowed a small plastic baggie of cocaine. Arresting officers recovered some from his mouth and placed it in an evidence bag. In a subsequent investigation by Michigan State Police and the county's prosecutor, the arresting officers indicated that they told an officer supervising the jail about Marshall's ingestion of cocaine. In a suit later brought by the Marshall family, the attorney charged that the jail did not follow its policy that officers were to contact EMTs or take arrestees to the hospital when they faced possible danger of an overdose. EMTs did arrive at the scene ninety minutes after Marshall's admission but were too late to save him. Because Marshall had been held in a municipal jail run by the Westland, Michigan, Police Department, the city, not the county or state, eventually had to pay out $3.75 million to settle the wrongful death suit brought by Marshall's estate. The twenty-four-year police veteran assigned to the jail that night, who was subsequently fired, complained he was scapegoated for the death.[6]

About a third of local police departments, those in cities with a population of at least 10,000, operate at least one temporary lockup facility for adults separate from a county jail. Most with populations of less than 2,500 operate none.[7]

Tulsa, Oklahoma, Jail

The city opened its own municipal jail in 2017 to save money, so local police would not have to transport arrestees to the county jail. The jail is open 24/7, including holidays, and is managed by the Tulsa City Police Department with a staff of twenty-five detention officers, a manager, and a police sergeant. The facility has beds for twenty-five males and five females, interview rooms for attorneys, and other facilities. The jail can hold prisoners up to ten days pursuant to state standards. The City of Tulsa has an agreement with the Okmulgee County Criminal Justice Authority to be used for overflow capacity and for the occasional municipal sentence longer than ten days.

Junction City, Oregon, Jail

The city police department municipal jail has just two 8' by 12' cells, each with two beds. It houses inmates convicted of misdemeanor crimes committed within the city limits up to one year. According to its website, the municipal jail holds 1.9 inmates a day.

Irving City, Texas, Jail

The city jail is limited to "the temporary confinement of pretrial individuals involved in the judicial process, as well as those individuals serving time assessed on misdemeanor Irving Municipal Court cases." The jail has a maximum capacity of 172 adults.

MUNICIPAL JAILS

Some states also have municipal jails, limited jurisdiction facilities for people convicted of things likes city ordinance violations or petty crimes tried in separate municipal courts. They're the lowest tier of criminal courts in the states that have them. Municipal jails vary widely as revealed by their websites.

TRIBAL JAILS

There are more than ninety tribal jails located on reservations and pueblos. Three-quarters are run by tribes and a quarter by the U.S. Bureau of Indian Affairs. The jurisdiction of tribal police forces is limited, so tribal jails hold those arrested or convicted of lesser offenses. Major offenders are sentenced in federal courts to federal prisons.

PRIVATE PRISONS

There are also a number of private prisons throughout the county run by for-profit companies. The majority of these house immigrants or sentenced offenders who would otherwise be held in state or federal prisons, not county or municipal jails. There are, however, a few county and municipal jails run by private companies scattered throughout the country, especially across Texas. The Jack Harwell Detention Center in Waco, Texas, for example, is run by LaSalle Corrections. GEO Group–owned CEC runs short-term jail facilities in Dallas and Houston. GEO also runs jails in California, including the Alhambra Jail for the City of Alhambra, the Fontana City Jail, the Ontario City Jail, and the Garden Grove City Jail. CoreCivic runs the Marion County Jail for the County Sheriff's Department in Indianapolis, Indiana.

Under the Obama Administration, a 2016 memo ordered the Justice Department to reduce the use of private prisons after a Justice report revealed private prisons had higher rates of contraband, violence, and use of force than public prisons. This directive, coupled with declining incarceration numbers, led many who opposed private prisons to believe that economic realities would lead to the facilities going out of business. But in 2017, then attorney general Jeff Sessions rescinded that memo. The Trump administration went on to embrace the use of private detention facilities, in part to facilitate its family separation policy for immigrant detainees. Private county and municipal jails got a new lease on life.

2

A Step Back

How America Invented Prisons

When Alexis de Tocqueville came to the United States in 1831, it was not with the intent to do research for his subsequent book *Democracy in America* (1835). He came to examine firsthand America's novel and innovative prisons and penitentiaries. The modern penitentiary was conceived in Benjamin Franklin's living room in the 1780s. At a salon Franklin hosted, attendees, including the physician Benjamin Rush, read a Quaker-inspired pamphlet detailing a "house of repentance," in which criminals would (ideally) benefit from the solitude imposed by incarceration rather than suffer from the humiliation brought by widely used public punishments of the time, like the stocks and gallows.

The result? The Eastern State Penitentiary, which opened in 1829 in Philadelphia. To this day, it's considered a model for numerous prisons built after its design (a circular, or radial, floor plan, not unlike a panopticon). The idea behind the penitentiary was that in complete isolation (prisoners were escorted blindfolded to and from their cells), the corrupting influence of other people would be removed, and the inmates would get closer to God. It may have worked if only pious Quakers were imprisoned. However, for many, the absolute isolation led to madness and despair.

Perhaps an omen of things to come, the first detainee in the new penitentiary was Charles Williams, described as having "light black skin." He received a two-year sentence "with labor" for stealing a watch, a gold seal, and a gold key.

The next iteration in correctional innovation occurred in New York with the construction of Auburn State Prison. The New York reformers rejected the isolation of the penitentiaries as cruel and inhumane. Also, they found them to be expensive. Although the Pennsylvania cells had workbenches for inmates to do piecework, their labor did not begin to cover the costs of their imprisonment. The New York prison substituted work outside the cells for quiet reflection within them. Armed with whips, guards could efficiently supervise work crews. Auburn turned a profit.

Ironically, labor became an even more important component of incarceration with passage of the Thirteenth Amendment outlawing slavery following the U.S. Civil War. The amendment has a loophole, prohibiting servitude except "as a punishment for crime whereof the party shall have been duly convicted." With slavery no longer legal, many states and counties came to rely on this constitutional loophole to both extract free convict labor and keep former slaves from realizing their rights as citizens.

Prison labor provided the means to help rebuild the country after the Civil War, and African Americans provided a disproportionate means to help fill the prisons. Arresting African Americans "en masse ... for extremely minor crimes like loitering or vagrancy" accomplished both of these goals, as described by author and civil rights advocate Michelle Alexander in the documentary film *The 13th.*[1] Their free labor powered the economy, and racist propaganda (like the 1915 film *The Birth of a Nation*, portraying black men as dangerous, particularly to white women, and glorifying the Ku Klux Klan) powered their arrests.

As inmates became the new slaves, law enforcement, especially Southern sheriffs, took over the role of slave owners.[2] Sheriffs were empowered to arrest black people for nearly anything, including congregating in public, being out at night, or being unemployed. Sheriffs then leased their black prisoners as laborers to continue an economy based on slavery. The sheriffs also helped to ensure the labor movement would not make headway by supplying inmates as strike breakers.

In North Carolina, for example, legislators increased the penalties for minor crimes, making them felonies so that inmate chain gangs could be assigned to build state roads when the county road system was deemed insufficient for the state's transportation needs. Corrections was contained in public works departments, in fact, until the state created its first Department of Corrections in 1960.

Sheriffs' powers were nurtured and expanded to promote pro-segregation Southern leaders, affording resources to defy federal efforts to enforce civil rights laws and voting rights through the twentieth century. In the 1960s, many sheriffs were members of the KKK, including the notorious Sheriff Jim Clark of Dallas County, Alabama, who led the police in the assault of John Lewis and other peaceful demonstrators at the Pettus Bridge in 1965. More recently, the overt racism of these sheriffs found expression in the Christian Identity movement. As Minister William Potter Gale explained, "The Constitution was a divinely inspired document intended to elevate whites above Jews and racial minorities."[3] Later, this movement morphed into the Constitutional Sheriffs movement, a right-wing organization whose members include many of the sheriffs overseeing many of the jails highlighted in the following pages.

This appeal to white Southerners to subjugate blacks through the criminal justice system was a deliberate political move carried out first by Democrats and then perpetuated by Republicans in the race to appear more tough on crime than rival political candidates. In *The 13th*, activist and philosopher Angela Davis describes how politicians used coded language to attract white Southerners to the Republican Party, with words like "crime" and "criminals" standing in for black activism and the civil rights movement. The "war on drugs," which Nixon began in the 1960s, served as a politically acceptable way to perpetuate a war against Nixon's opponents—the "antiwar left and black people"—according to his advisor John Ehrlichman.

"We knew we couldn't make it illegal to be either against the war or Black," Ehrlichman went on, describing the 1968 Nixon campaign's big push to crack down on, supposedly, drugs. "But by getting the public to associate the hippies with marijuana and Blacks with heroin, and then criminalizing both heavily, we could disrupt those communities. We could arrest their leaders, raid their homes, break up their meetings, and vilify them night after night on the evening news. Did we know we were lying about the drugs? Of course we did."[4]

Following Nixon, President Ronald Reagan adopted an even more severe stance on drugs, waging the "war" in primarily black neighborhoods where crack ran rampant, the possession, use, and sale of which carried much more severe sentences than that for the powdered cocaine more prevalent in white neighborhoods. Reagan announced that spending for law enforcement related to drugs would triple during his presidency, further perpetuating a tough on crime trend that jails are still grappling with to this day.

Jails and Prisons Today

THE NUMBERS

The U.S. Department of Justice Bureau of Justice Statistics (BJS) last report on U.S. jail populations came out in March 2020 but only covered up through 2018.[1] The data are based on a nationally representative survey of all county and city jail jurisdictions and all regional jails in the country. The states with unitary state and local correctional systems—Alaska, Connecticut, Delaware, Hawaii, Rhode Island, and Vermont—are not included, although fifteen locally operated jails in Alaska are. Most of the jurisdictions maintain a single institution, but some maintain multiple jail facilities, like Allegheny County in Pennsylvania, which encompasses Pittsburgh and maintains four jail facilities. The BJS report aggregates data by each jurisdiction. Based on its survey, BJS estimated that there were approximately 2,851 jail jurisdictions across the country, with approximately 3,200 jail facilities.

At midyear 2018, a third of people in jails, 248,500, were sentenced or awaiting sentencing after conviction, while two-thirds, 490,000, were awaiting court action on a pending charge or for other reasons, mostly inability to raise cash bail required to be released pending trial. Inmates spent an average of about twenty-five days in jail in 2018. Even though the midterm jail census sat at a little under three-quarters of a million, the total number of admissions in 2018 for all jails was almost eleven million, 10,700,000. Every week, 55 percent of the jail population turned over. The bigger jails held people more than twice as long as the smaller jails (thirty-four vs. fifteen days), probably reflecting much busier court schedules delaying trials and court hearings.

While major urban jails had reduced their populations even before COVID-19, dropping 18 percent from 2013 to 2019, the population of the nation's 3,100-plus jails overall increased. It went up 27 percent in rural counties and 7 percent in small to midsize cities. Incarceration rates rose for whites by 12 percent and declined for blacks by 28 percent and for Hispanics by 33 percent. Despite the decrease, black people were still jailed at exceptionally high rates—at 592 per 100,000, as opposed to 182 for Hispanics and 187 for whites. The rate is also high for Indigenous Americans and Native Alaskans, at 401 per 100,000. Although the male incarceration rate dropped slightly over the past decade and the rate rose for women, for men, it is 397 per 100,000 and, for women, 69 per 100,000. In 2018, half of jail inmates were white (368,500), a third were black (242,300), and 15 percent were Hispanic (109,300). In addition, there were 9,700 American Indians and Alaskan Natives, 4,600 Asians, and 3,900 listed as "other," including Pacific Islanders, Native Hawaiians, or persons of mixed races.

The increasing number of jailed women, 115,000, is particularly concerning as "more and more are arriving in need of medical attention or with debilitating health conditions that strain the capacity of lockups typically designed for men. Thousands arrive pregnant each year. Most suffer from mental illness—at far higher rates than their male counterparts—and they're more likely to experience drug and alcohol addiction."[2]

The jailed population is not distributed evenly across the country or within states. On an average day, a little more than a third of the nation's jail jurisdictions hold only 50 people, while 28 percent hold 2,500 or more. The country's largest jails holding people from its largest cities hold nearly 20 percent of all those jailed.

BJS estimates that the nation's jails employed almost a quarter million full time, 80 percent of them correctional officers who spend the majority of their time with inmates. Most officers are male (69 percent), and the inmate to correctional officer ratio is 4.2 to 1 nationally. In contrast, the majority of noncorrectional officer jail staffs (565) are female.

COVID-19 JAIL EXODUS

These numbers all changed radically during the spring and summer of 2020, when prisons and jails scrambled to downsize to prevent COVID-19 infections. Jails began releasing detainees in March 2020. In Pennsylvania, for example, by mid-April, the Allegheny County (Pittsburgh) Jail released 912 individuals, Bucks County Jail 250, Montgomery County Jail 468, Northumberland Jail 60, and Philadelphia more than 300. In Michigan, Wayne County (Detroit) Jail released 384, and the Dallas County Jail in Texas released about 1,000. By May, jails across Oregon had slashed their populations almost 50 percent. The reductions allowed many Oregon jails to limit one person to each cell. According to the Bureau of Justice Statistics, between March and June 2020, about 208,500 detainees received expedited release. By June 2020, occupied bed space in jails dropped from 81 percent in midyear 2019 to 60 percent. People held for misdemeanors dropped by 45 percent, felonies by 18 percent.[3]

In addition, many courts and police departments began reducing the number of new admissions. Police stopped arresting people for minor crimes, and the courts released more people on their personal promise to return, not imposing cash bails. The Fresno, California, sheriff, for example, complained in April that the state had ordered a "get out of jail free" card by ordering zero bail for most criminal charges. His jail released 131, and another 297 were released after the state's chief justice recommended that detainees within thirty days or less of their sentence remaining be released early. Similarly, in the Clarke County Jail, judges released 530 by altering the terms of their bail since the state Supreme Court declared a judicial emergency on March 13, putting a halt to most proceedings except bond hearings.

Jails	2017 Census	Spring 2020 Census
Los Angeles, CA	19,836	12,000
Rikers Island, New York City, NY	13,849	3,855
Harris County (Houston), TX	10,000	8,000
Cook County (Chicago), IL	9,900	4,567
Maricopa County (Phoenix), AZ	9,265	4,500
Curran-Fromhold (Philadelphia), PA	8,811	3,935
Metro West (Miami), FL	7,050	3,209

Whether these numbers represent the beginning of a new trend or merely a blip remains to be seen. After the initial COVID-related releases, many jails began to refill. The population of the Cuyahoga County Jail in Cleveland, Ohio, for example, rose from 900 in March 2020 to 1,511 in September (still below its average 2015 population of 2,168). The population of Cook County Jail in Chicago also rose, to 5,518 by November 2020.[4] By December 2020, the Los Angeles County Jail population was up to 15,427, the Rikers population had risen to 4,805, and the Harris County Jail population had increased to 8,790.[5] By March 2021, Rikers population rose again to 5,500.[6] The Harris County Jail population also inched up to 8,790 by 2020.[7] Despite drops in Dallas and Travis, by 2021, Texas's statewide jail population was about what it was before the pandemic.[8]

The sad fact remains, however, that even at their lowest levels, detainees were still dying in record numbers in the nation's jails, including detainees not infected with the coronavirus. A report by Disability Rights Oregon, for example, released in February 2021, documented that despite a drop in jail populations across that state, the number of people dying in the state's jails *increased* between January and October 2020. The leading cause remained suicides, not COVID infections.[9]

Another search of "jail death" on Google News on October 19, 2020, during the initial peak of the pandemic featured nine jail death stories. They included: (1) "Outajamie County Jail inmate dies after medical emergency," *Post-Crescent*, Appleton, Wisconsin; (2) "Inmate found dead in OTC [Otter Tail County] jail identified," *Valley News*, Fergus Falls, Minnesota; (3) "East Bay Sheriff's Office investigating apparent suicide at county jail," *East Bay Times*, Richmond, California; (4) "Linn County jail death blamed on 'medical episode,'" KIMT 3, Cedar Rapids, Iowa; (5) "Man died after catching COVID-19 in Durham jail, Why didn't the county or state say so?" *News & Observer*, Raleigh, North Carolina; (6) "Authorities investigating death of an inmate at the Kossuth County Jail," *Explore Okoboji*, Algona, Iowa; (7) "Texas Rangers, Starr Co. sheriff's office investigating death in county jail," *Monitor*, McAllen, Texas; (8) "After two recent inmate suicides, Delaware County Jail changing ventilation grates," *Columbus Dispatch*, Columbus, Ohio; and (9) "Sullivan County man fatally stabbed in Marion County Jail," WBIW, Indianapolis, Indiana.

4

How Did America Become the World's Biggest Jailer?

While America represents 4.4 percent of the world's population, it holds 21 percent of the world's prisoners. As of 2018, the United States had the highest documented incarceration rate in the world, at 698 per 100,000 people. In comparison, Canada imprisons 114 per 100,000, United Kingdom 139, France 102, and Denmark 59.[1]

The U.S. national rate does not reveal the wide variations among states. Oklahoma, for instance, incarcerates 1,079 per 100,000 compared to 487 per 100,000 in Hawaii.[2] And statewide jail rates do not account for variations among jails within the same state. The following chart compares a sample of Texas and Florida populations in 2020.[3]

Texas County	Jail (Daily) Population 11/1/2020	Rate per 100,000	Florida County	Jail Daily Population 9/2020 (Average)	Rate per 100,000
Armstrong	2	105	Palm Beach	1,588	110
Travis (Austin)	1,841	142	Miami/Dade	3,585	130
Harris (Houston)	8,632	183	Hillsborough (Tampa)	2,357	160
Tarrant (Ft Worth)	4,167	198	Orange (Orlando)	2,497	180
Dallas	5,497	208	Sarasota	896	210
Galveston	836	244	Leon (Tallahassee)	936	310
Nueces	965	266	Duval (Jacksonville)	3,290	340
El Paso	2,302	274	Citrus	656	440
Nacogdoches	261	400	Baker	465	1,650

CASH BAIL AND BAIL BONDSPERSONS

While defendants can be held in jail before trial in some states because they have been found to constitute a danger to specific victims or the community, most defendants are held because they are poor. They can't afford to pay a cash bail imposed by the court. The cash bail system is exclusive to the United States and its former colony the Philippines. If the defendant pays the bail assessed, he or she walks and gets the bail back when they return to court. If the person cannot pay the bail, he or she is incarcerated. The words "bail" and "bond" are often used interchangeably. But bail is the money that a defendant must pay to get out of jail. A bond is posted on a defendant's behalf, usually by a bail bond company, to pay for the defendant's release.

In most states, bail bond agents will guarantee a defendant's bail bond, but the defendant must pay 10 percent of the assessment to the agent. That's the bond agent's fee, which the defendant doesn't get back. In turn, the bond agent guarantees the full bail on behalf of the defendant and assumes the risk of its loss if the defendant fails to return to court. Laws governing bail bonds vary by state. Bond agents generally maintain standing security agreements with local courts, under which they post irrevocable "blanket" bonds to be paid if the defendant for whom they are providing surety fails to appear in court. Arrangements with insurance companies, banks, or other credit providers enable bond agents to draw on such security outside normal business hours, eliminating the need to deposit cash or property with the court every time a new defendant is arrested and eligible to be bailed out.

The courts have come to increasingly rely on cash bails for defendants' release. The overall share of defendants required to post bail to avoid pretrial detention increased from a little over half in 1990 to almost three-quarters in 2009, while the share of defendants released without bail dropped by 15 percentage points. The share of defendants who were denied bail decreased slightly during this period, but those jailed because they could not afford to pay it increased by 6 percentage points.[4]

Even at 10 percent, the bond fee is too much for many defendants. As of November 2020, according to the nonprofit Chicago Appleseed Fund for Justice, 529 persons were in the Cook County Jail because they could not afford to post $5,000 or less in bond themselves or 10 percent of that amount to a bondsperson.[5] In Dallas County, the lowest recommended bail is $1,500, ensuring many arrestees will remain behind bars before trial. The statewide average for pretrial detention is twenty-one days, but it goes up to sixty-eight for those charged with felonies, for example, in Houston. As of February 1, 2016, persons awaiting trial constituted 62 percent of that state's jail population, or 40,300 detainees. Cash bails are the root of Louisiana's tremendously high pretrial jail rate. While the median annual income in the state is only $27,027, the median bail set for detainees locked away in jail is $24,000.[6] It is less in Harris County, Texas, but at an average of almost $3,000 for misdemeanors, it is still prohibitive for many.[7]

Most pretrial detainees who are jailed because they cannot buy their way out end up being low-risk defendants, while many high-risk defendants

---

East Baton Rouge Parish Jail

Marcus Morris, 61, had a history of homelessness, mental illness, and "extensive medical problems" when police arrested him and booked him in jail in December 2020. Morris was unable to raise bail for charges stemming from his failure to appear in court for multiple minor offenses over the previous months, including public drinking, urinating in public, theft, and simple battery. Unable to pay a $5,800 bond, he remained in jail for five weeks until he died in his cell from seizures. After his death, the mayor promised to replace the jail's medical provider, CorrectHealth, long criticized for the quality of its detainee care.

Arriba County, New Mexico, Jail

Juan Archuleta's body was found in his cell, the day after he was jailed for not showing up to court after receiving a public drinking ticket. A judge imposed a $500 bond, which Archuleta could not pay. Supposed to provide a reason for monetary assessments, the judge provided none. Although the sheriff's office said no foul play was suspected in the death, Archuleta's mother took photographs of his body, which showed bruises and multiple cuts.

Sources: L. Skene, "Baton Rouge jail inmate, locked up for failure to appear in court, dies in hospital," *Advocate*, December 8, 2020, https://www.theadvocate.com/baton_rouge/news/crime_police/article_f5f8113c-38cb-11eb-966f-bfbb3d3978c3.html; T. Lopez, "Mother wants answers after son found dead in New Mexico jail," KOB4 Eyewitness News, December 10, 2020, https://www.kob.com/new-mexico-news/mother-wants-answers-after-son-found-dead-in-new-mexico-jail/5948457/.

(those most likely to harm) can pay and get released.[8] According to the American Bar Association, at any given time, half a million people are in jail because they can't pay bail before trial.[9]

While most people held awaiting trial spend only several weeks in jail, others can spend months, even years in jail awaiting trial. In 2021, for example, in thirty-two California counties that supplied data, 5,796 had been jailed more than a year awaiting trial. Most of these detainees were people of color. While black people make up 5 percent of San Francisco's population, for example, 50 percent of inmates held more than a year awaiting trial were black.[10] Studies suggest that racial bias plays a big role in bail assignments. Compared to white defendants, black defendants are more likely to be assigned bail and on average receive bail amounts that are about $10,000 higher.[11] Studies have

---

Cuyahoga County, Ohio, Jail

After a number of jail deaths and related criminal convictions against jail administrators and staff, the county hired consultants to analyze the jail's population. They looked at all detainees booked between May and November 2019 and found one-third had serious mental illness or substance abuse problems. On average, those inmates stayed in jail 77 percent longer than other detainees, averaging 39 rather than 22 days. A quarter of those charged with felonies who could not afford bail stayed in jail an average of 104 days. Overall, the average length of stay for the entire population of the county's jails and detention center was 30 days, but the average length for the population suffering from mental health issues was 117 days.

Harris County, Texas, Jail

Among the 8,790 inmates in the jail in 2020, the average stay was 209 days. One reason for this length of stay was that the bond amount for 58 percent of the 7,553 pretrial detainees was greater than $10,000. Half were black, non-Hispanic; 16 percent Hispanic; and 33 percent white, non-Hispanic. Eleven percent were homeless, 68 percent had an indicator of mental illness, and 35 percent were receiving psychotropic medication.

Sources: Criminal Justice System Assessment, Cuyahoga County, Criminal Justice Center Master Plan, August 7, 2019, presentation PowerPoints, PMC & DLR Group; Harris County, Texas, "Jail population statistics," https://charts.hctx.net/jailpop/App/JailPopCurrent, downloaded December 7, 2020.

also found that detained persons suffering from substance abuse or mental disorders spend more time in jails because they are less able to raise funds for release. This also increases the health vulnerability of jail populations.

One of the reasons many prosecutors oppose bail reform is because being incarcerated pending trial also increases the likelihood that defendants will agree to plead guilty to expedite release even if they are not guilty. Mothers want to get home for their children. Employees want to keep their jobs. Even if they are not guilty, many find the quickest way to get out of jail is to admit guilt.[12] Advocates have long opposed cash bails. In 2014, New Jersey became the first state to move away from them. The state eliminated cash bail for most crimes and established nonmonetary bail alternatives for release. In the first year of the law, the state's pretrial jail population fell by 20 percent.[13] California followed by eliminating cash bail in 2018, substituting a pretrial assessment of whether the defendant might flee or reoffend for those charged with felonies. But the multibillion-dollar bail industry, which represents some 2,500 bail agents in that state, got a referendum put on the 2020 ballot, and the law was repealed by voters.

As of June 2020, state bail reform laws were limited at best. Alaska had eliminated it, but a new Republican governor rolled back the reform a few months later. Implementation of bail reform in New York in January 2020 initially resulted in a 40 percent decline in pretrial jailing. But three months into the reform, after a firestorm of criticism caused by sensational media coverage stoked by resistance from prosecutors and police, the state amended the reforms to reimpose cash bail for more offenses. Researchers predicted the new revisions will increase New York City's pretrial jail population by 16 percent.[14]

DEINSTITUTIONALIZATION

Whether or not the United States continues to lock up more people than almost any other country in the world, who it locks up has remained and will likely remain consistent.

The best data come from a couple sources, including a National Association of Counties survey completed in 2015, which it combined with earlier BJS reports. It revealed a very fragile population, physically and mentally. Forty percent had a chronic medical condition, with high blood pressure/hypertension as the most common.[15]A third of these were receiving medical

Benton County, Washington, Jail[·]

Marc Moreno struggled with mental illness throughout his short life. In 2016, after his most recent psychosis emerged, his family took him to the Lourdes Hospital. The hospital discharged him after a few days. Its associated counseling center refused to admit him, directing the family to take him to the Benton County Crisis Response Unit, which they did. Moreno was still delusional when he began hitting himself in the face, and someone at the crisis unit called the police (even though, ironically, this unit typically receives people undergoing mental crises brought to them by police). When officers learned Moreno had been discharged from Lourdes Hospital a few days earlier, they didn't have "many options," according to a Kennewick Police lieutenant. When a computer search revealed that Moreno had old warrants lodged against him for driving with a suspended license and failing to transfer a vehicle title on time, the officers booked him into the county jail. At the jail intake, Moreno, who had been diagnosed as bipolar and schizophrenic, made suicidal statements, so he was placed in a "safety cell," a padded cell with no toilet, bed, or sink. A jail social worker interviewed him through the closed cell door, noting he demonstrated "bizarre and illogical behaviors with evidence of mania and psychosis," but no treatment or referrals for treatment were made. He died eight days later of dehydration and arrhythmia, naked and covered in his own excrement on a cell floor. He was thirty-eight pounds lighter than when he entered the jail eight days earlier and was eighteen years old when he died. Subsequently, the county medical examiner's office ruled he died from accidental asphyxiation with acute methamphetamine intoxications as a contributing factor.

Kalamazoo County, Michigan, Jail

Held on $100,000 bail after setting a fire in the mental ward of a hospital, Chase Lovell, 29, was held in the Kalamazoo, Michigan, jail. Diagnosed with bipolar disorder and believed to have schizoaffective disorder, he had been sent to the hospital because he said he'd heard voices encouraging him to commit suicide. Jailed, he was able to do so the second day when left unchecked for two hours. The sheriff's investigation found no wrongdoing on the part of the jailers, but the family announced it was suing for jailers deliberately ignoring Lovell's condition.

Charleston County, South Carolina, Jail

Palmetto Lowcountry Behavioral Health, an inpatient facility, called the cops on Jamal Sutherland, 31, when a fight broke out between patients.

Sutherland, diagnosed with bipolar disorder and schizophrenia in his teens, received regular treatment at the facility. His parents voluntarily checked him in for treatment when his symptoms surfaced. They had brought him there in November and again in January when he heard voices and became paranoid. According to the incident report, Sutherland was not involved in the initial scuffle between two patients but became agitated, damaged property, and then tackled a staff member. Responding police arrested him for assault and battery and took him to the Charleston County Jail. The next morning, he was dead. The lawyer for the family found that jailers had used a stun gun six times and pepper sprayed him before he died. The sheriff's office promised to be transparent about the death . . . but only after the State Law Enforcement Division completed an investigation. Subsequently, a suppressed jail video was released, described as "horrifying," suggesting that the death was, in fact, "murder." The coroner, however, attributed the death to an "excited state with adverse pharmacotherapeutic effect during subdual process." Nonetheless, Charleston County approved a $10 million settlement. Said a councilman, "I am so happy that it was a unanimous decision to do what is right." In May 2021, two more people died in the jail.

Sources: L. Kamp, "An Eastern Washington teen went to a mental health clinic for help. Eight days later, he died in a jail cell," *Seattle Times*, November 1, 2020, https://www.seattletimes.com/seattle-news/an-eastern-washington-teen-went-to -a-mental-health-clinic-for-help-eight-days-later-he-died-in-a-jail-cell/; K. Kraemer, "Benton's ex-healthcare company destroyed evidence in teen's death," *Tri-City Herald*, June 7, 2020, https://www.wenatcheeworld.com/news/northwest/benton-jails -ex-healthcare-company-destroyed-evidence-in-teens-death/article_68fd8e0c-a9aa -11ea-afbb-6b5e472bfa42.html; City News Service, "Jail inmate who died in January suffered from Asphyxiation, with Meth use a factor," Times of San Diego, March 25, 2021, https://timesofsandiego.com/crime/2021/03/25/jail-inmate-who-died-in-january -suffered-from-asphyxiation-with-meth-use-a-factor/; R. Boldrey, "Man charged with arson in Kalamazoo hospital fire found dead in county jail," MLive, December 24, 2020, https://www.mlive.com/news/kalamazoo/2020/12/man-charged-with-arson-in -kalamazoo-hospital-fire-found-dead-in-county-jail.html; M. Krafcik, "Family plans legal action after son dies in Kalamazoo County Jail," WWMT TV, April 8, 2021, https://wwmt.com/news/i-team/family-plans-legal-action-after-son-dies-in-kalamazoo -county-jail; G. Gyee, "Questions emerge in death of inmate at Charleston County jail, family's attorney says," *Post and Courier*, January 12, 2021, https://www .postandcourier.com/news/questions-emerge-in-death-of-inmate-at-charleston-county -jail-familys-attorney-says/article_91222bea-54e0-11eb-8493-8ba238b4ea94.html; B. Hicks, "Hicks: Video of Charleston County jail death is coming, and it's not good," *Post and Courier*, May 11, 2021, https://www.postandcourier.com/columnists/hicks -video-of-charleston-county-jail-death-is-coming-and-it-s-not-good/article_294732fe -b25f-11eb-843b-3f3d586e5260.html; "$10 million settlement approved in death

of inmate at South Carolina jail," NBC 10 Philadelphia, May 26, 2021, https://www
.nbcphiladelphia.com/news/national-international/10-million-settlement-approved-in
-death-of-inmate-at-south-carolina-jail/2827156/; "Jail inmate hangs himself inside
jail cell with bed sheets," Charlotte Alerts, May 23, 2021, https://newsmaven.io/
charlottealerts/news/jail-inmate-hangs-himself-inside-jail-cell.

treatment in the month prior to entering jail. Almost two-thirds (64 percent) had a mental illness.[16] A small percentage, 15 percent of male detainees and 31 percent of female detainees, had what was judged a "serious mental illness," including depressive disorders, bipolar disorders, schizophrenia, delusional disorders, and psychotic disorders. More than half of those with mental illness also suffered from substance use disorders.[17] According to the county sheriff, 21 percent of Fulton County Jail detainees were on medication for mental health issues as of December 2019.[18]

Why have so many mentally ill people ended up in the nation's jails?

State after state began closing their mostly archaic state-run psychiatric hospitals starting in the 1950s. They were supposed to be replaced by an array of local mental-health-care providers, but the money and commitment to support these alternatives never materialized. With no other options, American jails filled the gap. Too often, families end up calling 911 in a desperate attempt to secure assistance for a mentally ill family member having a psychotic episode or who is off their medication. Or police tire of being called repeatedly to respond to a homeless person loitering by a local business and arrest the person, who is then held in jail, unable to make even a nominal bail.

California operated a network of state hospitals that housed thirty-seven thousand patients in the 1950s. With the creation of antipsychotic medications and pressure by advocates, California and the rest of the country deinstitutionalized the mentally ill. By 1968, new governor Ronald Reagan signed that state's deinstitutionalization law, which called for an end of involuntary commitments of the mentally ill. State hospital populations fell to twenty-two thousand. Today, in California, that number is down to fewer than twelve thousand, most of whom courts have ordered into treatment until they are "competent to stand trial."

In Michigan, the state's three adult psychiatric hospitals include 480 beds. By comparison, the Wayne County jail has 2,951 beds. Wayne County jailers say 80 percent of their incoming inmates "have connections to mental health or substance abuse issues." According to the Missaukee County sheriff, "Obviously the way we used to do it, warehousing people in mental institutions, isn't the right way, but the pendulum has swung so far the other way. People end up in jail and the temporary fix is Community Mental Health tries to work with them, but as soon as they make bond, they're dumped back out on the street. To be blunt, the community mental health system is broken. Out of 39 mental health facilities in Michigan, only nine will accept an incarcerated individual in crisis."[19]

While mentally ill people make up about one-third of the San Diego County jail population at any given time, they represent about half of the 140 in-custody deaths that have occurred since 2009.[20] In 2020, the sheriff's department spent more than $83 million on inmate health care. Despite this, as of June 2020, three more inmates had died by suicide in its jails. The jails still lead all large California counties in in-custody jail deaths, averaging more than one every month going back more than ten years.

As the undersheriff of Benton County, Washington, where 18-year-old Marc Moreno died, explained to the media, most of the jail's detainees suffer from mental illness—making it the largest mental health provider in the region. "I get frustrated because I feel like we're the dumping ground at times," he said, going on to reveal that the jail was not designed to house the mentally ill as they had to be kept in holding cells where it is "loud and noisy and lights remain on 24/7," hardly a "therapeutic environment." Years ago, he lamented, the jail could automatically send mentally ill to the Eastern State Psychiatric Hospital. Now the jail has to vie with thirty-nine other counties for a bed in the few remaining psychiatric facilities. Making matters worse, during the jail's initial evaluation of entering inmates, it is increasingly difficult to know if people are detoxing or suffering a mental crisis until they "calm down," so the jail "uses a chair with straps and binding for safety." But, he assured, the sheriff's office had worked with county commissioners and partners to improve mental health care within the jail, developing a "multidisciplinary team of a psychiatric provider, a registered nurse, mental health professionals, mental health advocates, case managers, chaplains, and jail classification and operations representatives to give detainees better continuity of care." Ironically, many were the same partners who paid out millions of dollars to settle the lawsuit over Moreno's death two years after this interview.[21]

Deinstitutionalization is also widely responsible for homelessness. According to reports, there are more than 550,000 unhoused people on U.S. streets at any given night, with almost half suffering from mental illness, half of whom are seriously ill, according to the U.S. Department of Housing and Urban Development.[22] Lifetime arrest rates for unhoused people range between 62 and 90 percent, making them eleven times likelier to be incarcerated than the general public.[23]

Many mentally ill homeless find no more safety in jail than on the streets. The three detainees who died in the Cuyahoga County Jail in Cleveland, Ohio, for example, in 2020 all had been homeless when arrested. All were diagnosed as mentally ill. Lea Daye, 28, who died of an overdose in August 2020, was jailed because she could not raise $10,000 bond on charges stemming from a fight outside the homeless shelter where she was then living. The last to die that year, Shone Trawick, 48, had been arrested wandering in someone's backyard naked and intoxicated after punching a man on the street. He was beaten to death by his cellmate Edmond Hightower, 31, who himself had a long history of mental illness. Hightower had been found not guilty by reason of insanity in 2016 for a weapon with a prior felony conviction charge. He had been committed to the Northcoast Behavioral Healthcare facility and remained there for the maximum period permitted for commitments for criminal charges, three years. Three days after he was released in December 2019, he assaulted his mother's boyfriend. He was remanded to jail on a $10,000 bond he could not raise. Instead of being isolated in the jail where mentally ill inmates are usually housed, he was released to the general population along with Trawick.[24]

RACISM AND THE WAR ON DRUGS

Before 1970, the nation's incarceration rates were dropping, down to 200 per 100,000 that year. Then Richard Nixon launched the "war on drugs" in 1971. Incarceration rates rose steadily, topping 700 per 100,000 by the end of the 1990s. The "war on drugs" filled the jails with minorities. Two-thirds of those incarcerated for drugs were people of color due to their disproportionate arrest, conviction, and sentencing in courts. Although the number of black people arrested for crimes of violence fell in the 1980s and 1990s, the number of those arrested for drugs soared.

As of 2007–2009, BJS researchers reported that 63 percent of jail detainees suffered from what is now called substance use disorders (SUD).[25] Considering the rate of substance use disorder among the general adult population was only 5 percent at that time, this demonstrates how skewed jail populations were to those suffering substance abuse disorders, a continuing legacy of the war on drugs. Back when BJS completed this report, the most common drugs regularly used by those sentenced to jail were marijuana (64.4 percent), cocaine or crack (38.5 percent), hallucinogens (22.5 percent), depressants including barbiturates (20.8 percent) methamphetamines (19.8 percent), and heroin/opioids (18.9 percent). Of course, these data were collected before the opioid epidemic. Jails today house even more persons with substance use disorders.

The war on drugs was always about easy arrests—picking off people using marijuana, despite hype to the contrary. As late as 2018, 40 percent of drug arrests in this country were for marijuana, 663,000 out of 1.65 million. Most were for simple possession. Only 25 percent of the arrests were for heroin, cocaine, or their derivates.[26] As mentioned, it was also about racial bias. The ACLU documented in 2020 that despite roughly equal usage rates, blacks were 3.73 times more likely than whites to be arrested for marijuana.[27]

SUD among those jailed has only gotten worse since the last BJS report. In 2019, not only were more than a million Americans arrested for drugs, but 40 percent were on drugs at the time of the offense for which they were subsequently jailed. Of those arrested for property crimes, 40 percent committed them to feed their drug habits.[28] A study examining yearly trends in Kentucky's inmates from 2008 and 2016 found that prior heroin use had increased by 204 percent. Officials attributed the increase to policy changes meant to curb the opioid epidemic, which made it harder for users to obtain prescription pills. Instead, they switched to street heroin. The report found that the most recent incarcerated population had more severe use patterns than the general population.[29]

American jails house more mentally ill and drug-addicted people than all the psychiatric hospitals and drug treatment facilities in the country. That makes them the nation's de facto primary psychiatric and drug treatment facilities. It also means they have become the treatment provider of last resort for the most vulnerable and sickest . . . and, to put it bluntly, they suck at it.

PROBATION AND PAROLE, RECYCLING INMATES

Although probation and parole were designed to be alternatives to incarceration, the war on drugs ironically resulted in them becoming major contributors to jail overcrowding. Most people convicted of crimes are not imprisoned, at least not initially. They are placed on probation. In 2020, 3.6 million people in the United States were on probation. Many don't serve their full sentences; they are paroled. In 2020, 840,000 were on parole.

Judges impose probationary sentences, generally after a person admits or has been found guilty of a crime. Founded by an evangelical opponent of alcohol in the 1840s, probation was designed to provide a jail alternative whereby defendants could prove their worth in the community. People on probation may be supervised by a probation officer or unsupervised. The first condition of probation is not to commit a new crime. Additional conditions vary but may include mandatory regular office visits with a supervising officer, payment of restitution to crime victims or fines, stay-away orders from intimate partners or geographical areas, and the like. For those with substance use disorders, conditions often include abstinence and mandatory treatment. In some states, peoples may receive short-term jail sentences as a condition of probation. These "shock" sentences are then followed by probation supervision in the community. In other states, a judge may impose a split sentence including jail time followed by a period of probation.

If a person on probation commits a new offense or violates any condition of probation, called "technical" violations, he or she can be brought back before a judge and jailed after a "quasi-criminal" hearing. They are "quasi-criminal" because the judge has only to find it more likely than not (preponderance of the evidence) that the violation occurred. This is way below the legal standard of "beyond a reasonable doubt" required for a criminal conviction. The rules for revocation hearings are less stringent, too. Evidence that is not allowed in a criminal trial, like hearsay and illegally obtained evidence, may be used to prove a probation violation. Because of the differences in legal standards, a person on probation can be found not guilty of a new crime but still be found in violation of probation for committing that crime. While the evidence may not have supported a conviction beyond a reasonable doubt, it may have supported a violation on the lesser preponderance standard. Or, although the defendant is found not guilty, the trial may have revealed that the defendant was under the influence of drugs at the time, possessed a firearm, or was in an area prohibited, which constituted a violation of the other terms of probation.

When persons are charged with violating their probation, judges can immediately send them to jail. There is no right to bail because probationers have already been found guilty of the crime for which they were placed on probation. For example, a judge sentenced Lee Creeley, 34, to jail in Chatham County, Georgia, for a probation violation in September 2020. He violated probation by failing to inform his probation officer that he had changed his address, having moved from a motel to a house so his two boys, 12 and 7, could have their own bedrooms. He died in his cell four days later.[30] He was not alone. At least two other probationers died that same month, including George Adams III, 46, who died in the Chesterfield County, Virginia, Jail for a probation violation[31] and Calvin Cunningham, 44, held for a misdemeanor probation violation, who collapsed and died in the Athens-Clarke County, Georgia, jail.[32] As of December 2020, six hundred of the detainees in the troubled Allegheny jail in Pittsburgh, Pennsylvania, were there for probation violations. At least a third, according to state officials, were there as a direct "byproduct of substance use disorder."[33]

Parole is like probation except it is for people released early from prison or jail and placed under parole supervision by the paroling authority, not a judge. The same terms and standards for enforcement generally apply as for probation. In most states, parole officers are from a different agency than probation officers. If parolees are thought to be in violation of their parole, parole officers take them before parole boards or designated hearings officers. If found in violation, they can be returned to prison or jail to serve out the remainder of their sentences.

Probation and parole populations grew 239 percent from 1980 to 2016. By the latter date, one in fifty-five U.S. adults were on one or the other.[34] As the drug epidemic intensified, more and more persons under probation or parole supervision were ordered into drug treatment and/or ordered to remain abstinent from drugs and/or alcohol. Up until the 1980s, it was expensive to enforce abstinence conditions. Blood tests were pricey and took time. Probation and parole officers did not have access to police breathalyzers nor the training to administer them for alcohol use. However, the invention and widespread marketing of inexpensive, instant urine drug testing changed all that. A small drop of urine could reveal drug use. While not as accurate as

Wright County, Missouri, Jail

Daniel Moore, 44, used a blanket to hang himself in the jail while awaiting a hearing for violating his probation. The sheriff said no foul play was suspected.

Waseca County, Minnesota, Jail

Diana Balderas hanged herself in the jail less than an hour after being booked on a probation violation. The jail failed to remove her shoelaces or perform a mental health screening assessment.

Kenosha County, Wisconsin, Jail

Timothy Nelson, 25, hanged himself in the jail while held for a possible probation violation involving misdemeanor theft. Police were investigating his involvement in a possible subsequent theft, but no charges had been filed against him.

Santa Fe County, New Mexico, Jail

Carmela DeVargas was jailed for a probation violation—a missed appointment. She died a month later, shackled to a hospital bed even though she had developed quadriplegia from an infection she'd gotten in jail. Her family is suing the county because, they claim, jailers failed to provide her appropriate medical care.

Alachua County, Florida, Jail

Erica Thompson was jailed for a probation violation as well as a traffic charge. She was having contractions when deputies arrested her and took her to jail. She gave birth in jail. The baby subsequently died after being taken to the hospital. Protestors demanded that the sheriff take responsibility for the failure to care for the mother and stop defending it. As one protestor declared, it was "heinous and horrific."

Sources: C. Six, "Sheriff shares what led to the death of a Wright County inmate," KOLR, February 16, 2021, https://www.ozarksfirst.com/local-news/local-news-local-news/sheriff-shares-what-led-to-the-death-of-a-wright-county-inmate/; A. Lagoe, B. Stahl, & S. Eckert, "KARE 11 Investigates: Flawed—often toothless—jail death investigations," KARE 11, September 29, 2020, https://www.kare11.com/article/news/investigations/kare-11-investigates-flawed-often-toothless-jail-death-investigations/89-0255d498-8679-4961-959a-6f19c4a9e040; D. Smith, "Man found hanging Feb. 9 at Kenosha County Jail has died," *Kenosha News*, February 17, 2021, https://www.kenoshanews.com/news/local/

man-found-hanging-feb-9-at-kenosha-county-jail-has-died/article_42721274-da49-5739-93c7-773eb180fa49.html; I. Alves, "Father files wrongful death lawsuit on behalf of his late daughter," *Albuquerque Journal*, March 1, 2021, https://www.abqjournal.com/2364809/father-files-wrongful-death-lawsuit-on-behalf-of-his-late-daughter-ex-carmela-devargas-allegedly-became-ill-and-died-while-incarcerated-in-the-santa-fe-county-jail.html; T. Simpson, "Protestors want ASO to take accountability, for a baby that died as her mom gave birth in jail," WCJB, August 21, 2021, https://www.msn.com/en-us/news/crime/protesters-want-aso-to-take-accountability-for-a-baby-that-died-as-her-mom-gave-birth-in-jail/ar-AANAiFr.

blood tests or those administered in laboratories, they met the standard for probation and parole hearings, more accurate than not. As a result, probation and parole officers could more easily enforce abstinence.

After posting his $200,000 bond, 18-year-old Baxter Stowers was released from the Baxter County, Arizona, jail on the condition of drug abstinence, for example. He got weekly drug tests, passing his first the day the court issued the order. The second showed positive for "THC/Marijuana." His attorney argued that it was absurd to send his client to jail because even if he consumed marijuana, it did not make him a danger to the community. The judge, however, found he was in violation and revoked the release order, returning him to jail.[35]

While a failed drug test only offers proof that addiction is, in fact, a relapsing disease, in the world of probation and parole, it represents a willful violation of a court or parole order. This creates a vicious circle. First, judges or paroling officials order probationers or parolees to remain abstinent and often to attend drug treatment in lieu of jail or prison. The probationer or parolee, however, doesn't get instantly "cured," relapses, tests positive for drugs or alcohol, and then is jailed for their failure to get better. All of this is greatly facilitated and made routine thanks to cheap, portable urine screening.

The result? Approximately 25 percent of the individuals who are incarcerated each year are not jailed for new crimes but are recycled probationers or parolees. Overall, up to a third of jail populations are persons committed for probation or parole revocations.[36] In 2016, at least 168,000 probationers were incarcerated for "technical" (noncriminal) violations as were almost 100,000 parolees.[37] Incarceration rates for violations vary widely. In New York City, in

Hennepin County, Minnesota, Jail

Naajikhan Powell, 23, had been diagnosed with schizophrenia, bipolar disorder, and PTSD and had been repeatedly committed to a mental hospital before being sent to the jail. Less than two hours after he was booked in the jail, the county petitioned to have him sent to a local hospital because he was "posing a risk of harm due to mental illness." He'd been sent to jail for a probation violation, namely failing to take antipsychotic medication as prescribed and failing to complete treatment. In other words, a young, mentally ill man was jailed for a technical violation of his probation for continuing to suffer from mental illness. He died in jail from an apparent suicide.

Source: B. Stahl, A. Lagoe, & S. Eckert, "KARE11 Investigates: Mother sues Hennepin County following son's jail death," KARE 11, March 4, 2021, https://www.kare11.com/article/news/investigations/kare-11-investigates-mother-sues-hennepin-co-following-sons-jail-death/89-e6609d63-4122-4a34-893f-031fafe2118b.

2019, technical parole violations accounted for 8.6 percent of the jail population, up 12 percent from 2016. A study of thirty rural jails in five states in the fall of 2019 by the Vera Institute found people jailed for supervision violations ranged from an average of 14.6 percent to more than 25 percent.[38]

Instead of serving as an alternative to jails, probation and parole have come to serve as back door to them. Research also reveals that blacks and to a lesser extent Hispanics are much more likely to be revoked than whites, contributing to the disproportional incarceration rates of minorities.[39]

5

Death in Jails

We don't really know how many people die in the nation's jails. The federal government didn't collect data until after 1995, when an investigative journalist estimated that more than one thousand people had died in local jails during a four-month period, many under suspicious circumstances. It took a few years, but Congress responded with the Death in Custody Reporting Act of 2000, which mandated that states report people who died in the process of arrest, en route to jail, or in jail or prison every three months. The Bureau of Justice Statistics (BJS), the agency charged by the Justice Department to collect crime data, was put in charge. Subsequently BJS gave up collecting police deaths because states failed to cooperate. BJS used its own budget to reach out to all state prison systems and most of the nation's jails. It reported that, between 2001 and 2016, 16,058 people died in local jails, nearly half by unnatural (nonillness) causes like suicide and drug overdoses.

On average, three people died in jails each day. Jails with less than fifty detainees had a higher death rate than larger ones. The higher fatality rates in small jails were obscured, however, because BJS only provides aggregate state information. It claims that identifying specific jails or prisons would violate the privacy of decedents. Besides, officials were concerned that if they tattled, individual jails with disproportionate death rates would stop sending them data. In effect, the Justice Department adopted a policy to cover up for the nation's deadliest jails.

In 2013, Congress amended the act to impose financial penalties on states that withheld information. But the law did not provide resources for states to reform their sometimes intentionally fragmented, archaic data collection systems. Further, Congress had enacted another law that forbids the government from using BJS data for law enforcement purposes. For this reason, the Justice Department put its Bureau of Justice Assistance (BJA) in charge of this data collection, creating additional problems because BJA is not in the data collection business, like BJS.

The threat to withhold monies to states for noncompliance also proved problematic because most of the data come from local and county law enforcement and correctional agencies, not state agencies—meaning states don't have that information. Realizing this, the Obama administration devised a plan to use media reports and other public records. The administration also announced it would begin to release deaths by each agency or facility. But then Donald Trump became president. Lobbyists from the Major County Sheriffs Association and other law enforcement groups convinced the Justice Department to scrap BJA's plans, including public disclosure of the data and cross-checking official data with media reports. After Reuters came out with its own analysis of jail deaths in October of 2020 based on more than 1,500 freedom of information requests, congressional leaders called on the U.S. Justice Department to do better.[1]

In April 2021, BJS released "Mortality in Local Jails, 2000–2018, Statistical Tables."[2] It reported 1,120 deaths in 2018, an increase of 2 percent from the year before and the highest ever reported since BJS began collecting the data. About half of the deaths were due to heart and liver disease or cancer. Suicides were the single leading cause of deaths, accounting for almost a third (30 percent). The mortality rate from drug or alcohol intoxication more than quadrupled since 2000, almost catching up to suicides. They were up 19 percent from just the year before, evidence of the opioid epidemic that continues to expand to this day. According to experts who examined 1,442 jail deaths associated with drugs and alcohol between 2000 and 2013, however, coding for alcohol- and drug-related deaths were grossly undercoded. They found, for example, that only 18 percent of deaths within seven days of arrest for alcohol intoxication were officially coded as involving drugs/alcohol intoxication.[3]

BJS noted that jail detainees had a lower mortality rate than that among the general American public, 146 per 100,000 compared to 322 per 100,000.

However, this is nonsense, failing to account for the fact that the general population death rate is based on deaths over a full year. By contrast, the jail detainee deaths generally occur during an average jail stay of just three weeks. Assuming the general public death rate is constant over a year, the death rate for a period of just three weeks would be less than 19 per 100,000, or just 13 percent of the jail death rate!

Researchers at Columbia School of Public Health and Wayne State University examined jail death rates from 1987 to 2017 across a little more than one thousand mostly larger, urban counties and compared them with nonjailed residents of those counties aged 75 or younger. The study found that a one per 1,000 population increase in these jails was associated with a 6.5 percent increase in death from infectious diseases, a 4.65 percent increase in deaths from lower respiratory diseases, a 2.6 percent increase in deaths by suicide, as well as smaller increases in deaths tied to heart disease, unintentional injury, cancer, and diabetes. Researchers concluded that their study joined the "growing body of evidence concerning the public health consequences of mass incarceration," especially for the disproportionate population of incarcerated impoverished, unemployed, and minorities. As researchers reported, "Racialized disparities are a central feature of the public health consequences of mass incarceration."[4]

According to the BJS data, most jail deaths occurred quickly, 40 percent within seven days of admission. The median time for drug or alcohol intoxication deaths was just one day, suicide nine days, and illnesses thirty-three days. Jennifer Leinberger, 64, died from the toxic effects of methamphetamine and amphetamine three hours after being booked into the Wise County, Texas, Jail for theft of property under $2,500. The medical examiner ruled the death was "accidental." Other than cell checks conducted every twenty minutes, the jail reported no medical withdrawal management.[5] Carlos Yazzie, 44, was incarcerated in a Navajo Nation jail in New Mexico on a bench warrant. Although his foot was swollen and his blood alcohol content was almost six times the legal limit, he was put and left in a small isolation cell. The next day when a guard came to give him a jail jumpsuit, he was dead from acute alcohol poisoning.[6]

Less than 2 percent of those who died by suicide were in a mental health unit, although a quarter were in the jail's medical unit. Almost as many, 20.6 percent, died in a segregation unit and the remainder in general housing. A little over 40 percent of those who died from alcohol or drug intoxication died in the medical unit, 9.8 percent in segregation, and 36 percent in the general population. Most people who died of heart diseases, AIDS, cancer, and other illnesses died in medical units, although more than a quarter who died of heart disease did so in general housing. Most who died in jail, 75 percent, had not been convicted of the crime for which they were jailed.

Seventy-eight percent of jails reported no deaths in 2018. Almost 14 percent reported one, and 8 percent reported at least two. The rate was highest for the smaller jails with fewer than fifty detainees.

BJS data, of course, is based on reports received from participating jails. According to BJS, 179 fewer jail jurisdictions provided mortality data in 2018 compared to participating jails in 2000. From other studies, it has been documented that many jails also underreport jail deaths. For example, when detainees are found "unresponsive" in their cells, jailers generally transport or alert EMTs to take them to local hospitals. Many either die en route or shortly upon arrival at the hospital. Some jail officials do not report these as "jail" deaths. On May 21, 2018, Patrick Flynn, 36, hanged himself in his Spokane County, Washington, cell with his bedsheet. He was transported to the hospital unconscious. He later died when the hospital removed life supports. County officials maintained his was not an in-custody death, and the death did not end up in the state's official jail death statistics.[7]

Even where states require it, some jails simply don't report deaths. A Reuters investigations found that multiple deaths in thirty-nine jails it examined were not reported to government agencies or the media.[8] Generally, no one is charged with or interested in enforcing accurate jail death reporting.

In Louisiana, Loyola University Law School announced in 2021 that it would begin doing what the state has failed to do: track jail deaths. Arnold Ventures, a philanthropic organization, provided $410,000 to fund the project over two years. Using public record requests, the school will gather data on all correctional deaths from 2015 to 2020 in the state's 130 correctional institutions. The data bank acquired will be open to the public, unlike the way Louisiana jails currently keep certain deaths secret. For example, the St. Bernard Parish sheriff's office released information on a January 2020 detox death but kept secret a similar death three months earlier. The Jefferson Parish sheriff's office obscured two suicides, both from hanging, until a third hanging death weeks later exposed all three deaths.[9] The *Louisiana*

Illuminator reported it documented 786 jail and prison deaths in the state between 2015 and 2019. Although the majority occurred in state prisons, it found that parish (county) jails had a far higher number of suicides, deaths from overdoses, and accidents and an equal number of violent deaths as state-run facilities. More than 60 percent of the suicides occurred in jails, and almost half of these, 43 percent, occurred when the person was being held in solitary confinement.[10]

In 2016, the *Huffington Post* tried to determine the number of deaths in local jails. It was prompted by the death of Sandra Bland, a 28-year-old black woman who was found hanged in a jail cell in Waller County, Texas, on July 13, 2015, three days after being arrested for a minor traffic violation. Although highly motivated, the *Huffington Post* found tracking jail deaths to be a "prohibitively difficult" task.[11] The *Huffington Post* found that some states, like Texas, collect county but not municipal jail deaths. Louisiana collects jail deaths but only of state prisoners temporarily housed in local jails, a tiny fraction of the jailed population. After tracking nearly a thousand jail deaths, *Huffington* researchers concluded, "Despite our efforts, the true number of deaths is still unknown." They were able to document that reports of jail deaths released by the U.S. Justice Department were inaccurate. Over the past decade, the department reported on average fewer deaths than the *Huffington Post* reporters were able to substantiate through news articles, interviews, medical examiner reports, and other sources. The *Huffington* reporters are not alone in their inability to track jail deaths.

After a spate of deaths in San Diego's county jails, the *Union-Tribune* completed a six-month investigation that resulted in a series entitled "Dying Behind Bars." Reporters found three deaths classified as in-custody deaths by the medical examiner or the Citizens Law Enforcement Review Board that were not reported as such by the sheriff to the state. Rogelio Torres, for example, was found "down and unresponsive" in his Central Jail cell early New Year's Day in 2016. Paramedics were able to jump-start his pulse before taking him to the hospital, where the 42-year-old San Diego man died fifteen days later. He was not listed among the fifteen inmate deaths the sheriff's department reported to the California Department of Justice that year.[12]

Not only do Hawaiian corrections officials who run the state prisons and jails not release the names of detainees who die, they often fail to announce their deaths. In 2020, sixteen died in the state's unified correctional system containing both the state's prisons and jails. The agency announced only two deaths publicly. Legislators filed bills in 2021 to mandate the release of detainee deaths reports. Previously, the department was only mandated to release the data to the governor, who then gave it to state lawmakers, who released heavily redacted reports to the public. The Department of Public Safety managed to get even those redacted reports embargoed.[13]

Investigators for Reuters filed more than 1,500 public records requests to gain death data from 2008 to 2019 from the nation's biggest jails, including the ten largest in every state and those with detainee populations higher than 750.[14] The data covered 523 jails or jail systems, accounting for 60 percent of the total jail population across the country. It discovered 7,571 deaths. Most alarming, the records revealed that death rates had climbed almost 10 percent in the last three years of the study period before the COVID-19 pandemic. Reuters found that black inmates accounted for at least 28 percent of the jail deaths, more than twice their proportion in the U.S. population. In accord with prior and subsequent BJS reports, Reuters found that two-thirds of the deaths occurred before trials. In fact, 300 of the deceased detainees had spent a year or more in jail but still died before their trials. More than a quarter of the deaths were suicides, and more than 10 percent were tied "to the acute effects of drugs and alcohol."

In addition, Reuters documented that an increasing number of women were dying in jail. Its examination of data from 500 jails revealed 914 deaths of female inmates from 2008 to 2019. In just the last two years, 287 died from drug and alcohol abuse. Again, black women were disproportionately represented in the deaths, at 24 percent. Like their male counterparts, most who died were awaiting trial. The dangers women faced in jail sometimes extended to their infant children, who were also dying behind bars in increasing numbers. Shade Swayzer's baby, for example, died unattended when she gave birth alone on a Milwaukee jail cell floor in 2016. Reuters estimates that up to 5 percent of the women entering jails were pregnant.

Breaking down deaths by states, based on the limited data representing each state's largest jails, Reuters found the jail death rate across the entire country was 146 per 100,000 detainees. South Dakota had the lowest rate across the ten in-state jails surveyed at 82, followed by Alabama's thirteen jails surveyed at 87. The highest death rates were found in the ten jails surveyed in West Virginia with a rate of 223, followed by Oklahoma's eleven jails surveyed at 216.

The data suggest that death rates have more to do with the specific jail administrations than the demographics of each county. California jails provide an example. The Alameda County Santa Rosa Jail, with an average of 2,365 detainees in 2019, had ten deaths for a rate of 434, while the Fresno County jail had only four with an average inmate population that year of 2,940 for a rate of 136. On the other hand, the San Diego County Central Detention Facility reported ten deaths for a daily population of only 1,018 for a rate of 982. Los Angeles reported thirty-two deaths in all its facilities for a death rate of 187. Two dozen of California's large jails had death rates that were twice the national death rate.

Assuming the BJS 2018 jail death data are not totally off, most jails can go at least a year with no deaths, which make the multiple deaths in other jails more outstanding. The Madison County Jail in Huntsville, Alabama, for example, was designated as Alabama's "deadliest jail" before the end of 2020 with nine deaths since 2019. Death rates rose in the last two years with people dying "from causes including medical emergencies, injuries sustained during assaults, and suicide." The sheriff, who oversees the jail, refused to release subsequent jail death statistics, but, according to media reports, at least four more detainees died in 2020, none attributed to the coronavirus, and another in July 2021.[15] The Tarrant County Jail that serves Fort Worth, Texas, had three detainees die in one week alone in mid-2020 according to the Texas Commission on Jail Standards. Twelve in all died over that whole year in the jail, only two from COVID-19. Most causes of death were not revealed on the medical examiner's website or were undetermined, but revealed causes included a suicide, a seizure disorder (that the family claims was due to medical neglect), heart disease, and untreated liver cancer, hepatitis, cirrhosis of the liver, chronic obstructive pulmonary disease, and sepsis. In December, two more detainees died in the jail, bringing the total for the year to seventeen, including four from COVID-19.[16] The East Baton Rouge Parish jail also had a state record for most deaths, according to local media, with forty-four from 2012 through 2020.[17] On average, one person died every six months in Erie County, New York, jails. Since the appointment and subsequent election of Sheriff Timothy Howard in 2005, thirty people have died in that county's jails, four in 2019.[18] In 2020, Bexar County, Texas, had a record high number of jail deaths, eighteen, up from ten in 2018 and twelve in 2019. A third of the deaths were suicides. Bexar was not alone. Across Texas, jails reported

974 deaths, up from 721 in 2019, representing the first time the number of deaths exceeded 800 across Texas. While some of the deaths were attributed to COVID-19, many facilities reported increases in suicides and deaths by "natural causes." The non-COVID deaths were called a "historic spike."[19]

Death rates are also high in tribal jails. Back in 2004, an Inspector General investigation found widespread inmate abuse, attempted suicides, inhumane conditions, and other issues in many of the tribal jails scattered throughout the United States, including in Arizona, New Mexico, Montana, Wisconsin, and Mississippi.[20] The Interior Department's inspector testified the jails were a "national disgrace." Although indigenous people have some of the highest substance abuse rates in the country, the tribal jails often lack basic medical resources. Although the total number of deaths in them are not known, at least nineteen people died in the almost two dozen tribal jails overseen by the federal Interior Department's Bureau of Indian Affairs from 2016 to 2021. Most were incarcerated for minor infractions as tribal police and courts have very limited jurisdictions.[21]

MEDICAL EXAMINERS, CORONERS, AND "NATURAL DEATHS"

The corrections officer said the detainee's vomit looked like "motor oil." Daniel Stout, 31, died a slow, painful, and preventable death according to the lawsuit filed against Missouri's St. Louis County Justice Center. The suit also charged that Stout was denied medical care despite vomiting coagulated blood and not having a bowel movement in eight days. Stout died one hour after he was transferred to the Eastern Reception Diagnostic Correctional Center in Bonne Terre, where he was to serve the remainder of his sentence for drug possession. The autopsy reported the cause of death to be "peritonitis due to a perforated ulcer."

Larry Reavis died in January after the St. Louis jail failed to provide medical care despite knowing he was detoxing and "had tremors, paroxysmal sweats, anxiety, agitation, headaches, diarrhea, nausea and vomiting." The autopsy listed the cause of death to be "chronic ethanol use." John Shy bled to death the next month from an intestinal hemorrhage despite two nurses observing him on the floor in a pool of blood for fifteen minutes before anyone entered his cell. His emergency call button had been muted, and he reportedly had been screaming for help for the prior seven hours. The only response had been a threat to put him into a restraint chair. The next month,

Lamar Catchings died untreated for leukemia. He told jail staff that he had lost hearing and stopped eating for the two weeks before his death. A week before his death, he needed a wheelchair to leave court after a hearing.

All these deaths were determined by medical examiners to be from "natural causes."[22]

Similarly, across the country in Bucks County, Pennsylvania, four deaths declared to be "natural deaths" were all revealed to have been due to opioid toxicity and the jail's failure to treat their withdrawals.[23]

There is nothing "natural" about these jailhouse deaths. It is not as if the vast majority, if any, of these detainees gently pass away while asleep in their bunks. Occasionally, medical examiners report jail deaths to be "accidental." They too may be the result of medical neglect or complete disregard for the individual's well-being.

When inmates die, medical examiners or coroners perform autopsies. They attribute deaths to one of four official options allotted for jail deaths: "natural causes," "accident," "suicide," or "homicide." In most cases, they choose "natural causes."

Medical examiners' and coroners' reports of jail deaths are almost always accepted at face value. Medical examiners and coroners have become key allies in helping jails sweep deaths under the rug. Often intentionally or through incompetence, they provide the first cover for these deaths, failing to raise the alarm when presented with even egregious examples of easily preventable fatalities. Many go out of their way to shield jail security and medical staff from any responsibility. Other may just be incompetent. Occasionally, one is held accountable.

The Tarrant County deputy medical examiner was placed on administrative leave after an audit of forty-one homicide cases found he made mistakes in at least twenty-seven between January 1 and November 9, 2020. The Tarrant County Criminal Defense Lawyers Association called for an independent investigation of the medical examiner's office.[24]

Although not a jail custody death, the nation saw how the county medical examiner who first examined the body of George Floyd in Minneapolis ruled that Floyd's death was due to a combination of his underlying medical conditions, being restrained, and potential intoxicants in his system. The actions of the police were not mentioned, nor was suffocation raised as a cause of death. It wasn't until the video surfaced and after Floyd's family paid independent

Dawson County, Georgia, Jail

Official reports determined 18-year-old Jonathan Sanford's death in jail to be from "accidental causes." The young man had been arrested for narcotics and driving under the influence of drugs. Shortly after entering the jail, he was found unresponsive in his cell. There were no reports of jail medical staff or others working to safely manage his withdrawal or reverse a drug overdose from what the medical examiner characterized as "combined drug intoxication." Sanford's father says that what the family was told "doesn't add up."

Luzerne County, Pennsylvania, Jail

Shaheen Mackey's daughter questioned the medical examiner's characterization of her father's death. "An accident? Natural causes? Natural causes? Really? Come on? That's no natural cause. They let him sit in that chair and take his last breath, and they didn't care." The chair referred to is a "restraint" chair, designed to immobilize unruly inmates. Mackey's "unruly" behavior was having a seizure. His family charged that instead of addressing his epilepsy, jail staff "yelled at him, physically restrained him, [and] tased him several times." He died two days later in the hospital. The family released on Facebook a video showing his agonizing last breaths in the chair. Those "natural causes" cost the county $3 million, the amount paid out to settle a lawsuit for Mackey's wrongful death. Determined to continue the coverup, the following September, the Luzerne County Council voted not to investigate Mackey's death, nor have it reviewed by an outside law firm.

Lycoming County, Pennsylvania, Jail

Ashley Cupp, incarcerated for a probation violation, died in her sleep in the county jail, officially reported from "natural causes." The coroner listed the cause of death to be cardiac disease due to substance abuse, noting she had had an aortic valve replacement. Although jail officials were aware of her serious mental and medical conditions that required daily medication, neither jail staff nor medical staff provided it to her. Any care she received was from other inmates who, according to the family, helped her get to the showers, dress, and brush her hair. They also submitted medical requests for assistance for her that went ignored. Fellow inmates told jail staff that she was having difficulty breathing and her legs were cold and lined in red. Attributing her condition to detoxifying from drugs, jail staff left her untreated. No doctor ever came to see her in the jail. The night she died, jail staff ignored her screams for help. They discovered her body the next morning when she failed to report for roll call. Her estate charges jail staff failed to act when it became apparent the contracted medical provider was mistreating or ignoring her medical needs from when she entered in October 2018 to when she died in February 2019.

Worcester County, Massachusetts, Jail

Michael Ramey, 36, was awaiting trial when he complained to jail medical staff of worsening conditions. He told a nurse his head "was about to explode." At various times, he couldn't walk, see, or hear. A jail medical report characterized Ramsey's complaints as "apparent medication seeking behavior" and concluded "no diagnostic intervention needed at this time." Shortly after, he died in jail of treatable meningitis. The jail reported the death was from "natural causes."

Sources: A. Popp, "Teen's death in Dawson County Jail ruled accidental by GBI," *Dawson County News*, July 24, 2020, https://www.dawsonnews.com/local/crimecourts/teens-death-dawson-county-jail-ruled-accidental-gbi/; C. Strub, "Video shows incident before inmate Shaheen Mackey's death," WNEP, August 5, 2020, https://www.wnep.com/article/news/local/luzerne-county/shaheen-mackey-luzerne-county-prison-video/523-470b3307-4822-4f7c-b0a1-874e5c963a0e; WNEP Web Staff, "Council votes against further investigation into inmate death," WNEP, September 8, 2020, https://www.wnep.com/article/news/local/luzerne-county/council-votes-not-to-investigate-inmate-death-any-further/523-062e29db-2ac8-475e-ac32-f3a1a5c4d1b6; J. Beauge, "Inadequate medical care was factor in Lycoming prison inmate's death, suit claims," PennLive, September 30, 2020, https://www.pennlive.com/news/2020/09/inadequate-medical-care-was-factor-in-lycoming-prison-inmates-death-suit-claims.html; C. Willmsen & B. Healy, "When inmates die of poor medical care, jails often keep it secret," WBUR, March 23, 2020, https://www.wbur.org/news/2020/03/23/county-jail-deaths-sheriffs-watch.

investigators to conduct a second autopsy that asphyxia (suffocation) was reported as the cause of Floyd's death. It was at this point that the medical examiner issued a revised report. The final report, though, still maintained that heart failure, not suffocation, was the cause of death and suggested that fentanyl intoxication and heart disease may have been contributing factors.

According to researcher Justin Feldman of Harvard's FXB Center for Health and Human Rights, county sheriffs, police, and other officials routinely pressure medical examiners to ensure death certificates do not paint in-custody deaths as suspicious. A survey from the National Association of Medical Examiners conducted a decade ago found 20 percent of respondents reported being pressured by officials to change death certificates involving in-custody deaths. Many reported retaliation for refusing.

The Harvard research also documented how medical examiners and coroners commonly use "junk science" to absolve jails for detainees who die from the actions of the correction officers or deputies. In more than half of the cases studied, it found in-custody deaths were blamed on drug intoxication or "excited delirium," caused by drugs, including cases where subsequent toxicity reports found no drugs in the deceased's body. "Excited delirium" is not accepted in the International Classification of Diseases. It is not accepted in the Diagnostic and Statistical Manual in the United States. But it is commonly accepted by many medical examiners and coroners. This allows them to rule that detainees who have been forcibly restrained, tased, placed in chokeholds, or injected with ketamine died from "natural causes," not the actions of officers.

According to the National Center for Biotechnology Information, "excited delirium syndrome" is the "go to" diagnosis for cause and manner of death when highly agitated persons are held and die in police custody, typically made when medical examiners have difficulty in identifying an anatomic cause of death but stimulants are involved. It is a "controversial and highly debated" diagnosis "precisely because the mechanism of lethality is unknown."[25]

"Excited delirium" was invented in 1985 by a forensic pathologist who theorized that someone who chronically abuses cocaine or other stimulants eventually develops a brain condition that causes mania, violence, and non-response to verbal cues or even pain. Not only do experts reject this theory, but as explained by Dr. Homer Venters, former chief of medicine for New York City's jails, "Excited delirium, which is not a medical diagnosis, has a long history of being used to absolve law enforcement of responsibility in the death of people, especially people of color." The company that makes Tasers has helped to advance the theory, however, by funding researchers who promote it. It's funded the same researchers to serve as expert witnesses to testify in cases involving Tasers. In some jurisdictions, a coroner's cause-of-death determination can be changed if challenged in court. The company has done this in deaths involving Tasers so that inmates' deaths are attributed to "excited delirium" instead of jail staff using Tasers on them.[26]

Richland County, Ohio, Jail

The coroner ruled that Alexander Rios, 28, died as a result of "excited delirium," noting he tested positive for amphetamines. However, after reviewing jail footage of Rios's death, a criminal justice expert concluded that officers who restrained Rios "demonstrated a gross disregard for the value of human life." The video, obtained by the *Mansfield News Journal* through a public records request, shows five deputies holding Rios down, stepping and kneeling on his back while another presses the inmate's head into the jail's concrete floor as they try to handcuff him. After being repeatedly shocked with a stun gun, Rios stops struggling and an officer is heard shouting that Rios was turning blue. He never regained consciousness and died in the hospital after being removed from a ventilator. The incident began when Rios refused to come down from a partition to be placed in a restraint chair, which officers told him was for his own safety. When officers opened the cell door, Rios raced out. That's when the five deputies tackled and subdued him. One officer can be heard on the video urging the others to "Tase him, tase him!" When a deputy asks if they should tase Rios again, the officer advised them to. Another officer punches him in the head as another places a foot on Rios's back and lifts his other foot off the ground so that his full weight presses on Rios. Rios can be heard gasping for breath. The entire incident took two minutes. The officers were so concentrated on their assault that they didn't notice that Rios was unconscious until he failed to heed their commands to get up.

Source: L. Whitmire, "'He's turning blue.' Family demands answers in Richland jail death after video surfaces," *Mansfield News Journal*, January 10, 2021, https://www.mansfieldnewsjournal.com/story/news/2021/01/10/ohio-richland-county-jail-death-video-alexander-rios-family/4128410001/.

Similarly, the *New York Times* has documented multiple instances in which medical examiners blamed sickle cell as a cause or major factor in deaths of black people in custody. As the *Times* reported, what makes this suspect is that in two-thirds of the deaths, the person who died had been "forcefully restrained by the authorities, pepper-sprayed or shocked with stun guns." However, the determinations on sickle cell trait created enough doubt for officers to avert criminal or civil penalties, according to the *Times*. For example, Army Sgt. James Brown, 26, turned himself in to the El Paso jail to serve a two-day sentence for drunken driving. He died in the jail "after five jailers in riot gear piled atop him, pulled a mesh mask over his head and bound him in a chair." The medical examiner ruled it a "natural death," caused by sickle cell trait. A grand jury declined to bring charges. As an outside expert pathologist declared, "You can't put the blame on sickle cell trait when there is a knee on the neck or when there is a chokehold or the person is hogtied." Most revealing, in none of the deaths did the *Times* find the deceased had sickle cell disease.[27]

There are about two thousand medical examiners and coroners across the United States, as last reported by the Bureau of Justice Statistics. About 80 percent work in county coroner's offices, most of which serve small jurisdictions. Sixteen states have a centralized statewide medical examiner system, seven a county medical examiner system, and thirteen mixed county medical examiner and coroner systems. They vary. In West Virginia, for example, unlike in most states, the medical examiner doesn't have to be a physician. In Georgia, the mayor can serve as the coroner in towns with fewer than five thousand people. In Nebraska, the county attorney serves as the coroner as do justices of the peace in Texas.[28]

In Washington State, as in many others nationwide, the system of death investigation is a patchwork led by professionals with wide-ranging experience. Only six counties in the state's most populous areas rely on the work of medical examiners who are doctors who specialize in forensic pathology. These medical examiners manage a staff of investigators, perform autopsies, and interpret toxicology results, among other duties necessary to determine causes of sudden, unnatural, or suspicious deaths. The remaining thirty-three counties, covering a population of about 2.5 million people, depend on elected coroners. In seventeen counties, candidates only have to check two boxes to make it onto the ballot: they must be eighteen years old and have a clean criminal record. And in the state's sixteen least populated counties, prosecuting attorneys investigate deaths, splitting their time between courtrooms and death scenes. The elected coroners also manage the death investigation process with little or no support staff, minus medical duties—because they often don't have any medical training. While some coroners in Washington have prior experience related to death and medicine, such as mortuary work and nursing, others don't have any relevant experience at all. They include a former chimney sweep and a farmer.[29]

Coroners are generally laypeople elected by county residents. In 1857, a committee of the American Medical Association recommended abolishing elected coroners, but 164 years later, they endure. Medical examiners are appointed, and many are board certified in a medical specialty. Competent forensic pathologists, whether serving as medical examiners or working for coroners, however, are few and far between. They can make much better money outside of government work. A 2012 report by the Scientific Working Group on Medicolegal Death Investigation cited a number of reasons for the shortage of forensic pathologists, including a lack of educational centers that teach the profession, lax funding to support that education, high dropout rates, tight budgets among states and counties, and the resultant low salaries that deter young people who may want to enter the field.

The national shortage of forensic pathologists means many in-custody deaths aren't even examined. A 2011 NPR, PBS, and ProPublica investigation found jurisdictions were cutting back on autopsies when the cause of death was purported to be obvious. As a retired examiner from Los Angeles explained, "When you only see one in every three cases, the possibility that a homicide's going to be missed are pretty great."[30]

The National Association of Medical Examiners has also condemned the inherent conflict of interest of county forensic investigators analyzing in-custody county deaths, calling for outside investigators instead. When the Colorado Department of Public Health tried to get death certificates to contain a check box if the death involved "legal intervention" in 2015, the state's coroners banded together to get the checkbox removed from the form so as not to alienate sheriffs and other law enforcement officials. Tellingly, the last successful effort to reform medical examiners in this country occurred during the brief period of Reconstruction when black people held office in the South immediately after the Civil War. They elected black coroners, considered important to control the deaths of black people by law enforcement officers and others.[31]

Medical examiner and coroner reports have helped to allow jail deaths to go unquestioned for years. When questioned, more often than not, it is found that the jail deaths were preventable. A grand jury investigation of jail deaths in Orange County, California, concluded, for example, "Like people on the outside, jail inmates die." However, over the last three years, it found that 44 percent of custodial deaths in Orange County jails (thirty-four) may have been preventable. "Delays in treatment, failure to identify health threats at intake, failure to diagnose serious mental illness, and lack of timely referral

Clark County, Nevada, Jail

The county coroner's office had already cost the county $75,000 in taxpayer money after fighting more than three years to keep one of its autopsy reports out of the hands of the *Las Vegas Review-Journal*. In November 2020, it announced it would continue to appeal the latest ruling after the state's supreme court declared that autopsy reports were public information but directed a lower court to determine if some of the content should be redacted for privacy considerations. The lower court judge had ruled that since the coroner had not redacted the last six hundred autopsies, the current report should be released unredacted. The lower court judge commented that "it is as if the coroner's office doesn't accept that they are a public servant. It's upsetting that this type of heel-dragging has been going on in such a public records case." The executive editor of the *Review-Journal* commented, "The failures of this system must be far worse than anyone imagined. Why else fight so hard and spend so much . . . to keep critical records secret? These documents tell an important story."

Wayne County, Michigan, Jail

When the *Detroit Free Press* asked the Oakland County chief medical examiner to review the Wayne County, Michigan, medical examiner's report on the death of Priscilla Slater, 38, in the Harper Woods jail, he determined it was "nonsense." The Wayne County medical examiner had determined that an irregular heartbeat caused by abnormally angled coronary arteries could have caused her death. The Oakland County medical examiner countered that "the most likely diagnosis . . . is she died from alcohol withdrawal." He continued, "If she was not monitored in the cell, that is a big problem." The jail video showed she had a seizure in her cell at 5:10 a.m. Officers did not discover her body until 12:30 p.m. The Wayne County prosecutor, investigating the death, said her office had not even been made aware of the possibility of alcohol withdrawal syndrome in the Wayne County medical examiner's report. She called for a third independent medical examination. Subsequently the prosecutor said the report attributing the death to a heart attack meant no criminal charges were warranted.

Los Angeles County, California, Jail

An LA deputy medical examiner ruled that Alan Ramos died in the Long Beach jail because he was "at risk for sudden cardiac death" due to an enlarged heart. The fact that he was tasered nine times and left handcuffed and face down when he died was dismissed as merely reflecting "the circumstances under which the death occurred." Ramos family's lawyer said the coroner's ludicrous ruling effectively undermined their civil lawsuit and probably ended any chance for a finding of criminal culpability for the officers involved. Long Beach officials, however, agreed to pay the family $325,000 before the details of Ramos's death became public.

Sources: A. Kane, "Coroner wants to appeal juvenile autopsy release, despite court order," *Las Vegas Review-Journal*, November 20, 2020, https://www.reviewjournal .com/investigations/coroner-wants-to-appeal-juvenile-autopsy-release-despite-court -order-2187415/; N. Kaffer, "Expert poses new theory on what really killed woman in Harper Woods jail," *Detroit Free Press*, November 12, 2020, https://www.freep .com/story/news/local/michigan/wayne/2020/11/12/priscilla-slater-autopsy-jail-harper -woods/6251487002/; N. Kaffer, "Wayne County: No charges in Harper Woods jail death," *Detroit Free Press*, May 20, 2021, https://www.freep.com/story/news/local/ michigan/wayne/2021/05/20/priscilla-slater-harper-woods-jail-death/5185358001/; J. Dobruck, "Police repeatedly Tased a man and left him on the jail floor," *Long Beach Post*, May 6, 2021, https://lbpost.com/news/taser-death-alan-ramos-jail-long-beach -police-heart-disease.

---

to a health-care professional have increased the chances that a detainee will not make it out alive." The grand jury reported that fourteen of the jail deaths could be attributed to "natural causes," including "cancer, liver or heart disease, stroke, etc." One death was a suicide, and one was a murder committed inside a jail cell. The cause of death for three others was not determined. The remaining fifteen deaths, it concluded, were preventable, including not giving entering persons urine drug screen tests "even though inmates are known to be a high-risk group for alcohol and drug use." Six of the deaths, occurring within seventy-two hours of admission, included cases of undiagnosed drug intoxication or delayed drug treatment. The jury also documented widespread deficiency in health-care delivery, including delayed attention, medical personnel errors, medication errors, missing or incomplete intakes, and housing assignment errors. Jurors even discovered that jail personnel often did more harm than good when they acted to save detainees with CPR. Nine of the twenty who received CPR suffered three or more broken ribs, a broken sternum, or damaged internal organs, "an excessive amount of damage according to the American Heart Association Guidelines." "In one instance at the OC Central Jail, CPR resulted in seventeen fractured ribs, the perforation of one of the heart chambers, and over three pints of blood flooding the chest cavity."[32]

SUICIDES

A quick search of "jail suicide" on Google News on February 18, 2021, similarly revealed ten different news stories on jail suicides. The included: (1) "Suicide attempt by inmate at Dane County Jail," *Enterprise & Press*, 17 hours ago; (2) "Peoria jail suicide did not show signs of mental distress, sheriff says," CIProud.com, 3 days ago; (3) "Sheriff's office investigates suspected suicide at Loudon Jail," LoudonNow, 5 days ago; 4) "'There is no way I'm getting out of here?' Kalamazoo County inmate asked parents before suicide," MLive, 6 days ago; (5) "Sheriff's office confirms inmate committed suicide at Gwinnett County Jail," *Gwinnett Daily Post*, 14 days ago; (6) "Corrections officer saved 2 inmates from committing suicide," WBBM, 6 days ago; (7) "Lawsuit filed in wake of suicide at county jail," *Enterprise*, 6 days ago; (8) "Jail suicides raise questions about mental health treatment behind bars," KMSP, 3 days ago; (9) "Suicide remains the leading cause of death in Oregon's jails, new report finds," Oregon Public Broadcasting, 10 days ago; and (10) "Weber County challenges civil suit's accusations over inmate's death in 2017," *Standard-Examiner*, 3 days ago.

Jail suicides appear to be something that jails have come to accept, as the jail suicide death rate has reportedly remained consistent for years. According to BJS, for example, suicides accounted for 32 percent of all detainee fatalities in 2000. Sixteen years later, they accounted for 31.1 percent of jail deaths.[33] The decline in jail populations accompanying COVID-19 has not resulted in a proportionate decline in detainees with mental health disorders.

Although its jail population was reduced by 35 percent, from 1,100 to 800 to reduce COVID-19 exposure, the mental health unit of the jail in Reno, for example, remained full in the summer of 2020, mostly due to detainees who had made suicide threats. Initial screenings of entering detainees continued to identify "75 to 80 percent of the inmate population dealing with some mental health issue." While some were dealing with the stress of their incarceration, according to the jail psychiatrist, 40 to 60 percent were suffering from illnesses serious enough "to warrant psychotropic medication." According to the jail, a total of 212 suicides were averted due to its screening and monitoring. Still, more than one suicide attempt took place each month at the jail. The sheriff told the media that on any given day, 20 percent of the daily jail population either think about suicide or attempt it. The jail was able to report, however, no deaths by suicide in more than a year. The sheriff pointed out that his jail is, in effect, the second-largest mental health hospital in Nevada—the first being the Clark County Detention Center.[34]

When accused sexual predator Jeffrey Epstein, 66, died by suicide in a federal facility in Lower Manhattan, many wrote about how he was just one of many examples of jail suicides. But Epstein was neither a typical defendant nor was his death typical. Although he died by suicide while awaiting trial, like most jail suicides, he was in a federal—not county or local—jail. More importantly, he was a multimillionaire financier who counted former and current presidents as friends, and he faced forty-five years in federal prison. Most people who die by suicide in jail do not face four decades in prison. Unlike Epstein, most people who die by suicide in jails are mentally ill, suffering from clinical depression, paranoia, trauma, and the like, often with a history of suicidal ideation and past attempts. Or they are withdrawing from opioids and other drugs. The U.S. Department of Health and Human Services advises in its warning against rapid opioid detoxification that the risks "include acute withdrawal symptoms, exacerbation of pain, serious psychological distress, and thoughts of suicide."[35]

Within the depressing and traumatic confines of jails, thoughts of suicide often lead to attempts. A 2010 study of jail suicides reported 47 percent of the deceased had a history of substance abuse, 34 percent had a history of suicidal behavior, 38 percent had a history of mental illness, 28 percent had a history of medical problems, and 20 percent had a history of taking psychotropic medications. It also reported that 20 percent of the victims were intoxicated at the time of their death. Most, 93 percent, died by hanging, with 66 percent using bedding and 30 percent anchoring the hanging device to the bed or bunk. Testifying to too many jails' failures to prevent suicides, the report noted that 8 percent of the deceased were on a suicide watch when they died by suicide. Part of the problem was that 38 percent of the victims were in isolation at the time of the death, leaving no cellmate to alert guards. This accords with the previously cited BJS report that more than 20 percent of suicides occurred in segregation units. The report also found that while 77 percent of the jails where the suicides occurred conducted intake screening to identify risk for suicide, only 27 percent made the effort to verify suicide risk from prior commitments, and just 31 percent checked with the arresting or transporting officer if the detainee was at risk for suicide. While most of the jail officials claimed to provide suicide training to staff, the trainings mostly lasted for just two hours and were not provided annually. The standard jail protocol for suicide prevention, adopted by the jails in the survey, is limited to checking inmates' cells every fifteen minutes.[36]

There is a consensus in the literature that suicide, addiction, and depression are all closely related and interconnected. Many who experience severe depression caused by major depression, bipolar disorder, obsessive-compulsive disorder, and other conditions self-medicate with drugs. Unfortunately, this typically increases the severity and duration of depressive episodes, greatly increasing the likelihood of suicidal ideation. Forced to withdraw from these drugs, the risk for death by suicide escalates. A University of Washington study examined suicides among individuals involved in the criminal justice system. It found that recent arrest status was associated with a higher prevalence of suicide attempts than being on parole, being on probation, or not being involved in the criminal justice system at all. The recent arrest group also had the highest prevalence of substance use disorders.[37]

Alarmingly, some jails have shown an inability to identify and prevent even slow-motion suicide deaths. The Shasta County, California, Jail, for example, ranked second-highest in California for total deaths for jails in 2018, two-thirds of which were suicides, making it number one for jail suicides in California that year. By comparison, only 13 percent of deaths in the Los Angeles County jail were suicides. Not surprisingly, one of the main reasons Shasta County jail suicide deaths were so high was staff concern for detainee well-being was so low. A Shasta jail 2018 video showed a detainee "screaming in agony" from methamphetamine withdrawal as officers laughed and insulted him rather than take him to a hospital. The detainee died two days later.[38] In the first four months of 2021, five more died by suicide, including one who died within an hour of admission to the jail.[39]

The Shasta County Jail is not a lonely outlier.

Too many jails' medical and security staff fail to appreciate or choose to ignore the heightened risk of suicide for people left untreated while withdrawing from drugs. The failure to treat opioid withdrawal elevates suicide risks. As an astute medical examiner in Oregon recognized, after conducting the autopsy of Chad Bomar, his suicide in the Deschutes County Jail "was likely related to symptomatic withdrawal from opioids."[40]

After the Bristol County, Massachusetts, jail had seven suicide deaths over two years, Correctional Psychiatric Services, its contracted medical provider,

Las Vegas, Nevada, Jail

It took forty-seven days for Stephen Burrell, a 26-year-old father of two, to die by suicide in the city jail. Although diagnosed as schizophrenic, he did well when on his medication. When not, he frequently got arrested for minor offenses. His last arrest was for sleeping at a fast-food restaurant and refusing to leave. Officers took him to city jail for trespassing. When arrested, he weighed 160 pounds, according to jail records, although his family claimed he was heavier. Jailers placed him in administrative segregation for a psychiatric evaluation. Within a month, official jail records noted that he was not eating so they began a food log. Seven days later, the log remained empty. A doctor was called and simply ordered that the food log continue. The log remained empty for the next seven days. Burrell also stopped showering. Four days before his death, officers increased monitoring to every fifteen minutes and recorded that he sat up five times in the four days. On his final day, an officer brought him a breakfast tray and asked if he would eat but found Burrell unresponsive. Jail staff performed CPR and transferred him to a hospital, but it was too late. He weighed 126 pounds. A forensic pathologist and former medical examiner told the media that he would rule the death to be "neglect" and turn the case over to the prosecutor. However, a year later, the media reported that it did not appear anyone was investigating the death nor taking actions regarding involved jail personnel. The jail, however, did institute a new policy. Staff were instructed to warn detainees who stopped eating that it was unhealthy and could lead to starvation.

Johnston County, Indiana, Jail

The 19-year-old detainee called his mother and asked her to contact the mother of inmate Eric Cruz because, as he told her, "I think he's gonna die." He made the call after witnessing jail staff neglect Cruz for days, "denying him clothes and a blanket and mat to sleep on — Cruz was on suicide watch — and ignoring him as he cried out for treatment." The young detainee was correct.

Delaware County, Pennsylvania, Jail

Thirty-five-year-old Janene Wallace, who suffered from mental illness, was in jail for a probation violation. She was held in solitary fifty-one of fifty-two days, locked up twenty-three hours a day at the George W. Hill Correctional Facility. When she threatened to strangle herself, a guard told her to "go ahead" and went to lunch. She did. Her family sued, eventually receiving a $7 million settlement.

Marion County, Kansas, Jail

The jail staff knew 38-year-old Julie Starks had previously been committed to the state hospital for mental illness. Upon entering the jail, staff failed to complete her processing because she was described as uncooperative. They did not take away her shoes and laces, waiting for her to calm down the next day. The employee with her at booking left for fifteen to twenty minutes while Starks went to the bathroom, where she hanged herself with the shoelaces. There was a camera for the bathroom, but no one was monitoring at the time.

Sources: J. Treanor, "Vegas Lost: Starved to death," KSNV, July 23, 2020, https:// news3lv.com/features/vegas-lost/vegas-lost-to-death-the-story-of-stephen -burrell; T. McDonald, "Family members of inmates who died allege negligence at Johnston County Jail," *Indy Week*, February 1, 2021, https://indyweek.com/news/ family-members-of-inmates-who-died-allege-negligence-at-john/; S. Cohen & N. Eckert, "Pennsylvania inmate threatened to choke herself," *Morning Call*, June 18, 2019, https://www.mcall.com/news/pennsylvania/mc-nws-pa-jail-suicide-20190618 -gcjwi77erzdabecu4757eendz4-story.html; A. Simone, "KBI probes inmate death," *Marion County Record*, December 10, 2020, http://www.marionrecord.com/direct/ kbi_probes_inmate_death+5212death+4b42492070726f62657320696e6d61746520646 5617468.

---

reported that six had previously expressed no suicidal ideations. It warned, "Given the likelihood of the prevalence of inmate suicide to increase due to the increasing opioid problem in Bristol County, *if* funding can be procured to implement the recommended changes in this report (including six additional full time mental health employees), the risk of suicide should decrease [emphasis added]."[41]

Relying on contracted medical and psychiatric service providers to prevent suicides often proves worse than useless as illustrated in a pending lawsuit. The estate of James Lynas is suing the medical staff at the Sherburne County, Minnesota, jail; a psychologist who scheduled an appointment with Lynas (a week after his jail suicide death); and the medical director and owner of the jail's medical services company, MEnD Correctional Care. Lynas had a history of drug and alcohol abuse. He was held in the jail the summer before for driving under the influence and tested positive for opioids and other drugs. He was re-incarcerated for another drunk driving charge in October 2017. An intake evaluation by a jail nurse reported he suffered from "depression and anxiety and was exhibiting suicidal ideation . . . due to pain association with withdrawal." A physician put him on mental health watch and ordered medication for him. According to the suit, no one followed up to see if the medication was working. A physician's assistant made an "urgent referral" for a mental health professional to see him, but that did not happen. The jail contends that the medical staff never said he was suicidal or Lynas would have been placed in a watch cell with a Kevlar gown. The lawsuit charges that MEnD Medical had only one doctor for four thousand inmates in thirty counties across the state in 2017, and the doctor spent almost all of his time on administration, not seeing patients.[42] In February 2021, the county's tax-payers and MEnd Correctional Care agreed to pay the Lynas family and their attorneys $2.3 million. The county had tried to get the suit dismissed, but the federal judge rejected its motion, writing that the officer's checks on Lynas amounted to no check at all. The county will pay $1.3 million and MEnD the rest. MEnD had tried to get the family to sign a nondisclosure agreement to keep the settlement amount secret, but the family refused. Both the county and MEnD insisted that the settlement not include any admission of wrongdoing.[43]

A number of statewide investigations have found their jails commonly fail to take remedial measures to prevent suicides.

The Associated Press and the University of Maryland's Capital News Service also completed an investigation of jail deaths by suicide in 2019. It revealed that "scores of jails have been sued or investigated in recent years for allegedly refusing inmates medication, ignoring their cries for help, failing to monitor them despite warnings they might harm themselves, or imposing such harsh conditions that the sick got sicker." After examining hundreds of local news reports, the investigators compiled a database of more than four hundred lawsuits filed in the last five years for mistreatment of detainees; 40 percent involved suicides in local jails, including 135 deaths and 30 suicide attempts. Not surprisingly, more than half of the lawsuit suicides occurred during the first seven days after entry, and many of those within the first forty-eight hours. Also, not surprisingly, 80 percent of the inmates were awaiting trial. Withholding medicine was just one of the means the joint examination found jails contributed to inmate suicides. It also revealed instances of inmates being given razors, despite clear warnings they might harm themselves. Many detainees rated high-risk for suicide weren't checked

Oregon Jail Suicides

Oregon Public Broadcasting, KUOW, and the Northwest News Network teamed up to examine jail deaths in Oregon and Washington in a series they called "Booked and Buried." They concluded, "Despite decades of concerns, jail leaders and elected officials have failed to protect inmates at risk of suicides." The investigation found between January 1, 2008, and December 31, 2018, at least 122 people died by suicide in the two states' county jails, representing 40 percent of all jail deaths. More than half occurred within two weeks of the person's entering the jails.

North Carolina Jail Suicides

Disability Rights North Carolina (DRNC) examined jail deaths in that state from 2013 to 2016, documenting a rising number of jail deaths by suicide. DRNC later updated the report to include suicides through 2018, noting that they had not gone down, nor had jails or the state adopted any of the reforms it had called for in its first report. Suicides accounted for almost half of jail deaths in the first report. In the second, their proportion of all jail deaths declined, but only because the number of nonsuicide jail deaths jumped dramatically. As in the Northwest investigation, almost all the suicides involved people being held after an arrest and awaiting trial. Twenty percent occurred within one day of entering jail; 65 percent within a week; and 80 percent within twelve days. Most involved people who were forty years old or younger. Comparing the jail suicides to those in the general population, the study found that a resident jailed in North Carolina was fifteen times more likely to die of suicide than those not incarcerated. Most, 85 percent, of the suicide deaths were caused by hanging, 10 percent from falls, and 5 percent from other self-inflicted causes. The state Division of Health Services Regulation, examining the last twenty suicides covered in the updated DRNC report, found an explanation. In almost half of the deaths, the jails were not in compliance with state Department of Health and Human Services regulations for jail safety. Jail staff failed to follow proper procedures regarding frequency and adequacy of cell checks. In 2019, the state reported twenty deaths by suicide in North Carolina jails, the highest number since North Carolina began keeping records of inmate suicides in 2013, representing an increase of 67 percent from the year before.

Minnesota Jail Suicides

In Minnesota, suicides were found to account for 60 percent of jail deaths. In five years ending in 2020, the Department of Corrections reported sixty-three jail suicide deaths, seven in the Hennepin County jail. The Hennepin County sheriff claimed that although seven died, the jail had stopped as many as 169 in 2017 and 20 in the first two months of 2021.

Sources: Disability Rights North Carolina, "Suicide in North Carolina jails, 2019 jail suicide report," June 2020, https://disabilityrightsnc.org/wp-content/uploads/2020/06/Report_Suicide-in-NC-Jails_June-2020.pdf; T. Knopf, "NC jail suicide and overdose deaths on the rise," North Carolina Health News, October 31, 2019, https://www.northcarolinahealthnews.org/2019/10/31/nc-jail-suicide-overdose-deaths-on-the-rise/; H. Critchfield, "North Carolina jail suicides reached record high last year, amid calls for reform," North Carolina Health News, June 4, 2020, https://www.northcarolinahealthnews.org/2020/06/04/north-carolina-jail-suicides-reached-record-high-last-year-amid-calls-for-reform/; B. Stahl, A. Lagoe, & S. Eckert, "KARE 11 Investigates: Minnesota jail failures costing taxpayers millions," KARE 11, October 29, 2020, https://www.kare11.com/article/news/investigations/jail-failures-costing-millions/89-519c65ec-0b35-4912-8966-b764e8bd2b5c.

---

regularly because of staffing shortages or inadequate training. Expanding its investigation beyond jail lawsuits, the reporters also completed an "exclusive 50-state reporting effort" to collect recent data on all suicides, not just those that engendered lawsuits. They found more than three hundred suicides in local jails from 2015 to 2017—in just the nine states that provided these data.[44]

After determining that its suicide rate from 2013 through 2018 was twice the national average, the Volusia County, Florida, Council hired an expert consultant to review the jail's suicide screening and prevention measures. Nearly all the detainees who died by suicide had been identified as at-risk. All but one had been placed on "suicide precaution" or housed in a mental health and detoxification special cell block. Two had died by suicide despite fifteen-minute interval checks by officers, two died while in the detox cells, and seven died after getting released from protective cells into the general population.

Lindsay Hayes, the expert consultant who had researched detainee suicides for the U.S. Justice Department Civil Rights Division, found the mental health assessment forms, including those for judging suicide risk, were inadequate. Second, mental health professionals were not involved in making determinations, and clinicians needed to take more detailed notes and develop treatment plans. Finally, detainees discharged from suicide precautions were not seen by mental health staff within twenty-four hours but after one week.

After the county council received the report, four more inmates took their lives in the jail. Hayes was invited back. He found the jail had continued to use the same assessment forms Hayes had found inadequate. The clinician notes still lacked key information. Correction officers, not mental health staff, were still assessing suicide risk. Treatment plans remained nonexistent. Once discharged from suicide precaution, detainees didn't get follow-up assessments until a week later, and it took a full month before they saw a clinician. Making things worse, the number of mental health-care professionals at the jail had dropped from five to three. Those remaining complained it was difficult for them to do their jobs because they could only ask detainees a few questions, as they were mostly forced to communicate through closed doors or food portals in loud cell blocks. During his second investigation, Hayes sat in on the jail's Suicide Task Force meeting, charged with examining suicides. He found the meeting, in which the task force reviewed four cases in less than an hour, "very problematic." The chairperson "appeared more concerned about incident reports having the correct signatures rather than thoroughly reviewing each case" to prevent future deaths.

After the second report, the county corrections director replaced the jail's contract with Armor Correctional Health Services, Inc., and required the new medical contractor to provide more staffing of licensed mental health-care professionals, including some who would work overnight hours. The director announced a psychiatrist would assume responsibility for discharging detainees from suicide protocols. Other reforms included a phone system to give more privacy to those receiving mental health evaluations; replacing metal bunks with safer concrete bunks; retrofitting cell grates to close gaps; an alert in the jail's computer system to tell staff whether a detainee had ever been on suicide protocols; a new step-down unit to assist detainees' transition to the general populations; creation of a detainee observer program where fellow detainees act as monitors, watching those who are detoxing from drugs or judged as potentially at-risk for suicide; training staff on "Mental Health First Aid" meant to provide basic skills on how to recognize and react to someone suffering a crisis; and asking families to inform the jail's staff about whether their loved ones have any history of suicidal thoughts or have shown signs of mental distress. However, the jail did not mandate time limits on how long individuals could be held in restraints. Hayes's report had criticized Volusia County jail staff for strapping detainees down for periods lasting forty-eight hours or longer. Hayes had advised that if strapped down for twenty-four hours, detainees should be hospitalized.[45]

What Hayes found in Florida was not unique. The Wisconsin Department of Corrections, charged with assessing the safety, sanitation, and fitness of local jails each year, found two violations in the Vilas County jail in January 2021. Tellingly, both involved failed suicide prevention efforts. The inspectors found that a qualified mental health professional was not authorizing the removal of detainees from suicide watch after an on-site face-to-face assessment. Removals were supposedly occurring based on telephone calls, but the jail did not identify the person on the other end of the telephone. The other violation was the jailers' failure to personally observe detainees on suicide watch at staggered intervals not to exceed fifteen minutes.[46]

Disability Rights Oregon investigated jail suicides in that state's jails in 2020 and similarly blamed the misuse of restraint practices, inadequate assessment of medical conditions, failure to provide necessary treatment, and often failure to take measures to prevent suicide, "even when detainees presented with known risks of suicide."[47]

After the national uproar over Sandra Bland's death by suicide in jail, Texas enacted legislation to prevent suicides of mentally ill persons arrested or incarcerated, including funding for electronic sensors or cameras for accurate and timely cell checks. Derrek Monroe, 28, soon demonstrated the limits of these reforms. In a central Texas county jail, he strangled himself with a phone cord. The officer on duty witnessed the act, but security rules barred him from entering the cell without at least one other officer present. It took ten minutes for another officer to arrive. Monroe died the next day in the hospital. Ironically, the jail at the time met the state's requirement of one jailer for every forty-eight inmates in a single-story jail or a jailer for each floor with ten or more inmates in a multistory jail. The standards are, of course, dangerously inadequate, especially for inmates like Monroe, who was already on suicide watch after attempting to kill himself the day before.[48]

Monroe was only the first suicide death after the Texas reform passed. Forty-eight jail suicides followed over the next two years.

The dismal conditions of many overcrowded jails can exacerbate mental illness, making suicides more likely. A lawsuit filed against the Clearfield County jail in Pennsylvania reveals a common scenario. Michael Duffalo died by suicide in the jail three days after his 38th birthday. Police had arrested

Cuyahoga County, Ohio, Jail

Brenden Kiekisz, 27, was jailed for failing to show up in court to answer for panhandling more than a year earlier. He suffered from PTSD, depression, and anxiety and abused opioids. He'd also informed officers that he had tried to kill himself days before his arrest. Three days after entering the jail, he was declared brain dead in a hospital from a suicide attempt and died two days after that. During the two days he was in jail, Kiekisz spent most of the time in forced lockdowns because the jail was short on correctional officers. The jail also had failed to give him his medication, according to his family. Kiekisz's death occurred just a month after U.S. Marshals had issued a scathing report on the Cuyahoga County jail, including denial of access to medical care and "red zoning," lockdowns that spanned entire days. It found that none of the 199 deficiencies documented in a prior 2015 audit pursuant to the federally mandated Prison Rape Elimination Act had been addressed. The report also found there has been fifty-five suicide attempts in the past twelve months, three of them resulting in deaths. Later, a former warden admitted that Kiekisz's death was "particularly preventable."

Spokane County, Washington, Jail

When Chris Rogers was sent to jail, pretrial services submitted a report that Rogers had mental health concerns—he had previously tried to hang himself. He was placed on suicide watch. When asked if he would tell staff if he had suicidal ideations, he said no, but later the same day, he talked of suicide. He was given medication for schizophrenia. The next morning, he was removed from suicide watch. A little more than a week later, he told medical staff that voices were telling him to kill himself again. After he was found with a towel wrapped around his neck, he was placed on suicide watch again after first being confined to a restraint chair. He was removed from suicide watch the next day. A little more than a week later, he hanged himself in his cell. In a subsequent lawsuit, the family alleged that the jail's medical provider, NaphCare, failed to evaluate Rogers for mental illness and never provided him any treatment.

Grundy County, Iowa, Jail

Jared Slinker was a 26-year-old mentally ill father of three. He tied a bedsheet around his neck and was left hanging for thirteen minutes because the one correctional officer who worked that night also doubled as a dispatcher. Jail policy prohibited him from entering a cell until another worker arrived, according to the lawsuit. The jail eventually settled the suit for $500,000. Slinker's father, a doctor, and Slinker himself had warned jail officials that Slinker was depressed and withdrawing from drugs. He had told a jail official he was delusional and was on an antidepressant, but the booking officer did not indicate this on his intake form.

Josephine County, Oregon, Jail

The last time Janelle Butterfield was jailed, her family e-mailed the jails: "If our Janelle were just another drug user, it would be hard enough to accept. But compound that with the horrible disease of PARANOID SCHIZOPHRENIA [emphasis in email], and you can begin to imagine what our hearts deal with on a daily basis. . . . We want to thank you for realizing that Janelle has people who love her dearly. We appreciate anyone who keeps our Janelle safe." Her public defender filed for a hearing to get her released to the state mental hospital so she could stand trial. The day a court transfer hearing was finally scheduled, she was found hanging from her top bunk, a bed sheet around her neck. According to a suit filed by her family, the jail did little to keep her safe. During her forty days of custody awaiting trial, she never saw a doctor, a nurse practitioner, a physician assistant, or a nurse from either the jail's medical or mental health provider. Further, the jail discontinued her antipsychotic medication after sixteen days when she said she didn't want it. She had prescriptions for several antipsychotic medications, aimed at treating schizophrenia, seizures, and bipolar disorder.

Edgecombe County, North Carolina, Jail

A detainee identified as S.N., a grandfather, committed suicide in 2018 in the jail. He had died by suicide after beating his own chest, trying to get his pacemaker to break. Jail staff responded by strapping him into a restraint chair and drugging him to keep him from harming himself. Then, inexplicably, they returned him to his cell without placing him on special watch, which would have increased cell checks from two to four per hour. Just hours after his return, guards found him hanging from a ceiling vent.

Sources: A. Ferrise, "Mother of man who died of suicide in Cuyahoga County Jail: 'They failed him,'" *Plain Dealer*, August 15, 2019, https://www.cleveland.com/metro/2019/08/mother-of-man-who-died-of-suicide-in-cuyahoga-county-jail-they-failed-him.html; A. Ferrise, "U.S. Marshals: Cuyahoga County deprives inmates of food, water, and Constitutional Rights among string of seven deaths," *Plain Dealer*, November 21, 2018, https://www.cleveland.com/news/erry-2018/11/9b3d3f3cc89150/us-marshals-cuyahoga-county-de.html; A. Ferrise, "Family of man who died of suicide in Cuyahoga County Jail after repeatedly warning jail staff sues county,"

Cleveland.com, December 21, 2020, https://www.cleveland.com/metro/2020/12/family
-of-man-who-died-of-suicide-in-cuyahoga-county-jail-after-repeatedly-warning-jail
-staff-sues-county.html; K. Riordan, "Family of man who died by suicide in Spokane
County Jail files wrongful death suit," KREM2, December 30, 2020, https://www
.krem.com/article/news/crime/family-of-man-who-died-by-suicide-in-spokane-jail
-files-wrongful-death-suit/293-a91b947e-21b6-430f-9418-df342891b669; S. Cohen &
N. Eckert, "AP investigation: Many U.S. jails fail to stop inmate suicides," AP News,
June 18, 2019, https://apnews.com/article/ap-top-news-ut-state-wire-ia-state-wire-ca
-state-wire-us-news-5a61d556a0a14251bafbeff1c26d5f15; C. Wilson, "Lawsuit reveals
details about Josephine County jail death uncovered in OPB investigation," Oregon
Public Broadcasting, May 15, 2020, https://www.opb.org/news/article/josephine
-county-jail-lawsuit-death-investigation/; Disability Rights North Carolina, "Suicide
in North Carolina jails, 2019 jail suicide report." June 2020. https://disabilityrightsnc
.org/wp-content/uploads/2020/06/Report_Suicide-in-NC-Jails_June-2020.pdf.

him the week before in a domestic disturbance where he threatened to kill himself, holding a knife to his head. However, they sent him to jail because he had an outstanding warrant for failing to appear on a misdemeanor theft charge. The suit charges that although police and jail officials knew Duffalo "was obviously suffering from a mental breakdown" and in need of medical treatment, they placed him in an overcrowded common living area. He was made to sleep on the floor under a jail-issued sheet, allowing him to remove a ceiling tile to expose a pipe and hang himself with the sheet. The suit blames his death on the jail's failure to provide a mental health evaluation, screen for suicide risk, or perform a drug test. After the death, the warden retired, explaining, "I've been doing this for 28 years, and it is grueling at times."[49]

As in this suicide, most jails provide the means. In addition to providing bedding that can be easily used for hanging, the standard jail response to at-risk inmates is to put them at greater risk. Jails put them in suicide smocks, deprive them of personal belongings, and place them in isolated lockdown in their cell notwithstanding a consensus among experts that human contact ameliorates risk of suicide. Further, the harsh treatment provided detainees deemed to be suicidal discourages detainees from reaching out for help.

Just providing different bedding could have prevented 65-year-old Elizabeth Gaunt's death. A former social worker with mental health and substance abuse problems, Gaunt was placed in a cell with a surveillance camera in Lake County, California. Jail staff was supposed to check on her every fifteen minutes. Over the twenty-five hours of her jailing, she begged for a doctor, screaming for help. She only stopped after she tore the bunk's blanket into strips, tested they were strong enough to hold her weight by attaching them to the sink/toilet apparatus, and then used them to hang herself. Although jailed after acting erratically, she had never been charged with a crime. The county subsequently paid out $2 million to settle her family's wrongful death suit. After Gaunt's suicide, the Lake County sheriff, Brian Martin, installed a larger surveillance monitor for guards to watch cells of high-risk inmates, added a registered nurse, automated the paper logs to better track cell checks, and replaced the blankets with tear-resistant ones.[50]

After attempted jail suicides tripled over three years, from twenty-three in 2016 to sixty-nine in 2018, the Cuyahoga County jail in Cleveland bought 2,000 specially constructed blankets that cannot be knotted or ripped apart. When announcing the purchase, jail officials said they expected between 500 and 750 detainees out of 2,000 would likely be provided the anti-suicide blankets. The new blankets did present a different problem. The jail had to figure out how to launder the blankets because they were too large to fit in the jail washing machines.[51] The Allegheny jail in Pittsburgh, Pennsylvania, reported that when it introduced the first 600 special blankets in one of its housing units, no one attempted suicide. It then bought 4,000 more for $237,000. Proving no good deed goes unpunished, the jail was lambasted by some critics who asserted the special blankets to be uncomfortable and unnecessary for most of the detainees.[52]

Chris Rogers, 24, had a long-standing delusion that he could save his family from a Martian attack by sacrificing himself. He was arrested in 2017 after running away from a mental health facility and stealing a car. In the Spokane County, Washington, jail, he was placed on suicide watch, initially requiring jail staff to check on him every fifteen minutes. For reasons not revealed, the suicide watch was withdrawn after several days, after which Rogers hanged himself with his bedding in his cell. Following a local newspaper investigation of his suicide—plus the suicide deaths of two other inmates who also used their bedsheets—the jail hired a suicide consultant and stopped providing inmates with bedsheets. In December 2020, Rogers's family sued the jail and its health-care provider, NaphCare, for his wrongful death.[53]

Some jails either don't take suicides seriously or don't accept any responsibility for preventing them. Jerome Thompson died by suicide in the

Mecklenburg jail in Charlotte, North Carolina. He threw himself off the second floor at the jail fracturing his skull. Earlier that very afternoon, a medical screener at the jail revealed Thompson suffered from "extreme" depression for which he was on multiple medications. However, Thompson was not placed on suicide watch. What makes this failure even more incomprehensible, Thompson had twice attempted suicide earlier that same day at the police station where he had been booked! He first stabbed himself in his artery with a pen cap and later intentionally and repeatedly fell backward from his chair to land on his head, requiring hospital treatment. Jailers were told of these suicide attempts, not to mention observing the bandage on his head from the injuries he'd sustained earlier that day. Thompson died six and a half hours after entering the jail. Within two months of his death, three other persons died in the same jail, including Kenneth Bigham, another black man, 39, who died by suicide while held in solitary confinement.[54]

Other jailers appear oblivious. In 2020, the City of Pasadena, California, finally settled a four-year-old lawsuit filed on behalf of a 32-year-old woman who suffered a traumatic brain injury after attempting suicide. Jail video revealed that Margarita Perez was preparing to commit suicide, including measuring her neck to the bedsheet. Not only did jail staff ignore this, but they also did not notice her hanging from a second story railing for nearly half an hour. The hanging left her paralyzed from the neck down, blind, and unable to communicate. The city settled for $8.5 million.[55]

Most inmate suicide attempts do not result in their deaths. Well-run jails with trained officers who maintain required surveillance of cells can and regularly do prevent suicide deaths. Deputies, in one example, prevented three suicides in one day at the Bexar County, Texas, jail. At 8:40 a.m.., a deputy saw a detainee hanging in his cell, rushed in, and removed a sheet around an inmate's neck. The detainee was rushed to the hospital, where he survived. Four hours later, a deputy conducting a cell check saw a detainee slouched on the floor with a sheet around his neck. He performed life-saving measures until medical staff arrived. Three hours after that, a deputy saw a detainee tying a sheet around his neck in a common area. The deputy ran over, removed the sheet, and summoned help. The detainee was taken to the hospital and survived. These three attempts brought the total number of suicide attempts in the jail that month to nine, down from eleven the month before. The sheriff's office also announced plans to establish a mental health hotline for family and the public to call if they had any concerns about a detainee's mental illness.[56]

A *Redding Record Searchlight* investigation of jail deaths in California points to San Francisco County's success in preventing jail suicides. After thirteen deaths from 2010 to 2012, only four occurred from 2017 to 2019, below the state's average. Sheriff Paul Miyamoto described how his office increased surveillance, monitoring, and check-ins. The latter, he explained, are critically important because they show detainees that the jailers care whether they live or die. Similarly, after paying out millions in lawsuits for the suicide death of Steven Neuroth, Mendocino County reduced its jail deaths in 2017–2019 to zero. Among other things, the jail required all entering detainees to be screened by registered nurses or high-level caregivers. It also got a new medical care provider.[57]

Preventing jail suicides requires immediate, sustained, and coordinated intervention. Finding that almost two-thirds of jails did not conduct reviews following jail suicides, the Vera Institute of Justice found that a vast majority of suicides are preventable, despite common perception that some deaths are inevitable. But to prevent suicides, it also found, jails need proper training, supervision, and communication.[58]

In a class action lawsuit filed by detainees against Missouri's St. Francois County Jail, one of the plaintiffs described how he saw another detainee attempt suicide with a makeshift rope torn from his blanket. When he tried to hang himself with it by jumping off a railing, the detainee pushed an emergency button to alert deputies. Deputies responded by telling him to stop pressing the button, but he continued until he was able to tell them about the attempted suicide. Seven minutes later, the deputies arrived and ordered everyone into their cells. The last the detainee who had alerted the deputies saw, deputies were wheeling the man who had hanged himself out in a wheelchair. He never saw the man again. He reported in the suit that he did hear one of the deputies who was wheeling the man out make fun of him for not knowing how to tie a knot.[59]

One of the problems many jails face is not enough staff. After the seventh attempted suicide in the Sandusky County, Ohio, jail since 2017, the sheriff testified to the county commissioners that he needed more funding to hire more officers. He had only four officers handing out medication and transporting detainees to court and four on suicide watch. The last suicide attempt was only prevented, he explained, because a corrections officer happened to notice toilet paper blocking a cell window. He had the cell opened to find the detainee hanging. Had he been five minutes later, the detainee would probably have died. An additional corrections officer would cost the county $63,000.[60]

After identifying a detainee as high risk for suicide, many jails make things worse by placing him or her in isolation or solitary confinement, often called "restrictive housing." Isolation potentiates suicide among those at risk. As the World Health Organization states, "Prisoners at risk should not be left alone, but observation and companionship should be provided."[61] A New York City jail study concluded that solitary confinement and serious mental illness were the strongest factors in suicide attempts.[62]

Solitary confinement has been found to also have long-lasting detrimental effects. A North Carolina study found people who spent time in solitary confinement were significantly more likely to die (of any cause) in the first year after release than inmates who did not, with the most common causes being death by suicide or opioid overdose. The more time individuals spent in solitary confinement, the more likely they were to be re-incarcerated or die compared to those who spent less than fifteen days in solitary.[63] Experts, summarized by the National Center on Institutions and Alternatives, recommend that housing assignments should be based on the ability to maximize staff interaction with the inmate, not on decisions that heighten depersonalizing aspects of confinement. It also should be noted that they recommend suicidal inmates be checked at intervals not exceeding ten minutes—although fifteen minutes remains the standard in most jails.[64] Disability Rights California spent two and a half years investigating the San Diego County jails where seventeen detainees died by suicide between 2014 and 2016. "The solutions . . . don't involve reinventing the wheel," concluded the Disability Rights' Litigation Counsel; the jails could simply stop excessively using solitary confinement on mentally ill inmates.[65]

In addition to ending overuse of solitary confinement, the accepted policy adopted by most jails to prevent suicides is for deputies to check on detainees identified as high-risk for suicide every fifteen minutes. However, investigations conducted after detainee suicides regularly find officers fail to make required checks that they recorded they made. When anyone bothers to investigate, these officers' failures are easily identified by a review of standard

Albuquerque, New Mexico, Jail

Albuquerque police arrested two suspects in a car that was reported as stolen. Each was held in a separate cell at a police substation. One used a set of shackles left in his cell to hang himself. An officer recorded on two detention log sheets he had checked on the man before his death. A subsequent internal affairs investigation, prompted by media coverage, viewed the video and found the cell checks had not been made. Further, when the officer did finally check and found the detainee on the floor with the chain around his neck, he kicked the man's leg and walked out, failing to render any aid or even check for signs of life. The investigators also found that *another* officer had also failed to render aid or call for medical assistance, and a supervising sergeant joined in submitting an inaccurate report. Internal affairs recommended the primary officer involved be fired. The police chief, instead, suspended the officer for 360 hours, which he allowed him to take as a few days PTO each week—essentially, a paid vacation.

Beltrami County, Minnesota, Jail

When Stephanie Bunker, 39, entered the jail, she told officials at her booking later that morning that she needed emergency care for kidney stones, was suicidal, suffered from depression and anxiety, and had tried to harm herself a couple months before. The standard suicide intake risk form revealed her score required intervention by medical staff and a mental health consult or institution of a suicide watch. She was placed on a fifteen-minute watch and provided a tear-resistant smock but was not required to wear it. But she was never seen by medical staff and was not checked on every fifteen minutes because a second suicide assessment indicated that she was not a suicide risk. The problem was, according to a lawsuit subsequently filed by the family, this assessment was completed *after* her death by hanging. The Minnesota Department of Corrections determined the Beltrami jail violated state rules by not requiring Bunker to wear the smock and repeatedly arriving late for her fifteen-minute checks. The same jail had also been found in violation of state jail rules in two other jail deaths, one that occurred the year before and one a year after Bunker's death.

South Fulton, Georgia, Jail

In a class action suit in 2019, an attorney representing detainees in the jail told the court that women with serious psychiatric disabilities were left in their cells for weeks and months on end. "In these conditions, they deteriorated, leaving them incoherent, screaming unintelligibly, laying catatonic, banging their heads against walls, and repeatedly attempting suicide." A U.S. District Court judge ordered the sheriff to allow detainees four hours out of their cells at least five days a week and to establish a plan for providing out-of-cell therapeutic activities. The sheriff appealed, arguing that the order would cause an "upheaval" by jail staff. He did not, however, contest evidence that solitary confinement is known to exacerbate mental illness.

Kern County, California, Jail

The jail "suicide watch" is a block of bathroom-sized isolation cells where individuals are kept alone twenty-four hours a day, dressed in a paper-thin set of clothes, and given a blue yoga mat to sleep on. Fluorescent lights reflected off the ash-white paint, and remained on 24/7. According to an investigation by the *Sacramento Bee* and ProPublica, the jail places hundreds of people in its suicide isolation watch, with some remaining in solitary for months. The sheriff explained the high-risk detainees are put "in an environment which is uncomfortable by design." The California Board of State and Community Corrections had previously informed the jail that the use of the yoga mats was in violation of state standards. The sheriff's response had been to buy one hundred more yoga mats. From 2015 to 2019, Kern had the highest suicide rate of California's ten largest jails, twice the statewide rate. While the Kern County behavioral health director agreed isolating suicidal detainees was harmful, he maintained it was much better than the indifference inflicted before on those detained in mental institutions. The county's behavioral health department doesn't provide treatment to detainees on suicide watch, although it does provide medication if people enter with prescriptions.

Sources: E. Kaplan, "APD officer violated policies in inmate's suicide," *Albuquerque Journal*, October 6, 2020, https://www.abqjournal.com/1504426/apd-officer-violated -policies-in-inmates-suicide.html; J. Gandsey, "Mother sues after 2017 inmate death," *Bemidji Pioneer*, July 6, 2020, https://www.bemidjipioneer.com/news/crime -and-courts/6563614-Mother-sues-after-2017-inmate-death-3rd-lawsuit-filed-against -Beltrami-County; K. Goggin, "Georgia sheriff argues against order requiring better jail conditions," Courthouse News Service, December, 16, 2020, https://www .courthousenews.com/georgia-sheriff-urges-panel-to-toss-order-requiring-better -jail-conditions/; J. Pohl & R. Gabrielson, "A jail increased extreme isolation to stop suicides. More people killed themselves," ProPublica, November 5, 2019, https:// www.propublica.org/article/a-jail-increased-extreme-isolation-to-stop-suicides-more -people-killed-themselves.

jail surveillance videos. The fact that officers continue to file false reports suggests they are confident no one will bother to check the videos even after a detainee's death.

Failure to prevent jail suicides often comes from the top. After a detainee was found dead by hanging in the Bradley County Jail in Tennessee, for example, Sheriff Steve Lawson announced, "From what I have seen, every one of my corrections officers did everything right. I commend my corrections staff for making timely cell checks and documenting in a manner of truthfulness, which is a testament to their commitment to the job and to the inmates. I also want to thank the jail's medical staff for all they have done in the wake of this situation."[66]

What the sheriff was basically saying is that jail suicides cannot be prevented. This, of course, is belied by actions taken by many sheriffs to prevent jail suicides. The Harris County, Texas, sheriff, for example, teamed up with mental health officials for a pilot program, providing detainees access to a suicide hotline. "It acted like a pressure valve," says Sheriff's Major Mike Lee. In Bexar County, Texas, where twenty-one detainees died by suicide from 2011 to 2018, a special team of deputies were organized to patrol the jail to identify detainees who may be at risk for suicide. The sheriff also began working with county officials to secure the release of nonviolent mentally ill detainees who may languish in jail because they can't afford a $250 bond.[67] After repeated suicides in the Lake County jail in Illinois and an undisclosed settlement with one of the victims' families who had sued for wrongful death, the sheriff revised policy to allow officers to call for an ambulance on their own initiative, even over the objections of the contracted medical provider. Since the change in policy, at least two detainees with medical emergencies received life-saving hospitalization in time, according to a jail sergeant.[68] Outside of Lake County, many jail administrators are reluctant to allow detainees to be sent to area hospitals because it requires officers to accompany them, costing the jail and limiting officers available inside the jail. The jail's contracted medical providers join them because, by contract, they may be financially penalized for failure to treat patients in-house.

Staffing shortages exacerbate the challenges many jails face in preventing suicides. In December 2020, for example, the Hampton Roads Regional Jail in Virginia had to transfer more than 250 inmates back to local jails because more than a third of the regional jail's positions, fifty-one, were unfilled. The jail, established in 1998, serves the Virginia cities of Chesapeake, Hampton, Newport News, Norfolk, and Portsmouth. According to employees, the lack of staff made the jail unsafe, especially as inexperienced officers replaced veteran staff. The officers reported that problems fed on each other, contributing to the shortage. Low pay, under $38,000 a year for some, made it hard to hire or keep officers. Short staffing means longer hours and tougher conditions for those who remain—so more leave, and the cycle continues. In 2020, the coronavirus made jail work even more fraught. The Hampton Roads Regional Jail is under U.S. Department of Justice oversight because it was found violating the rights of detainees in a 2018 federal investigation—the only jail to be put under such oversight during the Trump administration. In 2020, the jail and the Justice Department reached an agreement, a consent decree, to improve the facility by increasing staff and medical and mental health treatment. The federal monitor revealed that the staff shortage meant there were not enough officers to bring detainees for medical and mental health appointments or to get their medication. One of the reasons the jail was put under oversight was its excessive use of restrictive housing or solitary confinement for mentally ill detainees. But four years later, twice as many mentally ill detainees were in restrictive housing than when the initial investigation took place. A state study found the jail has suffered chronic staff shortages since it opened in 1998.[69]

Eight died in the Albuquerque jail between August 2020 and January 2021. Before 2020, there were ten deaths over four years, with none in 2018 and five in 2015. The deaths varied. Six died while detoxing from alcohol and drugs, two died as a result of suicides, and others from a heart attack, pneumonia, and other medical issues. While several correctional officers were suspended because of the deaths, others blamed poor medical care provided by Centurion, the jail's newly contracted medical provider. Making matters worse, however, was severe understaffing at the jail. The jail had 375 security personnel as of March 2021, though planned for 476. More than 20 percent of its positions were unfilled. Centurion's disorganization added to their burdens. The president of the correctional officers' association asserted that in one instance, barely trained officers had to do CPR for forty minutes while waiting for medical staff to take over. When inmate Vincente Villela died after officers subdued him, the association president said officers had to perform CPR on him because Centurion staff refused to assist "until their equipment arrived but then didn't have the keys to unlock the medical cart, the oxygen tanks hadn't been filled and the defibrillator wasn't charged. Things didn't get better from there."[70]

The Decatur County sheriff sued his county in 2021, demanding more money for his staff as the county had denied pay increases for years. According to the sheriff, his deputies got less than people employed at the local McDonald's. "Jailers were turning over so fast, it got to the point I didn't know who worked for me." The jail's current starting pay is $14.46 an hour.[71]

The failure of some jails to prevent suicides suggests more than incompetence, a critical lack of resources, even negligent deputies or the like. It suggests a basic lack of will or interest in doing so.

Jonathan Thomas was diagnosed as suicidal, paranoid, and schizophrenic. He tried to kill himself three times at the San Diego County, California, jail by jumping off upper tiers. One of the jumps shattered his pelvis. At the time of his third jump, Thomas had been returned from a state psychiatric hospital pending a hearing on whether he should be recommitted to the hospital as a "mentally disordered" offender. Despite his two prior jumps, jailers put him on what it called its "psych floor," located on the jail's sixth floor. According to a lawsuit, the sixth floor was not a "psych floor" with increased surveillance or medical attention. And it certainly did not prevent Thomas from jumping off the tier to his death. The jail's failure to implement a low-cost security fence, the lawsuit contended, demonstrated its deliberate indifference. Although fighting the suit in court, the jail subsequently added screening to prevent people jumping off upper tiers.[72]

RACISM AND BRUTALITY: THEY CAN'T BREATHE IN JAILS, TOO

The murder of George Floyd focused the spotlight on in-custody brutality on the streets. The same if not more can be found in too many of the nation's jails. This should perhaps not come as a surprise. Most jails are run by elected sheriffs who, as primarily law enforcement officers, stock their jails with other law enforcement deputies, poorly trained as jailers and too many possessing racist animus. At the height of George Floyd protests, the *New York Times* ran a story headlined "Three words. 70 Cases. The Tragic History of 'I Can't Breathe.'"[73] The story revealed, over the past decade, at least seventy people had died in-custody after saying the same words—"I can't breathe." More than half were black. The *Times* also noted that the people who died after

Bexar County, Texas, Jail

Burnt out by eleven years of staffing shortages, costing the county millions in overtime in a single year, deputies assert the impact has devastated their ability to do their jobs. Deputies, according to a report they commissioned, are working on average eighty to ninety-six overtime hours in a four-week period. The report said that due to pressure, the sheriff improved recruitment slightly, but poor retention rates were not addressed. The sheriff responded to charges that the jail constituted a "sweatshop" for employees, saying he didn't know of any sweatshops where people made $168,000 in a year.

Oklahoma County, Oklahoma, Jail

The screams of Brad Lane, 40, so alarmed another detainee in the jail that he unlocked his own cell door to investigate. He saw Lane bleeding on the floor of the cell. He called the jail medical number three times to summon help. When that didn't help, he called his girlfriend outside the jail to report the attack. He returned to Lane's cell to see Lane's cellmate continuing to beat him with a medical boot. He called medical again. Officers finally arrived, forty-five minutes after the first screams were reported, followed by medical staff. Documents revealed later that the jail corporal missed both her 6 and 7 p.m. pod checks because she was in the jail clinic at the time of the attack. The district attorney investigating the murder said his office and state investigators were attempting to determine if staffing deficiencies or other conditions contributed to any of the inmate deaths.

Saguache County, Colorado, Jail

Jackson Maes, 27, told his jailers he wanted to kill himself. They found his body eight hours later when they next checked on him. Lawyers for his family sued, alleging the county failed to properly fund the sheriff's office, leading to the hiring and retention of unqualified deputies, poor training, and inadequate health care at the jail. For years, the suit claims, the county was warned about unconstitutionally dangerous jail conditions that resulted from underpayment of staff, poor training, and aging facilities, but both the county commissioners and sheriff decided to devote their funds elsewhere. The county also ignored a previous audit by its insurance company directing the jail to remove items from cells that could be used for self-harm and to secure adequate medical services.

Sources: KENS 5 Staff, "Bexar Co. deputies' union says poor staffing is having a negative impact," KENS 5, December 9, 2020, https://www.kens5.com/article/ news/local/law-enforcement/deputy-sheriffs-association-of-bexar-county-says-poor

-staffing-at-jail-is-resulting-in-negative-consequences/273-e3206f2b-644d-4f25-be64
-d54b2c18fb43; P. Adger, "Court documents outline investigation into death at
Oklahoma County Jail," KOCO, January 11, 2021, https://www.koco.com/article/
court-documents-outline-investigation-into-death-at-oklahoma-county-jail-uncover
-problems-at-jail/35182691; E. Schmelzer, "Colorado jail deputies failed to check on
inmate after he made suicidal comments," *Denver Post*, March 4, 2021, https://www
.denverpost.com/2021/03/04/colorado-jail-suicide-jackson-maes/.

being restrained were "already at risk as a result of drug intoxication; others were having a mental health episode or medical issues such as pneumonia or heart failure." The *Times* concluded that too many in law enforcement have been falsely taught that "if you can talk, you can breathe."

To illustrate how widespread this belief is among officers, the *Times* described a posting of the erroneous advice on a bulletin board in Montgomery County (Dayton), Ohio, in 2018. The bulletin board was not in a police department. It was in the county jail. What made this example especially alarming was that a few years before, Robert Richardson, 28, had died in Montgomery County jail and the county had paid out $3.5 million to settle a lawsuit brought for his wrongful death.

Several more of the restraint deaths the *Times* cited also occurred in the nation's jails. Marshall Miles died in 2018 in the Sacramento County jail pinned down by sheriff's deputies. The same year, Vicente Villela died in an Albuquerque jail with guards holding him down with their knees. James W. Brown, an Army sergeant suffering from PTSD, died in the El Paso County jail after deputies placed a mesh-style mask over the lower half of his face. He pleaded with them to remove it because he could not breathe. He passed out and died the next day.

The death of Villela exemplifies the toxic and deadly mix of racism and brutality in jails. After his death, the deputy chief of the Albuquerque jail sent a text message to others, including the Metropolitan Detention Center (MDC) chief, that the Villela family called "disgusting." In it, the deputy chief used a racial slur to describe another detainee and referred to Villela as the "loser" killed by the correctional officer. Said the Villela family lawyer, "It speaks to the culture of indifference and the lack of accountability for the use of excessive force that has existed at MDC for years." He continued that the fact the deputy chief felt comfortable enough to effectively endorse in writing the killing of Villela is "a clear sign that the system at MDC is broken and needs drastic change." Equally telling was the fact that the MDC's chief ignored the message until it reached other county officials. He then claimed he had chewed the deputy chief out and referred him to sensitivity training. Later, the MDC's chief claimed he had also referred the case for investigation—but according to a subsequent investigation, an anonymous complaint initiated the county's investigation, not the MDC's chief. Two weeks after the text message, the deputy chief ordered it be deleted and threatened to fire the officer who received it. Four months later, a county panel recommended the deputy chief be fired, but he retired instead.[74] The county paid out $5 million to Villela's family to settle their wrongful death suit. The state attorney general, two years later, filed charges against the deputies involved for involuntary manslaughter.[75]

Unfortunately, the *New York Times* exposé of in-custody deaths just scratched the surface. Lawsuits for wrongful jail deaths caused by "positional asphyxia" have been filed against jails across the country.

Like within too many police departments, a correctional officer culture in many jails reinforces aggressive behavior, including brutality and racism. Sometimes the culture is set at the top by the sheriff. Correctional officer unions in larger jails also perform the same function as police unions, impeding accountability and reinforcing bad behavior. Also, as with police departments, correctional officers are amply supplied with weapons. Although firearms are not permitted in correctional institutions as a rule, correctional officers can be armed with Tasers, pepper gas, and the like. Many jails are equipped with devices, such as restraint chairs, spit masks, and restraint devices known as WRAPs, designed to be used to subdue inmates. If used excessively or incorrectly, all of these tools can and do kill.

The former Salt Lake City mayor Rocky Anderson described how toxic correctional officer culture had become in that city's jail in a two-hundred-page letter he sent to state lawmakers and the city's elected leaders. Based on the most recent deaths at the jail as just a few examples of how inmates were treated, he advised, "There is a systemic culture at the Salt Lake County Jail of immense disdain, even a cruelty, and certainly an indifference towards inmates, on all levels, including an indifference toward their serious medical problems. . . . People working for the county at the jail cause or allow this kind of devastation, and nobody holds them accountable. In fact, they don't

Kitsap County, Washington, Jail

When Sean Howell, 28, was booked into the jail, he was placed in a solitary "crisis cell." The next morning, he was seen tampering with the cell's sprinkler system. Officers entered his cell and restrained him (officers said Howell "violently resisted" them). Afterward, Howell showed signs of medical distress, according to the jail. Five days later, he succumbed to his injuries and died in a hospital. The coroner ruled that positional asphyxia was the cause of his death. The coroner explained, "It is when you get put into a position that is difficult for you to breathe. It is usually an unintended consequence." He ruled the manner of Howell's death was homicide.

Lansing, Michigan, Jail

Anthony Hulon, 54, died in April 2020 after four police officers handcuffed him behind his back and pinned him to the ground in the city jail. The county medical examiner ruled his death was caused by positional asphyxia and ruled it a homicide. According to a lawsuit filed by the family, the Michigan State Police recommended the state attorney general file criminal charges; however, no action had been taken by the time the lawsuit was filed in October. The next year, the attorney general said the officers did what they were supposed to do although the media warned that the video clip of the death released with the attorney general's statement was "disturbing."

Sources: A. Binion, "Kitsap jail inmate restrained by officers died of homicide from 'restraint asphyxia,'" *Kitsap Sun*, September 10, 2020, https://www .kitsapsun.com/story/news/2020/09/10/kitsap-jail-inmate-restrained-officers-died -homicide/3460421001/; K. Berg, "'I can't breathe': Wrongful death lawsuit filed against Lansing Police Department officers," *Lansing State Journal*, October 27, 2020, https://www.lansingstatejournal.com/story/news/2020/10/28/lansing-police -officers-jail-wrongful-death-lawsuit-back-work/3745749001/; C. Martinez & S. Lehr, "Attorney General: No charges against officers in Lansing Lockup," *Lansing State Journal*, April 9, 2021, https://www.msn.com/en-us/news/crime/attorney-general-no -charges-in-anthony-hulon-death-in-lansing-lockup/ar-BB1ftA9i.

even take the measures, usually, to find out what happened." The sheriff blamed the detainees. "Maybe," Sheriff Rosie Rivera explained, "some of those folks really should not be in a jail facility."[76]

There may be no greater example of racism in jail administration than what occurred in the Ramsey County Jail in St. Paul, Minnesota, when Officer

Derek Chauvin was held there after being charged with murdering George Floyd. Despite the national anti-racism demonstrations that followed Floyd's murder, despite heightened national alarm over racist behavior of police officers, what did the jail administration do when Chauvin entered the facility? It ordered all correctional officers of color to a separate floor and prohibited them from any contact with Chauvin because a supervisor said their race would be a potential "liability" around Chauvin, according to a copy of racial discrimination charges immediately filed on behalf of eight officers. When the actions of the jail became public, the chairwoman of the County Board of Supervisors said that they were "appalled and angered" over the order. As one shocked board member concluded: "Every supervisor should know that you cannot change someone's work duties or work assignments solely based on that person's race. That is civil and human rights 101." The jail superintendent was demoted, and the board asked the Human Rights Department to launch a probe into the county jail. Another supervisor specifically said the sheriff, who he said lacked accountability, perpetuated "racism and cronyism" in the department. He joined with colleagues in welcoming an external investigation into the sheriff's department. Prior to this incident, the board had butted heads with the sheriff, Bob Fletcher, over personnel. According to a supervisor, the board had worked hard to fire two employees, one for falsifying time sheets and the other for ongoing receipt of racist, sexist, and pornographic messages on his work e-mail. Sheriff Fletcher rehired them both.

Widespread racism in jails has been largely ignored. We know this because now, thanks to Black Lives Matter demonstrations, it is bubbling up to the surface. Just two years ago, for example, after an investigation by the Oregon State Police and a neighboring sheriff's office, the Washington County district attorney refused to charge a jail deputy for excessive force against a person being booked into the jail. A month after Floyd's death, the case was reopened when it was alleged the same deputy had used racial slurs in "online communication" for the last seventeen years at the jail! The deputy was placed on administrative leave, and the district attorney took the case to the grand jury. The jury returned an indictment for a misdemeanor charge of official misconduct in the first degree.[77]

Overt racism does not bar employment in some jails. Clayton County, Georgia, correctional officer Gregory Brown was fired for calling a detainee on suicide watch a "crazy [n-word]," overheard by other detainees and officers.

Nueces County, Texas, Jail

Although the medical examiner said David Johnson, 49, died from preexisting conditions, a subsequent investigation led to the indictment of three of his jailers for "official oppression and tampering with a governmental record" and one for "invasive visual recording" of his genitals without his consent. What they were "oppressing" was evidence of their assault on Johnson and then the failure of the jail to provide him any medical assistance despite his pleas as he was dying in his cell. He was later found on his cell floor, not breathing, with blood and vomit on his bunk and floor. A lawsuit filed by the family charged the jailers, the sheriff, Wellpath (the contracted medical provider), and four health-care workers with his wrongful death. After the death, the sheriff fired one of the three jailers.

Shasta County, California, Jail

The parents of John Adena, 31, filed a wrongful death lawsuit against the county and its medical provider, Wellpath, in April 2021. The suit charges that Adena, suffering from mental illness, was beaten to death in the jail, evidenced by cuts on the back of his head, a carotid artery dissection from trauma, extensive hemorrhaging on his neck, multiple bruises from blunt force trauma to his head and face, a chest cavity filled with blood, and severely bruised legs, ankles, and feet. He had marks consistent with having been beaten while handcuffed. He was also smothered to the point where his bottom teeth ripped into his lower lip.

Sources: B. Churchwell, "Federal lawsuit filed against Nueces County Jail in connection with 2018 inmate death," KIIITV.com, December 3, 2020, https://www.kiiitv.com/article/news/local/federal-lawsuit-filed-against-nueces-county-jail-in-connection-with-2018-inmate-death/503-118c462b-07a2-4902-a06b-22d9272a335f; A. Robinson, "Lawsuit filed against Shasta County Jail," KRCR, April 30, 2021, https://www.msn.com/en-us/news/crime/lawsuit-filed-against-shasta-county-jail-claims-beatings-lead-to-inmates-death/ar-BB1gcBVH.

What is revealing is that this was the third time Brown had been fired from a jail in the previous ten years, according to the Georgia Peace Officer Standards and Training Council's records. He was fired in 2010 from the Coweta County Jail for workplace violence. He was then hired by the Clayton County sheriff's office a year later but was fired in 2012 for "unsatisfactory performance during his probationary period." The sheriff's office rehired him the next year.[78]

Racism is not confined to the treatment of inmates. Anthony Eigner, a black man, was employed as a corrections officer at the King County jail in Seattle in 2014. He reported racist jokes and harassment. According to his wife, he refused to obey a sergeant who told him to fight a detainee. He also reported to supervisors about officers who used excessive force on brown and black detainees. Things got so bad, Eigner requested reassignment. His request was ignored. After a sergeant at the jail threatened him with a stun gun because they'd gotten into an argument, Eigner was fired for disobeying an order. He subsequently died by suicide. Anthony Eigner had survived the U.S. Marines, but he did not survive the racism and violence of the King County jail.[79]

Five other black corrections officers, three former and two current, told the media that what Eigner documented was merely a glimpse into the jail's institutional racism. The black officers reported that they have been punished and humiliated for complaining. One officer, a 38-year veteran of the jail, said that twice in the previous five years, someone has put human feces in the shoes in his locker. They report that two white officers wore MAGA caps at work to symbolize the antagonistic mentality of the white officers. At the same time, black officers had been confronted for wearing BLM and Obama shirts. As one black officer told KUOW of his white tormentors, "These are people that carry weapons, people in leadership roles."

Social media is rife with racist entries by white corrections officers. After the white teen, Kyle Rittenhouse, shot two demonstrators in Kenosha, one of the officers posted his picture and another wrote, "Great shot, two less for Uncle Joe [Biden]." Two white officers were placed on administrative leave for social media posts in September 2020. One of the officers that shared a racist meme had previously been sued for assaulting a black inmate in 2016, but the suit was dismissed. The black officers also reported being passed over for promotions and facing retaliation for filing complaints. With racist supervisors, they said, they had nowhere to turn.[80]

There are accusations of racism in the provision of correctional health care. Vermont has a unified correctional system, meaning the state runs both prisons and jails. A report issued by the state public defenders' Defender General on one black inmate's death charges that the death was the result of failures of both the prison's medical provider and correctional officials. It details concern about a "culture of dismissiveness" when it comes to complaints of inmates relative to medical care, compounded by racial bias. The report called for an independent panel to review medical care, misconduct, and racial bias. The Vermont corrections commissioner, James Baker, responded that "teasing out implicit bias isn't easy . . . but that's a very fair question." He replaced Centurion, the system's health-care provider, with VitalCore; hired a private law firm to investigate prison staff conduct on the specific case highlighted in the defenders' report; and created an office of professional standards to look into equity issues.

In the case that gave rise to the report, the detainee, awaiting trial, died from a tumor that blocked his airways. He had complained about not being able to breathe. Medical staff suspected a chronic inflammatory lung disease and gave him steroids. His symptoms got worse. When he complained more, guards threatened him with stricter confinement if he didn't "knock it off." He died that night. The correctional commissioner told the media, "No one should die in our custody the way [he] died."[81]

In August 2020, an *11Alive Reveal* TV investigation uncovered a video of a man detained in the Cobb County, Georgia, jail who is repeatedly heard by staff screaming that he could not breathe, while sheriff's deputies and medical personnel watch him die slowly. Although this occurred in September 2019, the sheriff did not release details about the death pending its investigation. It took many more months before the TV reporters could secure a copy of the video. The man who died, Kevil Wingo, a 36-year-old black man and father of three, had been arrested for drug possession. The jail video shows him knocking on the glass door of his cell in the infirmary where he had been taken for drug withdrawal trying to get a nurse's attention and collapsing five times. Although the video does not have sound, three employees told investigators that Wingo screamed he could not breathe and needed to go to the hospital. Two of the three believed him, but none took any action to assist him. A deputy did respond by telling him that if he could holler, he was breathing. A lab technician and a jail secretary were so concerned they asked a different charge nurse if they could at least take Wingo's vitals. She said no. Later the nurse said she refused because Wingo was rowdy, and he only wanted to go to the hospital to get drugs.

Instead of being taken to the hospital, jail staff put Wingo in a padded cell. The video revealed that Wingo was not rowdy nor was he attempting to hurt himself. He collapsed twice on being removed to the padded cell. It took

Sacramento County, California, Jail

Two years before George Floyd's murder, Marshall Miles, a 36-year-old black man, died at the jail, pleading with deputies on top of him, "I can't breathe." He had been arrested while experiencing a mental health crisis in a shopping center. Police charged him with two counts of vandalism. His death occurred less than fourteen hours after arriving in the jail, half an hour after being put in a segregation cell. When the three deputies had subdued Miles on the concrete jail floor, pressing their knees into his shoulders and back, he was shackled at his wrists and ankles. A jail video showed him wailing in agony. When deputies put him into the segregation cell, he laid motionless on the floor, face down. Thirty minutes later, when guards attempted CPR, it was too late.

His family filed a civil rights suit against the sheriff. Miles's family's lawyer deposed four of the deputies involved and told *The Appeal*, "There seems to be a huge discrepancy between what the sheriff says his cops are trained on and what the officers actually say they know. Of every deputy who physically acknowledged touching Marshall, none claimed to have ever been trained on where to place a knee or how to avoid asphyxiating someone. There seemed to be a complete ignorance and lack of knowledge about the safe way to restrain somebody on the ground in that manner." Commented a family member "[The sheriff's] gotta tell us that either his deputies weren't trained, or his deputies are wrong or not telling the truth." The family says since the death, the sheriff has taken no actions to improve the jail. The *Sacramento Bee*'s editorial board compared the sheriff to Bull Connor, the segregationist public safety commissioner who beat protestors in Birmingham, Alabama, in the 1960s.

Source: J. Iannelli, "Family of man who died at California jail after shouting 'I can't breathe' demands answers from sheriff," *The Appeal*, June 19, 2020, https:// theappeal.org/california-jail-death-sheriff/.

nine deputies to get him there, where he was left naked. Though jail personnel were supposed to check on Wingo every fifteen minutes, the video shows deputies walking right by the cell without bothering to look in. Within the hour, Wingo stopped breathing. Thirty minutes later, he was taken to the hospital, where he died. An autopsy concluded he died from complications of a perforated gastric ulcer.

According to the family's attorney, "At the end of the day, they didn't care. There was nothing he could have done to make them care. It's who they are."

The family established a website about the case. It alleges that the jail listed a Dr. Hindi as the doctor who saw Wingo there but that no such person exists. It is a pseudonym the jail's nurses use when they illegally perform a doctor's tasks. The sheriff's office concluded, after its investigation, what these in-house investigations typically find—that no one violated jail policy, therefore no one warranted discipline, much less criminal charges. The sheriff did respond to the TV investigators by saying, "At the end of the day, we are law enforcement officers, not medical professionals." The jail's medical provider, Wellstar Health Systems, responding to the video, admitted its nursing staff had failed Wingo. It called Wingo's death heartbreaking and unacceptable.[82]

The family asked the county district attorney to investigate. Wingo was just one of nine detainees who died in the jail between December 2018 and August 2020. The president of the Cobb NAACP is also calling for a complete investigation of all nine jail deaths.[83] The family filed a lawsuit against the jail and its medical provider the next month, alleging Wingo's constitutional rights were violated by sheriff's deputies and medical staff who did not treat him while he was in medical distress. It also charges that jail staff violated jail policy by not properly monitoring him after he was placed in a padded isolation cell. The family's attorney said the family had waited over a year to understand what had happened to Mr. Wingo and now wants to hold the defendants accountable.[84] Finally responding to mounting public pressure, the Cobb County district attorney, Joyette Holmes, announced that she had asked the U.S. attorney for the Northern District of Georgia to conduct an independent investigation into the jail deaths at the Cobb County Detention Center. She said the video should be part of the investigation into Wingo's death. Some welcomed the invitation, hoping it would bring attention to a broad set of problems at the detention center, including "lack of citizen oversight over the Sheriff's Office, poor transparency about inmate deaths, lack of proper food and water, policies of collective punishment, and little accommodation for veterans and people suffering from mental health issues." A lawyer for Wingo's family, however, charged the prosecutor was not asking for a specific investigation of Wingo's death but "a massive, broad investigation without any specific direction." Others pointed out that a federal prosecutor would be much more limited than a county prosecutor, as the feds only had jurisdiction to prosecute murders or civil rights violations. For her part, the district attorney refused to explain why her office would not conduct an investigation. She initially said her office could not investigate the case because of COVID-19 restrictions imposed by the Georgia Supreme Court. When the court lifted the restrictions, she said that a grand jury would be called to investigate the jail, but then called for the U.S. attorney instead.[85]

Federal investigations can get results in especially egregious cases. One looking into the Iberia Parish Jail in Louisiana documented widespread brutality and subsequent cover-ups. The investigation focused on the racial animus behind many of the beatings of black detainees. Sheriff Louis Ackal and a dozen staff at the jail were indicted for civil rights violations of prisoners. Ackal's 2016 trial included testimony of beatings and excessive force routinely used against black people. A guard testified that a supervisor once told him that he and a group of deputies needed to inform Ackal that they beat two black men. The guard said he was relieved by Ackal's response: "His remark was it sounds like a case of [n-word] knockin'." Nine deputies were convicted for brutality. The sheriff, accused of overseeing the whole operation, was acquitted, claiming ignorance and blaming his staff. He had been elected to his third term in office while the investigation was pending.

The sentences for those convicted were up to eighty-seven months in federal prisons. One beating in the jail that resulted in the largest lawsuit settlement involved a U.S. Marine, Derrick Sellers, who was permanently injured after guards broke his left cheekbone up to his eye socket and then stomped on his already broken face before pepper spraying him twice, once when he was in a fetal position. He suffered permanent brain damage. The sheriff's office paid out $2.5 million to settle his lawsuit. Other suits were settled, totaling another $3 million. The county's insurance company booted the county from the insurance pool that covers most of the state's other jails for costing it too much. Sellers's attorney declared that the culture that infested the jail under Ackal's watch gave license to the deputies. Even after the settlement, guards involved in the beatings remain employed at the jail.[86] When Ackal left office in 2019 after a decade as sheriff, more than one hundred cases brought by his office had been thrown out because of the federal investigation.[87]

But jail brutality has not been limited to jails in backwater, rural counties. Los Angeles jail presents a vivid example of a jail culture where officer brutality also came from the top down. We know this because Sheriff Lee Baca was sentenced in 2017 to three years in federal prison for his role in a scheme to obstruct an FBI investigation of pervasive deputy brutality against detainees in his county's jails. Although the prosecutor agreed to a plea deal to limit Baca's sentence to no more than six months, the judge, according to the *LA Times*, "unleashed a scathing rebuke of the man who ran one of the nation's largest law enforcement agencies for 15 years." He excoriated Baca for refusing to accept responsibility for overseeing and condoning the obstruction carried out by his subordinates. The judge expressed the hope that Baca's sentence would demonstrate that "blind obedience to a corrupt culture has serious consequences."[88]

For years, the ACLU of Southern California had reported on deputy abuse at the jail alleged by inmates to little effect. Then in its third report issued in 2011, it was able to substantiate what detainees had reported for years with eyewitness accounts by jail chaplains and others. Calling for the resignation of Sheriff Baca, the ACLU claimed a "pattern of severe and pervasive abuse of LA county inmates at the hands of deputies."

"This climate of violence has continued for years under the leadership of Sheriff Lee Baca, who has covered up and ignored claims of brutality." The legal director declared: "Deputy-on-inmate abuse has reached levels we've never seen before. . . . Contrary to what the Sheriff and his spokesperson contend, hundreds of inmates are telling the truth about deputy abuse. This . . . demonstrates that there is a salient pattern of unprovoked, excessive force and abuse against inmates, many of whom are not resisting. . . . The complaints reveal that deputies do not act alone; groups of them often attack non-resisting inmates. In other cases, they enlist other inmates to carry out their orders of abuse. In one instance, inmates sexually assaulted another inmate with a broomstick, while on another occasion others raped an inmate while holding his head in a flushing toilet; all with the apparent cooperation of the Los Angeles Sheriff's Department employees." A former FBI agent and assistant special agent in charge of the LA office agreed, "The violence is not the work of a few rogue deputies, but systemic. . . . It has continued unchecked for decades. Gang-like groups of deputies have been operating in the Los Angeles Sheriff's Department at least since the 1980s, and perhaps since the early 1970s, and these deputy gangs continue to operate today seemingly with impunity, right under the eyes of all levels of the current management of the Los Angeles Sheriff's Department."[89]

The case against Baca was one in a series of cases resulting from the investigation into county jail facilities in downtown Los Angeles that led to twenty-one convictions. Other lawsuits that have resulted in large payouts involved the "3000 Boys" and the "2000 Boys" at the Men's Central Prison. A jail official testified that deputy members would "earn their ink" by breaking inmates' bones. Defenders of the Los Angeles deputy gangs say they helped boost deputy morale.[90]

Sheriff Baca was not an outlier among sheriffs. The Cherokee County, North Carolina, sheriff and jail, for example, are currently being investigated after former guards revealed that detainees were ordered to beat up other detainees. The beatings were alluded to in a lawsuit filed by the family of Joshua Long. Intoxicated, Long died after receiving no medical attention until he collapsed on the jail floor without a pulse. The suit includes allegations that the jail perpetuated "an illegal cover-up" due to a "conspicuous lack of documentation." The suit points out that the paper trail for persons booked into jail is long, but for Long, they were mostly blank. Worse, before dying in his cell, Long shoved a piece of paper outside it. The paper, captured on video, disappeared and what was written on it was never revealed. It is also alleged that the jail sought to change Long's bond status, delaying the medevac helicopter to take him to the hospital for thirty minutes so that the jail would not have to foot any medical bills. By the time Long arrived at the hospital, he was dead from a methamphetamine overdose. Two investigations of the jail were reported to have been completed in 2019, including one of Long's death. The district attorney, however, would not reveal what was concluded, only declaring that she was working with partner prosecutorial agencies to determine what, if any, criminal investigations might be undertaken and which agency was the appropriate party to handle any prosecution. She failed to specify the identity of the partner agencies.[91]

Four months later, the prosecutor charged a former jail supervisor with aggravated assault and battery for using "unjustified and excessive force" on still another detainee. According to investigation documents, the detainee was noncooperative in putting on a suicide prevention smock. Two officers called their supervisor to assist them. The supervisor taunted the detainee and made him wrap himself in a blanket and walk to a room without a surveillance camera where the supervisor proceeded to beat him. The two officers intervened and placed the detainee in a restraint chair. The supervisor told the officers to leave the detainee there and have no contact with him, but one disobeyed and tended to the detainee's injuries from the assaults. Later, when the detainee was finally taken to the hospital, doctors determined that he had a broken wrist. The sheriff fired the supervisor the month before the prosecutor charged him.[92]

Deputies assigned to jails cover for those assigned to the streets. This may explain the death of Jorge Zuniga in the Hidalgo County, Texas, jail. In their lawsuit, the family alleges that Zuniga, a 23-year-old Hispanic man, was beaten by four deputies who arrested him for violation of an emergency management plan, public intoxication, and resisting arrest after those deputies, while responding to another call, found him asleep in a trailer park's grounds. The charges were subsequently dismissed, but during arrest he was, according to the suit, "tased multiple times, pushed to the ground, had his neck crushed, was handcuffed and placed in ankle restraints." He was later tripped then shocked with a stun gun, although he was fully shackled. The deputies took the seriously injured Zuniga directly to the jail, where fellow deputies did not acknowledge his injuries and did not provide a medical evaluation, even though the jail mug shot shows his head had to be held up by a deputy. Zuniga was placed in the "drunk tank" at the jail where he was found unresponsive twenty-one hours after being booked. EMS personnel found him hypothermic and with bradycardia, an 82.4-degree temperature, and injuries including a swollen, hyperextended neck. Doctors later found hematomas, accumulation of blood outside a blood vessel, on his left eye, right chest, upper arm, and nose. Doctors diagnosed Zuniga with a severe cervical fracture and a swollen spinal cord, resulting in him becoming quadriplegic. He spent a month in intensive care before returning home on a ventilator, completely paralyzed. He went back and forth to the hospital until he died several months later, suffering a heart attack due to acute respiratory failure. The lawsuit charges both the deputies on the streets and those in the jail of acting with the same deliberate indifference to Zuniga's medical needs.

Another lawsuit, this one filed by a victim's mother against the Guilford County Detention Center in Greensboro, North Carolina, details a laundry list of atrocities perpetrated by law enforcement against a jail detainee. According to the lawsuit, the body of Tasharra Thomas, a 33-year-old black woman who died in that jail after three days, had her nipples ripped off, bite marks and bruises on her body, some of her hair ripped out, and some possibly broken bones. The sheriff at the time did not allow the family to see the body or video of her death in the jail, but in 2020, a newly elected sheriff

Miami-Dade County, Florida, Jail

Darren Rainey, a 50-year-old black man suffering from schizophrenia, was jailed for cocaine in Miami-Dade County. Four Dade correctional officers threw him into a jail shower turned up to 180 degrees, hot enough to steep tea. As a punishment, they kept him there for two hours. His pleas to be released were met by laughter from the guards, asking him, "Is it hot enough?" Rainey died in the shower. His body temperature was too high to register on a thermometer according to the jail nurse. His skin fell off at the touch. An investigative reporter for the *Miami Herald* subsequently reported that jail guards used the showers routinely to scald and punish detainees who act out or upset them. That series led to lawsuits, some firings, rule changes, and a public hearing.

Madison County, Georgia, Jail

After being exposed by a Reuters investigation, state and federal legislators demanded that the jail be investigated for the death of Harvey Hill. Guards first kicked the 36-year-old black inmate apparently in retaliation for striking a guard with a lunch tray. They then punched him and slammed him into a wall. But then, as documented on jail video obtained by Reuters, guards led Hill to a shower, away from cameras where they beat him while he was handcuffed. They then took him to an isolation cell where he died. The autopsy ruled it a homicide, but no charges were ever brought against the officers by the district attorney. Jail officials said the guards' response to Hill's "combativeness" conformed to its use-of-force policy. The head of Mississippi's NAACP chapter says the case illustrates "why criminal justice has to be reformed." A suit filed by the family was settled by the sheriff and the jail's contracted medical provider, Quality Correctional Health Care, for undisclosed amounts.

Alameda County, California, Jail

Two former Alameda County, California, sheriff's deputies avoided jail by taking a plea deal for assault under the color of authority. They were charged with orchestrating a feces- and urine-throwing attack against a detainee. The detainee had allegedly been disrespectful to one of the deputies.

Sources: J. Iannelli, "Rundle won't charge prison guards who allegedly boiled schizophrenic Black man to death," *Miami New Times*, March 17, 2017, https://www.miaminewtimes.com/news/florida-wont-charge-prison-guards-who-boiled-schizophrenic-black-man-darren-rainey-to-death-9213190; L. So, "Mississippi state, federal lawmakers seek inquiry after Reuters report of jail beating death,"

Reuters, November 2, 2020, https://www.reuters.com/article/us-usa-jails-mississippi
-idUSKBN27I2OP; A. Ruggiero, "Ex-Alameda County deputies avoid jail time for
inmate feces-throwing," *Mercury News*, January 21, 2020, https://www.mercurynews
.com/2020/01/21/ex-alameda-county-deputies-avoid-jail-time-for-inmate-feces
-throwing/.

allowed it. A cellmate also revealed she observed jail staff harassing Thomas repeatedly, including an officer visiting her cell to bully and threaten her. She said that Thomas expressed fear for her safety. On at least two occasions, Thomas was removed from her cell late in the evening for no apparent reason and returned despondent, quiet, and crying uncontrollably in pain and barely able to move. She told her cellmate, "You don't know what they do to me." Seven detention center employees, all of whom were on duty during Thomas's incarceration, were fired in the months after her death.[93]

Transgender detainees are frequent targets of jailer abuse, including deadly abuse. Lea Daye, a black 28-year-old trans woman, was found unresponsive in her Cuyahoga County, Ohio, jail cell. Community activists charged the jail continued to represent a persistent danger and inhumanity particularly to trans people.[94] The same occurred after the death of Layleen Cubilette-Polanco in New York City's Rikers Island jail.[95] A 2015 U.S. Justice Department report revealed that more than a third of trans inmates experienced at least one incident of "sexual victimization by another inmate or facility staff in the prior 12 months."[96]

WEAPONS OF DETAINEE DESTRUCTION: TASERS, WRAP, PEPPER SPRAY, AND RESTRAINT CHAIRS

As previously mentioned, correctional officers typically do not carry firearms in jails, but they are armed with Tasers, stun guns, pepper spray and other gases, as well as tools to restrain inmates. Jails are typically equipped with restraint chairs and WRAP restraint systems, used to immobilize detainees. The latter comes standard with "soft cuffs" designed to fit all adults. Both include locking shoulder harness, leg restraint, ankle strap, and tactical bag.

Excessive use of all the above is regularly tied to jail deaths—like a death in the Ector County Detention Center in Midland, Texas, in June 2020. The detainee, a 38-year-old man, got into a fight with another detainee in the holding cell upon entry. According to the jail report, when staff intervened to

Mississippi County, Missouri, Jail

Despite being diagnosed by a mental health counselor as suffering from paranoia, Tory Sanders, a 29-year-old black man, died when eight correctional officers and Sheriff Cory Hutcheson decided he needed to be subdued in his cell. Hutcheson himself led a team of officers into Sanders's cell. They wore helmets and vests and held a large shield, according to a lawsuit later filed by Sanders's family. Sanders was tackled, pepper sprayed, hit with a stun gun, and punched while "pleading for help and struggling to stay alive." As the lawsuit also alleges, the sheriff personally kept his knee jammed on Sanders's neck for three minutes, even as a police officer at the scene urged him repeatedly to stop. Sanders fell unconscious and never revived. In 2021, a federal judge approved a half-million-dollar settlement. Defendants asked the judge to require the Sanders family to accept another $2 million to settle the rest of the case—the amount its insurers agreed to cover.

Sources: D. Murphy, "'They're trying to kill me,' Tory Sanders told mother before fatal collapse in rural Missouri jail," *Riverfront Times*, May 10, 2017, https://www.riverfronttimes.com/newsblog/2017/05/10/theyre-trying-to-kill-me-tory-sanders-told-mother-before-fatal-collapse-in-rural-missouri-jail; Associated Press, "Family of Black man who died in Missouri jail offered $2.5 million," AP News, April 29, 2021, https://apnews.com/article/tennessee-michael-brown-crime-lawsuits-23ef061df841215cf0f85bbeb9eb7a76.

break up the fight, he "began to charge staff members." Staff responded with multiple Taser shocks, then placed him in a WRAP to restrain his arms and legs. They then moved him to a padded cell, where he was later discovered to be unresponsive. A little less than an hour later, he was pronounced dead, the second to die at that detention center in six months.[97]

Similar deaths have resulted in lawsuits, like by the family of Sterling Higgins, a 37-year-old black man who died while jail staff restrained and strangled him in March 2019 in the Obion County, Tennessee, jail. After he lost consciousness, jailers placed him in a restraint chair and wheeled him to a cell. The officer who admitted putting his hand under Higgins's chin and then standing on his shackled leg was later promoted.[98] Officers kept Billy Ames, 36, in a restraint chair for twenty-four hours at the St. Francis County, Missouri, jail despite the manufacturer's warning that after two hours in the chair, medical supervision is required. Jailers also deprived him of his needed anti-seizure medication, which he started taking following a brain injury years before.[99] The county eventually agreed to pay $1.8 million to settle the wrongful death lawsuit.

Use of restraint chairs is not exceptional in many jails. In 2019, for example, jailers at Luzerne County Correctional Facility in Pennsylvania used them twenty-nine times, down from sixty-four the year before! The decrease was prompted by the aforementioned death of Shaheen Mackey, put into the chair while having an epileptic seizure. Complementing its use of restraint chairs, the Luzerne jailers also employ an electronic immobilization device, or EID. They used the device seven times in 2018, according to jail reports.[100] The Marshall Project news organization linked the use of restraint chairs to at least twenty jail deaths in the last six years and at least nine lawsuits.[101] As a lawyer who sued the Maricopa County, Arizona, jail numerous times when Sheriff Joe Arpaio ran it said, "It is utterly essential" that jail staff be trained if they use restraint chairs, which he calls "medieval." He adds, however, "They are damn difficult to use safely even with good training."[102]

Death investigations involving restraint chairs reveal that officers involved are often untrained in their use. The investigators of the restraint chair death of Sean Howell, led by the Washington State Police, for example, identified eleven "areas of concern," including inconsistent training and understanding on how to use the chair, use of a primary instructor for restraint chair training who had not received any formal training herself, no formal review process for uses of the chair, training materials available from the manufacturer not utilized, and more. Investigators found that officers bent Howell over at the waist while strapping him in, suffocating him. When officers pulled him back up, they eventually noticed that he was no longer breathing. Although Sheriff Gary Simpson refused to read the investigators' report, saying he would wait to see if there would be more investigations, he announced he was confident in his officers' work. Asked if the chair would still be used, he responded, "Absolutely," adding, "I don't think it's a tool we want to remove just because it is associated with a death."[103]

Jailers also kill detainees without equipment. John Neville died from injuries sustained after a guard placed him in prone restraint for fourteen minutes at the Forsyth County Jail in North Carolina. Guards entered his cell when told by a cellmate that Neville had fallen from a top bunk and might be having a seizure. Though confused, he was able to follow commands to

Starr County, Texas, Jail

Police arrested Alberto Peña, 29, after his father called to say his son was highly intoxicated and under the influence of drugs. He was taken to the jail to be booked for criminal mischief and causing minor property damage, less than $750, but was pronounced dead six and a half hours later. The initial autopsy revealed he had cocaine, marijuana, and alcohol in his system and his death was a "cardio-respiratory arrest," judged "accidental." Officers had placed him in a detox holding cell where, according to the sheriff's office, he became violent. As officers tried to calm him down, he reportedly hit his head on the cell door. Jailers then placed him in the roll cart for the WRAP restraint system. However, he managed to get out of the roll cart and hobble to the cell door and kick it. Officers placed him into restraints again. But, as the subsequent jail report emphasized, "Alberto made no outcry or notified the jail staff of any medical distress or trouble breathing." However, less than twenty minutes later, he was found unresponsive. Officers unwrapped him, removed him from the roll cart, and started CPR. He was transported to a hospital where he was pronounced dead. The cell video revealed he stopped breathing an hour before.

Cuyahoga County, Ohio, Jail

On what would have been his 32nd birthday, Esteben Parra's family sued the jail for his death. Parra entered the jail intoxicated at 9:30 p.m. but wasn't seen by medical until after 2 a.m. In the interim, both correctional and medical staff ignored warning signs that he was in medical distress. Instead of managing his withdrawal from drugs, jailers merely strapped Parra to a restraint chair. It took twelve hours before they sent him to a hospital, where he died three days later of a drug overdose. Commented Parra's sister, "The laws protect correction officers. Some detainees may need to be controlled. Some may have to be removed involuntarily from their cell. But there is a right way and a wrong way to subdue someone."

Sources: N. Puente, "Inmate dies in custody at Starr County jail," KGBT-TV, August 20, 2020, https://www.valleycentral.com/news/local-news/inmate-dies-in-custody -at-starr-county-jail/; C. Frye, "Cuyahoga County sued by family claiming improper medical care in death of former inmate," WOIO, June 25, 2020, https://www .cleveland19.com/2020/06/25/cuyahoga-county-sued-by-family-claiming-improper -medical-care-death-former-inmate/.

walk to another cell and kneel on the floor. That is where the guards lowered him into the prone restraint. Neville's hands were cuffed behind his back and his ankles were raised to his wrists. The autopsy report said Neville told the guards he could not breathe and cried out for his mother. After three minutes, he stopped talking. After four, he stopped moving. At fourteen minutes, guards released him from the prone restraint and left him alone in the cell. The nurse told the guards she didn't think Neville was breathing. Five minutes later they started CPR. None of the guards got in trouble for their actions. One even received a merit raise.[104]

For decades, experts have warned against "prone restraints" because they lead to positional asphyxia, when one person's weight presses against the other's diaphragm and prevents them from breathing. The U.S. Department of Justice National Law Enforcement Technology Center issued a bulletin about positional asphyxia in 1995, following a study of unexplained in-custody deaths. It advised, "As soon as the suspect is handcuffed, get him off his stomach."[105] Despite its ban in the state's prisons, state regulators allow prone restraints in local jails, like in Forsyth County.

Many jails have special "extraction" or "crisis" teams called in when detainees are out of control. These teams' training varies, but often their responses consist of brute force. The Jackson County, Missouri, jail had what it called a "Critical Incident Response Team" to quell disturbances. Officers on the team had eight hours of special training. After four incidents where officers on the team allegedly brutalized detainees, a nurse reported one of the injured detainees had suffered a broken back, neck, punctured lung, and two broken wrists. The FBI was called in to investigate, and though the results of their investigation were not made public, the four guards left the jail. The sheriff never revealed if they resigned or were fired.[106]

In many cases, untrained officers and even medical personnel misinterpret detainees having seizures or experiencing drug side effects as resistance to authority. Methamphetamine, cocaine, and other stimulants can make people extremely agitated and aggressive and induce psychotic symptoms like hallucinations and paranoia.[107] Detainees withdrawing from these substances, especially if the jail does not provide medically responsible withdrawal management, are at extreme risk from correctional officers who misinterpret their intoxication and withdrawal as defiance. The U.S. Substance Abuse and Mental Health Services Administration guide on stimulant treatment advises,

"For clients who exhibit severe symptoms of intoxication, consider pharmacological treatment, for example benzodiazepines, for acute management of agitation and distress, antipsychotic medication for psychosis/paranoia/hallucinations." For the many jails that provide none of these medications, the consequences often prove deadly.

Everett Palmer Jr., 41, died on April 9, 2018, in the York County, New York, jail two days after entering on a warrant for drunk driving. Withdrawing from methamphetamine, he became agitated and banged his head against his cell's bars. In response, five officers opened the cell door with a tactical shield and Tased Palmer twice before shackling him, putting a hood on him, and strapping him in a restraint chair. The "scuffle" lasted twenty-three minutes, according to the coroner. Once belted to the chair, Palmer was taken to the jail medical unit, where staff found him "unresponsive." He was then taken to the hospital and confirmed dead. His official cause of death: "complications following excited state, associated with methamphetamine toxicity, during physical restraint," with sickle cell disease as a likely contributing factor.

Palmer's family hired a forensic pathologist and neuropathologist to perform a second autopsy. He agreed with the coroner on cause of death but not the manner. He declared the cause to be "homicide," adding that Palmer would not have died but for being violently restrained. The family had initially grown suspicious when the first person who was not a county official to view Palmer's body told them to look at the bruising around Palmer's neck. The family also knew that Palmer didn't have sickle cell disease. Although there was video footage of the events leading up to Palmer's death, the family was not permitted to view it.[108] Subsequently, a grand jury convened by the prosecutor found that no one involved in the death was criminally negligent. Palmer's family also amended their lawsuit, charging that one guard provided methamphetamine to Palmer and that use of excessive force by guards was a "widespread custom and practice" at the jail.[109]

JAILS' TOXIC ENVIRONMENTS

It is often difficult to pinpoint a single cause for jail deaths. Isolation, racism, brutality, improperly trained or supervised deputies, inadequate medical providers, and overpopulated and understaffed facilities all add up to a lethal mix—particularly for the disproportionate number of detainees with

Bristol County, Massachusetts, Jail

The Massachusetts attorney general concluded that the sheriff's office violated the civil rights of detainees, engaging in "unnecessary use of force" that left three detainees in the hospital and several others in solitary confinement when they should have received medical treatment. The incident began when the sheriff pushed and threatened a detainee. According to investigators, officers in gas masks then entered the fray with a flash bang grenade, pepper ball launchers, shotguns with beanbag rounds, two battering rams, and K9 units. The congressman from the district accused the sheriff of "launching a paramilitary-style" force inside the jail to punish immigrant detainees.

Richmond, Virginia, City Jail

A class action lawsuit was filed against the jail for tear-gassing detainees after several spoke up about exposure to the coronavirus in their pod during the height of the pandemic. Instead of addressing their concerns (which proved valid, as one of the detainees tested positive after being transferred to their pod), according to the suit, officers in riot gear shot a tear gas grenade into the pod after first shutting off ventilation (increasing risk for COVID-19 exposure) and water supply so detainees could not wash their eyes. Evidence in the lawsuit included a grenade label warning that it should be used outdoors only. Many of those gassed were locked in their cells at the time, including detainees with asthma (yet another COVID-19 risk factor). Guards also repeatedly pepper sprayed detainees after the incident, per the lawsuit.

Sources: S. Betancourt, "Healy: Civil rights of ICE detainees violated," *CommonWealth*, December 15, 2020, https://commonwealthmagazine.org/immigration/healey-civil-rights-of-ice-detainees-violated/; J. Lazarus, "Federal lawsuit filed over tear-gassing of inmates at Richmond Justice Center," *Richmond Free Press*, December 3, 2020, http://richmondfreepress.com/news/2020/dec/03/federal-lawsuit-filed-over-tear-gassing-inmates-ri/.

mental illnesses. A lawsuit filed by a group of detainees against the Allegheny jail in Pennsylvania offers a summary of all that is too typically wrong with jails. According to the sixty-page federal lawsuit, the jail, where 64 percent of detainees are reported to have a mental health condition, has one of the highest jail suicide rates in the country. The suit cites an environment where staff belittle, abuse, and mock mentally ill detainees. Seeking class-action status, the suit lays out detailed allegations of excessive use of solitary confinement and restraint chairs, as well as implications by officers that detainees ought to kill themselves as punishment for suicide attempts. The lack of care, the suit charges, leads to psychological pain, increased disciplinary infractions, excessive use of force, and an elevated risk of self-harm. Detainees leave worse than when they enter due to correctional officers' hostility and psychiatrists' failures to meet and treat their patients. It further claims that the jail medical facilities are inadequate and its providers severely understaffed and untrained. The lawsuit seeks injunctive relief to prohibit the staff from continuing to violate the plaintiffs' rights, require the jail to provide adequate mental health care, and prevent staff from punishing plaintiffs when they seek help.

The managing attorney at the Pennsylvania Institutional Law Project, one of the three organizations supporting the suit, declared it appalling that the jail's top health care and mental health facilities administrators have no health care experience at all. Further, the suit charges, "due to the severe staffing shortages and lack of appropriate training, rather than provide any meaningful counseling, mental health staff simply 'make rounds' during which they only ask patients how they are doing and whether they want to hurt themselves." There was no full-time psychiatrist at the jail for seven months in 2020, and as of August 6 that year, 40 percent of the total health care positions were unfilled. Worse, in the absence of meaningful mental health services, correctional officers resorted to brutality. "OC spray, tasers, stun shields, extraction teams, forced nudity and immobilization in a restraint chair [while] facing a blank wall, is common and often lasts for hours." Officers were ordered to withhold privileges or use force against anyone requesting mental health care "to compel the person requesting help to be silent." The suit goes on to claim that the "widespread use of solitary confinement on people with psychiatric disabilities ... causes severe harm, resulting in class members leaving ... in worse condition than when they arrived, causing additional burdens and challenges to successful re-integration, and thereby contributing to a cycle of recidivism." Jail racism plays a role in officers' brutality, as the suit noted 67 percent of the jail population is black. "The Allegheny County Jail operates as the dark vortex of racial oppression in this county, fueling the cycle of trauma and violence."[110]

When the news organization *Public Source* tried to review the jail's mental health and suicide prevention policies, the county explained revelation of its policies "would likely result in a substantial and demonstrable risk of physical harm to or the personal security of an individual." Lamented one jail advocate, "If outsiders cannot get access to these policies, then how can the jail ever be held to account to whether it is even complying with its own policies?"[111]

DRUG AND ALCOHOL TOXICITY AND WITHDRAWAL

It was inevitable that once Big Pharma and the nation's doctors collaborated to expand opioid addiction across America, jails would feel the fallout. In 1980, there were reported 40,900 people incarcerated for drug offenses; by 2020, there were 157,000 in U.S. jails alone.[112] Considering that most drug arrests were for personal possession, this meant the number of people with substance use disorders cycling through the nation's jails has exploded. Many enter jail under the influence of opioids, pain pills, heroin, fentanyl, morphine, and/or buprenorphine, often mixed with methamphetamines, cocaine, alcohol, and benzodiazepines, often in life-threatening amounts or combinations. Without appropriate medical care, many leave the jail in ambulances to hospital emergency rooms or in coffins.

A 2019 review of jail deaths in the State of Washington found drugs or alcohol played some part in at least 38 percent of all its jail deaths, the percentage significantly higher for women than men. Drugs or alcohol were likely at least a contributing factor in 54 percent of women's deaths. The jails' drug- or alcohol-related deaths included overdoses and alcohol poisonings, deaths caused in part by poorly managed withdrawal, and deaths caused by other serious medical conditions whose symptoms jail staff mistakenly attributed to withdrawal. Like suicides, the Washington data revealed that the drug and alcohol jail deaths occurred quickly. Substance use–related deaths made up 67 percent of the deaths that occurred within the first seventy-two hours of admission and 58 percent during the first week.[113] Although medical examiners and coroners routinely declare these deaths to be from "natural causes," an increasing, but unknown, number of people entering jails die withdrawing from drugs and alcohol because of the jails' medical malpractice or nonfeasance. Tragically, almost all jail withdrawal deaths are easily preventable.

Jails have become by default the largest drug and alcohol detoxification centers in the United States. It is estimated that in 2016, 2,620,725 people withdrew from opioids in jail or prison. This number far exceeded the estimated 299,165 people detoxified in residential rehabilitation centers and 64,801 in hospitals during the same period.[114] No jail is immune. The warden of the Westmoreland jail in Pennsylvania, for example, testified to the county prison board that in February 2019, more than 80 percent of new detainees arrived addicted to drugs or alcohol. Of the jail's 187 detainees, 152 needed its detoxification services, 73 for opioids.[115]

According to the U.S. Department of Justice, as of 2009, only 2 percent of jailed individuals withdrawing from substances were provided specific withdrawal treatment.[116] It hasn't gotten much better. A later study of jail detoxification services across Colorado, for example, concluded: "County jails were not set up to treat people with addictions ... [putting] Colorado sheriffs on the front lines of a public health crisis they are currently ill-equipped to handle." Of the state's fifty-seven jails, as of 2019, only two routinely provided medication-assisted withdrawal management. In Montezuma County, Colorado, although nearly half of its detainees suffer from drug addition, the facility's medical resources consisted of one registered nurse.[117]

Throughout the last decade, most people entering jails in need of drug detoxification were on opioids, pain pills, heroin, or fentanyl, often mixed with alcohol and methamphetamines. It is a widespread belief that detoxing from opioids, though agonizing, is not dangerous. That has proven a dangerous myth, particularly when it comes to jail populations. As Dr. Jeffrey Keller explains in *Jail Medicine*, "Yes, young healthy patients can tolerate being sick with no lasting problems from withdrawal. But what about someone who is not healthy to begin with? Someone with asthma or heart disease? Or with underlying sepsis acquired from sharing needles? Or malnourished and dehydrated from not eating? Add physiological stress of withdrawal, of course they can die."[118] Health risks, including fatal ones, multiply if the person withdrawing is on more than one drug. Seizures, for example, do not usually accompany opiate withdrawal, but if the individual is also withdrawing from benzodiazepines, the risk of seizures increases.[119] The American Society of Addiction Medicine (ASAM) and the Substance Abuse and Mental Health Services Administration (SAMHSA) have issued the following edict regarding withdrawal management: "For

Duval County, Florida, Jail

According to the wrongful death lawsuit, Lina Odom, 28, died because the jail and its medical provider, Armor Correctional Health Services, failed to provide her medical care despite knowing she was subject to withdrawal seizures. Staff ignored her pleas for help until she died on her sixth day in jail—the day she was scheduled for release.

Salt Lake County, Utah, Jail

Lisa Ostler died withdrawing from opioids in the jail. Her family filed a wrongful death suit blaming the jail's "recklessness and indifference." The suit charged that jail nurses failed to conduct mandatory assessments for patients experiencing withdrawal symptoms. Ironically, the medical director at the jail had authored a treatise on managing opiate withdrawal, describing it as "a life-threatening medical condition" that "can frequently result in death if not managed appropriately."

Thurston County, Washington, Jail

Lummi tribal police arrested Joseph Cagey, 28, for drug paraphernalia before sending him to the Niqually jail (having no tribal jail, the tribe contracted with Niqually at that time). Although Cagey first denied he was on opioids, his withdrawal symptoms didn't lie. A video showed him in significant distress before he collapsed the same day he was booked. The coroner determined Cagey died of complications of opioid withdrawal, likely suffering from dehydration and electrolyte imbalance. Based on the autopsy, video footage from the jail, and medical records, the coroner ruled his death to be a homicide. The evidence, he concluded, showed Cagey did not receive the care that he should have in the jail. The Lummi tribe voted unanimously to end its contract with the jail.

Sources: First Coast News Staff, "Wrongful death lawsuit filed in 2018 death of woman in JSO custody," *First Coast News*, October 16, 2020, https://www.firstcoast news.com/article/news/crime/wrongful-death-lawsuit-filed-in-2018-death-of-duval -county-inmate/77-aedc4c34-c52a-46c5-8f81-f8f4829fdaad; T. Wilcox, "Managing Opiate Withdrawal," cited in J. Miller, "Deaths at the Salt Lake County Jail," *Salt Lake Tribune*, June 7, 2020, https://www.sltrib.com/news/2020/06/07/deaths-salt-lake -county/; S. Gentzler, "28-year-old deemed homicide victim in latest probe of inmate death at Nisqually jail," *Olympian*, September 16, 2020, https://www.theolympian .com/news/local/article245722615.html.

alcohol, sedative-hypnotic, and opioid withdrawal syndromes, hospitalization (or some form of 24-hour medical care) is often the preferred setting
for detoxification, based on principles of safety and humanitarian concerns.
*When hospitalization cannot be provided, then a setting that provides a high
level of nursing and medical backup 24 hours a day, 7 days a week is desir-
able* [emphasis added]."[120] As previously mentioned, research also links
substance-use disorders with higher risks for suicidal ideation, attempts,
and deaths, especially with central nervous system depressants like opioids,
benzodiazepines, and alcohol.[121]

People with alcohol- or substance-use disorders, typically detained in the
nation's jails, are disproportionately likely to be in poor health. Since 2018,
for example, the Philadelphia Department of Prisons, which runs the county's
jails, has tracked the medical conditions of the several thousand detainees
referred to its pioneering medication-assisted treatment program each year
for those with opioid-use disorder. Through fall 2020, the jail's medical staff
found that 27 percent also suffered from asthma, 22 percent from Hep C, 13
percent from hypertension, 8 percent from alcohol-use disorder, 4 percent
from diabetes, and 3 percent from HIV. Almost 20 percent suffered from two
or more of these disorders, as well as their opioid addiction.[122]

Mix in benzodiazepines (Valium, Xanax, Ativan, Librium, Klonopin,
Restoril), alcohol, and other drugs, and detoxification becomes even more
dangerous. Many entering detainees do mix, like the Cuyahoga County,
Ohio, detainee who died after being arrested and booked for cocaine and drug
paraphernalia in his car. Jailed, he began vomiting and hallucinating. When
his symptoms continued, the jail sent him to a hospital, where the arresting officers should have taken him in the first place. The medical examiner,
completing the autopsy, reported the drugs in his system included ecstasy,
marijuana, cocaine, and liquid PCP.[123]

Too many jails also force detainees on prescription opioid medications,
including methadone and buprenorphine, to detox from these medicines, the
latter prescribed by their doctors and the former obtained through opioid
treatment programs (OTPs). One of the more horrifying detox deaths, for
example, occurred in a Macomb County, Michigan, jail involving a 32-year-
old man being treated with methadone, an FDA-approved medication for
opioid-use disorder, as well as prescribed benzodiazepines for anxiety. His
cause of death, after spending days in agony and losing more than fifty

pounds, was determined to be "acute withdrawal from chronic benzodiaz-epine, methadone and opiate medications." The jail video revealed a naked, emaciated young man curled in a fetal position on the floor of his cell. It is alleged that correctional officers had alerted the physician covering the jail to the man's condition but were told that the symptoms they described were normal for opioid withdrawal.[124]

It has taken multiple federal court orders for individuals to get a handful of jails to continue providing them methadone or buprenorphine, another FDA-approved medication for opioid-use disorder. So far these court deci-sions have only covered individual plaintiffs. Fortunately, several of the jails that were ordered to provide the medication to a specific individual have gone on to implement medication-assisted treatment programs, providing opioid medications to detainees with prescriptions, as well as others with OUD when deemed appropriate. The number of jails that provide agonist opioid medications, including methadone and buprenorphine (usually combined with naloxone), however, remains very limited, numbering fewer than several hundred as of winter 2021. More jails provide antagonist medication only, usually injectable naltrexone marketed as Vivitrol, also an approved FDA opioid medication. Before naltrexone may be provided, however, persons must be opioid free for seven to ten days, requiring complete withdrawal from opioids. Methadone may be provided immediately, obviating the need for opioid withdrawal, and buprenorphine may be provided when opioid symptoms are reduced, usually after a day. Inmates provided an injection of Vivitrol are usually given it immediately before release, covering them for the first twenty-eight days in the community, a time of extremely high risk for overdoses for released addicts.

One of the complicating factors for continuing patients on methadone is that methadone cannot be prescribed for opioid treatment. Jail physicians can only prescribe methadone to opioid users during pregnancy until the baby is born, to protect the fetus from abrupt withdrawal, but not for the mother's addiction treatment. Doctors may also prescribe it for temporary pain relief, but to obtain methadone for opioid-use disorder, patients must be enrolled in DEA-approved Opioid Treatment Programs (OTPs). Very few jails in the United States are licensed to be OTPs, mostly those in major cities, includ-ing New York, Chicago, Albuquerque, and Baltimore. In order for jails to provide incarcerated persons methadone, they either have to transport them to the nearest OTP in the community every day or arrange for a community OTP to come into the jail every day to physically bring the person his or her daily dose. When the Middlesex County Jail in Massachusetts partnered with a community OTP to be able to offer methadone to detainees, the DEA required the jail to install a safe in which to store the medication—a measure meant to safeguard methadone from being stolen from community OTPs. The Middlesex County Jail discovered that it had to reinforce the floor holding the DEA-approved safe due to its weight.

Opioids are not the only drugs that may require clinical withdrawal management. Buprenorphine withdrawal can also be deadly. For this reason, medical experts recommend if detainees are not going to remain in jail for a long period of time, jails should not even attempt to detoxify them. In the community, with time, psychiatrists recommend weaning patients off benzodiazepines by reducing doses by 10 percent every four weeks. For long-acting benzodiazepines like Valium, a detainee may not show withdrawal symptoms for two or three weeks. If not continued on benzodiazepines in the interim or carefully monitored, the patient can then, seemingly out of the blue, suffer a seizure and die. Detoxing from alcohol is the most complicated of all. Chronic drinkers can experience delirium tremens and seizures unless carefully managed.

A leading expert on jail withdrawal, Doctor Kevin Fiscella, warns, "Newly admitted jail detainees and inmates have high rates of alcohol and opioid dependence. Acute withdrawal from these substances is common in correctional facilities. Unrecognized and untreated alcohol (and chemically related sedative/hypnotic) withdrawal can be fatal. Untreated opioid withdrawal results in needless suffering, potential interruption of vital treatments such as antiretroviral treatment for HIV, and masking of symptoms from other life-threatening illness. In the presence of significant chronic illness, untreated opioid withdrawal has resulted in deaths. Even in healthy patients, untreated opioid withdrawal results in needless suffering, diversion of opioids within the facility, and behavioral challenges for custodial staff."[125]

In addition to agonist medications that can be used to taper people off opioids, the FDA has recently approved the first non-agonist medication, Lofexidine, that mitigates the symptoms of opioid withdrawal. Most jails don't use any of them. Almost no jails provide the latter, and few use agonist medications to safely taper people off opioids. Utah jails are typical. According to a state legislative report, the Salt Lake County jail alone offers various FDA-approved withdrawal drugs, including methadone, buprenorphine, naloxone, and naltrexone. All of the other counties either did not have withdrawal protocols for detainees, did not submit them if they did, or offered only non-narcotic-based withdrawal treatments, using off-label medications for diarrhea or nausea. Generally, the smaller jails had no protocols and provided no medications. The state legislature ordered the report after at least two detainees died in 2016 from opioid withdrawal in two of the state's counties, resulting in wrongful death lawsuits.[126]

The recent increase in methamphetamine has presented jails with additional withdrawal challenges, evidenced by a corresponding increase in lawsuits for jails' failure to also treat methamphetamine toxicity and withdrawal. In addition to presenting medical issues, people withdrawing from methamphetamines can be paranoid, aggressive, and out of control. The behavior is called "tweaking," a slang term referring to the irrational actions and behaviors that can take place after meth use.

Most jails either don't have or don't follow appropriate clinical protocols for withdrawal management and detoxification. The Whatcom County, Washington, jail provides a typical example. In the summer of 2018, police arrested Kirk Powless on suspicion of identity theft, possession of stolen property, and possession of a controlled substance, heroin. Powless admitted to the arresting officer that he was a daily user. Police took Powless to the county jail, where staff also knew him to be a heroin user because of prior contact. Upon admittance to the jail, Powless was given a "health screening," performed by a non-medically trained jail deputy. Despite knowing of his heroin addiction and his arrest for possession, the jail did not institute a detoxification protocol. However, that would have made little difference at the time as it was jail policy to deny medication for people detoxing from opioids. Powless, in a second-floor cell by himself, died alone and was not discovered until almost an hour after he died. Powless's family's wrongful death lawsuit alleges the jail's policy of making persons detox "cold turkey," without medical supervision, allowed Powless to die a "terrible and easily preventable death, suffering pre-death pain, anxiety and terror."[127]

Other jails may not have an explicit "cold turkey" detox policy but simply fail to provide medical care in general, including for high-risk withdrawal.

Buncombe County, North Carolina, Jail

Michele Smiley, 34, died when left alone in her cell after being jailed for a probation violation. She apparently ingested methamphetamine she possessed at the time of her apprehension to avoid getting caught with the drug. A state review by the Division of Health Services Regulation, which oversees jails in North Carolina, found that the jail had failed to meet detainee supervision rules. A lawsuit filed after her death said that she exhibited signs of a "severe medical reaction to the methamphetamine overdose" but received no treatment. Witnesses said she told jailers about ingesting the drug and complained of convulsing, vomiting, and "burning up" inside. Allegedly, jail staff reassured her that she needn't worry—she was just going to get "really high." The county settled for $2 million. The medical provider also settled, but the amount was kept secret because it is a private company. Since the settlement in 2019, the jail now requires all persons who report being on drugs to be taken directly to a local hospital first for a medical assessment.

Summit County, Ohio, Jail

Timothy Strausser Jr. was booked in the jail at 4 p.m. on drug charges. He became agitated and hostile, according to the medical examiner's report, enough so that officials removed a neighboring detainee. The next day, the judge came to Strausser's cell to arraign him because officers could not get him to cooperate with transportation to his court hearing. Later that day, paramedics responded to his complaints of shoulder pain, reporting he was still combative, but they evaluated him. The jail kept a cleaning crew out of his cell because of his behavior. His behavior apparently kept officers away, too, because shortly before 5 p.m., a day and an hour after he first arrived at the jail, an officer found him hanging in his cell by his bedsheets, his knees almost hitting the floor. The officers cut him down and tried to revive him, unsuccessfully. The toxicology report revealed both methamphetamine and THC in his urine.

Sources: J. Boyle, "Buncombe County reaches $2M settlement in jail death," *Asheville Citizen Times*, December 18, 2019, https://www.citizen-times.com/ story/news/local/2019/12/18/buncombe-county-reaches-2-m-settlement-jail -death/2678255001/; B. Morehead, "Medical examiner rules jail death a suicide," *Barberton Herald*, August 12, 2020, https://www.barbertonherald.com/2020/08/12/ medical-examiner-rules-jail-death-suicide/.

Teton County, Wyoming, for example, paid out $377,500 to the family of Scott Millard, who died withdrawing from alcohol in the county jail. He entered the jail with a blood alcohol content (BAC) almost four times higher than the legal limit for drunk driving. In addition, he suffered from diabetes and hypertension and was experiencing severe tremors, agitation, and anxiety. Rather than send him to a hospital to manage this extremely risky withdrawal, his care was left to correctional officers, as there were no medical personnel on duty. He was dead within forty-eight hours.[128]

Further west, police arrested James Wippel while he smoked methamphetamine in his car outside a casino and took him to the Jefferson County, Oregon, Jail, where he remained unable to raise $7,500 bail imposed for the drug charges. Staff put him on the jail's seventy-two-hour detox program. They later admitted that they had expected his withdrawal to be "pretty rough." He told the jail nurse he was using a gram of heroin a day. An officer saw him later in his cell that evening rocking back and forth, complaining of stomach pain. She also noticed blood in the toilet and reported her concerns to the corporal on duty. However, since no nurse was on duty at night, the corporal said there was nothing they could do. During the officer's next round, she saw more blood on the floor of Wippel's cell. The next morning, when asked how Wippel was doing, another officer said he was faking a medical emergency. Wippel soiled himself and was moved to another cell, limping with labored breathing, where staff gave him Gatorade and breakfast. He died shortly thereafter. A jail video showed a pool of blood on the cell floor and more blood sprayed on the wall near where Wippel's head had been. The corporal in charge denied noticing anything other than a little bit of blood on the floor. Another officer testified, "The only thing I was told is that he was detoxing off heroin, really bad. And I'm not familiar with heroin, or how people detox, other than what I'd seen in the movies." Apparently, those movies failed to reveal that vomiting blood is not a normal part of heroin withdrawal.[129]

Jails are frequently absolved of any responsibility for drug withdrawal deaths. Medical examiners and coroners typically rule them to be "accidental." The courts and the media generally accept these verdicts from medical examiners. A brief South Bend, Indiana, story offers a typical example. The report quotes Indiana State Police saying that the autopsy and toxicology results determined 37-year-old Jason Peters died of "heroin, fentanyl, and meth toxicity. Peters was found unresponsive in his jail cell back on September 2. His death has been ruled accidental." The story did not question whether jail medical staff tried anything to prevent Peters's death, whether the jail even had a medical protocol for high-risk detoxification, or whether there were any available trained medical staff to implement it.[130]

Sometimes medical examiners rule overdose deaths to be "natural." Michelle Bewley, 35, was placed on suicide and "disintox" (short for "disorderly intoxication") watch, requiring checks every fifteen minutes. She spent her first day and night in the Clay County, Florida, jail screaming in pain, according to another person incarcerated at the same time. Though given Pepto-Bismol for nausea and Ativan for anxiety, she vomited up the medication. After twenty hours, nurses gave her an Ativan injection, which they repeated four hours later. The last time a nurse checked on Bewley, her skin was cold, and she was moving around too frantically to let the nurse listen to her breathing. Concerned, the nurse called the off-site, on-call doctor but got no answer. Bewley was left in her cell to be checked every fifteen minutes by officers. Log records document that officers did check every fifteen minutes for the next two hours, but they failed to discern that Bewley was already dead when most of the checks occurred. A medical examiner reported that the death was "natural," the result of hypertensive heart disease, with "chronic drug abuse and opiate withdrawal as contributing factors." Bewley had been jailed for shoplifting.[131]

The U.S. Food and Drug Administration warns that the combination of drugs Bewley was on in the jail—benzodiazepine like Ativan mixed with opioids like fentanyl—can be deadly, especially for people with underlying heart conditions. Nonetheless, the Clay County sheriff declared the treatment jail staff provided to her to be acceptable. A Florida Department of Law Enforcement charged with investigating jail deaths also found no deficiencies in the jail's response. However, the jail did begin a special medical unit overseen by nursing staff. The sheriff maintains the reform was coincidentally instituted after Bewley's death, not because of it.[132]

There is no consensus on specific withdrawal protocols for jails, where medical providers tend not to have the luxury of extended periods of time to gradually taper people off drugs or alcohol over several months. However, there is absolute agreement that "clear and valid criteria are needed for initiation of medical detoxification" so that all inmates who experience appreciable withdrawal are treated and that those who do not experience such symptoms do not undergo needless treatment.[133]

Many jails refuse to accept any responsibility for withdrawal management, affording it a low priority or asserting they have no money to pay for it. The sheriff in Alamosa County, located in Colorado's rural San Luis Valley, for example, admitted that although the vast majority of detainees were addicted to opioids and methamphetamine, he didn't have the resources for medication, let alone qualified medical staff to administer it. The only thing the jail could do, he explained, was closely monitor those in withdrawal, which he admitted "looks like something out of a scary movie." He put men and women together in a 10 by 10 foot holding cell with nothing but a hole in the floor and a mat to sleep on. They are given paper uniforms and blankets aimed at preventing suicide.[134]

The Washington report on alcohol and drug deaths discussed earlier also diagnosed why so many detainees were dying in the state's jails. Most of Washington's jails had no protocol for monitoring withdrawal, and fewer than half of the jails surveyed provided any medications to those withdrawing. In 2018, the Spokane County, Washington, Jail launched a new program to prevent inmates from dying of opioid withdrawal. With its contracted medical provider, NaphCare Inc., it began providing buprenorphine, a synthetic opioid, to inmates withdrawing from opioids who present with "sufficiently severe withdrawal symptoms."[135] There is also evidence that a single high dose of buprenorphine may provide rapid treatment for suicidal opioid-dependent patients.[136] After the death of Powless described earlier, the ACLU filed an unrelated federal civil rights lawsuit against the jail for not providing opioid medication to a detainee with a prescription. The ACLU argued the jail's failure violated the Americans with Disability Act, as addiction is considered a disability. In a settlement, the jail instituted a medically supervised detoxification program using the FDA-approved medication buprenorphine to taper people safely and humanely off opioids. It also now provides medication-assisted treatment (MAT) for all those who desire it. The State of Washington also subsequently provided funding to expand MAT in jails. These Washington State jails, however, remain the exceptions, not the rule, though Denver and several other Colorado jails have now instituted medically appropriate withdrawal management programs, as well.

A review of wrongful withdrawal jail death lawsuits reveals most die from simple dehydration. Their symptoms and metrics are not hard to observe, even if observers have not completed medical school. The person cannot hold down food or liquids. They vomit and have diarrhea, further depleting their body of hydration. They lose weight rapidly. A pending wrongful death lawsuit from Michigan demonstrates how jailers and their medical providers can inexplicitly fail to act.

The RAND Corporation assembled a panel of experts on jail and prison deaths in 2017, which concluded that "most forms" of death in corrections are preventable with proper interventions. It made the following

---

Macomb County, Michigan, Jail

David Stojcevski, 32, died from acute withdrawal from chronic benzodiazepine use among other drugs sixteen days after entering the jail. He'd been jailed for failure to pay traffic fines. Jailers watched him writhe in pain, hallucinate, and lose fifty pounds in a little over two weeks, more than a quarter of his body weight. In the last two days of his life, he lay listless on the floor of his cell, first on a thin mattress and then on the cement floor. He was found there, struggling to breathe, before being taken to the hospital, where he died. The autopsy found cause of death to be acute withdrawal, dehydration, electrolyte imbalance, and either seizures or seizure-like activity. Though initially placed in what the jail purported to be a three-day detox program, Stojcevski was released before his withdrawal symptoms surfaced. He was then transferred to a high-observation mental health unit. In spite of his hallucinations and convulsions, however, jail medical staff found no need for intervention, telling concerned correctional officers that his symptoms were typical for drug withdrawal and he was no doubt faking seizures to get meds. According to a class action lawsuit, his death was "completely avoidable." Dehydration can be prevented by a simple IV drip. The suit charged, "All of the named defendants were so deliberately indifferent to David's mental health and medical needs, that [they] . . . monitored, watched and observed David spend the final ten days of this life suffering excruciating benzodiazepine withdrawal symptoms."

Source: C. Guyette, "Lawsuit targets billion-dollar company making life-and-death medical decisions in Michigan jails," *Detroit Metro Times*, March 12, 2020, https://www.metrotimes.com/news-hits/archives/2020/03/12/lawsuit-targets-billion-dollar-company-making-life-and-death-medical-decisions-in-michigan-jails.

recommendation to reduce jail withdrawal mortality: (1) provide medical and mental health services at a community-level standard of care; (2) better manage organizational and cultural conflicts between security and care objectives; (3) greater capacity for medical, mental health, and substance abuse care, both within facilities during incarceration and in the community after release; (4) expand medication-assisted therapies and drug overdose countermeasures; (5) more-uniform adoption of best practices in suicide risk assessment and prevention; (6) compliance with national standards for medical screening and care provisions; and (7) greater electronic information sharing between and among correctional institutions and community-based health providers.[137]

Decades ago, Congress created a state and U.S. territory grant program to promote prison and jail drug treatment. Although recently amended to promote opioid medications in prisons and jails, it focuses on treatment for sentenced defendants. It does not address, much less mandate, jails providing withdrawal management for the millions who enter them each year. The Justice Department's technical assistance provider for prison and jail drug treatment programs, however, produced a training video on a model jail program that provides an excellent example of jail withdrawal management and treatment for opioid-use disorder.[138]

The Philadelphia Department of Prisons that runs that city's jails has been able to both mitigate risk of withdrawal deaths and advance opioid treatment. It began in 2008 instituting a medical intake for all entering detainees that must be completed within four hours of arrival. Anyone who enters under the influence of alcohol or drugs or is determined at-risk for suicide is pushed to the front of the line for clinical intervention. For those who come in with prescriptions for methadone, a contracted methadone program for the jail provides their regular dose as prescribed, the same for those with buprenorphine prescriptions. While withdrawal is clinically managed for anyone in need, those who wish to be induced on buprenorphine (with naloxone) receive ameliorating medications until their withdrawal symptoms are reduced enough to begin taking the medication. That usually takes no more than a day or so. As a result of providing medication-assisted treatment that obviates days of agonizing withdrawal symptoms, the Philadelphia jails are now the largest opioid medication program in the state and perhaps in the country. As of 2021, on average more than 3,300 detainees each year are released on buprenorphine medication and another 700 on methadone. It also offers naltrexone injections for those who want it in lieu of the agonist medication. Once released, the detainees are referred to a network of community clinics that provide counseling and in-house pharmacies for continuing care and medication in the community.

Detainees also die in jail by overdosing on drugs they obtain *after* being incarcerated.

San Diego County, California, Jail

The San Diego sheriff finally reported that a detainee, 31, had died in one of his jails two months earlier of "acute fentanyl, alcohol and citalopram intoxication (an anti-depressant)." The detainee had been jailed in July and died the following December. The sheriff's office did not disclose how the detainee, described as struggling with drug addiction for years by his brother, obtained the drugs and alcohol. A month later, Omar Hasenin, 41, was found unresponsive in his cell. The San Diego medical examiner's office determined he died of fentanyl toxicity, with a contributing cause of cardiovascular disease. Hasenin had been booked into the jail a month earlier. Again, there was no report on where he obtained the drugs. Months later, Jonathan Whitlock, 35, died of an overdose. He had been in the San Diego jail for a year. The medical examiner ruled his death due to "acute fentanyl intoxication with a contributing factor of obesity."

Bartholomew County, Indiana, Jail

After two inmates died of overdoses in the jail, both on methamphetamines, the county invested $179,000 in a new body scanner to prevent drugs being smuggled into the jail by hiding them in body cavities in 2019. The county coroner ruled a June 2021 jail death to be an overdose on fentanyl.

Sources: KUSI Newsroom, "Sheriff: Jail inmate's death was due to drug overdose," KUSI, December 8, 2020, https://www.kusi.com/sheriff-jail-inmates-death-was-due -to-drug-overdose/; City News Service, "Autopsy: Inmate died of accidental drug overdose," Fox5, January 12, 2021, https://fox5sandiego.com/news/local-news/ autopsy-inmate-died-of-accidental-drug-overdose/; S. Pascoe, "County authorities say jail inmate died from fentanyl overdose," *San Diego Union-Tribune*, August 5, 2021, https://www.sandiegouniontribune.com/news/public-safety/story/2021-08 -05/county-authorities-say-jail-inmate-died-from-fentanyl-overdose; Staff Reports, "Jail inmate died of fentanyl overdose," *Republic*, August 18, 2021, http://www .therepublic.com/2021/08/19/jail_inmate_died_of_fentanyl_overdose/.

As part of his plea bargain for obstructing investigations into the deaths of multiple inmates, the former warden of the Cuyahoga County Jail in Ohio agreed to sit down with the state attorney general and FBI. According to transcripts obtained by the media, ex-warden Eric Ivey admitted that drugs "poured" into the jail. Four of the nine people who died between June 2018 and May 2019 in the Cuyahoga County Jail died of a drug overdose. Ivey suspected correctional officers of smuggling in the drugs. He explained that the officers stationed at the entrance to the jail didn't screen fellow officers because they didn't want to be in the position of policing colleagues. Despite his suspicions, he said he could not stop the influx of drugs. The sheriff's detectives, in charge of investigating wrongdoing at the jail, were "no help." When alerted to possible drug smuggling by officers, the sheriff put the investigation "on the back burner," waiting for concrete evidence, although the jail had no independent investigators to provide it. The U.S. Marshals, however, corroborated Ivey's contention. In their report on the jail, the Marshals found the sheriff failed to investigate jail overdose deaths (as well as criminal cases against officers for beating detainees). Subsequently, an officer was charged with drug smuggling in the jail, as a result of an investigation of inmate Kenneth Evans's overdose on fentanyl in his jail cell. Medical staff had to give him two shots of naloxone to prevent him from dying. The investigation found the correctional officer was working with gang members in and out of the jail to run a drug-smuggling ring. Prosecutors charged that the officer helped turn the jail into a "lawless zone where drugs were easier to access than on the streets."[139]

While the Cuyahoga County Jail may be an extreme outlier, it is certainly not unique.

New York City, New York, Jail

Six correctional officers and fifteen detainees at Rikers Island, New York City, were charged with smuggling and bribery to funnel drugs into the city jails. Said the city investigator, "Contraband smuggling enterprises have long plagued city jail facilities. The arrests today are another example of a pattern in which inmates and outside conspirators identify correction officers vulnerable to corruption and use them to carry drugs and other illegal substances into the jails."

Lancaster County, South Carolina, Jail

A detention officer was arrested for smuggling drugs into the jail to a detainee with whom she was romantically involved. The officer was charged with misconduct in office, two counts of distribution of drugs, conspiracy to deliver drugs to inmates, furnishing inmates with contraband, and attempted furnishing of contraband to inmates.

Duval County, Florida, Jail

An officer was charged with smuggling methamphetamines and marijuana into the facility. According to the news report, the officer is the tenth sheriff's employee arrested in the same year, although it did not break down how many worked in the jail.

Atlantic County, New Jersey, Jail

A correction officer allegedly made thousands of dollars bringing in contraband to the jail. The president of the corrections officer union released a statement, "Let me start off by stating, no one and I mean no one, dislikes a dirty officer as much as a good officer!"

York County, Pennsylvania, Jail

A corrections officer was charged with plotting with an accused murderer to smuggle drugs into the jail. His attorney alleges that while the officer received money, he had no intention of delivering on the drugs. However, a search of his car led investigators to almost $3,000 in the trunk and seventy-five Suboxone strips, a buprenorphine/naloxone medication for opioid use disorder subject to abuse. The state police revealed in the court hearing that there was also a separate investigation into a second drug-smuggling ring in the county jail. The detainee accused of involvement with the officer was reported to be a regular buyer of Suboxone (a synthetic opioid) and is accused of shooting someone during a drug deal.

Sources: C. Marcius, "Rikers Island correction officers, inmates charged in drug smuggling scheme," *New York Daily News,* January 14, 2020, https://www .nydailynews.com/new-york/ny-rikers-island-officers-inmates-charged-narcotics -bribes-contraband-20200115-geohurt4n5acrdkdazqygk7rve-story.html; A. Dys, "Lancaster S.C. detention officer arrested in plot to smuggle drugs to inmate," *Herald,* November 14, 2020, https://www.msn.com/en-us/news/crime/lancaster-sc -detention-officer-arrested-in-plot-to-smuggle-drugs-to-inmate-cops-say/ar-BB1b0355; *First Coast News* Staff, "Jacksonville corrections officers arrested," *First Coast News,* November 2020, https://www.firstcoastnews.com/article/news/crime/jacksonville -corrections-officer-arrested-charged-with-smuggling-meth-marijuana-contraband

-into-jail/77-0130cf28-5573-4935-997c-43751b75157c; L. Cohen, "Corrections officer allegedly smuggled drugs, cell phones into Atlantic County jail," *Breaking AC*, October 16, 2020, https://breakingac.com/2020/10/corrections-officer-allegedly -smuggled-drugs-cell-phones-into-atlantic-county-jail/; L. Scolforo, "Police: York prison guard accused in drug-smuggling plot still being actively investigated," *York Dispatch*, August 5, 2020, https://www.yorkdispatch.com/story/news/ crime/2020/08/05/police-york-prison-guard-accused-drug-smuggling-plot-still-being -actively-investigated/3297790001/.

SECURITY AND MEDICAL PROVIDERS TEAM UP TO DEPRIVE CARE

While perhaps no one should expect America's jails to compete with the Mayo or Cleveland Medical Clinic for those in need of care, one would expect that they at least operate like competent MASH units, triaging patients and sending those with life-threatening physical and mental conditions to better-staffed hospitals and other care facilities. And one would be wrong.

Jail detainees, withdrawing from alcohol and drugs or not, represent a disproportionately medically fragile population. Among those in jail, rates for HIV, hepatitis, asthma, heart disease, and other conditions are disproportionately high. These conditions are exacerbated by the fact that 80 percent of people entering jail have had limited medical care prior to their last arrest.[140] Less than a quarter of those re-entering the community who have a diagnosis of chronic conditions have been found to see a physician in the year following release, suggesting that even those with chronic conditions have little medical care.[141]

Hospitals and care providers outside of jails aren't perfect, of course. Patients die from preventable deaths. However, even a cursory analysis of jail deaths finds obvious patterns of medical malpractice and neglect that account for a disproportionate number of avoidable deaths in jail. Withholding needed medications and failing to provide any medical treatment at all provide two of the clearest examples.

Although coronavirus-related deaths have been the result of a hopefully rare global pandemic, these deaths in jail cannot be dismissed as inevitable. They, too, represent the dismal failure of jail administration and health care. Suffice it to point out, that like the jail deaths covered in this book, some jails avoided all COVID-related deaths, while others reported multiple deaths—many accounting for the hot spots in their cities or counties. On the one-year anniversary of the start of the pandemic, for example, the San Francisco sheriff was able to report no COVID-related deaths in the jail. He credited collaboration between his office, jail health services, and other "justice partners." The director of health attributed the jail's success to "the decision to intervene early, such as providing masks and limiting jail personnel to essential workers, which paid off in saving lives." Contrast this to many state and federal prisons that reported 51 percent more deaths from COVID than the mortality rates for those who share common demographics outside the walls. Local Bay Area jails have seen both detainee and employee COVID deaths. These same jails, like the Santa Rita Jail, also see high rates of detainee deaths in general, many of which are featured in these pages. The same year the San Francisco jail had no COVID deaths, the state prison system reported 216.[142]

Withholding prescribed medication and medical care is a regular practice in many jails. The death of Roderick Pendleton, 51, in Suffolk County, Massachusetts, jail exemplifies the inadequacy and cruelty that too often defines jail medical care. He died from a bowel obstruction. Detainees told investigators that he was "way beyond sick," saying he was skinny with a strangely distended belly. He was moaning and throwing up in a pail for days just a few feet from the nurses' station, so they could hear his screams. An officer found him lying on the floor, gasping for breath, and pleading for help. Jail staff finally brought him to the hospital, where he was pronounced dead three hours later. He was one of 127 people the local NPR station identified who died in Massachusetts jails for medical causes over the last decade. Many, according to the report, like Pendleton, were simply ignored or their symptoms were not believed.[143]

It took Lanekia Brown's family two years to get the death certificate, but once they did, it confirmed their belief that their pregnant daughter died because Madison County, Mississippi, jailers ignored her pleas for assistance. They left her to die in the medical unit, never seen by a doctor or transferred to a hospital. In their lawsuit, the family accuses the jail of simply lacking concern for incarcerated black and brown individuals.[144]

It should also be noted that contracted, privately run jails are especially deadly, combining the worst of poorly run government jails and contracted for-profit medical providers. For example, CoreCivic's Marion County Jail in Indianapolis has had twenty-three suicides in recent years, fifty-four since 2008 through April 2021. According to a local TV news report, the reason for the jail's dramatic death rate is that it has only thirteen deputies working the floor for a population of around eight hundred. Because the wages are so low compared to neighboring counties, it has trouble attracting and retaining staff, although the total revenues for the company in the first quarter of 2019 were $484.1 million, up 10 percent from the prior year quarter (dividends were up to 28 percent from the prior year quarter). According to news accounts, its death rate is two to three times the national average.[145] In July 2021, there was another suicide by hanging at the jail. The detainee was not on suicide watch but "was experiencing substance abuse withdrawal."[146]

JAIL MEDICAL PROVIDERS (MAKING MONEY, LIMITING CARE)

Inadequate medical care for those withdrawing from drugs and alcohol is only the tip of a very large iceberg. The largest proportion of jail deaths are detainees dying of illness and medical conditions, including an unknown number whose deaths can be attributed to negligent or nonexistent jail medical care.

When police jailed Timothy Kusma, 31, a diabetic, in the Naples Jail Center in Florida in March 2019 for driving with a suspended or revoked license, he was in "good condition," his blood sugar levels "normal."[147] Though he'd long been diagnosed with Type 1 diabetes, Kusma managed the condition with regular insulin use. However, when the Naples Jail Center's contracted, for-profit medical provider, the Miami-based Armor Correctional Health Services, failed to give Kusma his medication, his condition deteriorated quickly. The day after his arrest, Kusma told Armor staff and jail employees that his blood sugar levels were too high and that he had not been given enough insulin to lower them. Kusma repeated his pleas for medical attention for days as Armor continued to neglect his worsening condition in jail. Kusma told medical staff that he felt sick, was coughing up blood, and was experiencing severe nausea, pain, and shortness of breath. Still, staff failed to provide Kusma with the medical attention he needed. Two weeks after his arrest, Kusma collapsed and died on what would have been the day of his release.

Later, when Kusma's father filed a lawsuit against Armor, Armor maintained that it was not responsible for Kusma's death. In a statement provided to the *Naples Daily News*, a spokesperson for the company declared Armor had "conducted a thorough investigation" into Kusma's death that showed "no reasonable grounds to believe that Armor and its medical providers at the jail were negligent in [his] care or treatment." The family's attorney

St. Bernard Jail, Louisiana

Nimali Henry, 19, had a rare and potentially fatal blood disorder that was successfully treated with medication. She did not have the medication on her when she was arrested and jailed. Within two days, other detainees realized her distress and alerted deputies. Henry was in excruciating pain, barely able to walk, and died ten days after entering the jail. According to her family, she never got her medication, and deputies never called an ambulance to rescue her from a slow death. Explained Sheriff James Pohlmann, the jail had a "shortfall" at the time. The attorney representing the family in a suit against the jail said what surprised him most when he saw the video of her death "is the fact it's obvious that Nimali Henry needs medical attention, and she did not receive any medical attention. All they had to do was call an ambulance and take her to the hospital and she would be alive today."

Tuscaloosa County Jail, Alabama

Arrested for missing a child support payment, Phillip Anderson, a young black man, told jail officials that his medical conditions required daily prescription medications. The jail staff withheld it, and he spent the week until his death unable to eat, in pain, and screaming for help. His fellow detainees, seeing that his abdomen was distended, called out for deputies to help him. He collapsed in their arms before deputies arrived to put him on the floor with his face in a pool of urine until an ambulance arrived to take him to the hospital, where he died from a duodenal ulcer that had perforated. The family's wrongful death suit was settled, according to the family's lawyer, for $300,000.

Muskogee Jail, Oklahoma

A lawsuit filed by the estate of Floyd Patterson III, 35, charges that police officers were deliberately indifferent to his "obvious distress" when he was apprehended for public intoxication. The officers brought Patterson directly to the jail, where staff did not complete a medical evaluation or treat him despite obvious signs of a life-threatening medical condition—and the fact that Patterson had told jailers of his diabetic condition on a medical questionnaire earlier. When he died, his glucose level was nearly five times higher than normal.

Wilkinson County Jail, Georgia

Cynthia Mixon turned herself in to the jail for two drug offense warrants. A lawsuit filed by her family charged the jail didn't screen her for medical problems and never followed up to find what medications she needed. A friend had brought her prescribed medication to the jail, but the jail administrator, Thomas "Buster" King, refused to give it to Mixon. Responding to a suit filed after she died, King declared, "We're not running a rehab center here. We're going to dry these people out." In allowing the civil suit to go forward, the judge ruled that King knew Mixon had a valid prescription and denying her medication put her at serious risk. The judge ruled her symptoms were consistent with opioid withdrawal, but "King took no steps whatsoever to treat Mixon's condition or otherwise provide her with medical care." The lawsuit alleged that the county sheriff allowed King to make all decisions about which detainees needed medical treatment and medication, though King had no medical training. The county settled the suit for $420,000.

Sources: A. Killion, "WDSU Investigates: Videos show final hours of St. Bernard woman who died in jail without medication," WDSU, February 10, 2021, https://www.wdsu.com/article/wdsu-investigates-videos-show-final-hours-of-st-bernard-woman-who-died-in-jail-without-her-medication/35470942; E. Enfinger, "Lawsuit settled over Tuscaloosa jail inmate's 2015 death," Tuscaloosa News, February 17, 2021, https://www.tuscaloosanews.com/story/news/local/2021/02/18/lawsuit-over-death-phillip-david-anderson-settled/6718767002/; D. Smoot, "Officer's testimony sought in lawsuit stemming from inmate's death," Muskogee Phoenix, January 5, 2021, https://www.muskogeephoenix.com/news/officers-testimony-sought-in-lawsuit-stemming-from-inmates-death/article_767831c2-c947-5623-a8d7-710f7d788fd0.html; B. O'Donnell, "Wilkinson County to pay $420,000 settlement in woman's jail death," WMAZ, January 2, 2020, https://www.13wmaz.com/article/news/local/wilkinson-settlement-lawsuit-woman-jail-death/93-7f9a63bc-4298-4f81-a575-2a1bc2628200.

commented: "The saddest part about this case and what really should enrage people is that Timothy was in for suspicion of driving with a suspended license. There's certainly no reason he should have gotten the death sentence for allegedly driving a car with a suspended license."

Armor Correctional Health Services provides a sad but not unique profile of for-profit correctional medical providers.

By 2018, Armor was reportedly handling health care for more than forty thousand mostly jail detainees in eight states. Founded by Jose Armas, a physician, Armor obtained its first contract in 2004, though the Broward County Sheriff's Office had to alter its bid specifications to allow the company without prior correctional work to win. In the months prior to its selection, Armas, his business, and his employees had donated heavily to the sheriff's reelection campaign. (The Broward sheriff was subsequently imprisoned for unrelated corruption.) Armor expanded quickly across Florida thanks to wooing local sheriffs with $300,000 of contributions through 2019 and promises of better health care at lower prices. Its medical care, however, has not been as successful, resulting in at least thirty-four lawsuits for detainee deaths. Settlements have included $7.8 million for a New York and $6.75 million for a Wisconsin jail death. The latter death made national headlines as Armor medical personnel ignored a mentally ill detainee slowly dying of thirst. After allegations of placing detainees at risk, the company paid $350,000 and agreed not to bid on any contracts in New York state for three years in a settlement with the state's attorney general. The *Miami New Times* revealed court depositions by Armor nurses in two suits that provide a glimpse of the company's business model. The first, who was fired after a Sarasota County, Florida, detainee death, testified that there was a culture where "if you actually care for a patient, you are blackballed as a pushover." The nurse admitted the company had an "unwritten policy," which she described as "very cruel," of cutting detainees off all psychiatric medication. Another nurse testified in a Nassau County, New York, jail death that she was not allowed to perform an EKG that would have saved the detainee's life because of "the costs associated with various tests and medications." The nurse was so disturbed with Armor that she quit her job and reported the company to the New York agency overseeing nurses. In other court filings, multiple attorneys accuse Armor of chronically high staff turnover, poor record-keeping, and a pattern of delaying sending patients to a hospital or outside specialists. One of the nurses also testified that there was a "strong corporate push for the doctor not to send patients out" due to money. When detainees are sent to hospitals, generally two jailers must accompany them. Armor accused both nurses of having grudges against the company.[148]

Medical providers like Armor, as well as Wellpath, CorrectHealth, Corizon, NaphCare, and other for-profit correctional health-care providers, have not just let sick people die in jail but have taken or failed to take actions that have directly caused those detainees' deaths—to save money and expand profits. Then, these for-profit medical providers, and their army of attorneys, generally refuse to accept any responsibility for these avoidable fatalities.

Privatization of jail medical care first took off in the 1980s, picking up speed as jail and prison populations soared over the next several decades. A

Reuters review found that by 2018, 62 percent of the nation's jails used privatized medical services.[149] In looking at five hundred jails from 2016 to 2018, Reuters observed that those with the highest death rates used one of the five largest for-profit medical providers: Wellpath Holdings Inc., NaphCare Inc., Corizon, PrimeCare Medical Inc., or Armor Correctional Health Services Inc. Jails that used medical services run by government agencies had significantly lower death rates in that same time period, 3.86 per 100,000 compared to 5.01 per 100,000. While 587 died out of 152,000 detainees in facilities with in-house medical care, 691 died out of fewer detainees, 138,000, with for-profit medical providers.

Armor stands out as a particularly deadly provider. In that three-year period, the death rate of those in the company's care reached 188 per 100,000. The only medical provider with a higher death rate was NaphCare, at 202 deaths per 100,000 detainees. Corizon, Wellpath, and PrimeCare each had around 160 or 150 deaths per 100,000 detainees. Overall, death rates at jails that contracted for-profit medical providers exceeded those of jails with government-run services by anywhere between 18 percent and 58 percent, depending on the county.[150]

Companies contracted to provide health care to incarcerated people constitute a multi-billion-dollar industry, worth $12 billion as of 2016.[151] Wellpath, based in Nashville, is worth roughly $1.5 billion.[152] Across thirty-four states, 352 jails contract Wellpath to provide health care to more than 135,000 detainees. Corizon says that it's contracted to supply medical services to approximately 180,000 people per day, and the Florida-based Armor says it serves more than 40,000 detainees across eight states.[153] From jails across the southeastern United States, CorrectHealth earned upward of $45 million in contracts in 2019.[154]

With outsized death rates at jails with for-profit medical providers serving as a cautionary tale, it may seem surprising that so many of the nation's jails opt for this kind of care for their detainees. However, there's one very significant factor in these jails' decisions—money. The deadly shortcuts Armor, Wellpath, and others take can save counties thousands, even millions, at least in the short run until wrongful death settlements begin to mount. Since providers are often paid based on per day, per detainee rates, medical companies work to ensure that their expenses don't exceed those amounts. They do this by avoiding taking detainees to the hospital, failing to provide prescription medications, and not hiring enough medical professionals to meet detainee needs.

As the attorney of Kenneth McGill, who suffered from a stroke in the Jefferson County, Colorado, jail in 2012, revealed to the *New Yorker*, the medical provider at that jail, Correctional Healthcare, had to pay the first $50,000 detainees incurred with every hospital visit. After McGill began experiencing stroke symptoms in the jail, Correctional Healthcare staff waited "more than 12 hours" before getting him to a hospital—trying to avoid paying steeply for the visit. McGill has since sued the company and says ever since the stroke, he's been unable to fully move his right arm and experiences vertigo.[155]

Hector Garcia died in the Doña Ana County, New Mexico, Jail from a perforated ulcer that ultimately caused sepsis, according to a lawsuit filed after his death. Garcia had told jail staff that he was experiencing intense pain and pleaded for help. "If he weren't in jail and anywhere else and looked like this and collapsed the number of times he had, he would go to an emergency room in an ambulance," said Garcia's family's lawyer. However, Garcia was never taken to the hospital. Instead, jail staff put him in a medical unit at the facility. Garcia's family's lawsuit alleges that the contracted medical provider, Corizon Health Inc., declined to call an ambulance for Garcia because doing so would be too expensive. "[Garcia] paid with his life because a private corporation was trying to save money." Garcia had been jailed for unpaid fines.[156]

Cost-cutting, deadly practices pervade Corizon's business model. According to Reuters, a Corizon nurse testified that during her orientation in 2014, the company's then regional medical director instructed that it "costs too much money" to send detainees to the hospital to get medical care; same for medications. The nurse testified she was instructed not to prescribe medications she "felt were necessary" to detainees.[157] Wellpath has also been revealed to have instructed its staff to deny detainees their prescription medications. In May 2020, a suit against Wellpath, the medical provider for the Grand Traverse County Jail in Michigan, by three detainees charged the company "cut [them] off" from their medications, which included Vyvanse, a stimulant, for one detainee. A Wellpath supervisor testified in court that because Vyvanse is "considered a stimulant . . . there is no need to provide that medication" in jails, as detainees are not "going to their jobs, or in school." Later in her testimony, the supervisor admitted that other medications, including suboxone (to treat opioid abuse), were also "not provided" by Wellpath in the jail. Well-path also skimped on the medical staff it provided to the jail. The company contracted just one psychiatrist there, who worked at the jail for only two hours a week. The *Traverse City Record Eagle* disclosed that the same doctor was listed as a weight loss specialist at a Skin & Laser Clinic with offices in three locations across Michigan.[158]

Wellpath was not alone in failing to provide adequate staffing to meet its contracts. In 2018, Milwaukee County audited Armor and found that, between November 2015 and August 2017, the company *never* fulfilled its 95 percent staffing requirement, which it supposedly needed to maintain its $16 million contract with the county's jail.[159] A 2020 lawsuit over a detainee's death in Minnesota, against MEnD Correctional Care, alleged that the for-profit provider employed only one doctor to oversee four thousand jailed patients across thirty counties—and that doctor spent "90 percent of his time on administrative duties."[160]

Chronic understaffing in correctional facilities kills. Kenneth "Buddy" Staley died in August 2019 after becoming severely ill in the Grainger County Detention Center in Tennessee, in part because the doctor serving the jail made "infrequent visits" there, as charged in a lawsuit filed after his death. Staley had a fever and body aches and was acting disoriented for three days in the jail while staff ignored him and other detainees who requested Staley get help. Finally, he was taken to the hospital, but it was too late. He died there of septic shock, with pulmonary embolism and pneumonia. The suit alleged that the doctor at the jail "could not oversee the provision of medical care with the attention required."[161]

In Virginia, Tyrone Lee Bailey died of lung cancer when he was in Virginia's Hampton Roads Regional Jail. His chemotherapy treatments had been periodically delayed—in one case by seventy-seven days—and twelve were cancelled during the last year he was in custody. A jail supervisor had contacted Wellpath, the jail's medical provider, to ask why treatments were cancelled. Wellpath's scheduler said they were just "slowed down" because the company needed to limit the number of outside appointments to five per day "due to workload of the transportation officers."[162]

By cutting costs on essential jail medical services, for-profit medical providers become increasingly appealing to small and medium-sized jails that have tight budgets, Reuters found. At one Savannah, Georgia, jail, for example, medical costs decreased by roughly 53 percent after Corizon took over care from the previous provider in 2012. At the same time, the company's jail profit margins went up from 21.5 percent in 2012 to 24.2 percent in 2013.

Although their cost-saving measures may increase fatalities and wrongful death lawsuits, the companies have found that paying out settlements for lawsuits arising from jail deaths, illness, or injuries is less damaging to the bottom line than providing the medical services. Letting detainees die generally saves more money than providing them proper health care. In 2019, the *New Yorker* reported that, combined, Corizon and Wellpath had been sued around 1,500 times over the previous five years. These suits covered alleged malpractice, wrongful death, and neglect. "More than 100" of these suits ended in settlements, but confidentiality agreements prevented the *New Yorker* from obtaining more detailed information. However, the lawsuits that require for-profit medical providers to pay up hefty sums are relatively rare— but when they do happen, they pale in comparison to the companies' profits. Roughly four years after Madaline Pitkin died while withdrawing from heroin in Oregon's Washington County jail in April 2014, for example, a federal judge approved a $10 million fine against defendants, including the county where Pitkin died and Corizon, the jail's medical provider. Corizon paid for all of it, the largest amount the company has publicly paid.[163] Although this payment was an extreme outlier when it comes to jail death lawsuits, it was still dwarfed by Corizon's profits. In 2015 alone, Corizon made $1.5 billion in revenue.[164]

Sometimes county or city officials sign contracts with for-profit medical providers that keep them from having to pay out anything for jail deaths notwithstanding their culpability. After a settlement required New York City to pay out $6 million over the death of a former Rikers Island detainee, for example, the jail's for-profit provider, Corizon, was able to pay nothing. Its contract with Rikers specified that it would not be financially responsible for any malpractice claims.[165]

CorrectHealth, a for-profit correctional health-care provider started in 2000 by physician Carlo Musso (initially as Georgia Correctional Health), has been particularly adept at evading financial culpability in lawsuits related to its (abysmal) ability to provide care to detainees. By the end of 2014, CorrectHealth accounted for the health-care needs of fifteen thousand people

Chatham County, Georgia, Jail

Chatham County jail contracted CorrectHealth in 2016 at $7 million per year. The company immediately began its contract by failing to conduct medical intakes at the jail and understaffing. The independent monitor who, per CorrectHealth's contract, was required to oversee its operations at the jail recommended the county fine CorrectHealth $5.2 million for these initial failures. The Chatham County commissioners ended CorrectHealth's contract in 2017. However, CorrectHealth founder Carlo Musso, meanwhile, had become one of Chatham County Sheriff John Wilcher's biggest donors. The sheriff stood by Musso, putting pressure on the county commissioners to get rid of the independent monitor and called their ending CorrectHealth's contract "micromanagement" of his jail. The commissioners rehired CorrectHealth on a short-term basis, which CorrectHealth accepted on the condition that the independent monitor be banned from the jail. The county agreed. It also never got the $5.2 million the monitor had suggested CorrectHealth pay out for its lapses in providing medical care to detainees. The following year, Chatham County awarded CorrectHealth a $22 million, three-year contract.

Source: M. Blau, "For sheriffs, healthcare for inmates can be a burden," *Atlanta,* October 12, 2019, https://www.atlantamagazine.com/great-reads/for-sheriffs -healthcare-for-inmates-can-be-a-burden-for-one-doctor-it-has-been-the-opportunity -of-a-lifetime.

held at forty jail facilities spanning four states. Musso and his jail health-care companies had been sued "at least 90 times" but had "never lost in court." Musso's approach to lawsuits has been proactive. Around 2005, he hired an attorney in-house to help train CorrectHealth staff on how to circumvent litigation. He also used the entity CorrectHealth Companies as a wider organization that encompassed his other correctional health-care companies to spread culpability (if one company got sued, his entire collection of companies wouldn't bear the brunt of the penalty). Meanwhile, Musso made sure to remain in good favor with politicians. Between 2006 and 2019, *Atlanta Magazine* found he and his companies had donated more than $470,000 to political causes.[166]

6

Getting Away with Murder

The Failure to Hold Jails Accountable

Deadly jails have largely avoided accountability for their lethal incompetence and irresponsibility.

There is little real oversight of jails, even when multiple people die in the same jail in a short span of time. Sheriffs, who run most jails, occupy powerful political positions in their counties. They also wear two hats—that of law enforcement and jail administration—and so are charged with conducting investigations of deaths in the jails that they run. Even if these investigations did not represent a blatant conflict of interest, county prosecutors are generally sheriffs' colleagues, relying on them to be able to prosecute crime. As the Orange County Jails project coordinator with the ACLU of Southern California explained, the relationships between local officials constitute another obstacle to accountability even where investigations are allegedly independent "given the close relationship between the sheriff's department and the district attorney's office."[1] To avoid this inherent conflict, New Jersey enacted a law that requires the state attorney general to investigate all cases of people who die in custody, rather than county prosecutors. But New Jersey is the exception. According to the American Jail Association, fewer than 20 of the nation's 3,100-plus jails have any independent oversight.

Even if there were an appetite to investigate jail deaths, at-fault jails are as likely as not to be shielded by incompetent or complicit coroners and medical examiners, prosecutors, county commissioners, and state investigators. In

addition, county officials, sheriffs, jail administrators, and jail medical providers have found it more efficacious to settle wrongful death lawsuits than to
safeguard inmates. For the mostly for-profit correctional medical providers,
settlements are part of their business plan, given the savings provided through
the nondelivery of detainee care.

Jails and sheriffs are regularly absolved of any responsibility for jail
homicides. Take Lorenzo Hayes, a 37-year-old black man, who was jailed
in May 2015 in the Spokane County, Washington, Jail. He didn't make it
to the holding cell before officers "took him to the ground" and wrestled
him into a restraint chair where he stopped breathing and died. He was
withdrawing from methamphetamines, and while officers restrained him,
he aspirated his own vomit. Although the medical examiner ruled the death
to be a homicide, a subsequent investigation by the Spokane Investigative
Response Team exonerated the jail officials involved. The Hayes family
charged the local investigation was not independent as it involved investigators who were part of the same law enforcement community as those
running the jail. Although exonerated by the county prosecutor, the county
subsequently paid out $500,000 to settle a suit brought on behalf of Hayes's
seven children.[2]

When Sheriff Cory Hutcheson assisted in killing Tory Sanders in a Missouri jail, the country prosecutor turned the case over to the then state attorney general, Josh Hawley. One might expect that a state official, far removed
from local officials, would hold jailers accountable. One would be wrong, at
least in Missouri. Although, at the time, the NAACP and others pressed for
justice for Sanders, Hawley declined to act. He said that the medical examiner
report that Sanders died of "excited delirium" ended the matter. The attorney
general's refusal to hold the jail accountable, as well as Missouri legislature
weakening of the state's antidiscrimination law, prompted the Missouri
NAACP to issue a "travel advisory," warning travelers not to drive into Missouri. It took three years and the national revulsion over George Floyd's killing in Minnesota for the Missouri NAACP and black lawmakers to revive the
case. Noting the parallels to the Floyd killing, they renewed their campaign
to get the local prosecutor to charge Hutcheson with murder. Hawley had
moved on to the U.S. Senate. A new state attorney general at least met with
NAACP officials and promised to review any new evidence to see if the case
should be reopened but subsequently decided there was not enough evidence

to convict for murder, and lesser charges could not be filed because the statute of limitations had expired thanks to Hawley's inaction.[3]

An FBI investigation for civil right violations didn't yield any better results in Michigan. After the egregious death of David Stojcevski Jr. in the Macomb County jail, the FBI's Civil Rights Division found no criminal wrongdoing on the part of the jail or its medical contractor, Correct Care Solutions, now Wellpath. Looking at each death individually, investigators miss even egregious patterns of misconduct. The same medical provider in the Stojcevski case, for example, in other cases had been found to effectively cut mentally ill patients off their medications first and ask questions later.[4]

SHERIFFS INVESTIGATE THEMSELVES

Here's a typical jail death headline: "Sheriff investigates death in the county jail." This KOEL News story superimposed the headline on a picture of the Clayton County Law Enforcement Center in Iowa. The Clayton County sheriff is also, as his website proclaims, the "custodian of the county jail and is responsible for all prisoners committed to him until discharged by law." He is also the "principal peace officer in the county." The article relates that the sheriff was investigating "an incident" in the county jail. The "incident" was the death of a 51-year-old female detainee by suicide. Although the sheriff released news of her death on September 23, 2020, it took place weeks earlier.[5] Tellingly, the next year the state's governor called for the sheriff's removal from office as he was being sued in federal court for abusing a detainee in retaliation for a personal grievance.[6]

The same day, WDEF in Chattanooga, Tennessee, ran a story that the Hamilton County Sheriff's Office Internal Affairs Division would investigate the death of a detainee "showing signs of a drug overdose." The county district attorney, according to the sheriff's press release, asked the Sheriff's Office to investigate the case. The sheriff referred to the investigation as a "common practice with all in-custody deaths."[7] A couple weeks later, the Monroe County, Michigan, Sheriff's Office similarly reported both a detainee suicide in its jail and that the "incident" was under investigation by the Sheriff's Office Detective Bureau.[8]

To say sheriffs are not enthusiastic about investigating their own is an understatement. To say it's a "conflict of interest" is not. Another newspaper headline concludes, "As Cuyahoga County Jail inmates died in record numbers, county investigations into the deaths were minimal, records show."[9] It took an outside investigation by U.S. Marshals, which came after the Cuyahoga County Jail's first seven deaths, for the sheriff's investigators to even begin to probe these deaths.

Even when independent law enforcement agencies take over jail death investigations, flawed or incomplete initial sheriffs' investigations compromise these new investigations. During the handover, pertinent records, videos, and other evidence can "disappear" or be altered. When sheriffs do ask another law enforcement organization to investigate, it is either because the jail has nothing to hide or because of mounting public pressure. The sheriff of Washington County Detention Center in Fayetteville, Arkansas, for example, immediately asked the Fayette Police Department to investigate the death of a man found hanging in his cell. The sheriff released a video that showed an officer talking to the detainee at 7:29 p.m.; another checked on him between 8:10 and 8:12 p.m. A deputy, dispensing medications to detainees, found him hanging in his cell at 8:35 p.m. In other words, there was nothing to indicate criminal culpability on the part of the sheriff's jail staff.[10]

In contrast, more culpable sheriffs go to great lengths to avoid outside scrutiny.

To avoid oversight, these sheriffs limit media access so that what happens in jails stays in jails. In the case of the Cuyahoga Jail, for instance, it took the local newspaper more than a year after it requested records to obtain them for eight of the nine jail deaths that had occurred within eleven months, eight of which took place within six months. When it finally got the sheriff's records, reporters found that the county sheriff's reviews were minimal, failing to include "any of the systemic issues within the facility and among its staff that officials could change to prevent another death. The probes were inconsistent, with investigators sometimes reviewing jail surveillance video, and sometimes not." Further, "deputies failed to follow-up on clear leads, find out how drugs ended up in the hands of inmates who overdosed, or pinpoint how an inmate who reported suicidal thoughts ended up in the general population instead of a part of the jail where staff could better monitor them."[11]

What broke the story wide open was an independent U.S. Marshals Service investigation because the jail had a contract to house federal prisoners. The Marshals' report castigated the jail death investigations. It said that the county never performed postmortem reviews and that it didn't review its

Jefferson County, Washington, Jail

Joseph D'Amico sought documents from the jail pertaining to the death of Thomas Lorecki, who'd reportedly hanged himself in the jail. D'Amico had sponsored Lorecki at both in-patient and outpatient drug rehab centers and went to high school with Lorecki's older brother. He was not satisfied with how the then sheriff had exonerated his own staff in the death, rather than bringing in an outside law enforcement agency. When D'Amico finally won his suit to gain access to the records, he found them blackened out. Finally, two years later, the county approved a $187,365 settlement "to avoid costly ongoing litigation over inadvertent errors the county readily admits, and to cap potential damages." Said D'Amico, he had no intention of bankrupting the county. "I just wanted Tommy Lorecki to have his story told and ensure this didn't happen to anyone else in the future."

Los Angeles County Jail, California

According to a correctional consultant who has spent decades investigating jail deaths, the inmate was an unresisting homeless person who was placed in a four-point restraint in the LA County jail. He died of asphyxiation when a group of deputies kneeled on his throat and torso. An internal affairs investigation by the sheriff who is responsible for the county's jails exonerated the deputies "since none of them had kicked or punched the victim."

Sources: Leader News Staff, "Jefferson County commissioners approve settlement in public records case," *Leader*, September 10, 2020, https://www.ptleader.com/stories/jefferson-county-commissioners-approve-settlement-in-public-records-case,71136; E. Press, "Dying behind bars," *New Yorker*, August 23, 2021, https://www.newyorker.com/magazine/2021/08/23/a-fight-to-expose-the-hidden-human-costs-of-incarceration.

policies, procedures, or any other possible contributing factors to the deaths. The U.S. Marshals Service investigation found that the jail's corrections officers threatened, beat, and deprived inmates of food, water, and medical care. Prompted by the report, not the deaths when they occurred, the Ohio Attorney General's Office and FBI also launched a criminal investigation that resulted in charges against several jail officers accused of beating inmates and dealing drugs. It also charged the former jail director for making the jail unsafe.

When questioned about the lack of thorough investigations and any follow-up to improve the jail, the county's spokesperson refused to answer or reveal the policies and procedures for how the sheriff's deputies should investigate jail deaths. Here, too, the county has a conflict of interest because it is liable for county jail deaths. In fact, the Cuyahoga County spokesperson referred reporters to an assistant county prosecutor representing the county in lawsuits filed against it for jail deaths. The assistant prosecutor naturally told reporters he could not answer their questions either because of the pending suits. A county inspector general's report, obtained by the newspaper, revealed that jail officials shared "a sentiment that any problems were overstated or were caused by external factors, and that the jail itself was well run." After the U.S. Marshals' report, the jail did begin slowly to initiate reforms. Following two more jail deaths that were more thoroughly reviewed by deputies, actions were taken including hiring more officers and increasing their salaries and changing the contracted medical provider for one that instituted screening measures for inmates reporting mental or physical health issues before being booked into the jail.

It would be nice to conclude that the Cuyahoga jail is an extreme outlier. Unfortunately, it has company. After press coverage of seven deaths in less than two years, the sheriff of Cobb County, Georgia, for example, was pressured to ask for an independent investigation . . . almost. Instead of going to a truly independent authority, the sheriff asked a local law firm to review the jail's operations, including use of force, racial biases, discrimination, and allegations of neglect for the previous five years. The same law firm had successfully represented the sheriff earlier when a former opponent had accused him of failing to notarize his qualifying documents for his last election. The law firm revealed it had been approached by the sheriff at a prayer rally and was not charging for the review. It vowed the review would reveal what the sheriff "is doing well at the jail and what areas need to be improved." The ACLU of Georgia that had pressed for an investigation denounced the move, demanding a transparent review by a separate constitutional office with an independent examiner. An attorney hired by the family of one of the seven men who died in the jail dismissed the sheriff's ploy as a "political move." The attorney said he, however, hoped he was wrong and the private law firm's investigation "unveils the systemic racism that transfers from our police departments to the jails where citizens wrongfully die."[12]

After the sheriff asked the law firm to investigate, two more detainees died, including the jail's first death of a female detainee. Meanwhile, one of the suits against the sheriff progressed, but the county prosecutor came to the sheriff's aid. In January 2020, the Cobb County Attorney's Office, representing the sheriff, filed an emergency protective order to limit discovery in the jail suit filed by the family of Reginald Wilson, 54. He died of dehydration after spending nine days in the jail. Never assessed by a psychiatrist, the suit charged Wilson had been showing obvious signs of psychosis, including not drinking water and smearing his own feces. The sheriff refused to release to the family pictures, videos, or reports. Eventually, the court required the sheriff to turn over a list of witnesses that could testify to jail practices, jail logs, documents on food and drink intake, policies and procedures for mental health care, recordings, photographs, and videos of Wilson and an incident report related to his death.[13]

Meanwhile, after being accused by her political opponent in her reelection as district attorney for Cobb County that she had taken no action on the jail deaths, the district attorney said the state supreme court had halted grand juries due to COVID-19. She promised when the ban was lifted, her office would "send another grand jury to inspect the jail" as she had done in the past. Her opponent pointed out, "To admit that the Grand Jury investigates the jail on a monthly basis, tells us that such investigations are a walk-through without substance as to the daily procedures and working of our Adult Detention Center." He also criticized the law firm's investigation of the jail as lacking independence.[14]

Certain cases are even more inappropriate for sheriffs to investigate. A 36-year-old man, for example, died in the Manitowoc County Jail in Wisconsin of an overdose. The local sheriff announced that his investigation determined criminal activity related to narcotics distribution that was "occurring by another inmate in the jail." His detectives, according to the sheriff's press release, would be referring charges to the county prosecutor, pending a toxicology report on the deceased detainee. As complicit as the suspected detainee might have been, he probably did not escape from the jail one night and then sneak back into the jail with the smuggled drugs! When it comes to smuggled drugs in jails, jail staffs, at worst, are involved or, at the very least, have failed to stop it. Even the best-intentioned sheriffs are in a "catch-22" situation. The better job they may do uncovering staff's crimes or incompetence, the worse it may be for their chances of reelection.

Some sheriffs' offices have internal review boards for jail deaths, but as in San Diego, the reports may be secret and their impact on deputy accountability nonexistent. The San Diego Sheriff's Department's internal board is called the Critical Incident Review Board. The Sheriff's Department's chief legal adviser serves on the board but only in a nonvoting capacity. The remaining four board members are high-ranking commanders from each of the department's bureaus. The board operated in unchallenged obscurity for twenty years—until deputies forcibly subdued Paul Silva, 39, in one of the county's jails. Silva's mother had called police for help with her son's mental health emergency at a medical facility, but they arrested him instead, charging him with being under the influence of drugs. A urine screen subsequently found marijuana and benzodiazepine, commonly prescribed for patients diagnosed with schizophrenia like Silva. His second day in jail, deputies tried to take Silva for a medical evaluation, but a jail video showed him being "visibly disturbed." The deputies used tasers, pepper spray, and water balls to subdue him, eventually pinning him to the ground with a body shield that left him unconscious. He was then taken to the hospital but remained in a coma until he died a month later. The review board completed an investigation, part of "its robust efforts to hold deputies accountable," according to the sheriff. But the report was kept secret. Silva's family filed a suit asking the federal court for access to the board's report, charging that the review process was, in essence, a sham that contributed to an environment that allows officers to kill with impunity.

Normally motions for discovery are not earthshaking but in the Silva family's suit, according to the press, "piercing some holes in the county's veil over its review activities" broke new ground and was especially helpful in multiple other San Diego jail death suits. Said one attorney who has sued the jail, "I've been trying to get [board] records forever." As an ACLU lawyer commented, opening these reports just puts the sheriff in the same position as everyone else. A sheriff's official admitted that the review process had been initially created twenty years ago to "keep the public safe without incurring unnecessary liability." The Silva family charged that the nonvoting lawyer had only been put on the review committee so the committee could claim client-attorney privilege and avoid complying with the state's Public Records Act. In fact, the committee's attorney had authored an article for *Police Chief Magazine* years before advocating putting lawyers on these boards for that very reason.

While a Citizens' Law Enforcement Review Board, an obscure independent review panel, found no evidence to support allegations of procedural violation, misconduct, or negligence of the deputies, a U.S. District Court judge subsequently denied the county's motion to dismiss the Silva lawsuit. The judge also declined to dismiss the case against Coast Correctional Medical Group, which provided the jail nurse who gave no treatment to Silva during his thirty-six hours in custody.[15] In April 2021, the county paid the family a record breaking $3.5 million to settle the suit.

Nonetheless, the San Diego jail continued to keep a tight grip on information on jail deaths. Within hours of Omar Arroyo's death, the first inmate to die in the jail in 2021, the sheriff's office sealed information, refusing to tell his widow what happened to her husband shortly after he was jailed. Three months later, the medical examiner's office said the death was "accidental." The report indicated that there were no illicit drugs, prescription medication, or alcohol found in his system, although he had been arrested on suspicion of being under the influence of methamphetamine. The report raised questions that the sheriff refused to address, including that sheriff's detectives' report that Arroyo had possibly swallowed a baggie of drugs before his arrest. Although the medical examiner found Arroyo might have choked on his COVID mask, none of the responding medical staff noticed that Arroyo was choking or had a mask in his throat. The jail video reveals he was sitting on a bench in the holding cell and collapsed, experiencing a "seizure-like activity." According to the jail's policies, detainees suspected of being under the influence of drugs like Arroyo were supposed to be in "a protective environment" with special observation. Again, the family had to sue for answers.[16]

When the Kitsap Critical Incident Response Team in Washington reviewed the suffocation death of Sean Howell through the improper use of a restraint chair in the Kitsap County Jail, the sheriff's office first impeded it, then ignored it. The team, led by the state police and local officials, requested documents from the sheriff's office. Officials responded by turning over "thousands of pages" of mostly irrelevant records, requiring detectives to laboriously search for anything material to their investigation. Eventually, they identified fewer than a dozen relevant documents. The officers involved, after making initial statements, refused to cooperate with investigators. The sheriff, Gary Simpson, announced he had not read the investigators' report and would not do so until he determined that the investigation was over. He did announce, however, he trusted his officers and was "confident in the work they do." The sheriff took no action regarding the four officers involved in Howell's death. The sheriff also declared that their failure to follow the instructions for placing persons into the restraint chair issued by its manufacturer was justified because the instructions did not cover situations when a person resisted being placed into the chair. It is unclear what the sheriff thought would be the "normal" use of the restraint chair.[17] It was revealed that the last training provided to his deputies on how to use the restraint chair properly was eight years earlier.[18] The county prosecutor covered for the sheriff, announcing the next year that although the killing was "not justifiable," it was "excusable." Prosecutor Chad Enright explained that since the officers were untrained, they did not know that their actions would be lethal. He also blamed Howell's "own conduct rather than the conduct of the officers" for the death.[19]

There are, of course, refreshing exceptions. The Bexar County sheriff in San Antonio, Texas, charged one of his deputies with tampering with government documents. After a detainee attempted suicide and was rushed to the hospital in critical condition, investigators found that the detainee was not on a suicide watch and was not checked as required. Yet a detention deputy's report indicated he was. That deputy was also placed on leave. Sheriff Salazar declared the public deserves "an agency that holds ourselves accountable."[20]

Holding sheriffs accountable is not easy. In forty states, they are elected. Once elected, sheriffs tend to stay in office term after term, facing no or little competition. Without having to face the voters, and usually invisible but for the propaganda they release, sheriffs can accrue enormous political power. In many regions, sheriffs have wide jurisdiction and primary law enforcement responsibilities, but unlike police chiefs, they operate largely unfettered by civilian authority. They don't report to a mayor, city council, or even county supervisors. As noted in a law review article, "Long tenures with limited oversight allow some to run their counties as small fiefdoms, subject to their own rules."[21] Sheriffs in Missouri, for example, got the legislature to require every defendant brought to court, found guilty or not, to pay an unconstitutional $3 fee to bolster sheriffs' retirements. After almost a decade of suits, the state's supreme court finally ruled the bounty unconstitutional and ordered the lower court to decide on reimbursing millions to the defendants who had been forced to pay it.[22] As history has taught us, power without accountability can be dangerous. And it has proven deadly for people incarcerated in America's jails.

The 2020 election posters against Grand Traverse County, Michigan, sheriff Tom Bensley, first elected in 2008, read: "Shame on you sheriff for dodging accountability." At that time, the captain who ran the sheriff's jail was facing multiple felony charges for allegedly sexually assaulting detainees as well as embezzlement and more; female detainees were denied basic hygiene products; and the jail health care provider, Wellpath, had been sued, accused of cutting detainees off from their psychotropic medications to increase corporate profits. The Northern Michigan for Accountable Government advocates found two years earlier that the jail's problems were systemic and laid them at the sheriff's feet. To their chagrin, in their subsequent campaign to hold Bensley accountable, they found a lot of people in the county didn't realize the sheriff was elected. Answering critics, Bensley explained that his office was big, and he couldn't oversee everything all the time. After winning the Republican primary with 75 percent of the vote, he was challenged by a Democrat promising jail reform whose mother had been incarcerated at the county jail and ended up in a hospital when the jail failed to provide her with medical care. Bensley was reelected for a fourth term, outpolling fellow Republican Donald Trump.[23]

The *Post and Courier* ran an exposé on South Carolina's sheriffs in 2020, under the headline, "Not exactly Mayberry." It found "a startling number had abused their positions and lined their pockets on the public's dime, using fear to silence whistleblowers." One in four of South Carolina's forty-six counties in the past decade had seen their sheriffs accused of breaking laws they swore to uphold. As the paper explained, the sheriffs "enjoy enormous powers not ordinarily given to other law enforcement officials." Their power is matched by lack of state oversight. "Reform is a challenge, in part, because sheriffs derive their authority from the state constitutions. Any major change in their powers requires amendments." The voters did pass such an amendment directing legislators to at least establish sheriffs' qualifications. And the South Carolina legislature responded by raising the bar, requiring the state's sheriffs to *both* have a high school diploma and not be convicted of a felony, at least before taking office![24]

The Marshall Project, a nonprofit news organization covering the criminal justice system, ran a story capturing succinctly in its headline how sheriffs' jobs become virtual annuities, despite long histories of abuse within their jails. The story was headlined: "Your local jail may be a house of horrors. But you probably wouldn't know it, because sheriffs rule them with little accountability."[25] The article featured a profile of Sheriff Daniel Bullock in Missouri's Ozarks St. Francois County, who had been reelected every four years since 1992. The fact that he runs what is widely conceded to be the second worst jail in the state has not impeded his career. (The St. Louis Workhouse was considered the worst but was recently closed.) Jailers were accused of holding "Friday Night Fights," pitting detainees against each other to toughen them up for state prison. In 2018, federal marshals ended a contract with the jail to house federal prisoners after an inspection found inadequate nutrition, water leaks, vermin, and a lack of natural light because cell windows had been covered in black paint. After losing the contract, Sheriff Bullock declared, "I'm not running a Hilton Hotel here." Until the Ames family hired the only attorney in the county considered brave enough to sue the sheriff, the long history of abuse, sexual assault by guards, and corruption at the jail was mostly only rumored. The Ames suit prompted a flood of accusations against the jail on Facebook. Within six months, fifty former detainees, as well as multiple former employees, told their stories to the Marshall Project. A new meme was posted calling the jail "Missouri's New Death Row." Family members of two other detainees who died in the jail within a few months of Ames came forward. The sheriff was forced to call for the state highway patrol to conduct an investigation into two of the jail deaths. In addition, the jail administrator retired, allowing the sheriff to appoint a new "reform" administrator.

Like a lot of sheriffs, Bullock focused his attention on law enforcement, not corrections. He proudly traces his roots in law enforcement back to the first sheriff of Deadwood, South Dakota, whom he claims as a relative. His desk is adorned with pictures of Wild Bill Hickok and Wyatt Earp, as well as a statue of a Confederate soldier. In August 2020, Bullock switched parties to become a Republican and won his primary with 60 percent of the vote, ensuring his twenty-eight-year reign would continue notwithstanding the twenty-six lawsuits filed against the county for injury and death at the jail.[26]

In Ramsey County, Minnesota, after the racism scandal in the jailing of Derek Chauvin, a county commissioner questioned electing the sheriff: "There is this pattern of abuse of power. I am angered and saddened that with all the good work this county is moving forward on, that we spend so much time on the harm the sheriff is causing in our community. It just sucks the air out of the room." Other commissioners agreed to evaluate pertinent legislation to identify the appropriate process for either electing or appointing the sheriff. The board also requested the sheriff to use a vacant position to hire an "accountability officer," who would report to the deputy county manager and work closely with the county's chief compliance and ethics officer. The sheriff countered, "Our elected sheriff's office has a strong, trusting relationship with the community. What we really need is an elected county manager . . . instead of the seven politicians who have confused accountability with control."[27] In short, he contended that individuals who are elected are "politicians," but not sheriffs.

Some have characterized sheriffs as representative of a rural-urban divide in the country. State officials are voted in by more liberal urbanites, while sheriffs represent more conservative rural voters (with some obvious exceptions already highlighted).[28] Scarily, the conservatism of many sheriffs veers toward fascism. In 1994, a group of sheriffs in Arizona and Montana sued the federal government, challenging a law that required them to perform background checks on people who wanted to buy handguns. The Supreme Court ruled in the sheriffs' favor. Encouraged, one of the sheriffs went on to found the Constitutional Sheriffs and Peace Officers Association, advocating that sheriffs not enforce laws that they believe to be unconstitutional. In a nutshell, the group believes that they as sheriffs are the ultimate authority to decide what is legal and what is not, superseding mayors, county commissioners, governors, the federal courts, and the rest of the federal government. One of the more notorious leaders of this movement was Maricopa Sheriff Joe Arpaio, who housed detainees in tents, issued them pink underwear, and blithely defied a federal judge. Another was Milwaukee Sheriff David Clarke. In his final term in office, at least four people, including a newborn, died under his watch in jail. The county had to pay out almost $7 million to the family of just one of those who died of profound dehydration after jailers denied him water.[29]

Not all sheriffs resist accountability for jail deaths. Guilford County, North Carolina, Sheriff Rogers, for example, put out a press release concerning the death of Tasharra Thomas (mentioned previously), who died in the Greensboro Detention Center three days after entering but before the new sheriff took office. The release explained how people could access the autopsy report.

Rogers also went to the demonstration protesting her death and met with Thomas's mother to express sympathy for her loss. He vowed to continue to cooperate with the family's lawyer to share all available information. The sheriff reached an agreement with the family's lawyer to release the video of Thomas's time in jail once approved by a judge.[30]

COUNTY PROSECUTORS COVER FOR DEADLY JAILS

Too often, county prosecutors join with sheriffs' and jailers' efforts to evade oversight and culpability for inmates' deaths. They use grand juries. Prosecutors often take jail death cases to grand juries to determine criminal culpability. Some do so, however, not to ensure jails are held to account but to avoid having to hold them accountable. One of the first jail death scandals to get national attention was the aforementioned death of Sandra Bland in Texas. The prosecutor took the case to a grand jury to determine if anyone should be held criminally responsible for her death. The grand jury subsequently absolved the sheriff and his jail staff of any liability. At the same time, however, the Texas Commission on Jail Standards documented the jailers' many failures, and the county and the Texas Department of Public Safety paid out almost two million dollars to Bland's family, who sued for her wrongful death.

These exonerations of jails by grand juries tell more about prosecutors than the criminal culpability of jailers. After the grand jury exonerated jailers in Rockdale for Tilson's death, another death followed the next month and two more after that. When a grand jury does not return an indictment, it is typically because the prosecutor didn't want it to—but wanted to be able to pin the blame for his or her inaction on the grand jury. Or the prosecutor who brings the case to the grand jury is incredibly incompetent. As the expression goes, "A good prosecutor can indict a ham sandwich in front a grand jury." The grand jury is the original kangaroo court. Only the prosecution presents witnesses in secret sessions. No one represents the defense nor is the subject of the grand jury present to refute the evidence. The prosecutor decides what and whom the jury hears and does not hear. In the rare instances when the grand jury does not do what the prosecutor intends, it is called a "runaway" grand jury because that is so exceptional.

After the Ector County grand jury refused to hold anyone criminally accountable for Howell's death, the prosecutor told the media he thought the deputies involved should be investigated for using excessive force. The

Ector County, Texas, Jail

The grand jury opted not to indict jail employees involved in the death of Wallace Howell, a 38-year-old black man who had been arrested several months earlier for allegedly evading arrest. He died in the jail after jailers tased him multiple times and placed him in a padded cell with his arms and legs restrained, according to an investigation conducted by the Texas Rangers. The jail alleged that Howell had assaulted another detainee. But the sheriff would not release further information because of a suit filed against the jail for Howell's death. Howell was the second detainee that year to die in the jail.

Rockdale County, Georgia, Jail

Shali Tilson, 22, died in a solitary cell after police arrested him for disorderly conduct. He died of blood clots to his lungs caused by dehydration. According to his parents, Tilson suffered from bipolar disorder and schizophrenia and was on the verge of a psychotic break when arrested. In jail, the solitary cell where he stayed had no water source, and he was given none during the three days he spent in jail before his death. It came out that the deputy who was supposed to be monitoring Tilson falsified the suicide watch log. But a grand jury found that although his death was preventable, no one would be held criminally responsible.

Lancaster County, Nebraska, Jail

A grand jury on July 29, 2021, reviewed five jail and prison deaths for assorted causes including suicides, suspected COVID, and unspecified medical conditions. One of the jail detainees who died by suicide had been taken off suicide watch. His record was subsequently sealed. The jury cleared the prison and jail for all five deaths as well as two other deaths of suspects involving local police officers.

Sources: C. Randle, "Employees not indicted in death at Ector County jail," *Midland Reporter-Telegram*, September 1, 2020, https://www.mrt.com/news/article/Employees-not-indicted-in-death-at-Ector-County-15533309.php; S. Abusaid, "Rockdale inmate dies of apparent suicide, officials say; GBI investigating," *Atlanta Journal-Constitution*, August 14, 2020, https://www.ajc.com/news/rockdale-inmate-dies-of-apparent-suicide-officials-say-gbi-investigating/DVAD7O3UNRECJCFUVMF2S6MLNY/; L. Pilger, "Grand jury review recent deaths at prison, county jail," *Lincoln Journal Star*, August 19, 2021, https://journalstar.com/news/local/crime-and-courts/grand-jury-reviews-recent-deaths-at-prison-county-jail/article_0dd3b040-e20d-5474-9938-edffa5a17a83.html.

attorney for Howell's family found the prosecutor's statement "extremely unsettling when viewed in the light of the grand jury's refusal to indict any of the officers involved." He continued that it "creates a cloud of uncertainty into the actions surrounding [Howell's] death and the subsequent actions of law enforcement in Ector County."[31]

The Higgins death in Obion County, Tennessee, previously described, demonstrates how prosecutors use grand juries to avoid prosecuting jail deaths. After the grand jury exonerated the jailers, the Higgins family discovered that the prosecutor had kept the video of the officers restraining Higgins from the grand jury. As the family's lawyer explained, "Imagine if a district attorney had empaneled a grand jury in the wake of George Floyd's death—for the purpose of determining whether to file criminal charges. Imagine if he withheld the video we've all seen and only presented the officer's version of events. And imagine if no charges were filed because of this. Videos matter. They don't lie. Not showing the grand jury the videos in this case was a grave miscarriage of justice." Confronted in the wake of the George Floyd case, the Obion County prosecutor put the blame on the medical examiner, claiming he would have had a case for homicide but for the autopsy report that concluded that "excited delirium due to a methamphetamine overdose" was the cause of death. Of course, the prosecutor could have easily challenged the report before the grand jury, especially since there would be no one appearing to defend it! And, of course, there was good reason to have refuted the medical examiner's report, as previously explained.

As the legal director of the Massachusetts ACLU explained, prosecutors' investigations don't work unless someone is really willing to follow the truth wherever it leads. To date, he charged, prosecutors' reviews of jail deaths in Massachusetts were "cursory." Under Massachusetts law, the medical examiner is charged with looking for negligence in death cases and turns them over to prosecutors. However, because the office is, according to a state audit, "woefully behind" in its investigations, investigations are closed long before officials obtain the official cause of death from the medical examiner.

Some prosecutors don't even bother to take cases before the grand jury. After Darren Rainey died in the 180-degree Miami-Dade County, Florida, shower jail staff forced him into, the county prosecutor, Katherine Rundle, investigated the incident. She investigated for five years before finding "the

Travis County, Texas, Jail

Tyler Grist committed suicide in his padded cell, allegedly banging his head against the cell wall almost thirty times unobserved by jailers. Finally, when seen shaking on the floor by a corrections officer, he summoned a nurse. The nurse informed the officer that Grist was safe in his padded cell. Later that morning, Grist's unresponsive body was found in the cell. Two years later, the Travis County district attorney took the case to the grand jury because, he explained, he feared he would lose at trial. The grand jury did not indict any officers or the nurse. The prosecutor's office announced it did not plan to take other jail deaths to a grand jury. The prosecutor insisted, however, that his office "takes the work of presenting all the facts and evidence to a grand jury very seriously."

Pottawatomie County, Oklahoma, Jail

The district attorney declared that he could not charge anyone responsible for the death of Ronald Given despite the state medical examiner ruling it a homicide. A video revealed a jailer kneeling on Given's neck until he was unconscious. The Oklahoma State Bureau of Investigation did not find criminal culpability. The prosecutor explained that without an affidavit from a law enforcement officer, he couldn't file criminal charges, nor could he conduct his own investigation. His chief investigator was a member of the jail trust. "In a perfect world, I would hope that we could get an investigator with the [state] or the federal government and do something with it," the prosecutor concluded.

Sources: K. Hall, "Grand jury declines to indict correctional officer, nurse in Travis County inmate's death," *Austin-American-Statesman*, August 13, 2021, https://www.statesman.com/story/news/2021/08/13/travis-county-inmate-death-jail-correctional-officer-nurse-not-indicted/8105853002/; B. Mangold, "Oklahoma district attorney says he will ask OSBI to reopen investigation into 2019 jail death," News 9, August 16, 2021, https://www.news9.com/story/61173882cb160e0c0778fcd5/oklahoma-district-attorney-says-he-will-ask-osbi-to-reopen-investigation-into-2019-jail-death-.

evidence does not show that Rainey's well-being was grossly disregarded by the correctional staff." Although the jail nurse had reported that Rainey's skin slipped off his body due to the torture, the prosecutor concluded that the slippage could have been due to "body decomposition" rather than burns. Rainey's family later revealed that they had been pressured to rapidly cremate his body at the time. A *New Yorker* investigation of the case detailed how a whistleblower at the jail was bullied, harassed, and finally forced into therapy after speaking out about abuses at the jail. Finally, George Floyd's death made the news, and the Rainey case made the news again when prosecutor Rundle was challenged for reelection. It turned out that not only had Rundle not charged the officers in this case, but in her twenty-seven-year career as head prosecutor, she had never charged any police officer for any on-duty killing. Her challenger promised in the campaign to bring accountability to the county. Rundle won her seventh term in August 2020 with 62 percent of the vote.[32]

Rundle's success is unfortunately not rare. Responding to a tip from an inmate, the *East Bay Express* newspaper investigated the case of Christian Madrigal in an Alameda County, California, jail. The reporters were told the inmate had been acting bizarrely, either under the influence of drugs, suffering from mental illness, or probably both. Officers placed him in an isolation cell and were ordered by a lieutenant to chain him to the cell door using a waist restraint even though it violated the jail's policy. The inmate was left there and later found with the chain wrapped around his neck because he'd either put it there or become accidentally entangled. Unconscious, Madrigal was taken to a hospital, where sources indicated he was taken off life support and died about two weeks later. This death occurred after the county's district attorney had just investigated another death in the same jail, also caused by the deputies using restraints.[33]

In June 2020, the Alameda district attorney cleared officers involved in both of these deaths. Prosecutor Nancy O'Malley admitted, however, to "shortcomings in the care" provided by the jail and called the decision to leave Madrigal "secured to the restraint chain . . . concerning," as well as the sheriff's personnel neglect to check on him as required. Tragically, Madrigal's family had initially called police to get him to a psychiatric hospital. He had been released recently from a medical center. Once police responded to the house, however, they decided he didn't meet the standards for a psychiatric hold, but since his stepfather had indicated he might have been on drugs, they arrested him and took him to the jail. The stepfather told them that a nurse had advised him to call police so that Madrigal could be taken to the care facility and pleaded with them not to take him to jail.[34]

When the jail finally released body camera videos, it showed no visual evidence of Madrigal thrashing, kicking, punching, spitting, or behaving violently in any way. According to a news report, "throughout the one hour and 49 minutes of video provided, Madrigal is constrained in a WRAP, which is similar to a straitjacket, and wears a spit mask over his face. Madrigal's head is down and he walks slowly. He is also seen lying down in much of the footage. Madrigal, who was six feet tall and weighed 132 pounds, was always surrounded by 10 to 12 deputies."[35] Madrigal's stepfather called the district attorney's decision not to file criminal charges in the case "ridiculous." The family's attorney calls it "not surprising," claiming that Prosecutor O'Malley, like her peer in Miami-Dade, has been siding with police against brutality cases "her entire career."[36]

After the video was made public, the sheriff disavowed the actions of the exonerated officers. "We do not in any way, shape or form condone those types of restraints." He then pinned the blame on the individual lieutenant who ordered the restraint but made no mention of the officers who stood by and did not try to intervene. He announced the department was seeking to have the lieutenant in question fired.[37] The county settled the family's wrongful death lawsuit for $5 million, the largest settlement since 2015.

The lack of prosecutorial oversight has helped make the Santa Rita Jail in Alameda County, the fifth-largest jail in the nation, also one of its deadliest. According to media reports, in the last seven years through 2020, forty-eight people died in the jail, seventeen by suicide. In 2019, ten died; in 2020 three died, and another died in February 2021. That year, the California state auditor castigated the jail for not disclosing information about the mental health of detainees. The audit found that lacking sufficient information regarding whether detainees have mental illness, the jail cannot make critical housing, supervision, and care decisions to keep them safe. According to the auditors, deputies at the jail only conduct mental health assessments if detainees admit to being mentally ill or exhibit noticeable, specific behaviors. Ironically, the auditor also uncovered a $135 million surplus that could have been spent on increasing mental health screening and treatment at the jail.[38]

Although they had been told that her transfer to a psychiatric hospital had been delayed, the Bucks County, Pennsylvania, commissioner chair had assured 28-year-old Kim Stringer's family that their daughter was safe and would be protected in the county jail. Although not a great option, the commissioner explained the jail was "very, very empty" at the time and was "providing the safety and time-out necessary for a real plan with judicial teeth to be implemented." Stringer had a long-documented history of mental illness and police and jail involvement. In jail, Stringer got worse, cutting herself, sticking items into an electrical outlet, pounding her head onto the sink and wall of her cell, soiling her prison anti-suicide smock, and refusing to shower. Detainees alerted Stringer's family that all was not well with their daughter, revealing jailers had repeatedly pepper sprayed her and that she was on a suicide watch and unresponsive. When the media picked up the story, the county district attorney announced his office would investigate the allegations of abuse. He described a video of guards pepper spraying Stringer as "very difficult to watch." A prison board's investigation found her treatment "horrific and sickening." Nonetheless, the district attorney found the guards were following proper protocols, their treatment of her "fair." After all, he noted, they had repeatedly ordered Stringer to comply each time before they sprayed her, and afterward, they had her examined by medical staff for any injuries. Stringer's mother aptly retorted, "I don't know in what universe pepper spraying someone on suicide watch is proper protocol!" She also noted that the district attorney and commissioners sit on the jail oversight board despite the fact the district attorney has responsibility for investigation of incidents within the jail. They are in an ideal position, in effect, to be able to approve their own coverup of jail abuses. Later, it came out that jailers had never bothered to file a motion with the courts to get Stringer committed to a psychiatric hospital as they had promised to do.[39]

Some prosecutors stick to their stories even when contradictory evidence comes out later to disprove them, as illustrated by another Pennsylvania jail death. When officers and medical staff at the Luzerne County jail in Pennsylvania responded to a detainee having an epileptic seizure with brutality instead of assistance, resulting in Shaheen Mackey's death as previously described, the county manager called on the district attorney to investigate. The district attorney, Stefanie Salavantis, exonerated the jail. At the time, the prosecutors refused to let Mackey's family, or their lawyer, see a video of his death. A year later, however, Mackey's family finally got the video. It showed officers attacking Mackey. The family released the video on Facebook. Mackey's daughter lamented, "It's not fair. It shouldn't have to come to this, us putting out a video for people to see the truth. . . . You see the video, but you don't see the crime that's being committed, how? I don't know how because it's right there. It's clear, it's clear. How could you go around that for two years?" The Luzerne City Council unanimously voted to settle with the family for $3 million and announced some jail reforms. A measure to fire the county manager and the director of corrections, however, failed.

Notwithstanding this, Prosecutor Salavantis stood by her ruling. The family pleaded in vain to the media, "See the truth. Don't see skin color, don't see that because it's not about that. He's a person, that's first, and that's all I gotta see. Imagine being him. Imagine being in that chair, imagine feeling how he felt. Just close your eyes, and take yourself out your own body, put yourself in his shoes. Imagine being his child, and you gotta see this. Nobody cared about him. Nobody." The officers who brutalized Mackey were all white, as is District Attorney Salavantis. Mackey was black.[40]

Even prosecutors who take seriously their responsibility for investigating jail deaths become strict constructionists when it comes to determining criminal culpability. The district attorney of Lackawanna County, Pennsylvania, for example, announced that the death of a jail inmate was caused by "woefully inadequate" conduct by the jail's medical staff who showed "no sense of urgency" responding to the detainee's medical emergency. He also found that the detainee who had been treated for mental illness had been deprived of his psychiatric medication by the jail even after repeatedly telling officers that he was hearing voices and threatening to harm himself. But, although "tragic," the prosecutor said there was no criminal wrongdoing.[41] Similarly, the South Carolina Circuit prosecutor covering Charleston County Jail declared after investigating the killing of Jamal Sutherland that "error after error after error" led to his death, including "clear negligence" by deputies. But since the deputies, after all, were following jail policy, she could not find criminal intent.[42] The use-of-force expert called the training of what is essentially the jail's SWAT team "ridiculous," "sadistic," and possibly even "criminal."[43]

Since 2015, New York jail death reviews have been bumped up to the Office of the Attorney General. As the death of a Rockland County detainee illustrates, it has not meant prosecutors have gone very far out on a limb to hold jailers accountable. In that particular death, a medical examiner "quite unequivocally" attributed it "to sustained compression of the neck" by corrections officers restraining the detainee. They broke his neck while struggling to place him into a restraint chair. However, another pathologist questioned if the officers' actions could cause the kind of harm to a person's brain "necessary to trigger a cardiac arrest." Rather than let a judge or jury decide, the attorney general announced that the disagreement made it "all but impossible to prove beyond a reasonable doubt" that the officers caused the death. Instead, she suggested that Rockland officers receive additional training "to properly handle inmates who are experiencing health complications." She did note, however, that the jail should make sure jail cameras are positioned to avoid obscuring the view of an inmate being placed in a restraint chair.[44]

It is apparent that jail accountability will never come from prosecutors like the Shasta County, California, district attorney. He found county jail deputies' use of force resulting in the death of Teddy Abbie to be reasonable—if you ignored, as he admitted he did, "issues of policy, training, tactics, or civil liability." According to the jail staff, concerned that Abbie would carry through on his threats to hurt himself, they'd decided to move him to a "safety cell." When he refused to leave his cell unless he was provided his medication, twelve officers removed him. A deputy used a "leg sweep" to knock him down. On the ground, he kicked and struggled with the deputies. Three deputies handcuffed him and, with the help of the other deputies, put his legs in restraints. He then walked to the safety cell as directed. In the safety cell, after lying on his stomach as ordered, Abbie began kicking again and rolling around when deputies tried to remove his clothing. He was pepper sprayed but continued to struggle, biting one of the officer's legs. By the time they got his clothes cut off, he had stopped struggling and his breathing was labored. Jailers injected him with Haldol and Benadryl to calm him down. His restraints were removed. A subsequent check found that he had stopped breathing. The autopsy found that heart disease was likely his cause of death, with the violent struggle with deputies and restraint being a contributing factor. Abbie had several fractured ribs. The prosecutor found the deputies' actions were reasonable. "Unfortunately, Abbie's own actions led to his death" because "correctional staff has no other option than to use force to keep him from hurting himself or others." The justification is reminiscent of the general in the Vietnam War who supposedly declared after a bombing, "We had to destroy the village in order to save it."[45] Shasta County Jail remains one of the deadliest in the state, ranking second among the state's ten county jail systems with ten thousand to eighteen thousand bookings a year. And its deaths are increasing, with nine between 2006 and 2012 rising to sixteen between 2013 and 2019. Two-thirds of its deaths were by suicide. It had five more in 2021.[46]

As in Shasta County, prosecutors, as well as agencies responsible for jail oversight, can set very low bars for jails. Both the New York City Department of Investigation, charged with overseeing city employees and contractors, and the Bronx district attorney, for example, exonerated New York City jail officers in the death of a transgender woman, Layleen Cubilette-Polanco, who died the year before, in 2019, on Rikers Island. Although she was supposed to have been checked every fifteen minutes, the investigation found that she had been left alone in her cell for forty-seven minutes when she died in solitary confinement. As a result of a civil suit filed by her family, a video was subsequently released that suggests the investigations had employed a rather loose definition of checking on detainees. The video shows guards tried and failed to wake her up for one and a half hours before bothering to call for help. According to the medical examiner's report, she died after an epileptic seizure in her cell. Her life could have been saved, the family claims, if she had received any medical attention. When confronted with the video, a Rikers spokesperson claimed that detainees had the "right to a nap." Rikers officials initially stated that its officers found her unresponsive while making rounds at 2:40 p.m. The video, by contrast, revealed that at least five jail staff knocked on her cell door for the hour and half before they finally opened her cell door to find her unresponsive. The family also contends that Polanco should never have been placed in solitary confinement given her epilepsy, schizophrenia, and the fact that she had already had two seizures while in custody. Jail staff had moved her to solitary confinement for assaulting an officer, according to jail officials. The Bronx prosecutor who had found no criminal culpability declined to comment after the video was released.[47]

A subsequent report by the Board of Corrections (BOC) found that the issues contributing to her death extended beyond the failure of a handful of officers to follow jail guidelines. In solitary, Polanco had broken down, had suicidal thoughts, and appeared delusional. She was hospitalized in a Queens hospital for nine days where she received psychiatric treatment. When she returned to Rikers, officials refused to put her with cisgender women, so they put her in solitary confinement again despite a psychiatrist's refusal to clear her for restrictive housing because of her history of seizures. The psychiatrist's call was reversed by another Correctional Health Services doctor less than a week later. The report concluded that placing her in this unit was "unsuitable to manage both her medical and mental health needs."[48] Eventually, after a public uproar continued over the death, the City Department of Corrections announced disciplinary actions against seventeen staffers, suspending three officers and one captain without pay. The New York City mayor called what happened "absolutely unacceptable" and stressed the importance of jail accountability.[49] The city also announced it would end solitary confinement in its jails, effective immediately for medically vulnerable prisoners and then, in a few months, for everyone else. Polanco's family settled its lawsuit with the city for $5.9 million.[50]

In the rare instances when jail staff and sheriffs are held accountable for a jail death, it is often not for the death itself but the coverup. Remember the LA sheriff was imprisoned for the coverup of brutal deputies, not for the brutality of his staff. On the other side of the country, a police officer assigned to the Niagara Falls, New York, police lockup was also charged after an investigation revealed he'd failed to conduct required checks on detainees, including of a man who died there in 2020 while withdrawing from alcohol. Not only had the officer failed to complete the required checks; he also falsified the records to say they had been made. The officer was first placed on paid administrative leave but several months later was charged with both felony and misdemeanor counts of tampering with public records.[51]

Like sheriffs investigating themselves, there is an inherent conflict of interest when it comes to prosecutors bringing cases against jails. At the same time the prosecutor is prosecuting jail staff for wrongdoing, they're also charged with defending the county against lawsuits that may have arisen out of the jailers' behavior. It was this conflict of interest, for example, that led to the prosecution of the Cuyahoga correctional officers in the Arquillo death by the state attorney general, not county prosecutors. The prosecutors' role as county defenders may make them less likely to root out wrongdoing in counties' jails in the first place. Even if prosecutors were interested in holding jails accountable for the death of detainees, the problem remains that they are limited to determining only criminal culpability. That requires, except in the most extreme cases of criminal negligence, proof of intent. Often, the poor training and incompetence of jailers ironically clears them.

For example, William Honeycutt, 39, died in the Sebastian County jail in July 2020 after he'd ingested methamphetamine earlier that day. He did not admit this to jail staff. No one at the jail conducted a clinical intake or even a spot urine test that would have readily alerted the jail of his toxicity. The jail didn't realize he was in trouble until he began having seizures the next day. His cellmate made the diagnosis and alerted officers and a nurse. Honeycutt was pronounced dead upon arrival at a local hospital. The autopsy found the primary cause of death was related to heart disease, with "the contributory effects of methamphetamine add[ing] an unnatural element to the cause of death, and the manner cannot be classified as natural." The report explained that methamphetamine, a cardiac stimulant, is extremely dangerous for someone with coronary artery disease. Five months later, the county prosecutor cleared the jail of any criminal culpability in his death. Their failure to conduct a proper intake screening cleared them from their failure to prevent his death. Like Sergeant Shultz in *Hogan's Heroes*, they chose to "see nothing."[52]

STATE REVIEW OF JAILS TEPID AND IGNORED

Twenty-four states have government bodies that have some regulatory power over jails and may review jail deaths. After the death of Sandra Bland, for example, the Texas legislature enacted the Sandra Bland Act in 2017, forcing jails to appoint third-party investigators, often the Texas Rangers, to look into all in-custody deaths. However, with some recent exceptions, these reviews, including those conducted by the Texas Rangers, traditionally haven't amounted to much. They result in toothless admonishments or are turned over and ignored by county prosecutors.

Many states either do not take their oversight responsibility of local jails seriously or lack the authority to enforce their standards. Even if they took their responsibility seriously and had the authority to require compliance, the standards are generally minimal. In at least six states, there is no authority to enforce the standards.[53]

In Pennsylvania, state law, for example, requires "all inmates admitted to [county jails] receive a health care screening performed and recorded by a person with health care training within 24 hours of admission." According to the state Department of Corrections charged with inspecting county jails, the Allegheny County Jail in Pittsburgh was in full compliance with the required standards: "Inmate medical records were observed to ensure that the inmates are being seen by medical [professionals] within 24 hours of commitment for an initial health risk assessment." Meanwhile a former nurse at the jail revealed jailers would leave detainees waiting to be screened "in the same clothes, sitting in those chairs, for days." A psychiatrist who also had left the

Red River County, Texas, Jail

When previously jailed, Chris Cabler cut himself and swallowed razor blades. A few months later, he returned to the same jail, where he requested, in vain, mental health medication. Jailers instead placed him in a single-person cell equipped with materials he could use to hang himself, which he did successfully. The Texas Rangers' investigation found from the jail video that the preparations he took for his death were obvious if anyone had bothered to observe. The Texas Commission on Jail Standards subsequently conducted an inspection, finding three violations, noting the jail had not updated its "mental disabilities/suicide prevention program" in nineteen years. The jail continued its noncompliance two years later. A repeat inspection found it still violated "a minimum standard regarding intake procedures for a person observed to be mentally disabled and/or potentially suicidal."

San Diego County, California, Jail

The Citizens' Law Enforcement Review Board, which conducts independent investigations into jail deaths, found no one did anything wrong after reviewing the suicide death of Joseph Morton. He had been released back into a regular cell from a seventy-two-hour psychiatric hold for trying to kill himself. Once returned to the regular cell, he did what he told jail staff he intended to do. He wrapped a blanket around his neck and hung himself from a top bunk. The exoneration of jail staff was not because they did everything correctly. It was because the jail video cameras were inoperable so the board could not determine if deputies checked on Morton during the last three hours of his life. Also, the board has no jurisdiction over the jail's medical staff so it could not determine why they had determined that Morton was not suicidal. Said Morton's sister, "To be blunt, it sounds like a not-so-subtle cover-up attempt on the part of the county jail. Clearly people were negligent. They ignored pleas for help from a desperate suicidal young man, and didn't even check on him per their own regulations." In a suit filed against the jail, the family claims that one of the jail psychologists found he was a low risk for suicide because he asked to be fed and asked about bail, while another declared he was faking his suicidal ideation so he could use a phone.

Sources: M. Garcia, "Family files federal lawsuit of man who committed suicide in 2019," KKYR, February 5, 2021, https://kkyr.com/family-files-federal-lawsuit-on-man -who-committed-suicide-in-2019/; J. McDonald, "Broken cameras, lack of evidence limit inquiring into Vista jail suicide, review board finds," *San Diego Union-Tribune*, August 9, 2021, https://www.sandiegouniontribune.com/news/watchdog/story/2021

-08-09/lack-of-evidence-limits-investigation-into-vista-jail-suicide-last-year; City News Service, "Family of man who committed suicide at Vista Jail files wrongful death lawsuit," *Times of San Diego*, August 10, 2021, https://timesofsandiego.com/crime/2021/08/10/family-of-man-who-committed-suicide-at-vista-jail-files-wrongful-death-lawsuit/.

jail after three years revealed that jail medical errors were so frequent that "if a hospital had those types of medication errors, they would be shut down."[54]

In Oklahoma, the Oklahoma Department of Health Jail Services Division is responsible for jail oversight. It has the authority to investigate detainee deaths and issue misconduct reports. But it cannot fine or impose sanctions on jails that fail to provide adequate care.[55] Oklahoma jails have the second-highest death rate in the country according to Reuters, more than three times the national average. The Texas Commission on Jail Standards has the authority to shut down jails that don't correct deficiencies documented by the commission but rarely exercises it. In California, despite multiple deaths in its fifty-six counties with jails, the state has done little to change how they're run—except to make conditions worse by increasing overcrowding. In 2011, state legislators voted to realign corrections, transferring thousands of inmates from the overcrowded, constitutionally violating state prison system to the county jails. Billions of dollars went to the counties to accommodate the increases in jail populations. Additional state oversight, however, was not included. The California Board of State and Community Corrections, charged with inspecting local jails and maintaining minimum jail standards, has no authority to make jails comply. Despite finding twenty-seven violations in the Kern County Jail, for example, all the board could do was ask the county sheriff, "If you choose to address the noncompliant issues, please provide your corrective plan to the [board] for documentation in your inspection file." When questioned about the Kern overuse of solitary confinement for mentally ill detainees, the California governor called the jail's isolation practices "unacceptable," declaring, "County jails should not hold people in their custody in isolation indefinitely, no matter what the situation is. This is troubling, and it is this Administration's hope that the findings in the reports issued by the Board of State and Community Corrections will catalyze change and reforms at the local level, where authority to make those changes ultimately resides."[56]

Minnesota offers an example of how states have failed to provide jail oversight, as well as their potential to do better. The state's Department of Corrections is responsible for licensing and inspecting county jails. In September 2018, Hardel Sherrell, a 27-year-old black man, died in the Beltrami County, Minnesota, Jail. After conducting its routine review, the Minnesota Department of Corrections absolved the jail of any responsibility. Investigators found no violation of state standards and protocols. This was despite the fact that Sherrell's mother had sent the Department of Corrections a letter she had received from a whistleblower employed by the jail's contracted medical provider. The whistleblower purported to have seen Sherrell while he was sick in the jail. The writer revealed that she, herself, was traumatized by how he was treated, explaining it was like "witnessing a murder right before your eyes." The whistleblower reported seeing Sherrell lying on his back on the floor, his mat full of urine, his body drenched in sweat. He begged the whistleblower to believe him that he was not faking and that he had lost feeling from the waist down. She could tell he wasn't faking his agony, but still, jail staff refused to allow him to be sent to the hospital.

Following this whitewash, KARE 11, a St. Paul TV station, reviewed the department's investigations of multiple county jail deaths. It identified fifty-six detainee deaths between 2015 and the end of October 2020. It found the department "repeatedly failed to identify failures at county jails that contributed to inmate deaths. Even when problems have been identified, records show the DOC has often failed to force local jails to make corrections." Its review of cases revealed "a pattern of investigations that regularly miss or dismiss critical evidence which indicated that deaths could have been prevented." It cited the example of James Lynas, who repeatedly expressed suicidal thoughts at the Sherburne County jail before dying by suicide, but the department review found the jail committed no violations. When the family sued, their lawyer said that the jail displayed "complete deliberate indifference." Although Lynas was on a special watch, jail staff only looked on him through a small window providing little visibility, obscuring critical areas of the cell. A federal judge concluded the jailers' checks "amounted to no checks at all."

KARE 11 also cited the Todd County Jail's inspections. For more than two years, department inspectors documented that guards had not just failed to make required well-being checks, but they were also filing false reports of checks they never made. Yet the department never required the jail to make changes. When a detainee died there the third year after the initial inspection found fraudulent guard reports, the department again found delayed checks and falsified records and did nothing. A month later, another detainee died. Court records from the lawsuit that the county settled with the detainee's family revealed that if guards had performed the well-being checks they recorded, they would have seen the detainee lying on the cell floor "with a sheet wrapped around his neck." The department also found that the Waseca County Jail didn't have a suicide prevention or intervention plan. Five months after the finding, Diana Balderas hanged herself less than an hour after being booked on a probation violation. The jail failed to remove her shoelaces or perform a mental health screening assessment upon her arrival. Two years after her death, the jail still lacked suicide prevention or intervention policies in its manual.[57]

Other media picked up the story. Apparently, the letter Sherrell's mother sent to the Department of Corrections was suddenly "found in a complaint drawer." The corrections commissioner announced that not only was the state's Beltrami County Jail review lacking, but the state's overall process for reviews needed an overhaul. A second DOC investigation "uncovered a myriad of issues," according to Fox 9, which stayed on the story. Most glaring, the new report found that the jail failed to follow a medical directive to return Sherrell to a hospital if his condition worsened. The jail ignored this directive, apparently, because personnel there believed Sherrell was faking his medical condition. The commissioner wrote the jail that if it continued its violations, the state would take action to suspend or revoke the county's license to operate a jail.[58]

After police officer Derek Chauvin killed George Floyd, Sherrell's mother was invited to speak before the Minnesota legislature on behalf of mothers who lost children to police brutality and negligence. She told the media, "It's not just the police brutality, but a corrupt and broken and failed system across the board. The whole system needs to be uprooted and gutted out and started over. Because I cannot, as a mother, see another mother go through what I am going through."[59] The Department of Corrections, completely reversing its initial finding, pressed for an independent law enforcement agency to investigate possible criminal charges for Sherrell's death. The commissioner also directed an analysis of all prior department reviews of deaths in Minnesota jails conducted over the past five years.[60] The commissioner also later revealed he had placed the official in charge of the inspection and licensing of county jails on paid administrative leave. The department said the decision was based on an active internal investigation by the department's Office of Professional Accountability that had been ongoing for a while.[61]

Commissioner Paul Schnell declared, "It shouldn't take a mother's determination for the truth to come to light. Minnesota law gives DOC oversight responsibility for county jails. Our recent re-review of Hardel Sherrell's death uncovered longstanding and problematic processes that led to a failure to uncover the truth about what occurred during Mr. Sherrell's nine-day incarceration. . . . I have directed the DOC's Jail Inspection and Enforcement Unit to redouble its efforts to ensure that conditions of confinement meet the legal, constitutional, and moral obligations of a civil society. Additionally, based on recently uncovered information, we are coordinating with the Minnesota Bureau of Criminal Apprehension to refer the matter to an independent law enforcement agency to explore possible criminal charges related to the circumstances of Mr. Sherrell's death. I have also directed an analysis of all Department of Corrections reviews of deaths in Minnesota jails over the past five years. The DOC is committed to the truth. We will be transparent. We will be thorough. And we will work to earn Minnesotans' trust that we are doing it right."

Its born-again commitment to review jail deaths competently and honestly now makes Minnesota's Department of Corrections an exception. A Georgia State Police investigation of an Appling County jail death is more representative, unfortunately. Police arrested Kelsey Rayner while he sold fruit from his truck for not having a license and theft. Before a judge, Rayner asked to be taken to the hospital for pain and fever. Instead, he was returned to the Appling County jail. Video later showed that deputies watched Rayner lying on his cell floor in agony for five hours. At one point, a deputy entered to try to get him up. "He just stayed, you know, pretty much acting stubborn, but he was still breathing." The deputy left Rayner on the floor where he died two hours later, never receiving any medical assistance during his two-day stay. A doctor had visited the jail the day before Rayner died, but he did not see Rayner because the jail nurse had not done a test ordered. Rayner died of sepsis, a deadly infection caused by a ruptured colon. A jail corporal explained, "When you're schizophrenic, you know how they behave, I took it as if that's behavior of a schizophrenic." Another officer explained that when they tried to get Rayner off the floor, he was "not talking, kind of making noises, not painful noises."[62]

The Georgia Bureau of Investigation completed its standard Georgia jail death investigation. The Brunswick district attorney reviewed it, finding no wrongdoing. For three years, Rayner's family believed he had died due to "natural causes" as the sheriff's office had told them. Then they learned more details, saw the jail video, and couldn't understand why the Brunswick prosecutor did not proceed with criminal charges. They eventually realized the sheriff's work in the district attorney's office constituted a conflict of interest. They also suspected racism, as the sheriff also worked with one of the three men charged in the racist shooting death of Ahmaud Arbery, another black man like Rayner. The men were only arrested for Arbery's murder after it became a national media scandal.[63]

It often takes media attention to change the default posture of state agencies charged with investigating jail deaths. Rarely do investigators otherwise listen to or pay attention to the closest witnesses, other people detained in the jail. After Rhonda Newsome died three months into her stay at the Anderson County jail, the Texas Rangers, for example, found no criminal wrongdoing by the sheriff's office or the jail medical providers. The county prosecution then used the grand jury to officially clear everyone of criminal wrongdoing.[64] Then, thanks to Pulitzer Prize–winning journalism by the local *Palestine Herald-Press*, the truth broke through.

Filing a Freedom of Information request, the paper got ahold of the Texas Rangers' report. It found that Newsome had died seven hours *after* the regional medical center alerted jail medical staff that her blood test results indicated danger of imminent death without immediate medical care. But the only care Newsome got was from jail staff, who—using a defibrillator that didn't work—tried to revive her when she was later found unresponsive in her cell. The coroner's report revealed that Newsome suffered from multiple health issues, including hypertension and Addison's disease. She also had a history of mental illness. Several former detainees revealed that Newsome was swollen on her left side, was bleeding from her mouth, and pleaded for hospital treatment several days before she died. Jeffrey Gerritt, the *Herald-Press* editor, wrote a series of reports entitled "Death Without Conviction" and ten editorials exposing Newsome's death in the jail and how it reflected a wider trend of misconduct and neglect in jails across the entire state of Texas. Gerritt filed dozens more public information requests to obtain Texas Rangers' reports. He found out Newsome's death was not unique. The Rangers documented a variety of discrepancies, "including excessive force, falsified time logs and delays in medical attention" across the state. Because, apparently, the Rangers failed to uncover shootouts at the OK Corral, they never did more than report their findings.

After the media attention, the Texas Rangers reopened its investigation of Newsome's death. The family also filed a $10 million wrongful death lawsuit against the sheriff, the county, the medical providers, and others. Meanwhile, the tiny *Herald-Press* launched a campaign to get the state legislature to require jails to make their videos public as is required in other states. The paper's editorial advised, "Across the country, falsifying jail observation logs is one of the easiest and most widely used ways to cover negligence, incompetence, and misconduct. That's one reason the *Herald-Press* has filed more than a dozen open-records requests, with four local and state agencies, for video related to the June 15, 2018, death of Anderson County prisoner Rhonda Newsome."[65]

In the summer of 2020, a Texas Rangers' report was finally used to hold a jail accountable. The Midland County prosecutor took a jail death case to the grand jury, and five contract nurses were indicted for the death of Savion Hall the prior summer. They were charged with manslaughter, criminal negligent homicide, and tampering with government records. The charges alleged first, the nurses recklessly caused the death by failing to maintain adequate records pertaining to Hall to allow for proper medical care; second, that by failing to keep medical records, Hall did not receive proper medical care; and third, they knowingly made false entry on a government record.[66]

But other Texas jails have found a way to continue to escape scrutiny. Within twenty-four hours of a detainee's death, jails are supposed to notify the Texas Commission on Jail Standards, as well as an independent law enforcement agency, usually the Texas Rangers. But the *Texas Observer* documented at the end of 2020 that jails were able to avoid these inconveniences. At the same time Hall died in the Midland jail, Holly Barlow-Austin died in the custody of the Bi-State Jail in Bowie County, a for-profit jail run by LaSalle Corrections. The jail neither notified the commission nor any law enforcement agency of her death because, it asserted, it had released her to a hospital for "medical reasons" just before she died. By that point, she'd stopped being able to eat or drink, had gone blind, and had the heart rate of someone who'd just run a marathon. After a lawyer representing Barlow-Austin's family charged, "The failure to investigate this atrocity is an atrocity in and of itself," the commission did eventually investigate. It found multiple violations, including the jail's failure to provide Barlow-Austin with the prescribed medications her husband brought to the jail for her HIV, her bipolar disorder, and to prevent fungal infections. A subsequent lawsuit charged LaSalle jailers also falsified cell check logs.[67] According to the Texas Jail Project's director, there were at least seven other cases of last-minute release of detainees so they could die somewhere other than the jail to avoid scrutiny. LaSalle's Texas jails have been on the commission's noncompliance list every year from 2015 to 2019, but they remain open.[68]

A former Washington County, Oklahoma, Jail assistant administrator charged the county sheriff for firing him for bringing hundreds of jail violations to the attention of his superiors, which they ignored. When he was fired in 2019, he contacted the Oklahoma State Department of Health, as well as the state police and attorney general, to tell them, among other things, that the jail was not reporting serious suicide attempts, injuries, and even an escape that led to damage significant enough that it closed a whole pod of the jail. When local media investigated, it obtained department reports confirming three of the incidents alleged. Reporters also discovered that although the state attorney general or county district attorney are authorized to investigate jails that do not correct deficiencies cited by the Oklahoma Commission, the former does not typically investigate jail complaints. Neither does the state Bureau of Investigation, unless invited to by the sheriff or the county district attorney. When asked about the whistleblower's allegations, the sheriff commented that the demands of the job were "not for the faint of heart."[69]

The Ohio Department of Rehabilitation and Corrections Bureau of Adult Detention provides another example of failed oversight. Mark Simms died in the Gallia County jail after jailers denied his request for an ambulance, despite the prior recommendation of EMS that Simms be transported to a medical facility for observation. He died two days later of a heart attack. Lacey Wolford died in the same jail of an overdose. Officers went to revive him with naloxone but arrived too late to administer it. The Ohio Bureau of Adult Detention jail inspector then found that the jail was out of compliance for seventy-seven state jail standards. While many of the issues revolved around the layout and age of the seventy-year-old jail, others concerned practices or policies that needed to be updated. Confronted with these failings, a bureau spokesperson declared, "Historically, the jail will remain non-compliant, and the Bureau of Adult Detention will act as a resource in bringing the jail up to standard." This was a somewhat baffling remark considering the jail had only seventy-one standard violations the last inspection three years before.[70] The next year, the Gallia jail had two separate lawsuits pending against it in federal court, one filed by one of its own correctional officers.

The New York Commission of Corrections provides another example. The commission monitors jails statewide, including annual evaluations, and can issue citations if jails do not comply with the state's minimum standards. Other disciplinary actions include issuing a directive, petitioning a court if the directive is not followed, or ultimately closing the facility. The commission can recommend an outside agency review circumstances surrounding an inmate's death to determine if a crime has been committed or an individual's civil rights have been violated, but it has no statutory authority to direct another agency to investigate. At what was recognized as the "second worst" jail in the state, after a detainee at the Greene County jail was found dead of an overdose in his cell, the commission sent the county jail's administrators a fourteen-page report citing the facility's inadequacies to include security and supervision, discipline and visitation policies, food services, sanitation, commissary, nondiscriminatory treatment, grievance program, good behavior allowance, educational services for youth, and chemical agents policy. Sheriff Greg Seeley was asked to submit comments responding to the citations within the month. The commission received no response and sent Seeley another letter requesting an immediate reply. It wrote again when Seeley still failed to respond. This time, it threatened that Seeley better provide a response "to avoid judicial enforcement by the Commission" and gave a deadline. This worked no better. The commission finally reduced the jail's certification for maximum facility capacity to twelve beds due to staffing deficiencies "well below the level required by the Commission." The letter added that to make things worse, jail security staff continued to abandon their required jail posts outside the jail, resulting in "violation of facility staffing regulations." These were the same findings reported to the jail previously. The commission continued to cite the jail for its deficiencies not addressed by the lowered capacity.

Finally, two years after the first report, the county attorney addressed one of the commission's earlier letters, claiming the jail was in compliance. The commission responded the next month asking the sheriff about the jail's outstanding citations. The county attorney responded the same month reiterating his assertion that the jail was mostly in compliance but acknowledged the county jail's classification policy may be lacking, which he attributed to the age of the 1908 facility that did "not permit nor lend itself toward full compliance with state minimum standards in this regard because the physical plant lacks the space for classification and separation of inmates during intake procedure." Subsequently, Sheriff Seeley testified before the county legislature, "I was elected by the people of Greene County here to be the sheriff of this county and I do designate people to answer letters and they do. I don't answer to Tom Beilein, Commissioner of Corrections, okay? He didn't elect me to be Greene County sheriff." When questioned about his failure to respond to the commission, Seeley admitted, "I'll be honest with you, is [the jail] unfit? Is it unsafe? Absolutely. But do you want me to be out there screaming and yelling and saying that to everybody out there? Absolutely not. I've never said a word about it. 'It's totally unsafe, unfit.' We all know it is. Take a tour, come down and look, everybody." Notwithstanding his remarks to the county, a month later, Seeley wrote the opposite in a letter to the commission arguing against closure of the facility: "It is the position of the Greene County sheriff that the Greene County jail facility is not unsafe, unsanitary or inadequate to provide for the separation and classification of prisoners."

The commission followed up with another site visit. It found the jail administration was not reporting required incidents, including "assault, sex offense, contagious illness, contraband, maintenance/service disruption, disturbance, natural/civil emergency, escape/abscondence/erroneous release, fire, discharge of firearm, group action, hostage situation, physical injury or hospitalizations and death." After the inspection, the commission again asked the jail's administration to address issues with the facility's system of reporting incidents, along with other citations. The jail's administration did not review or revise the policy as required, according to another site evaluation by the commission. Later, the commission complained to the jail, "These findings were brought to your facility's administration attention at an exit interview that took place at the conclusion of the evaluation." The commission gave the jail another deadline to respond. "Such response," it admonished, "shall include actions taken or to be taken to address the findings contained within this report." Failing to respond, Seeley was directed to appear at a hearing to "show cause why the Greene County Jail shall not be ordered closed." The hearing was postponed and then cancelled when Seeley finally responded days before the rescheduled hearing. Although he continued to maintain that the one hundred-year-old facility should stay open, eight days after the death of another detainee, Sheriff Seeley informed the commission, "Our mapping of the [jail] defects shows . . . that under a seismic event or wind storm that would be considered possible for our area, this wall could collapse." The county decided to permanently shutter the Greene County Jail. The commission responded, five years after its inspection found the first seventy-one deficiencies, that it agreed with the decision "to immediately vacate the jail and approved substitute jail orders to transfer custody of all committed inmates to other jails."[71]

In Michigan, the Sheriff's Special Investigation Network (MISSION) investigates jail deaths. It conducted a two-month investigation into the death of Amber Bills in December 2018 in the Montcalm County jail. It found, unsurprisingly, that no jail policies were violated and no criminal acts were committed. A couple months later, Bills's husband filed a lawsuit against the sheriff and county, as well as the Montcalm undersheriff, two sergeants, twelve correctional officers, a doctor, and his medical practice. An autopsy found Bills had an undiagnosed perforated ulcer. She died after five excruciating days in the jail, having been put on detox protocol after she spent a day vomiting and in pain—pain she insisted was not due to her withdrawal. "Amber continued to complain of abdominal pain and was vomiting 'weird green bile,'" according to one detainee, while another said she noticed Bills's toes "curling in pain." Medical staff gave her medication to ease withdrawal symptoms. She continued to plead to be taken to the hospital. Officers refused and told her to "suck it up." Before she collapsed in her cell, according to the lawsuit, she had lost feeling in her feet.[72]

In 2003, Maine enacted a law requiring each county to create an outside oversight board to review each county jail and make recommendations about its operations and how to better serve inmates with mental health diagnoses. Eight years later, most had yet to comply. According to the media, only a handful had formed their boards although at least one county board, the Franklin County Board of Visitors, filed its first report in July 2020. The

Maine Department of Corrections that has oversight responsibilities over county jails was unaware of how many counties were in compliance with the state law.[73]

Some states don't even make a pretense of overseeing jails—they shield jails from accountability. The family of Michael Ostby, 28, filed a wrongful death lawsuit against Yellowstone County, Montana, for his jail death in 2015. After three years, the suit was finally scheduled for trial when a federal judge dismissed the suit declaring that although timely filed to meet federal requirements, Montana state law holds that actions for claims against counties that have been rejected by the county commissioners must be commenced within six months after rejection. In other words, when counties are accused of wrongdoing, the county commissioners can short-circuit the rights of those wronged to sue them by simply denying guilt. In Ostby's case, the lawsuit was filed a crucial month and twenty days too late because the county had agreed to mediation. The mediation subsequently failed because the jail refused to accept any responsibility for Ostby's suicide, despite Ostby repeatedly telling his jailers that his mental condition was deteriorating. He had attempted suicide twice while in custody. Jailers had found torn bedsheets and a shank in his cell three days before he hung himself. The jail's defense was that it had prevented the first two attempts, and it maintained that the torn bedsheet was not indicative of his intent to attempt suicide again.[74] Finally, in 2021, while not admitting any wrongdoing, the county paid Ostby's family $156,000, so as not "to put the family through more litigation."[75]

Removing jail death investigations to state prosecutors does not necessarily advance local jail accountability as they are hesitant to proceed with cases that are not a slam dunk.

The failure of these states to hold local jails accountable is in marked contrast to actions of the North Dakota Department of Corrections. When a detainee died in the Rolette County Jail on June 4, 2020, the department temporarily shut down the jail as soon as it discovered it had violated specific standards, including completion of medical screening upon that person's admission to the jail and failing to place the detainee under observation as he showed signs of intoxication.[76] The jail was allowed to reopen once it implemented certain changes, including a new classification system, daily rosters of detainees, and weekly staff reports. The number of days the jail was allowed to

Erie County, New York, Jail

The New York attorney general's office called the death of inmate India Cummings, 27, a "terrible tragedy" but refused to bring criminal charges against the jail. Cummings died in 2016 after sixteen days in the Erie County Holding Center, where she'd been talking to herself and laying in a puddle of her own urine. The state Commission on Corrections had declared her death a "homicide due to medical neglect," caused by a "massive pulmonary embolism resulting from acute renal failure, rhabdomyolysis, dehydration and fracture of the humerus." The Erie County pathologist had previously said he was unable to classify the death as a "homicide," saying his pathologists found that she died from complications stemming from an untreated broken arm and the tissue breakdown it caused—a break for which they did not know the cause and could therefore not fault the jail. The commission, however, called the jail's care of Cummings "so grossly incompetent and inadequate as to shock the conscience." The sheriff had dismissed the state commission report as "no more than an opinion."

Bannock County, Idaho, Jail

The attorney general of Idaho declined to bring charges against jailers for the death of Lance Quick because the jail's dysfunctional management and lack of coordination among "command staff, jail sergeants, deputies and contract medical personnel" meant there was no one in charge who could be blamed. The investigation had concluded that the conduct of the sheriff's employees "contributed in significant ways." Police had arrested Quick for suspicion of drunk driving, though he may have been going through a manic episode, as he had been diagnosed with bipolar disorder and PTSD. During the six days he spent in the jail, his condition worsened as he was forced to withdraw from his prescribed antipsychotic medication, which jailers did not provide to him. By the third day, Quick was too incoherent for arraignment in court, meaning the court could not set his bail. He remained in jail for three more days—on the floor of his cell, covered in self-inflicted bruises and his own excrement—until he was finally taken to the hospital, dying from dehydration and starvation. Bannock County paid out $2.1 million to the deceased's family with the stipulation that all parties would remain mum about the death and there would be no criminal charges filed.

Sources: H. McNeil, "Attorney general finds no one criminally culpable in death of India Cummings," *Buffalo News*, October 2, 2020, https://buffalonews.com/news/

local/attorney-general-finds-no-one-criminally-culpable-in-death-of-india-cummings/
article_dde72c90-04f0-11eb-a77a-b31610125251.html; S. Harris, "Idaho AG now
involved in investigation of local jail inmate Lance Quick's 2018 death," *Idaho State
Journal,* October 28, 2020, https://www.idahostatejournal.com/news/local/idaho
-ag-now-involved-in-investigation-of-local-jail-inmate-lance-quicks-2018-death/
article_0728bc0b-0507-522c-9245-bcca43e9669a.html.

hold detainees was limited. In two months, the department indicated it would review the progress at the jail to see if it could return to holding detainees for longer. The sheriff admitted there was room for improvements and vowed to seek the department's assistance in making them though blaming the "overwhelming drug problem" in the community for causing the detainee's death.[77] Unfortunately, the North Dakota state oversight appears to be the exception, not the rule.

Other states have no state agencies that exercise jail oversight. In Washington, for example, the sheriff decides whether to invite a neighboring sheriff's office or a regional team of deputies to investigate a death in his jail or to do it within his own office. After examining how Washington and Oregon reviewed jail deaths, analysts concluded: "Deaths in Northwest jails rarely result in swift personnel actions, trigger multiple investigations or lead to sweeping changes in how jails are managed." In Oregon, where there are state jail standards, the state Sheriffs Association inspects jails biannually. In Washington, there are no such standards.[78]

At least 217 people have died in four metro Atlanta county jails since 2004. Only one of those deaths was investigated by an outside state agency. The others were investigated in-house by the sheriffs' offices. All these investigations cleared staffs of any wrongdoing. In 2020, a legislator finally filed a bill to create Georgia's first state jail oversight. As the legislator asked, "If they are the ones causing the problems, how can you ask them to investigate themselves?" The legislator said the impetus for the bill came from the 11Alive reports of Cobb County jail deaths, specifically that of Kevil Wingo, caught on video begging to be sent to the hospital for eight hours before he collapsed and died. The Cobb County sheriff investigated the death and exonerated his own jail staff. The legislator said he modeled his bill after the law Texas enacted following Sandra Bland's death in custody.[79]

U.S. JUSTICE DEPARTMENT ENDS CUSTODY DEATH INVESTIGATIONS

In the past, the U.S. Justice Department and its civil rights division investigated some of the more egregious jail deaths. But that ended with the election of President Trump. The department did complete an investigation toward the end of the Trump administration, asking the Hampton Roads Regional Jail in Portsmouth, Virginia, to enter into a consent decree requiring it to improve dismal medical care for inmates. The action by the Justice Department made it one of the first times it had proposed such a resolution in four years. The rare event followed a multiyear investigation into the jail where investigators found unlawful conditions, including unconstitutionally inadequate mental health care. The investigation followed the death of Jamycheal Mitchell, a 24-year-old detainee who had bipolar disorder and schizophrenia. Charged with stealing about $5 worth of snacks from a convenience store, he was sent to the jail where he died about four months later of heart failure and severe weight loss.[80] He joined at least twenty-two people that had died at the jail since 2015. The president of the Portsmouth NAACP, commenting on one of the jail deaths, said, "Now it's a pattern. . . . There's no accountability there whatsoever. The board that oversees the jail—the city managers and the sheriffs that send people over there—they're not going to make a fuss because it's not in their interest."[81] In the first two months of 2021, four more died at the jail. Reuters later reported that from 2008 to 2020, a total of forty-nine inmates died at the jail, making it the deadliest jail in Virginia.[82] Other than this, the Justice Department stood down during the Trump years.

FIGHTING ACCOUNTABILITY

Some of the sheriffs whose jails regularly prove to be the most lethal have adopted the most aggressive (and successful) campaigns against reform and accountability. They typically employ several strategies. First, they keep the details of jail deaths secret, even from the decedents' families. Second, they disparage critics as misinformed and unworthy. Third, they lie and cover up their failures. Fourth, failing to silence critics, they get the counties to settle quietly, keeping the amounts paid out secret where possible.

Two graphic examples from either end of the country demonstrate these sheriffs' unwillingness or inability to stop their jails' death tolls. More than 140 people died in the San Diego jail from 2009 through May 2020, including

Cobb County, Georgia, Jail

An Atlanta broadcast news station finally filed a lawsuit against Sheriff Neil Warren, accusing him of violating the state's Open Records Act by refusing to release investigative files of three jail deaths. The sheriff told the media that there were active investigations of all three deaths that prevented him from releasing files. The attorney for the TV station correctly charged that the sheriff "manufactured an investigation" to claim exemptions from the law. As mentioned, the so-called investigation was being done for gratis by a private law firm with no expertise, except that it had represented the sheriff in personal matters.

Contra Costa County, California, Jail

After ten people died in the county jail in almost as many years, advocates called for reform, transparency, and accountability. Benito Carrasco, 35, died most recently, of an overdose of methamphetamines and fentanyl, according to a pathologist. The coroner's inquest jury ruled the death was an accident. However, no "accident" caused the illegal drugs to get smuggled into the jail and given to Carrasco. The sheriff, however, accepted no responsibility, dismissing any criticism of his deadly jail as "nonsense" from "political radicals."

Harrison County, Mississippi, Jail

After correctional officers beat, pepper sprayed, hogtied, and wrapped up Jessie Williams Jr. "like a suitcase," leaving him to die in a restraint chair, the coverup began immediately. First, the jail shut off its phone system for prisoners for several days to prevent them from revealing what they had seen or heard. Then the sheriff's office synchronized stories and filed false reports. Sheriff George Payne announced that Williams had a history of fighting with police and that guards at the jail "had to fight him." He added, "They pepper-sprayed him, and it didn't slow him down. It cranked him up even higher, which it does when they're on crack or meth or something like that." In truth, Williams tested negative for drugs. The misinformation and secrecy continued for months. An attorney for the family and the *Sun Herald* fought in court to gain access to information that should have been public in the first place, including the autopsy and videotape of Williams's death.

Sacramento County, California, Jail

Despite six deaths in the jail in the first eight months of 2021, the sheriff's office publicly revealed only one. On the day Deyyj Watts died, the sheriff put out a press release featuring a photograph of a deputy dressed as "Deputysaurus Rex" and another as "McGruff" extolling the sheriff's crime-fighting prowess.

New York City Jail, New York

Tamara Carter revealed, "I had to find out he was dead on Facebook." Brandon Rodriguez died by suicide in the jail. Two days before he hanged himself, he suffered a broken eye socket. It was later found that there was a "documented use of force by staff" against him, according to officials.

Sources: K. Dixon, "TV news station sues Cobb sheriff over alleged open records violation," *Atlanta Journal-Constitution*, September 24, 2020, https://www.ajc.com/ news/atlanta-news/tv-news-station-sues-cobb-sheriff-over-alleged-open-records -violation/WGTAMA3UTNDUTOUTOBBAXWO67Q/; N. Gartrell, "Man died of drug overdose in Contra Costa jail," *Mercury News*, September 23, 2020, https://www .mercurynews.com/2020/09/23/man-died-of-drug-overdose-in-contra-costa-jail-days -after-he-was-arrested-and-briefly-hospitalized/; J. Fitzhugh, "Fatal 2006 beating of inmate by Coast jailers brought denials, then justice," *Sun Herald*, September 10, 2018, https://www.sunherald.com/news/local/crime/article218153040.html; J. Pohl, "People are dying in Sacramento County jails. The sheriff isn't telling the public," *Sacramento Bee*, August 17, 2021, https://www.msn.com/en-us/news/crime/people -are-dying-in-sacramento-county-jails-the-sheriff-isnt-telling-the-public/ar-AANqdW1; G. Rayman, "NYC mom who learned on Facebook of son's Rikers suicide demands answers from city," *Daily News*, August 17, 2021, https://www.nydailynews .com/new-york/nyc-crime/ny-brandon-rodriguez-suicide-rikers-mother-20210817 -4oqqvrtemzd7zgoecj3ju3ywki-story.html.

forty-one suicides. After completing a six-month review of the jail deaths, the *Union-Tribune* published a series called "Dying Behind Bars." It found that the jail had the highest jail-mortality rate among California's six largest counties, costing the county millions of dollars in legal settlements and awards. According to the report, the county on average paid out $5.5 million a year for the past thirty years, excluding a recent jury award of $12.6 million for the jail's failure to address a detainee, arrested for suspicion of public drunkenness, who had fallen in his cell and eventually suffered permanent brain damage from an ignored brain bleed. Five years before that award, a jury had awarded relatives and attorneys of Daniel Sisson, age 21, $4.2 million after he died from an asthma attack exacerbated by heroin withdrawal, having been left unattended for three hours.

After the newspaper investigation, the sheriff announced that he had increased some staffing and health services. He also instituted another new policy. The jail would go silent and no longer reveal in-custody deaths until internal investigations were completed, a process to delay public announcement for months. The new reforms, however, did not stop the deaths but did interfere with family members', much less the public's, knowledge of them. In May 2020, for example, Joseph Morton died by suicide, the second in-custody San Diego jail death that year. While his family was notified of the death, they received no details from the jail or the medical examiner. A liaison they were assigned at the jail told them not to call.[83] By mid-October 2020, at least another five inmates had died in the San Diego jail, including Adams Rogers, 32, whose family was also provided no details. Local media were also unable to obtain any information on his death. After the medical examiner ruled the cause of death to be "undetermined," the family stopped a planned cremation to get a second opinion they were hoping to be able to afford. Rogers's brother reported a correctional officer told him they had found a white substance and black residue in Rogers's cell and the officer asked the brother if Rogers had a drug problem. The brother said Rogers's drug problem had led him to be incarcerated. As the *Union-Tribune* reported, although the sheriff's department had established drug withdrawal protocols, no medical records were released to reveal if these policies had been followed.[84] Other California sheriff's departments announce jail deaths within twenty-four hours.[85]

In addition to staying mum, the San Diego sheriff's department launched a counterattack against the media. It challenged the jail death data used by the newspaper, claiming that the San Diego jail suicide rate was lower than that in the community (based on the nonsensical BJS calculations that did not control for the brief time most detainees spend in jail). More tellingly, it insisted it was unfair to compare its suicides with other jails, the standard approach also used by BJS, because while the rate in the San Diego jail was 74.8 per 100,000, compared to 25.8 in Los Angeles, San Diego's jail had a higher proportion of whites who were more suicide prone than other demographics.[86]

Worse than its public defense, months after the media first focused on the jail, a medical records clerk revealed that she was threatened with retaliation if she told the truth about how she had confronted a San Diego jail sergeant who had refused to put a detainee who had died at the jail four years earlier on suicide watch. In her court declaration, the clerk, who had worked in the jail for fifteen years, confessed she lived "with guilt and remorse for staying quiet." She said she had been ordered to "stand down" by the sergeant on duty when she offered to file the paperwork to transfer the detainee to a safety cell. That night, the detainee used two T-shirts to choke and strangle himself to death. Ironically, the clerk finally spoke out while being deposed on *another* lawsuit brought for a different jail suicide that took place later. She revealed that county officials had altered documents in that case, which the county eventually settled for more than half a million dollars.[87]

(Three more inmates died in the San Diego jail in November 2020 even though the jail's population was as low as it had been in years, about 4,000 as opposed to its usual 5,500. With the three additional deaths in November, twelve total died in the county's jails that year, thirteen if you count an unresponsive inmate who died in a hospital after he was formally released from the sheriff's custody.[88] It took less than a month for the first San Diego jail death to occur in 2021.)

Across the country, in Chatham County, Georgia, seven deaths in thirty months led the county to hire a jail monitor to scrutinize the jail's health-care services. The monitor made four reports on the jail's health care, all described as "scathing," listing staff shortages and unclear health guidelines, including its policies for detainees at risk for suicide and failures to provide prescribed medications. The monitor warned the company's failures could trigger loss of life. In response, the Chatham County sheriff kicked the monitor out of his jail. (Ironically, at the time, the National Commission of Correctional Health Care awarded its first-ever certificate for mental health services to the jail, immediately after yet after another detainee had died by suicide. The sheriff did not inform the commission about the suicide although the NCCHC vice president later excused the sheriff because the death occurred after the commission had inspected the jail, although before the certification.[89])

Later, the sheriff did fire four correctional officers after Lee Creely was found unresponsive in his cell. One of the four officers had falsified records of cell checks.[90] In March 2021, the sheriff revealed the facility has spent $300,000 on a new "guardian system" to prevent suicides. "It has a camera on it, it can monitor everything. It said [sic] were the inmates laying down, were they standing up, if they tore their cell up. It takes a photograph of the inmate." That same week, a detainee was found dead in her cell after hanging herself.[91]

Testifying to the power of sheriffs, politicians often mobilize to protect them and their jails from being held to account. The North Carolina General Assembly, for example, quietly and swiftly passed a bill that shielded jails from public access to custody death investigations sent to medical examiners. Alarmed, the executive director of the state Prisoner Legal Services explained, "It's just really important that the public knows—that everybody has the ability to know—what's going on in our prisons and our jails just to ensure that everybody is doing the job that they're supposed to be doing." The state's chief medical examiner supported the new law because law enforcement would be better about providing her office with reports if they knew they would not be made public. Fortunately, the governor vetoed the legislation after a public and media outcry.[92]

The case cited by opponents of the vetoed legislation is instructive. Not only did the jail attempt to stonewall the aforementioned death of John Neville, but it also came out later that one of the officers eventually charged in Neville's death had been given a merit promotion and a retroactive pay raise! After a subsequent protest, the Forsyth district attorney charged the officer, four other former county detention officers, and a nurse at the jail with involuntary manslaughter for the death. The district attorney charged that by restraining and strangling Neville, they caused his fatal brain injury.[93]

The day after charges were filed against the Forsyth officers, the sheriff issued new restraint policies, basically outlining what was in the Justice Department guidelines issued in 1995. As the News & Observer noted, "Neville was in a medical emergency when officers and a nurse arrived, but the video showed efforts to restrain him took precedence over his medical needs." The Forsyth sheriff also issued a new policy that deputies must "follow the guidelines of medical personnel and put preservation of life over any other priority. The new policy gives medical personnel full autonomy over inmates in medical distress."[94] However, the sheriff also noted that he had little control over the jail's medical provider, Wellpath, despite charges that it had repeatedly ignored an inmate's high-blood pressure, leading to his death. The sheriff explained he was dependent upon the medical provider as it was "the only game in town."[95]

Although sheriffs run most jails, independent jail administrators have also proven resistant to reforms. In 2016, a federal judge approved a settlement to clean up Baltimore's dangerous detention facilities. The settlement called for an overhaul for their failure to deliver medical and mental health care. Twelve deaths later, in December 2020, the ACLU returned to court alleging little progress: "Now that Defendants have spent more than four years avoiding compliance with a single medical or mental health care provision of the Settlement Agreement, it is clear that a Court order mandating that Defendants develop a plan for compliance with a specific schedule, as well as specification of the tasks that must be completed . . . is necessary." The ACLU noted that an outside jail medical director had concluded that the twelve most recent jail deaths over the prior two years were "preventable had there been appropriate systems in place to identify individuals' medical and mental health needs." The deaths included multiple drug overdoses and suicides.[96]

Grieving Families Left to Attempt to Hold Jails Accountable

When all else has failed—sheriffs, medical examiners, prosecutors, state oversight agencies, the media—families' wrongful death lawsuits become the last hope to hold lethal jailers accountable. Despite legal obstacles plaintiffs face in these cases, jail death lawsuits are proliferating. Win or lose, these suits raise the only public awareness of many jail deaths.

Anthony Aceves, jailed for a probation violation, died in 2020. When the Orange County, California, jail wouldn't tell his mother how her son had died, she called the coroner's office each month to request his autopsy report. Finally, after eight months, the office told her he'd died of an "accidental" fentanyl overdose. The prosecutor eventually did release its investigation of the death, only to suggest that someone passed what appeared to be a suspect cookie under Aceves's cell door the night before he died. The district attorney concluded that there was not enough evidence to show the Sheriff's Department was culpable in Aceves's death and closed its investigation, failing to even note that a grand jury had issued a scathing report on the jail's deficiencies the year before. It had castigated the jail for its prior failures to prevent almost half of its multiple jail deaths. Aceves's mother was also not reassured to find the prosecutor's report misstated her son's criminal record, saying, for example, he had attacked his wife when, in fact, he had never been married. "My son was schizophrenic. He needed help. . . . Anthony was no throwaway. He was loved, and he's still continued to be loved. We fight for him." She filed a lawsuit against the county hoping finally to find some answers.[1]

Often the threat of a lawsuit prompts settlements. Jail death lawsuits have cost Minnesota taxpayers, for example, more than $10 million in settlements and legal fees over the past decade, and, as reported by KARE 11, "taxpayers may soon be on the hook for a lot more." There were fifteen more lawsuits pending or about to be filed in federal court for other jail deaths as of the end of October 2020. Cass County, Minnesota, paid out $2 million to the family of a detainee who died by suicide in its jail in 2018 before the family filed a federal wrongful death suit. The detainee, known to have suicidal ideations and mental illness, had been able to drink two cups of toxic windshield wiper fluid and slowly die in his cell. Officers knew of the poisoning but did not summon medical assistance.[2]

But success is not guaranteed in these suits. First, grieving families have to be patient. After the death of Clifton Harper by hanging in the Roanoke, Virginia, City Jail, for example, the family sued Sherriff Tim Allen, several deputies, and a psychiatrist for disregarding the 22-year-old's "clear and present threat to himself." Before the case was resolved, more than twenty different depositions were taken and multiple psychiatric experts recruited. Finally, the county paid $370,000 to settle the case after five years of litigation.[3]

Second, families must find a lawyer willing to take the case. Lawyers are reluctant to take cases they cannot win and understand that, in these lawsuits, lethal negligence is not enough. Police officers, sheriffs, county governments, correctional officers, and jail contractors also have qualified immunity, a legal principle that grants government officials performing discretionary functions immunity from civil suits unless the plaintiff shows that the official violated clearly established statutory or constitutional rights that a reasonable person would have understood. Courts have ruled that even after plaintiffs show the law enforcement officials had subjective knowledge of risk, plaintiffs must also prove these officials disregarded that risk by failing to take reasonable measures to abate harm.

A few months before Derek Chauvin killed George Floyd, a somewhat similar case in the U.S. Eighth Circuit Court of Appeals exonerated jail officers who had held a detainee in a prone position in a holding cell until he died. The man, Bryan Guilbert, who was white, was experiencing homelessness and addicted to methamphetamines. Arrested for squatting in a vacant building, he had removed his sweatpants and tied them to the bars in jail. Afraid he was going to hang himself, officers entered the cell to restrain him. According to the lawsuit, he hit his head on a concrete bench as multiple officers wrestled him to the ground. Two officers then proceeded to hold him on the ground for fifteen minutes after handcuffing him and shackling his legs. The city medical examiner called the manner of death "accidental" and said the cause of death was "arteriosclerotic heart disease exacerbated by methamphet-amine and forcible restraint." As in the later Floyd suit, the plaintiff's expert disagreed, saying Guilbert died by forcible restraint inducing asphyxia. The federal trial judge dismissed the lawsuit against the officers, ruling they had "qualified immunity." The Eighth Circuit Court went further, ruling that the prone restraint, even holding a man down for fifteen minutes until he could not breathe, was not unreasonable.[4]

The ignorance of jailers ironically offers them a legal shield. Judges have ruled, in effect, that the almost total incompetence of a sheriff and jailers to understand what they are doing qualifies them for immunity. The Weber County, Utah, jail provides an unfortunate example. The jail kept no logs of the last day of Ashley Jessop's life, meaning no records indicated whether guards checked on him as required. The jail did not fill out Jessop's medical records until after he was found unresponsive and taken to the hospital. Jessop, 35, according to a wrongful death lawsuit, told the booking officer that he was "almost suicidal, was taking psychiatric medications and had a seizure disorder." He was also intoxicated. Despite this, the officer indicated on the intake form that Jessop did not need medical attention, which also prevented Jessop from receiving his prescribed medication. The officer later explained the jail did not need to place him on a medical watch because he would be watched "coming off of alcohol or drugs or whatever he was on." The officer also noted that Jessop could walk at the time—a rather low bar for detainee health. A nurse's report filed retroactively said that "Jessop had been using his hand and fist to insert into his anus and rectum repeatedly during his booking stay." According to the lawsuit, Jessop repeated that behavior in his cell while screaming. Jessop died in a hospital after collapsing in the jail. The autopsy found he was suffering from "metabolic encephalopathy, rhabdomyolysis, kidney injury, end-stage liver disease, seizures, gastrointestinal bleed, alcohol dependence with withdrawal, and left side bruising and injuries." According to the lawsuit, this meant his skeletal muscle tissue died because Jessop's body

Orange County, Texas, Jail

Police arrested Robert Montano for public intoxication and put him in a special glass-walled detoxification observation cell. The glass walls did not serve their purpose, as staff had covered most of them with paper, so they could only see Montano when he stood up. No one assessed him for suicide risk, and over the four days of his detention, jail staff checked his vital signs only once. On the fourth day, medical staff observed that he was not breathing but still waited twenty minutes before calling emergency services. When jailers entering the cell, they found uneaten food and excrement on the floor. Montano's estate filed a civil rights action against the county for cruel and unusual punishment. They jury determined that even though the written jail protocol called for detainees to spend a maximum of eight hours in its detox cell, the four days Montano spent there constituted the county's de facto policy. The jury awarded $1.5 million for pain and suffering and almost $1 million for wrongful death. The court added almost half a million in attorney's fees. On appeal, the federal court vacated the jury's actions, finding the law could not support them.

Broome County, New York, Jail

The parents of Thomas Husar, 40, sued, claiming that though he entered the jail with a known, serious preexisting condition, the jail ignored his pleading for help for twelve hours immediately before he finally died from his chronic illness. In the three weeks he spent in jail, Husar lost thirty pounds and developed an ulcer. An officer had requested, in vain, that he be transferred to the jail's medical unit. Husar was the ninth inmate to die in the jail in less than a decade. The judge ruled that jail staff had qualified immunity and dismissed the suit.

Santa Fe County, New Mexico, Jail

Police arrested Ricardo Ortiz for stealing a handbag. When booked at the jail, he said he was in withdrawal. They also knew he had a serious liver disease and noted he looked "severely ill." However, jail staff offered Ortiz no treatment, even when he began to vomit blood. On Ortiz's fourth day in jail, he was found dead in his cell floor, naked and covered in blood and feces. His family sued. The court dismissed the suit. On appeal, the Tenth Circuit upheld the dismissal against all but one of the jail employees. In 2021, the county settled, paying $1 million to the family.

Sources: Montano v. Orange County, Tex., 842 F.3d 865, 882-882 (Fifth Cir. 2016); A. Borrelli, "How Broome County responded to a negligence lawsuit after man died in jail," Binghamton Press & Sun-Bulletin, October 24, 2020, https://www.msn.com/en-us/news/crime/how-broome-county-responded-to-a-negligence-lawsuit-after-man-died-in-jail/ar-BB1alTwC; Quintana v. Santa Fe County Board of Commissioners, Tenth Circuit. No. 19-2039, August 29, 2020; K. Davis & J. McDonald, "Investigators said San Diego deputy neglected to check inmate found dead in 2020," San Diego Union-Tribune, July 12, 2021, https://www.sandiegouniontribune.com/news/watchdog/story/2021-07-12/investigators-said-san-diego-deputy-neglected-to-check-inmate-found-dead-in-2020.

was lying on the cell floor for an extended period, releasing substances into the blood that caused the kidney failure.

The lawsuit charged that the sheriff violated Jessop's constitutional right to adequate medical care by failing to properly train and monitor his officers' compliance with policies regarding intake procedures, medical treatment, and safety checks. Four years later in 2020, U.S. District Judge Robert Shelby in Salt Lake City granted summary judgment to the county, ruling, in effect, that because the sheriff had no idea how his jail had treated Jessop, he was covered for immunity, as was the officer responsible for Jessop's intake because he had "diligently" completed the paperwork and understood that medical professionals would take over any medical issues.[5] Since the judge's ruling, there have been four more deaths in the jail, including two suicides.

Some states have specifically enacted laws to shield jails from suits. In 2018, Oklahoma acted to reduce the rights of detainees seeking money damages against the state or its subdivisions for constitutional torts. The law makes a specific exception to the state's waiver of liability for the "provision, equipping, operation or maintenance of any prison, jail or correctional facility." As a frustrated plaintiff's lawyer lamented, the state Supreme Court's broad reading of the law "makes it impossible to imagine any act of a prison's employee, done within the scope of employment, that is not also in furtherance of the operation of the prison. . . . Certainly an employee's act of moving an inmate from one part of the jail to another, if done within the scope of employment, must be viewed as an operation of the prison" and therefore "acts to bar any tort claim by the estate against the county in this case."[6] The

Jefferson County, Colorado, Jail

Although assigned to special housing for high-risk inmates, Susanne Burgaz, 54, was able to hang herself in the recreation room of the jail with a television cord when left unchecked. The judge ruled that because the jail deputies were not trained medical staff, they couldn't plausibly know of her risk for suicide. The judge further specified, "While the sufficiency of a walk-through may have bearing on whether a deputy breached the duty to perform his or her job responsibilities with reasonable care for purposes of a negligence claim, the failure to conduct a sufficiently rigorous walk-through, without more, is insufficient to demonstrate constitutional deliberate indifference to a particular risk to a particular inmate." He also granted qualified immunity to the staff.

Montrose County, Colorado, Jail

Dillon Blodgett, 23, was found unresponsive three days after entering the jail. Although staff knew he had suicidal ideations, he died by suicide. A federal judge ruled "deficient supervision" did not meet the legal requirement for a valid suit. The judge ruled the plaintiffs had not presented an expert witness to educate the jury about adequate medical care. The plaintiffs *did* have an expert witness who testified what care for inmates at risk for suicide required, but the judge ruled that the expert's testimony had no relevance to the jail and its mental health provider's specific policies and procedures or how those were applied in Blodgett's death. In short, when a jail or its provider has no standards for preventing jail suicides, it becomes impossible to show they were violated, much less that the violations were directly connected to a detainee's death.

Sources: M. Karlik, "Federal court dismisses lawsuit over 2017 suicide in Jeffco jail," *Colorado Politics*, January 22, 2021, https://www.coloradopolitics.com/news/federal -court-dismisses-lawsuit-over-2017-suicide-in-jeffco-jail/article_b3c58b58-5ce5-11eb -9151-8bc42ed25165.html; K. Heidelberg, "Suit over inmate's 2015 death ends in dismissal," *Montrose Press*, November 17, 2020, https://www.montrosepress.com/ news/suit-over-inmate-s-2015-death-ends-in-dismissal/article_68252b88-2859-11eb -8586-5fa6c60d2e5e.html.

lawyer was referring to the dismissal of claims of excessive force against the Muskogee County Board of Commissioners in a suit brought by the estate of Marvin Rowell, 42. He died of multiple blunt impact injuries, according to the chief medical examiner. These injuries occurred when deputies moved him, while handcuffed, to a restraint chair, the use of which plaintiffs alleged was "unjustified and excessive." Police had put Rowell in jail for public intoxication, where sixteen minutes after entry two deputies escorted him from the booking area of the jail when he fell and happened to hit his head on the concrete floor. The suit alleges that officers "without provocation or justification negligently injured Marvin Rowell when they pushed him . . . or caused or allowed him to fall." After a federal court ruled several of the defendants had qualified immunity, a state judge dismissed the remaining claim, citing the 2018 law.

Fortunately, not all federal judges and appellate courts are on the same page. A federal District Court in the State of Washington, for example, found that a plaintiff's suit in another jail withdrawal wrongful death was valid. The judge ruled that a jury could decide whether the Snohomish County jail had no policy or consistently failed to follow a policy for opioid withdrawal that led to the detainee's death. A reasonable jury could also decide, the judge added, that the jail customarily failed to provide medical care to detainees, resulting in deaths. The court noted that jail officials themselves had advised the county of the jail's lacking health care and staffing levels.[7]

And again, it's often not a detainee's death that makes jails liable but the coverup afterward.

Often, the facts of wrongful jail death cases are so egregious that defendants and/or their insurance companies so fear letting lawsuits get anywhere near juries that they settle. The same day the federal courts dismissed the suit in Colorado, for example, a federal judge in Virginia approved an almost one-million-dollar wrongful jail death settlement for the family of 18-year-old Davageah Jones, who died in the Hampton Roads Regional Jail in 2018. Jones had appeared in state court the day before he died. The judge had noticed Jones looked ill, suspended the hearing, and ordered the public defenders to contact the jail and get Jones treatment. The jail staff ignored the request and returned Jones to his cell where he died the next day of diabetic ketoacidosis, caused by lack of the insulin he required twice daily. The jail provided him no medication for more than two weeks. Afraid of a potential award of up to $18 million in court, the settlement was probably a bargain for the defendants.[8]

Even when counties successfully fend off suits, it can cost hundreds of thousands of dollars. An examination of jail cases in Utah, for example, found

Cumberland County, New Jersey, Jail

A federal judge ruled that a jury could hear the wrongful death suit against the jail alleging officers failed to make required checks on David Conroy, who hanged himself while on suicide watch. The judge noted that the warden was aware of a "perennial problem" of officers falsifying records of detainee checks they never performed. In Conroy's case, jail video shows that two officers lied about checking on him every fifteen minutes, but supervisors had never watched the video to verify the officers' claims. As a result, the judge ruled it was up to the jury to determine if the two officers had shown "deliberate indifference."

Benton County, Washington, Jail

After the aforementioned, slow death by thirst of 18-year-old Marc Moreno in the Benton County, Washington, Jail, the family sued. The federal court found a "stunning obstruction of justice," as the jail's contractors deliberately destroyed e-mails and other potentially damning records relating to his death. The judge issued a rare "default judgment" against the contractors. It was revealed a year later that the jail's contracted medical provider, now called Wellpath, quietly paid out $4.5 million and the county another $1.2 million to the family, the largest jail settlement in Washington over the last twenty-six years. The jail's contracted mental health provider, Our Lady of Lourdes Hospital and Lourdes Counseling Center, also paid out an undisclosed sum.

Sources: J. Walsh, "Judge: Jury can hear lawsuit over Cumberland County Jail suicide," *Courier Post,* December 22, 2020, https://www.courierpostonline.com/story/news/2020/12/22/cumberland-county-jail-suicide-lawsuit-david-conroy/4008867001/; L. Kamp, "An Eastern Washington teen went to a mental health clinic for help. Eight days later, he was dead in a jail cell," *Seattle Times,* November 1, 2020, https://www.seattletimes.com/seattle-news/an-eastern-washington-teen-went-to-a-mental-health-clinic-for-help-eight-days-later-he-died-in-a-jail-cell/.

"an experienced cadre of private defense attorneys" paid by the taxpayers "play dominant and decisive roles" in defending jails. While these experts make it difficult for plaintiff lawyers to win claims of negligence or wrongdoing inside jails, they don't come cheap. The state government created the Utah Counties Indemnity Pool so counties could work together to share legal costs. According to one source, the pool paid out more than $2.5 million to cover losses and settlements to litigants and pay law firms in 2019.[9]

In attorney Rocky Anderson's letter describing deaths in Utah's jails, he included how Salt Lake County refused to even negotiate with the family of one of the inmates who died but then settled the case for $950,000, more than the family had initially requested. As Anderson explained, the settlement did not begin to include the costs of the county's two years of intensive, extremely expensive litigation, including thirty-seven depositions and numerous motions, consuming thousands of hours of staff time at the district attorney's office. Costs will continue to rise for Utah's jails because a federal judge ruled at the end of 2020 that a "reasonable" jury could conclude one of its counties was deliberately indifferent in another lawsuit involving the death of Heather Miller, 28. The Tenth U.S. Circuit Court of Appeals subsequently upheld the ruling.[10]

The elevated death rate in private prisons was revealed through wrongful death suits. A *Utah Law Review* article detailed: "In the past two years, [GEO Group–owned CEC jail facilities] has been under scrutiny for a number of health and safety issues. It is currently facing a wrongful death suit from a Dallas family that alleges their family member was given improper medical care while in CEC custody, leading to his death. CEC is also under investigation for the 2015 deaths of two prisoners in a single week at a Houston, Texas jail." The journal article concluded that the jail's violations, ranging from minor to severe, "are a constant feature for privately run jails, marking a definite worsening of conditions from government-run jails."

To be worse than some government-run jails is no small achievement.[11]

JAIL WITHDRAWAL WRONGFUL DEATH LAWSUITS AWARDS/ SETTLEMENTS GROWING

Despite legal barriers, it appears that most suits at least result in settlements, if not admissions of responsibility on the part of jailers. In 2019, Alexander Klein, my son, completed a Westlaw analysis of 109 wrongful death jail lawsuits then still pending or recently settled involving detainees who died while withdrawing from drugs and/or alcohol. It offers an insight into jail death lawsuit outcomes. Half of the studied lawsuits were resolved with payouts, including either settlements or court awards, totaling more than $67 million (not including ten settlements where the amounts were not disclosed). The amount also did not include separate undisclosed payments made by private contracted medical providers. The more recent payouts were the largest, with nearly $25 million paid out in 2018 alone. The largest award was for $10 million; the smallest $10,000. The average was $1.73 million per death. Plaintiffs dropped or courts dismissed only eight of the 109 civil suits. Because it takes years for these suits to be resolved, the suits involved deaths that occurred six years before. This means these deaths occurred before the current opioid epidemic hit its peak in the United States, meaning many more such suits have come and will continue since this analysis.

Generally, the suits' defendants were the counties where the jails are located, sheriffs if they run the jail, the jail security and medical staff that are jail employees, and any contracted private medical providers. However, in the final settlements, the defendants were usually limited to the county and the contracted medical provider, who have deeper pockets than individual employees. Payouts by the contracted medical providers were usually not disclosed. When these companies bid on jail and prison contracts, the last thing they want potential bidders to know is past payouts. Despite even the largest payouts made, the defendants rarely agree to accept responsibility for deaths.

The Howard County, Indiana, Sheriff's Department paid out $62,000 to the estate of James Patterson, who died by suicide in its jail. A joint stipulation of dismissal with prejudice was filed by both sides, ending the legal proceedings. The county attorney explained, "Through the county's insurance company, the risks were weighed going forward, and it was determined that it would be better for the taxpayers if some type of settlement was reached." The family had sued alleging that the jail had a "regular practice and policy of permitting its correctional officers to disregard the fact that an inmate was suicidal." The sheriff denied the jail had a "culture of indifference to the serious medical needs of its inmates."[12]

The withdrawal lawsuits underscore how poorly many jails manage detainee medical needs or their contracted medical providers. It is just inexcusable that some jails were found to rely on Tylenol or Pepto-Bismol, rather than FDA-approved medications. In a Swisher County, Texas, jail lawsuit, for example, the jail's detox "protocol" relied solely on "honey and orange juice."[13] In Utah, a nurse failed to inform the contracted off-site physician about a detainee's increasing weight loss due to severe vomiting, even though correctional officers, noting the woman's deteriorating health, had removed her from the general population to a single monitored cell. She died before a physician made regularly scheduled rounds at the jail. The only "treatment" the detainee received was Gatorade.[14] In Vermont, a detainee died in solitary of bacterial endocarditis, a heart infection often associated with intravenous drug use. Although he complained of an aching chest, shortness of breath, and dizziness during the sixteen days before his death, a jail employee described as a "medical staffer" gave him a word search puzzle book to distract him.[15]

Other jails simply lacked the resources to ensure safe detoxification. The Brown County, Wisconsin, jail, for example, had only one nurse available for up to seven hundred inmates. In many other jails, medical personnel were available for only part of the day or in some cases just once or twice a week. One Kentucky jail had contracted with a local physician through Southern Health Partners, a private correctional medical group. That same physician, however, was contracted with twenty-one other county jails, making him the sole doctor for 3,500 inmates located across the state. Another physician in Wisconsin was responsible for inmates at a jail located more than three hundred miles from his practice.[16]

Even where jails had medical protocols, staff often ignored them. Consequently, even if diagnosed properly, the information was not relayed to correctional officers and/or nurses who were responsible for the care.[17] For example, the nurses in the Central Virginia Regional Jail took note of Shawn Berry's withdrawal risks and recommended specific anti-seizure medication after observing moderate to severe withdrawal symptoms. Berry was never given the medication before he died in the jail. A specific withdrawal protocol at the Kalamazoo County jail called for inmates experiencing withdrawal to be given Clonidine. However, staff ignored the protocol in cases like Andrea Armstead's. She displayed severe symptoms, including vomiting and diarrhea, but was not given any medication until she started having seizures immediately before her death.[18]

Most of the documented withdrawal deaths resulted from dehydration and subsequent heart failure, but sometimes the cause was incidental to the symptoms of withdrawal. Multiple detainees, for example, died from blunt head trauma after falling from bunk beds during seizures. It was also common for detoxifying detainees to have preexisting and untreated medical conditions, making their withdrawals more dangerous. For example, an inmate in the San Diego County jail died from an asthma attack induced by his withdrawal from heroin. (The settlement was for $3 million.)[19]

8

Signs of Hope

It goes without saying that the jails featured in these pages are not wholly representative of the more than 3,100 jails throughout the country. As BJS probably reports accurately, in any given year, the majority manage to keep all their detainees alive, even as most must rely on for-profit medical providers. They negotiate and enforce contracts that ensure quality medical services for detainees. Some even provide better health care than many of their detainees receive in the community. A couple hundred jails initiated model medication-assisted treatment (MAT) programs, for example, before most community substance use disorder treatment agencies offered patients these medications. It is clear, however, that too many jails are either unable or unwilling to safeguard the lives of increasing medically fragile detainees. The situation continues to be both a tragedy and a scandal. It is a scandal because when held accountable, jails that were literal death traps have shown they can do better.

Even some of the jails with the worst cultures and conditions have proven to be remediable. Overcrowding, dismal health care, deplorable conditions, and violent staff long plagued the Boyd County jail in rural Kentucky. In one month alone, eight women held there overdosed on heroin. A civil rights investigation by the U.S. Justice Department found that jail officers regularly violated people's constitutional rights, including excessive use of chemicals and Tasers and humiliating women and men by having them wear suicide

Santa Rita County, California, Jail

The Santa Rita jail had the highest number of jail deaths in the Bay Area in 2019, even higher than the more populated jails in Los Angeles County. At least forty-five inmates had died since January 1, 2014, at least seventeen dying by suicide. The county paid out more than $25 million in suits between 2015 and 2020, nearly five times the amount paid out by San Francisco and Oakland over the same period. But by the end of 2020, with only two jail deaths, the jail had gotten a lot safer. Further, jailers had successfully prevented twenty-five suicide attempts. Thanks to a class action lawsuit brought against the jail, more deputies worked mandatory overtime. As a lawyer who had sued the jail concluded, "It helps when you have more bodies."

Maricopa County, Arizona, Jail

Before "Constitutional" Sheriff Arpaio took over the jails, there were between three and five deaths in the Maricopa County jail each year. Under his mismanagement, it jumped to nine in 2013 and eleven by 2015. In his last year in office, ten died. Within two years after he left office, deaths receded to their pre-Arpaio levels. Lawsuits against the jail also declined. Commented a lawyer who had sued the jail multiple times in the past, "I think [the new sheriff] actually paid attention to trying to increase the quality [of detainee care] and the risk management [staff] is trying to pay attention to the lessons." In 2018, all the deaths were attributed to "illness," perhaps indicating that the jail, like most, is still saddled with inadequate medical care providers.

Dauphin County, Pennsylvania, Jail

As previously detailed, the Dauphin County jail had more than a dozen deaths in the last decade, including a young black man who died of an inflamed brain after officers restrained him. Committed to "changing the narrative," the county spent more than half a million dollars for 125 cameras for all officers to wear. Every officer on duty is required to turn on the camera anytime they interact with inmates "if a situation is escalating." Employees in the control room can also activate the cameras if officers can't or won't do so. Explained an activist alarmed over the jail's previous death count, "It is a 'win,' when more light is shed on what is happening behind jail walls." In addition to the body cameras, the jail instituted dozens of policy changes and provides electronic tablets for inmates. The staff also went through crisis intervention training to help them better recognize and deal with mental health issues.

Sources: A. Komarla, "Guest Commentary: Another suicide at Santa Rita Jail sparks cry for sheriff oversight in Alameda County," *Davis Vanguard*, April 21, 2021, https:// www.davisvanguard.org/2021/04/another-suicide-at-santa-rita-jail-sparks-cry-for -sheriff-oversight-in-alameda-county/; L. Fernandez, "Father blames son's fatal drug overdose on Santa Rita jail guards' negligence," KTVU, September 13, 2020, https://www.ktvu.com/news/father-blames-sons-fatal-drug-overdose-on-santa-rita -jail-guards-negligence; J. Kelety, "Inmate deaths in Maricopa County decrease under Sheriff Paul Penzone," *Phoenix New Times*, December 3, 2020, https://www .phoenixnewtimes.com/news/inmate-deaths-maricopa-county-sheriff-paul-penzone -arpaio-lawsuits-11517648; C. Vendel, "Dauphin County Prison guards start wearing body cameras," *Patriot-News*, January 18, 2021, https://www.pennlive.com/ news/2021/01/dauphin-county-prison-guards-start-wearing-body-cameras.html.

smocks without underwear, exposing their genitals. Four detainees died in the jail in 2019, including Michael Moore, who died of blunt force trauma after officers tipped his restraint chair and slammed his head into the ground. One of the officers involved later pleaded guilty; four others are contesting more serious manslaughter charges. The county paid out $1.75 million to settle a wrongful death suit. After the county jailer (elected in Kentucky) was also indicted for willfully neglecting the discharge of his official duties and resigned in 2018, the jail transformed. Jail administrators added cameras, switched medical providers, and increased officer pay and training. Use-of-force incidents decreased significantly. Although still overcrowded, the jail initiated a new diversion program to reduce its population. As an officer explained, before the reforms, "The people that did care, or spoke up? You didn't have a very good time there. . . . They'll run you out of there. But they'll also let you know that if something ever happens, they're not coming to help you."[1]

Few jails have topped the Cuyahoga County Jail for detainee deaths, overall dysfunction, and downright criminal conduct. But even there, signs of hope have emerged. When county officials finally acted to reform the jail, they increased the number of correctional officers, changed the top management, and transferred responsibility for inmate medical care to MetroHealth, a nationally ranked nonprofit public health-care system located in Cleveland. MetroHealth provided the jail with a full-time physician medical director, more than eighty nurses and medical technicians, a dedicated pharmacy along with specialty services in psychiatry and OB/GYN, a real-time "virtual visit" telemedicine program, on-site chronic disease program (CDP), expanded in-house X-ray/ultrasound imaging and laboratory support, and ongoing skills training (e.g., wound care, orthopedics, suturing) designed to improve the standard of care while reducing the need for inmate transports to the hospital. Electronic medical records connect MetroHealth specialists systemwide. In addition to providing health care for seventy to one hundred daily patients, MetroHealth offers a six-week counseling program for substance abuse and antagonist medication-assisted treatment in collaboration with the Greater Cleveland Drug Court, as well as buprenorphine treatment during pregnancy. It was news in July 2020 when a detainee died in the jail because the jail had gone fourteen months without a death![2]

Even the Greene County Jail in New York, rated the second worst jail in that state for years, shows promising signs. Sheriff Seeley retired after another detainee died on his watch and the county settled a multimillion-dollar law-suit. His successor, Sheriff Peter Kusminsky, brought a new jail superinten-dent on board. His transition team is preparing procedures for a new facility due to open shortly, in accordance with guidelines set by the Commission of Correction. In addition to monitoring and evaluating construction, the team is working with the commission to write and prepare new policies and pro-cedures to assure the facility will be in complete compliance with state rules and regulations when it opens next summer. Kusminsky also announced he would get the Sheriff's Office Corrections Division state accredited.[3]

HOLDING CORRECTIONS OFFICERS ACCOUNTABLE

As these turnarounds illustrate, successful jail reform requires accountability, beginning with correction officers. Post George Floyd, officials, as well as the public, will have greatly reduced tolerance for in-custody deaths, whether on the streets or within jails. In Harper Woods, Michigan, the city fired the deputy chief and a police officer when it was revealed "that members of its police department attempted to conceal and manipulate evidence of the 'in custody death investigation' of Priscilla Slater." The Slater family's attorney suspected police denied her medical attention for hours and let her suffer so badly that they sought to conceal and destroy the evidence, perhaps position-ing her body after she died. "Maybe they didn't kneel on her neck . . . [but they've] done exactly what the people who have been accused in the George Floyd case of doing."[4] Subsequently, one of the fired officers filed his own lawsuit, claiming a superior officer ordered the change in the written account of Slater's death.[5]

In Collins County, Texas, following the death of Marvin Scott III, a 26-year-old black man, the sheriff placed seven jail employees on leave, including a captain, a lieutenant, two sergeants, and three detention officers. Sheriff Jim Skinner announced that both the Texas Rangers and his own internal affairs personnel would investigate the death.[6] The family's lawyer said Scott died after officers forcefully restrained him, pepper sprayed him, and put a spit hood over his head. Skinner confirmed these facts, indicating the restraint was in response to Scott "exhibiting some strange behavior."[7] Protestors called for no more bookings at the jail until the seven officers were arrested. They announced they would return every day until Scott's funeral. A week later, the sheriff declared, "Everyone in Collins County deserves safe and fair treatment, including those in custody at our jail." He fired the seven officers.[8] The prosecutor, however, did not show the same commitment, failing to convince his grand jury to indict the officers. A civil rights attorney commented, "Local hands should be off of investigations, and the case should proceed immediately to a special prosecutor." The district attorney's office declined to comment. The family is seeking federal charges.[9]

The newly created commissions to certify police officers are also bringing a new vehicle for sheriffs' deputy accountability. In El Paso County, Colorado, for example, Deputy Russell Smith, a five-year jail veteran, was removed from the county jail because the Colorado Peace Officer Standards and Training (POST) Board revoked his certification as a law enforcement officer because he logged detainee checks that he hadn't actually performed. His falsification of records came to light in 2019 when another deputy reported injuries to a detainee that had occurred during Smith's shift. Comparing Smith's logs to camera footage, investigators found that Smith completely made up eleven of fifteen log entries. To make matters worse, at the time, Smith was serving as a detention training officer! The decertification of Smith in January 2021 was the first such action taken by the board since it was created two years earlier.[10] Unfortunately, almost two dozen state law enforcement certification laws specifically exempt sheriffs, although twenty-four states include correctional officers.[11]

Federal appellate courts may be getting less forgiving of officers' bad conduct. A Fourth Circuit panel reversed a federal district court judge's grant of qualified immunity for several sheriff's deputies sued for failing to act on an intoxicated man's obvious medical needs before he died in the Botetourt County, Virginia, jail. The man's brother sued, charging the jailers' failure to provide any medical care constituted cruel and unusual punishment. The initial federal judge ruled the officers had qualified immunity as their actions were covered by their job duties. The appellate panel, however, disagreed, finding the officers' actions were deliberately indifferent to the detainee's medical condition and ruling that the suit "plausibly alleges that [he] had an objectively serious medical condition requiring medical attention and that the officers subjectively knew of that need and the excessive risk of their inaction. That is enough to overcome qualified immunity and survive a motion to dismiss." The case went back to the district court for trial.[12]

INCREASING MEDIA COVERAGE

The media hopefully is making it increasingly more difficult for jail deaths to be ignored or covered up. As illustrated in several of the cases highlighted, the media has proved essential in holding jailers accountable. It was the media and its Freedom of Information suits, after all, that got the Minnesota Department of Corrections to stop covering up jail deaths.

KARE 11, for example, has not let up on exposing Minnesota's jails. In November, six months after its first investigation, it uncovered another jail scandal, involving the death of Bruce Lundmark, also in the Beltrami County jail, which raised no alarm bells when it occurred in 2019. An autopsy found the 63-year-old died of "natural causes" after being transferred from Beltrami to the Clearwater Jail due to overcrowding. However, when his brother retrieved Bruce's belongings from the jail, he found a handwritten note, "If I die, sue the . . . out of the Beltrami Jail." Also, detainees had contacted Lundmark's family to report that Lundmark had been in intense pain but staff ignored his pleas for medical help. Although the Department of Corrections' then standard jail death investigation had found no violations, the family's review of the medical files found clear evidence of lethal neglect. Subsequent medical review from independent physicians concluded that appropriate medical care would have saved Lundmark's life. Despite reports of severe pain and a stroke that left half his body numb, the only response of the jail's medical provider, MEnD, was to have him seen by a medical technician, who was only qualified to hand out medications and take vital signs. The day before

Lundmark's death, the technician noted that Lundmark's blood pressure was sky high, reaching the level of a "hypertensive crisis," as defined by the American Heart Association. Instead of sending him to the hospital, the jail put him in shackles and transported him to another jail where he was barely able to walk and died hours later. A forensic nurse called the care "profoundly inadequate, horrifically inadequate—negligent." The family hired the same lawyer who was suing the county over the death of Hardel Sherrell. Adding insult to tragedy, Beltrami County sent a notice to Lundmark's brother seeking payment of $32,000 for Bruce's medical care while in the jail. The brother told KARE 11 that the bill may have been a tactic to warn the family off suing.[13]

More recently, when Ricardo Duran, 32, died in the Pima County, Arizona, jail, the sheriff did not disclose the death, nor did the jail notify Duran's lawyer. In fact, the lawyer had scheduled a video call with his client and was kept waiting in front of a blank screen for half an hour before the jail terminated the call without explanation. But someone tipped off the local newspaper. After the *Tucson Sentinel* broke the story, the sheriff finally confirmed the death. The newspaper also uncovered another jail death, kept secret months before Duran died. That detainee had died during a "use-of-force encounter" with jailers. When a 27-year-old man died in the jail a few months later, the *Sentinel* continued to uncover the circumstances despite the sheriff's continued refusal to reveal any details because, he stated, the investigation was "ongoing." The paper reported that court records showed the man was being held on bail for shoplifting and related cases.[14]

It was the *Winston-Salem Journal* and the *News & Record* of Greensboro that petitioned the court in North Carolina to get the sheriff to release the video of John Neville's death in Forsyth County. The video would show, according to the lawyer for the family, that Neville told jailers twenty-four times that he could not breathe as they kept him under restraint. The sheriff's office did not publicly acknowledge the death for seven months and only released partial information *after* questioning by the *Journal*. In the court hearing, the attorney representing the media said it was important for the public to know what "did or did not happen . . . the more information, the better." He concluded the "case presents a compelling public interest that can't be denied." Other news organizations joined the two newspapers that initially petitioned for the video's release, including WXII, the Associated Press, WRAL, WUNC Public Radio, *Carolina Public Press*, WBTV of

Charlotte, and WTVD of Raleigh and Durham.[15] Subsequently, a Forsyth County Superior Court judge ruled that the release was "necessary to advance a compelling public interest." In his five-page decision, the judge noted that the sheriff's seven-month delay in releasing news of the death "only deepens the compelling public interest in a death allegedly caused by the actions of Forsyth County detention officers or personnel."[16]

Thanks to a media campaign, the district attorney of Cobb County, Georgia, finally announced that she would ask the U.S. attorney to conduct an independent investigation of the multiple deaths at the county jail. Her change of heart, she admitted, came about after *11Alive Reveal*, an investigative TV show, uncovered the 2019 video of Kevil Wingo collapsing in pain and begging to be sent to the hospital for more than seven hours at the jail. Following the TV investigation, the *Marietta Daily Journal* demanded that the district attorney request an independent investigation and condemned the sheriff for not doing so himself. The editorial, by a former county prosecutor, said the sheriff knew about the video of Wingo but "did nothing about it. The fact that the family has had to hold rallies and literally beg—beg for the attention for the district attorney, beg for the attention for the Georgia Bureau of Investigation—is atrocious." It concluded: "What is clear is that, as of this date, just two short weeks before the year anniversary of his death, there is still no justice for Kevil Wingo." If it hadn't been for media campaigning and 11Alive's public records suit, the sheriff's friendly law firm "investigation" (that the court ruled to be "bogus") would have been the last words on Wingo's death.[17]

(Unfortunately, although a newly elected Cobb County sheriff Craig Owens sent a letter to the director of the Georgia Bureau of Investigation to reopen the investigation of Wingo's death, the new head of the bureau, in a horrible irony, had been the former district attorney of Cobb County and refused to do so! Lamented the Wingo family attorney, "It has been almost a year and a half now and we still can't get anyone to do a proper investigation into Mr. Wingo's death . . . despite the clear evidence of criminal conduct being committed against him."[18])

Media throughout the country have discovered the story of jail deaths. The *Mercury News* called the Santa Clara sheriff Laurie Smith's conduct appalling for stalling an agreement to establish a civilian watchdog group to audit how her office runs the scandal-plagued county jails. In effect, the *News* charged that she was "thumbing her nose at the Board of Supervisors' desire to shape up conditions at the county jails."[19] Smith had been reelected for her sixth term in 2018, extending her twenty-year reign in that office and making her one of the longest-serving sheriffs in California despite costing the county $1.6 million to settle a suit brought by a detainee-rights group that sued the county over its brutal treatment of prisoners, shabby medical care, and excessive use of solitary confinement. The county also had to pay $200,000 a year for monitoring the jail's compliance with court-ordered reforms.[20]

Florida Today uncovered and released a jail video of Gregory Edwards's death in the Brevard County Jail that revealed, despite the sheriff's claim that deputies were not at fault, why the jail secretly changed its use-of-force policy to require deputies to continuously observe detainees who have been secured in the restraint chair while wearing a spit hood until the hood is removed. Corrections deputies are also now prohibited from using the hoods in conjunction with pepper spray. Publicly, the sheriff's office criminal investigation maintained that the spit hood had no role in Edwards's death.[21]

Calling it "an embarrassing failure here in our San Diego community," *San Diego Union-Tribune* columnist Charles Clark spared no adjectives describing one of the deaths. Clark called it "disturbing, shameful, horrific and the definition of a tragedy." Although someone had died in the San Diego jail every month for more than the past ten years, it wasn't until 2019 that Clark's newspaper wrote an in-depth exposé. Instead of serving as a wakeup call, the series, according to Clark, was unfortunately met with "pushback" from the sheriff. Nonetheless, the media attention increased pressure for counties to appropriate more funding for jail medical personnel. As Clark implored readers, "We can't become numb to the unnecessary deaths. We can't let it be white noise or ignore it. . . . A petty crime or addiction or mental health crisis shouldn't warrant an execution."[22]

Once they get onto the story, at least some newspapers hold on. After Washoe County, Nevada, sheriff Chuck Allen took office in 2015 and provided a $5.9 million no-bid contract to NaphCare, Inc. for the jail's health care, deaths increased 600 percent. The *Reno Gazette Journal* spent the next year investigating, leading to a four-part series profiling the thirteen people who died while awaiting trial in the jail. It continued with a fifth at the end of 2020.[23] After the series ran, the *Journal* continued to cover the jail, publicizing the revelation that the county commission did not realize it was required by law to monitor the condition of detainees at the jail! Although the sheriff's response was to attack the newspaper investigation, calling it "shallow, pick and choose tabloidism," he was pressured to call for an independent audit. Not surprisingly, the audit found serious deficiencies in the jail's management and health care, particularly for mental health. The National Commission on Correctional Health Care documented medical staff denying inmates their psychotropic prescriptions, taking at-risk inmates off suicide watch, and more. The jail began to implement some of the twenty-seven recommendations made in the audit.[24] In 2018, Sheriff Allen decided not to run for reelection. The two candidates running to replace him both called the jail's death rate "unacceptable," promising reform.[25]

INCREASING PROSECUTORIAL SCRUTINY

A new wave of progressive prosecutors is holding jails more accountable. Suffolk County, Massachusetts, prosecutor Rachael Rollins became the first black prosecutor in the state when elected in November 2018. When a public radio station exposé revealed that a county sheriff had failed to report a jail death, Rollins ordered that when someone died in her county's jail, even if there were no suspicious circumstances, she would expect a call: "They don't get to self-regulate and make that determination without our involvement." She added that the calls should include people who died in hospitals while in custody. The 2020 election saw a slew of additional progressive prosecutors elected in Los Angeles, California; Austin, Texas; Orlando, Florida; Detroit, Michigan; Columbus, Ohio; and elsewhere. George Gascón, who won the district attorney's race in Los Angeles County, ran as an anti–death penalty, pro-reform alternative to incumbent Jackie Lacey. Lacey, who almost never moved to hold officers accountable for in-custody deaths, raised $7 million for her failed reelection, mostly from police and deputy unions.[26] Monique Worrell won in Orlando County's Ninth Judicial District, promising to prosecute in-custody deaths and assaults. José Garza won in Austin, Texas, promising to address "the gross racial disparities in our criminal justice system." In Oakland County, Michigan, Karen McDonald won promising an end to cash bail. However, reformer Julie Gunnigle lost the race for Maricopa, Arizona, prosecutor, representing a big setback for reform.

Gascón also announced he would no longer seek cash bail for any misdemeanor or nonviolent, nonserious felony offenses and would not seek

Duchesne County, Utah, Jail

It took persistence by the Utah attorney general to charge a jail nurse for the death of Madison Jensen, a 21-year-old withdrawing from heroin who was found dead in her Duchesne County Jail cell in 2016. She died from a probable cardiac arrhythmia caused by severe dehydration. She had lost seventeen pounds in four days, according to a lawsuit filed against the county, the jail, and its medical staff. The attorney general's office charged the jail nurse with negligent homicide. A magistrate threw out the case, but the office appealed. A Utah appeals court reversed the ruling, paving the way for the nurse to face trial. The appellate court noted that other than checking on Jensen's blood pressure and giving her a sports drink, the nurse didn't take her vital signs, perform other tests, or contact the physician's assistant even after Jensen filled out a jail medical request form. The nurse's conduct was likely, the court agreed, a "gross deviation" from the standard of care expected.

Source: J. Miller, "A Utah jail nurse will once again face a criminal charge in dehydration death of an inmate," *Salt Lake City Tribune*, June 14, 2019, https://www .sltrib.com/news/2019/06/14/utah-jail-nurse-will/.

sentence enhancements based on gang membership.[27] Eli Savit, the new Washtenaw County prosecutor in Michigan, also announced his office would no longer ask for cash bails. The new DA in Athens-Clarke and Oconee Counties in Georgia announced she would stop prosecuting simple possession of pot and low-level drug possession, limit charges that included mandatory minimums, and, most importantly, stop probation from being a "back door to incarceration." The latter is of particular import in Georgia, which has the largest probation caseloads in the country. Much of Georgia probation is contracted out to a for-profit company, Sentinel Offender Services, which aggressively seeks jail if probationers, even if indigent, do not pay their monthly probation fees. Prosecutor Deborah Gonzalez says her office will stop charging probationers for technical violations like nonpayment of fees and other violations that are not new crimes. Joining her, the new sheriff for the same county defeated an incumbent on promises of not accepting donations from the bail bonds industry.[28]

It appears more county officials are beginning to demand jail accountability, even after prosecutors find that there is no criminal wrongdoing.

St. Louis County, Missouri, Jail

The St. Louis County Council voted in January 2021 for the county executive to launch an independent investigation of the county jail. The council adopted a resolution of a long-sought goal of the Justice Services Advisory Board, a panel the county revived in 2019 to help turn around the jail after five detainees died. A recent report by the nonprofit ArchCity Defenders identified an additional seven detainee deaths at the jail between 2009 and 2019. The executive agreed that this warranted an outside evaluation and that it would address each detainee death in the past five years, how misconduct complaints are handled, and how to implement national best practices.

Los Angeles County, California

The Los Angeles County Board of Supervisors unanimously approved a Restorative Justice Village to replace the deteriorating Men's Central Jail. Back in August 2019, the board canceled a $1.7 billion contract to replace the jail with another and instead decided to use the money for "care first, jail last." Last November, the majority of voters approved a ballot initiative to permanently set aside at least 10 percent of existing locally controlled revenues to go to community investment and alternatives to incarceration starting in fiscal year 2021–2022. As of 2021, the county had begun building 232 housing units for people experiencing homelessness because the board asserted, "Those who are incarcerated in Los Angeles County jails have histories of homelessness, substance use disorders, and medical and mental health needs."

Sources: N. Benchaabane, "St. Louis County Council backs call for outside investigation," *Post-Dispatch*, January 26, 2021, https://www.stltoday.com/news/local/govt-and-politics/st-louis-county-council-backs-call-for-outside-investigation-of-jail/article_3de86d07-939e-5dc7-a91e-d1c3ceeb4894.html; T. Walker, "As LA moves toward closing Men's Central Jail, county supes vote to move toward building a Restorative Justice Village," WitnessLA, January 26, 2021, https://witnessla.com/moving-toward-the-closure-of-mens-central-jail-la-county-supes-to-consider-plan-for-restorative-justice-village/.

After the Dauphin County district attorney in Pennsylvania, for example, ruled no crimes were committed, the county's Prison Board in late 2020 still suspended the director of corrections and voted to approve two independent investigations of the county jail, one for a medical review into the two most recent jail deaths and another for the director himself. The board said both investigations would be independent.[29]

ELECTING REFORM SHERIFFS

Compared to the movement to elect progressive prosecutors, the effort to elect progressive sheriffs has been limited but is hopefully beginning. Ed Gonzalez, for example, was elected sheriff of Harris County, Texas, in 2016, promising the state's largest and long-troubled jail would comply with state standards. He opened the jail to reporters to make it more transparent and was reelected in 2020. Craig Owens defeated Cobb County, Georgia, sheriff Neil Warren to become the county's first black sheriff. A police major, Owens promised to restore trust in the sheriff's office.[30]

After thirty-two years, Charleston County, South Carolina, sheriff Al Cannon was defeated by his Democratic challenger, Kristin Graziano. Within seven months of her election, she instituted a number of jail reforms to prevent a future Jamal Sutherland from being killed at the hands of jail deputies. First, she ordered deputies not to remove people from their cells who refused to attend bond hearings. Instead, they would be allowed to attend remotely. Further, before being booked at the jail, individuals in crisis would be evaluated by a special mental health crisis unit and medical staff alerted. Officers are directed to de-escalate and disengage when an individual becomes combative or uncooperative, not confront. Also, officers are mandated to report policy violations they witness among other officers. Graziano ordered those incarcerated to be called "residents," not "inmates." Unlike the prior sheriff, she supplied the federal court data it sought on Sutherland's death, indicating the delay was prompted by the discovery of material left in disarray by the former sheriff.[31]

Elections matter.

At the same time, however, Bill Waybourn was reelected sheriff of Tarrant County. His jail had become infamous when a mentally ill inmate gave birth unattended in her cell. The child died ten days later. Following this scandal, the state found the jail to be out of compliance with minimum state standards. Later, three of the jail's deputies were criminally charged after allegedly beating a detainee, who ended up with a broken neck, fractured ribs, and a collapsed lung. One of the deputies blocked the security camera so video would not capture the assault. Another deputy reported that such beatings were "normal" at the jail. Waybourn's challenger promised to establish a community oversight board to monitor the sheriff's office, but Waybourn, a right-wing celebrity, won reelection the next month with 53 percent of the vote. On a more positive note, Tarrant County Commissioners came out with plans to bypass the sheriff, supporting creation of a diversion center for mentally ill people arrested for nonviolent crimes. The center was also supported by the district attorney. Officials hope to have it open by October 2021.[32]

REBIRTH OF U.S. JUSTICE DEPARTMENT OVERSIGHT

Eclipsing the election of reform-minded prosecutors and sheriffs, the election of President Biden promises more active federal oversight and accountability of deadly jails. Despite a grand jury having found no criminal negligence in the death of York County, Pennsylvania, jail detainee Everett Palmer Jr., acting U.S. attorney Bruce D. Brandler for the Middle District of Pennsylvania declared, "Our office, in partnership with the Department's Civil Rights Division, will continue to thoroughly review the facts and circumstances surrounding Mr. Palmer's death, including information recently released in the York County Grand Jury report." The grand jury issued a 174-page report that included recommendations for systemic changes to prevent future jail deaths.[33]

Immediately after Trump's defeat, federal officials put Cumberland County, New Jersey, on notice of possible legal action if it did not immediately address the jail failings that contributed to the death of six detainees between July 2014 and May 2017. The U.S. Department of Justice said the jail was guilty of "numerous, specific and repeated violations" of detainees' constitutional rights. Its investigation concluded that the six who died were all denied opiate withdrawal medications, part of a "deliberate indifference to [their] serious medical needs." The investigation also concluded the jail failed to provide adequate mental health care to detainees at risk for self-harm and suicide. The jail was given forty-nine days to "adequately address" the heightened risk of self-harm and suicide for detainees "experiencing unmedicated opiate withdrawal; provide sufficient screening to identify inmates at risk of self-harm or in need of mental health care for a serious mental health condition; and provide sufficient mental health care to inmates with a clear need for care."

Importantly, for the first time, the Justice Department specifically asserted that medication-assisted treatment "is the standard of care for treating opioid use disorder and for preventing serious harm from unmedicated withdrawals." By denying MAT to those entering the jail, the jail acted with deliberate indifference to the serious medical needs of many detainees experiencing opiate withdrawal. If this proposition is accepted by the courts, it will require the 86 percent of jails that currently lack MAT protocols to institute them.[34] The report also condemned the "unnecessarily harsh conditions on suicide watch," including keeping detainees naked in empty cells, without any meaningful access to treatment other than brief assessments by a mental health professional that take place less than daily. The cells are approximately five by nine feet, with a narrow "window" in the solid steel cell door and a camera for observation. Inmates on suicide watch are prohibited from showering. The report noted that the conditions deter inmates from reporting suicidal thoughts. Mental health care was labeled to be haphazard, incomplete, and woefully deficient. Not surprisingly, in the absence of mental health treatment, the jail relied on "inappropriate restraint of prisoners in behavioral health emergencies," used not to "quell disturbances, but to punish inmates."

The Civil Rights of Institutionalized Persons Act (CRIPA, 42 U.S.C. §§ 1997 et seq.) gives the Justice Department license to investigate and sue deadly jails. The Biden Justice Department's Civil Rights Division head was opposed by Republican senators because they knew she would aggressively enforce these rights.

In 2021, the Biden administration also took several little noted actions that indicate its commitment to hold jails accountable. First, it abruptly ended its contract with the Bristol County, Massachusetts, jail run by Sheriff Hodgson. The secretary of homeland security declared the government would not "tolerate the mistreatment of individuals in . . . detention and subhuman conditions of detention."[35] Second, the U.S. Justice Department and the newly appointed U.S. attorney for the Western District of Louisiana finally prosecuted a Rapides Parish sheriff's deputy. He had tased three different detainees who were under restraint or not resisting, including one fifteen to twenty times while he was shackled to a bench by his ankles and secured in handcuffs. He had also deployed a taser into a detainee's back, causing him to fall to the ground, then sat on top of a table in the cellblock and continued to activate the taser four more times while the individual thrashed on the floor, screaming in pain. These all occurred in 2018.[36] In April 2021, the U.S. Justice Department found that Alameda County violated the civil rights of inmates by failing to provide proper mental health services, especially in its Santa Rita jail, which has had fifty suicides since 2014. It also found the jail's prolonged restrictive housing violated the constitutional rights of prisoners. It gave the county forty-nine days to correct these conditions.[37]

In 2019, California banned private jails. Both the Trump administration and the GEO Group sued but lost in the federal court in San Diego, which ruled that states had the authority to ensure the health and welfare of detainees. In 2021, the State of Washington followed suit. The law will close a large for-profit detention center in Tacoma when its current contract expires in 2025.[38] In 2021, the Delaware County, Pennsylvania, Council unanimously approved transitioning the 1,800-person county jail run by the for-profit GEO Group, Inc. to a publicly run jail. The move, according to a jail administrator, represented "a new mindset that a county jail is also an important and integral part of the county services to the community, and an investment in the health safety and vitality of our community."[39]

Shortly upon taking office, President Biden issued an executive order scaling back the federal use of private prisons. His move could cost the two largest for-profit prison companies as much as a quarter of their billion-dollar yearly revenue. The announcement also resulted in their stock shares plummeting to their lowest levels in a decade.

Perhaps the most encouraging sign that for-profit prisons are on the way out occurred in Alabama. When Governor Kay Ivey proposed working with private prison companies to build three new facilities and then leasing them to the companies for thirty years, advocates stopped her. They successfully pressured Barclays of London and KeyBanc Capital Markets to back out of financing the project. The advocates, joined together in a group called Communities Not Prisons, included a wide range of local and state organizations. They were joined by the American Sustainable Business Council and the Social Venture Circle, which represent more than 250,000 businesses that refunded Barclays' membership dues and sponsoring dollars to protest. The council chair declared, "We abhor the hypocrisy represented here and renounce the continued investment in the broken, unjust system of incarceration of this country."[40]

EVICTING FOR-PROFIT MEDICAL PROVIDERS

Some county politicians have begun to speak out against for-profit jail health-care providers—like in San Diego, where the county jail has been a death trap for detainees. In August 2020, activists and county workers came together with the county's supervisor, Nathan Fletcher, when he announced a proposal to end privatized health-care services in the county's jail. He suggested replacing them with the government's Health and Human Services Agency. The aim was to keep Sheriff Bill Gore from attempting to cut costs by contracting for-profit providers. Gore had said the Sheriff's Department's $90 million yearly detainee health-care costs could be cut and had asked to review some possible providers in a meeting with the county's Board of Supervisors.

Fletcher and activists started a petition asking to "Stop the Sheriff from Outsourcing Medical and Mental Health Services," saying that it both hurt the local job market and threatened detainees' health care. "We need a system of care driven by providing the appropriate care and preparation for release and reintegration into society," Fletcher said, "not a system designed to limit care to maximize profit."[41]

In New Mexico's Bernalillo County, the Metropolitan Detention Center's for-profit medical provider, Centurion Detention Health Services, decided to end its contract with the detention center six months early over growing concern about the nine people who had died in the jail over the past year as of April 2021 from drug or alcohol detox and in its medical units. A correctional union official charged that Centurion staff frequently left jail staff to deal with dire medical situations by themselves.[42]

Bernalillo County Manager Julie Baca said the county "expressed concern to Centurion over staff vacancies and continuity of care" in early April and asked Centurion to speak to these grievances. Instead of responding, Centurion ended its contract with the county. The contract had awarded roughly $13 million to Centurion for a year of providing medical services, and the county had paid the company about $40 million over the prior three years. To replace Centurion, the county hopes to install a local business. "Almost every person who goes to our jail receives community-based health care and mental health care from local providers," said an attorney advocate for detainees. "A big problem with Centurion is they failed to provide continuity of services to people when they came in and failed to arrange for continuity of services to those people when they leave."[43]

EVEN MEDICAL EXAMINERS?

Medical examiners and coroners may themselves be held more accountable. After Dr. David Fowler, a former Maryland medical examiner, testified that George Floyd's death should have been classified as "undetermined," five hundred physicians asked that all in-custody cases that occurred in Maryland during his reign of 2003 through 2020 be reviewed by an independent panel of pathologists. "There is a genuine concern that there may be an inappropriate classification of deaths in custody by the [Maryland Office of the Chief Medical Examiner] as either Accident or Undetermined to purposefully usurp a manner of death classification of Homicide." The Maryland ACLU accused the medical examiner's office of being "complicit in creating false narratives about what kills Black people." The governor and attorney general agreed that Fowler's cases be reviewed.[44]

Medical examiners and coroners may be showing a new commitment to accountability. After police shot and killed Andres Guardado, 18, as he ran from them, the Los Angeles medical examiner-coroner, Dr. Jonathan Lucas, called an inquest "in the interest of public transparency." The autopsy revealed Guardado had been shot five times in the back. Explained Lucas, "The Department of Medical Examiner-Coroner is committed to transparency and providing the residents of Los Angeles County an independent assessment of its findings in this case." This was the first official inquest in Los Angeles in more than thirty years. The Los Angeles sheriff, whose office conducted the initial investigation, had asked for a security hold to be placed on the case to keep the autopsy and other details from the public. Lucas removed the hold.[45] Hopefully the medical examiner will demonstrate the same commitment when it comes to jail deaths.

LAWSUITS BEAR FRUIT

Mounting lawsuit settlements and awards promise to increase pressure on legislatures and other officials to act on jail deaths. In 2020, 9News in Denver and KARE 11 in Minnesota reported for the first time on their year-long probe of restraint deaths by officers in jail and on the streets. They eventually found at least 107 people who died "facedown and on the ground since 2010," although there were likely more. Tragically, according to the two news organizations, "not even that figure has proven enough to convince law enforcement officers to do what they were advised to do back in 1995 when the U.S.

Department of Justice through its National Institute of Justice Program told officers: 'As soon as the suspect is handcuffed, get him off his stomach.'" In less than a year, they updated their investigation, finding at least 120 deaths with settlements and awards up to $126 million. More importantly, they were able to report that it may at long last have been enough to convince state legislators to take action. The update included the announcement: "Prone restraint banned in MN jails and prisons."[46]

As other wrongful jail death lawsuits mount and awards increase, it will become increasingly difficult for legislators and officials to ignore other common jail deaths.

Ending America's Deadly Jails

The long-term solution to deadly jails is to stop using jails as warehouses for society's most vulnerable, those experiencing homelessness, those with alcohol or substance use disorders or mental illness, or those suffering from trauma, as well as those who are simply poor and can't afford to buy their freedom or those who "fail" probation or parole because they don't get instantly better. This would require reform of each state's criminal codes, as well as the development of a health-care system sufficient to respond to the needs of the ten million people who now pass through the nation's jails each year. True jail reform will require full-scale societal reform.

Perhaps we see a glimpse of this in Baltimore, where the mayor declared: "Today, America's war on drug users is over in the City of Baltimore. We leave behind the era of tough-on-crime prosecution and zero-tolerance policing and no longer default to the status quo to criminalize mostly people of color for addiction. We will develop sustainable solutions and allow our public health partners to do their part to address mental health and substance use disorder."[1] Allegheny County has put out a Request for Proposals (RFP), "Rethinking the Allegheny County Jail Facility," to develop a plan to reduce the jail from 1,700 to as low as 500 with special emphasis on reducing racial and ethnic disparities.[2]

But more immediate steps can save lives now.

ENDING CORRECTIONAL MEDICINE THROUGH MEDICAID EXPANSION

The Supreme Court ruled in *Estelle v. Gamble*, 429 U.S. 97 (1976), that detainees have a constitutional right to health care. Unfortunately, the Court did not make it clear that the health care had to be decent. The domination of correctional for-profit health-care providers has resulted in substandard, even deadly "care." Even if correctional health care were not terrible, it inhibits any continuity of care for those passing in and out of jails. Especially for the disproportionate number of detainees with chronic health conditions, the lack of continuity of care jeopardizes their well-being. Even when jails do the right thing and help detainees receive life-saving medication, once released, detainees must scramble to re-enroll in Medicaid or other insurance coverage, find prescribers, and continue treatment in the community. Their medical records do not follow them when released, just as they did not follow them into jails.

One reform will go a long way to both end substandard correctional health care and ensure continuity of care upon release—allowing Medicaid coverage to cover incarcerated individuals. Currently, once committed, detainees lose their Medicaid eligibility. The costs of jail medical care rest on the county or state. The only exception is if the detainee is taken to a hospital outside the walls for more than a day—then Medicaid eligibility kicks in. Exploiting this exception has saved wiser state correctional systems tens of millions of dollars a year. However, this is more difficult for jails with a limited number of correctional officers available to transport and remain with detainees overnight in hospitals. And it shouldn't be necessary.

Continuity of care demands continuity of coverage for that care. When jailers sought to hold Centurion, a for-profit medical provider, accountable for multiple deaths in the Albuquerque Metropolitan Detention Center, the company exercised its right to terminate its contract. What a longtime advocate for inmates commented about Centurion is true for most correctional medical care providers: "A big problem with Centurion is they failed to provide continuity of services to people when they came in and failed to arrange for continuity of services to those people when they leave."[3] Maintaining persons on Medicaid when they enter jail would go a long way toward this end. If coverage were maintained, the same medical providers who care for the person in the community could continue to do so when he or she is jailed and then when released again. The advancement in telemedicine can now facilitate this continuity even if the community providers cannot readily enter

---

Minnesota Jails

Dr. Todd Leonard runs MEnD Correctional Care, which provides inmate health care to a third of Minnesota's jails, making it the largest jail medical provider in the state. He is the focus of a complaint made to the state medical board following the 2018 death of Hardel Sherrell in the Beltrami County Jail. A former MEnD nurse practitioner who cared for Sherrell filed the complaint. She alleged that despite Sherrell's deteriorating condition, Dr. Leonard never saw him. A few days after his death, Leonard told her he thought Sherrell had been faking his illness but likely killed himself or stuck a sock down his throat. He admonished her "not to jump to conclusions" because that "could jeopardize his company." As of 2020, MEnD was responsible for an average detainee population of 2,700 a day. KARE 11 has reported allegations that MEnD denied medical care in the deaths of three others including Bruce Lundmark and James Lynas, described earlier. Since 2015, records show at least twenty-five inmates have died where MEnD was the care provider.

Source: B. Stahl, "With his license on the line, doctor at center of jail deaths faces judge," KARE 11, July 12, 2021, https://www.kare11.com/video/news/investigations/kare-11-investigates-with-his-license-on-the-line-doctor-at-center-of-jail-deaths-faces-judge/89-85b61e38-79f2-45f6-b272-38aadbb77f0d.

---

the jails. The jails just need to provide detainee access to appropriate workstations. This should also reduce, if not end, dependency on for-profit correctional medical providers and would also save counties and municipalities billions of dollars in health-care costs. Telemedicine can offer even the most remote rural jail access to doctors and other health-care providers covered by Medicaid and other insurers.

Under the current for-profit correctional care system, there is a disincentive to provide medical care. If detainees were covered, the incentive would move in the other direction. Medicaid eligibility would also remove one of the barriers keeping jails from providing medication to treat people with alcohol and opioid use disorders, as well as schizophrenia and bipolar disorders, because it would cover the costs of these medications.

Although most of the lethal failures of correctional medicine can be directly tied to for-profit medical providers and their higher-than-average jail death rates, the records of nonprofit correctional medical providers also illustrate that the bifurcation of medical care inside and outside jails compromises the ability to deliver quality care. For twenty years, the Connecticut Department of Corrections that administers both jails and prisons contracted with University of Connecticut (UConn) Correction Managed Health Care to deliver its health care. UConn "assumed responsibility for all global medical, mental health, pharmacy, and dental service provision" beginning in November 1997. The Department of Correction fired them in 2018 for what lawyers characterized as "subpar medical care."[4]

In the meantime, correctional medical providers must be held accountable. We may see a glimmer of that happening in Minnesota.

INCREASING JAIL OVERSIGHT

A second major reform that will also go a long way to stop jail deaths would be state establishment of rigorous jail oversight. This may require removing jails from sheriffs' offices and placing them under the control of jail administrators who can be held directly accountable. It would also mean that sheriffs, as counties' chief law enforcement officers, would be able to investigate jail deaths without conflict of interest. It is difficult to wear two hats, and most sheriffs would probably rather be law enforcement professionals than professional jailers. The same holds true for deputies. The skills needed on the streets as deputies are different than those required within jails as correctional officers.

This is not to say that all sheriffs are terrible jailers or the 20 percent of jails that are not run by sheriffs are all paragons of excellence. But as the U.S. Justice Department recognized a couple years ago when it issued an RFP for the development of a training program for sheriffs, being elected a sheriff does not make you equipped to run the Los Angeles Jail with 16,000 inmates or even the Coffee County, Tennessee, Jail with 305. The RFP called for the creation of a curriculum for sheriffs including: "Role, Purpose, and Characteristics of the Jail; Liability and Standards; Critical Aspects of Jail Operations: Seeing the Jail as Part of the County Government's Agenda; The Sheriff's Leadership in Promoting Optimal Staff Performance; and Where a Sheriff Should Begin."[5] The Justice Department is not alone in recognizing the inherent limitations of sheriffs to run jails.

In October 2019, the Benton County Commission in Washington removed the jail from the sheriff's control. Benton County joined six other counties in the state making jails independent of the sheriffs' offices. The Commission initially considered the move in 2017, seeking more control of the jail that accounted for 28 percent of the county's budget and had generated multiple lawsuits and settlements. The Commission dropped the takeover when the then sheriff resigned and a new election for sheriff took place. However, when the new sheriff was accused of strangling his wife, his deputies labeled him a "tyrant," and he was accused of mismanaging the jail and not paying a local health center for jail services, the Commission removed the jail from his control. After his removal, the jail won national recognition for its model medication-assisted treatment (MAT) program.[6]

Simply removing sheriffs who are unsuited or uninterested in running jails is just the beginning. Some of the more deadly jails, after all, are administered by jail administrators under the control of county officials, including the deadly Allegheny Jail in Pittsburgh and the Cuyahoga Jail in Cleveland. After six detainees died in 2020 in the troubled, poorly designed Oklahoma County Jail, the county took the jail away from the sheriff and gave it to the Oklahoma Jail Trust to run. Nine detainees have since died under the Trust's watch. The district attorney said the jail's operation is worse than it was before. The Jail Trust chair admits it could take years to change the culture of the jail and get control of it. Ironically, the sheriff had previously complained that he had been forced to spend nearly all his time focusing on the jail, rather than on enforcing law throughout the county.[7]

States must assist jail administrators, give them the resources to do the job, and then hold them accountable to meet acceptable state or national standards. This requires routine and periodic inspections before multiple deaths occur. The state Jail Review Committee, for example, found that the Hampton Roads, Virginia, Regional Jail had shown "an egregious lack of concern for the health and safety of all who enter" and represented "a significant public safety threat to inmates and correctional officers." It recommended that the jail be decertified and everyone housed there be sent back to the city jails where they were originally housed. Tragically, the Committee only acted after the regional jail had been declared by the media to be the deadliest in the state and one of the deadliest in the nation. All of this had happened while the jail has been under federal oversight from the Department of Justice after a 2018 report that found conditions there violated detainees' constitutional rights, indicating that effective oversight—whether local, state, or federal—has to be real.[8]

Updating its rules for the first time in several decades, North Carolina now requires twice-annual jail inspections by the state Department of Health and Human Services. The state sheriffs' association opposed the reform out of concern that the new rules would require jails to have suicide prevention programs, suicidality screenings, and services for people with mental illness, developmental disabilities, or substance use disorders. In reaction, a legislator—also a former sheriff whose jail was found by the state to have been out of compliance—filed legislation to allow jails to challenge the state inspections.[9]

Currently, seventeen states have no mechanism for jail oversight. It is also clear that more is needed than merely holding the most egregious jailers accountable for criminal conduct alone. This was dramatically demonstrated when Michigan's attorney general ruled insufficient evidence to charge the Lansing police officers who were directly responsible for Anthony Hulon's death, pinning him to the ground in his cell while he was already handcuffed until he died. The lack of criminal charges allowed the chief to return the officers to active duty.

States must take over jails from counties that cannot afford to run them safely. States should not allow jails to operate that do not have staff required to secure the safety of detainees and staff, as well as detainee medical and mental health care.

State legislatures are beginning to demonstrate interest in jail reform. The *Boston Globe* ran a page-long editorial supporting legislation to require Massachusetts's Department of Mental Health to promulgate regulations requiring county as well as state corrections to have written suicide prevention plans and to ensure all detainees on mental health watches are housed in clinically appropriate settings and all who need it receive mental health treatment consistent with generally accepted professional standards. The *Globe* admitted the proposed legislation micromanaged corrections a bit, but that was necessary given failures of jails and prisons to follow their own policies. The editorial was a reaction to the release of a U.S. Justice Department investigation initialed by the U.S. attorney of the state correctional system. The *Globe* concluded it would take both the legislation and a federal court appointed watchdog to "drag state corrections into the 21st century."[10]

Georgia's Democratic legislators announced they would file legislation for greater oversight of the state's jails after the Reuters report on jail deaths documented the twenty-four deaths over a dozen years at the Chatham Detention Center. The legislators specifically cited the death of Lee Creely, 34, mentioned earlier in this book. According to Reuters, in addition to

Morrow County, Ohio, Jail

After two escapes and a detainee suicide, Sheriff John Hinton sought to reassure the public. These occurred as the jail's population tumbled from 196 to 90. Despite Hinton's reassurance that there was "nothing wrong with our jail," advocates questioned: "How much incompetence can one county jail exhibit, and continue to operate? Last night's jail break from the Morrow County Correctional Facility should be the last straw." The Ohio Immigration Alliance also called for it to be closed as it contained ICE detainees, charging "filthy conditions, inedible food, and other conditions causing low morale among inmates and for jailers." Hinton admitted being down nine officers because retention was compromised by low wages, with officers topping out at $18.47 per hour. The Alliance concluded that the tax base in the county simply could not support the jail. However, the county commissioners, siding with the sheriff, attributed the jail's problems to "a run of bad luck."

Source: D. Narciso, "Morrow County: COVID, escapes, suicide called 'run of bad luck' at understaffed jail," *Columbus Dispatch*, September 13, 2020, https://www.dispatch .com/story/news/local/2020/09/13/morrow-county-covid-escapes-suicide-called -lsquorun-of-bad-luckrsquo-at-understaffed-jail/114006270/.

withholding medication, CorrectHealth also failed to check his vital signs in violation of its own protocols. Following his death, the sheriff recommended a $500,000 bonus to CorrectHealth for its COVID-19 effort, which the county awarded. The proposed legislation includes mandatory state investigations of jail deaths even if the sheriff does not request them, requires oversight of health care, and proposes alternatives to jail for those with mental health issues or experiencing drug withdrawal. As one of the bill's sponsors declared, "No one should die in jail."[11] The newly elected reform sheriff of Cobb County testified on behalf of the proposed legislation.[12]

As the legislative session ended in 2021, Minnesota lawmakers passed sweeping corrections reforms including the Hardel Sherrell Act, banning prone restraint behind bars. Other measures considered would give the state Department of Corrections (DOC) more authority to investigate jails and take swifter action should it find problems, including the ability to more quickly revoke a jail's license to operate. The DOC would be able to establish minimum medical and mental health care standards for detainees, while requiring jails to establish codes of conduct policies for facility staff. Independent fatality reviews would be instituted for jail deaths. A proposed law would also require staff members to report any observation of neglect or wrongful use of force. If the reforms pass, they would be the most substantial changes to jail oversight since the DOC was first given the authority to license jails in 1978.[13]

In October 2020, California governor Gavin Newsom signed a bill into law that allows counties to create new oversight committees that would have subpoena power to keep an eye on their local sheriffs' offices. This would make it easier for families of people who die in custody to obtain information and details many sheriffs customarily conceal. Said proponents, "One of the big problems we have now is there's no information reaching the public about any of this. And because that's the case, the sheriff always has the advantage to put their spin on whatever happens, so they don't look like the responsible party."[14]

Also responding to the Reuters investigation, West Virginia legislators filed two bills specifically addressing jail deaths for the first time. The first would require jails to provide staff training to identify and respond to trauma symptoms among detainees. The second would require jail health-care contractors to promptly provide prescription medications to those incarcerated. Said one of the sponsors, "Nothing has been even brought up to me or the legislature about the amount of deaths we have in our jails. I'm flabbergasted at this data." Being in a poor state, detainees stay in jail longer, according to officials, because they cannot afford to pay bail. Legislators also declared that they would put more intense scrutiny on for-profit private jail health-care providers. At the same time, the state ACLU filed public records requests seeking contracts of all jail medical providers, explaining it had not realized the state's jail death rate was so high.[15]

In the waning hours of the 2020–2021 legislative session, Illinois lawmakers passed sweeping criminal justice reforms. Included was a requirement that the state Department of Corrections and local law enforcement investigate and report all in-custody deaths. It also requires the agencies to notify family members of the deaths and provide an accurate account of the cause. The Illinois Sheriffs Association had opposed the legislation, claiming jails were already required to report jail deaths to the Department of Justice and Corrections. The legislation also abolished cash bails effective January

1, 2023. Illinois prosecutors opposed that measure, asserting its elimination would endanger victims, although cash bails are supposed to be based on the likelihood of appearing in court, not the danger presented by those bailed. Defense attorneys counter that prosecutors fear freeing defendants pending trial will take away defendants' incentive to plead guilty to get out of jail quicker.[16]

New York enacted the HALT Act (Humane Alternatives to Long-Term Solitary Confinement Act), calling for an end to solitary confinement in jails and state prisons. The HALT Act bans solitary confinement for the young, the elderly, and the mentally ill; would cap the time in solitary in prisons and jails to fifteen days; and would require more programming and out-of-cell time. Although the governor had complained that the HALT Act would cost the state and localities large amounts of money, advocates had countered that the Act would save counties $18 million and the state $114 million in reduced lawsuit expenses for wrongful death suits and more.[17] New York is also considering a Jail Transparency Act that would require the jail division to report all serious incidents to both a state commission and county legislatures. Meanwhile, the state attorney general sued the Erie County sheriff on behalf of the state Commission on Corrections for failing to report serious incidents within twenty-four hours and filing incomplete reports. He is asking the court to appoint an independent monitor to audit the jail.[18]

In March 2021, the California Supreme Court found that state's bail system to be unconstitutional because it held people in jail simply because they were poor, not because they constituted a risk to public safety, disproportionately impacting poor communities of color. In the ruling, the court required judges going forward to assess a defendant's ability to pay bail when they set it. The court agreed that some defendants should be held pretrial to protect community safety despite an arrestee's "fundamental right to pretrial liberty." But, to detain a dangerous arrestee, "a court must first find by clear convincing evidence that no condition short of detention could suffice and then ensure the detention otherwise complies with statutory and constitutional requirements." Ironically, the ruling came down four months after the state's voters had rejected a proposition to eliminate cash bail.[19]

Conclusion

For each day that jail reform is delayed, several people die needlessly, like Elisa Serna, 24, who hit her head against the wall of her San Diego cell while collapsing during a seizure on her fifth day in jail in February 2021. When she did not respond to a deputy and a jail nurse who attempted to assess her condition, they left her on the cell floor. An hour later, she was found dead in the same position they'd left her in. An investigation determined she was unconscious when she had fallen to the floor, and an autopsy concluded that she died from "complications of chronic polysubstance abuse" with "early intrauterine pregnancy" noted as a contributing factor. The medical examiner also found that Serna was suffering from dehydration and acute pneumonia. She had informed the jail at intake that she used heroin shortly before her arrest. In jail, she complained to jail staff of dizziness, vomiting, and fainting episodes but was not placed on the jail's drug withdrawal protocol. She joined the more than 150 who have died at the San Diego jail since 2009.[1] A jail review board exonerated the deputy in her death because he "was not trained in advanced medical response."

After her death, the California state auditor announced her office would investigate detainee deaths in San Diego County jails over the past fifteen years after gaining approval from local lawmakers. The auditor will lead the investigation and also examine how the jail trains personnel, maintains facilities, and provides detainee health care within its seven facilities. Witnesses to be interviewed included the mothers of two detainees who died in the jail. The auditor said the investigation would take seven months.[2] The *San Diego Union-Tribune* followed up with an op-ed that San Diego Sheriff Gore "is not the only elected official that should be taken to task as it relates to our alarming jail mortality rate and the lack of accountability. San Diego County District Attorney Summer Stephan must also bear responsibility." Writer Genevieve Jones-Wright, head of Community Advocates for Just and Moral Governance, pointed out that despite the many deaths, "not one deputy sheriff responsible for any of those deaths has been held accountable by the district attorney." She charged that the district attorney was not prosecuting because of "law enforcement associations" and the fact that the sheriff or police chief have not "signed off on the prosecution."[3] The same time this op-ed ran, the San Diego Citizen's Law Enforcement Review Board found that a jail deputy failed to perform safety checks for one of the jail detainees who died of a drug overdose the year before. This case represented the third time in less than three years that the board has reported to the sheriff on safety check failures.

Maybe an audit will inspire the sheriff to transform the country's jail facilities. But more likely, his and the rest of America's jails will cease being death houses only when officials at every level of government and the public make up their minds that preventable jail deaths are simply unacceptable. In the meantime, American jails, like San Diego's, continue their deadly practices as a last quick search of "jail death" and "jail suicide" on Google News on July 20, 2021, reveals with thirteen news items: (1) "Custody death: Jacob Biddix's family still awaiting answers from Buncombe County jail," *Citizen Times,* yesterday; (2) "Lawsuit: Inmate death due to Miller County jailers' medical negligence," *Texarkana Gazette,* 6 hours ago; (3) "State police investigate death of 23-year-old inmate at Jackson County Jail," WXIN, 2 days ago; (4) "Inmate at the Guilford County Detention Center found unresponsive in jail cell, pronounced dead at the hospital," WXII, 6 hours ago; (5) "Inmate dies at jail," *Santa Barbara News-Press,* 4 hours ago; (6) "Shelby County Jail inmate's death under investigation," WBRC, 16 hours ago; (7) "Inmate dies in holding cell at Baldwin County Jail," WGXA, 19 hours ago; (8) "Family of man who died in custody at Chambers County Jail wants to review surveillance video, bodycam footage," Click2Houston.com, 13 hours ago; (9) "Travis County jail inmate found unresponsive in cell, dies at hospital," KXAN, 10 hours ago;

(10) "Santa Maria inmate dies after apparent suicide attempt in County Jail cell," *Santa Maria Times*, 10 hours ago; (11) "Lucas County jail inmate dies by suicide," WTVG, 16 hours ago; (12) "Santa Barbara County Jail inmate dies from suspected suicide," CalCoastNews.com, 21 hours ago; and (13) "Lawsuit over Waterloo inmate's suicide is settled for $125,000," *Iowa Capital Dispatch*, 19 hours ago.

Notes

INTRODUCTION

1. M. Carlisle & J. Bates, "With over 275,000 infections and 1,700 deaths, COVID-19 has devastated the U.S. prison and jail population," *Time*, December 28, 2020, https://www.msn.com/en-us/news/crime/with-over-275000-infections-and-1700-deaths-covid-19-has-devastated-the-us-prison-and-jail-population/ar-BB1ciyY1.

CHAPTER 1

1. L. Maruschak & T. Minton, "Correctional populations in the United States, 2017–2018," Bureau of Justice Statistics, August 2020, NCJ 252157, https://bjs.ojp.gov/content/pub/pdf/cpus1718.pdf.

2. D. Kaeble, "Time served in state prison, 2016," Bureau of Justice Statistics, November 2018, NCJ 252205, https://bjs.ojp.gov/library/publications/time-served-state-prison-2016.

3. T. Herring, "Jail incarceration rates vary widely, but inexplicably, across U.S. cities," *Prison Policy Initiative*, May 4, 2021. https://www.prisonpolicy.org/blog/2021/05/04/city-jail-rates/.

4. B. Forman, "Corrections data raise big questions," *Commonwealth Magazine*, March 4, 2020, https://commonwealthmagazine.org/opinion/corrections-data-raise-big-questions/.

5. M. Lofstrom & B. Martin, "California's county jails," Public Policy Institute of California, February 2021, https://www.ppic.org/publication/californias-county -jails/.

6. S. Vela, "Former police sergeant sues Westland, says he was a scapegoat in prisoner death," Hometownlife.com, May 29, 2020, https://www.hometownlife.com/ story/news/local/westland/2020/05/29/police-sergeant-sues-westland-after-prisoner -death-triggers-his-firing/5273233002/.

7. B. Reaves & A. Goldberg, "Local police departments 1997," Bureau of Justice Statistics, February 2000, NCJ 173429, https://bjs.ojp.gov/content/pub/pdf/lpd97.pdf.

CHAPTER 2

1. A. DuVernay, dir., *The 13th* (Los Gatos, CA: Netflix, 2016).

2. D. Blackmon, *Slavery by Another Name: The Re-Enslavement of Black Americans from the Civil War to World War II* (New York: Anchor Books, 2009).

3. A. Powers, "The renegade sheriffs," *New Yorker*, April 23, 2018. https://www.new yorker.com/magazine/2018/04/30/the-renegade-sheriffs.

4. T. LoBianco, "Report: Aide says Nixon's war on drugs targeted blacks, hippies," CNN, March 24, 2016, https://www.cnn.com/2016/03/23/politics/john-ehrlichman -richard-nixon-drug-war-blacks-hippie/index.html.

CHAPTER 3

1. Z. Zeng, "Jail inmates in 2018," Bureau of Justice Statistics, March 2020, NCJ 253044, https://bjs.ojp.gov/library/publications/jail-inmates-2018.

2. P. Eisler, L. So, J. Szep, & G. Smith, "As more women fill America's jails, medical tragedies mount," Reuters, December 16, 2020, https://www.reuters.com/investigates/ special-report/usa-jails-women/.

3. T. Minton, Z. Zeng, & L. Maruschak, "Impact of COVID-19 on the local jail population, January–June 2020," Bureau of Justice Statistics, March 2021, https://bjs .ojp.gov/content/pub/pdf/icljpjj20.pdf.

4. P. Sabino, "8th detainee dies from Coronavirus as Cook County Jail population swells again," Block Club Chicago, November 18, 2020, https://blockclubchicago .org/2020/11/18/8th-detainee-dies-from-coronavirus-as-cook-county-jail-population -swells-again-causing-concern-another-outbreak-coming/.

5. J. Cain, "Fears of more COVD-19 spread as thousands of L.A. County inmates await transfer to state prisons," *Los Angeles Daily News*, December 2, 2020, https://

www.dailynews.com/2020/12/02/fears-of-more-covid-19-spread-as-thousands-of-l-a
-county-inmates-await-transfer-to-state-prisons/.

6. N. Reisman, "Advocates: Reduce jail population to halt COVID spread," Spectrum
News, December 7, 2020, https://spectrumlocalnews.com/nys/central-ny/ny-state-of
-politics/2020/12/07/advocates--release-jail-inmates-to-halt-covid-spread; T. Closson
& J. Bromwich, "'A ticking time bomb': City jails are crowded again, stoking Covid
fears," New York Times, March 10, 2021, https://www.nytimes.com/2021/03/10/
nyregion/nyc-jail-covid.html.

7. Harris County, Texas, "Jail population statistics," https://charts.hctx.net/jailpop/
App/JailPopCurrent, downloaded December 6, 2020.

8. J. McCullough, "With a stalled court system, some Texas jails are dangerously
overcrowded in the pandemic," Texas Tribune, January 28, 2021, https://www
.msn.com/en-us/news/crime/with-a-stalled-court-system-some-texas-jails-are
-dangerously-overcrowded-in-the-pandemic/ar-BB1dbSnc.

9. Mental Health Rights Project, "Report: 9 of 10 people who died in Oregon jails
in 2020 had a disability," Disability Rights Oregon, February 8, 2021, https://www
.droregon.org/advocacy/report-9-of-the-10-people-who-died-in-oregon-jails-in
-2020-had-a-disability?rq=jails.

CHAPTER 4

1. P. Wagner & W. Sawyer, "States of incarceration: The global context 2018," Prison
Policy Initiative, June 2018, https://www.prisonpolicy.org/global/appendix_2018
.html.

2. Wagner & Sawyer, "States of incarceration."

3. Texas Commission on Jail Standards for the jails' census as of November 1, 2020,
and Florida Department of Corrections Bureau of Research and Data Analysis for
the average daily census for September 2020.

4. P. Liu, R. Nunn, & J. Shambaugh, "The economics of bail and pretrial detention,"
Brookings Institute, December 2018, https://www.brookings.edu/research/the
-economics-of-bail-and-pretrial-detention/.

5. M. Hendrickson, "Cook County Jail was one of the nation's largest COVID-19
hotspots last spring. It's worse now," Chicago Sun Times, December 15, 2020, https://
chicago.suntimes.com/coronavirus/2020/12/15/22165917/cook-county-jail-covid-19
-coronavirus-bond-release-reform-judge-kim-foxx-tom-dart.

6. A. Robinson, "Justice can't wait: An indictment of Louisiana's pretrial system," ACLU Louisiana, undated, https://www.laaclu.org/en/justice-cant-wait-indictment-louisianas-pretrial-system.

7. P. Heaton et al., "The downstream consequences of misdemeanor pretrial detention," *Stanford Law Review* 69, no. 3 (2017): 711–94.

8. N. Fennell & M. Prescott, "Risk, not resources: Improving the pretrial release process in Texas," Lyndon Baines Johnson School of Public Affairs, June 2016, https://lbj.utexas.edu/sites/default/files/file/Risk,%20Not%20Resources-%20Improving%20the%20Pretrial%20Release%20Process%20in%20Texas--FINAL.pdf.

9. J. Mathews II & F. Curiel, "Criminal justice debt problems," American Bar Association, November 30, 2019, https://www.americanbar.org/groups/crsj/publications/human_rights_magazine_home/economic-justice/criminal-justice-debt-problems/.

10. R. Lewis, "Waiting for justice," Cal Matters, March 31, 2021, https://calmatters.org/justice/2021/03/waiting-for-justice/.

11. D. Arnold, W. Dobbie, & C. Yang, "Racial bias in bail decisions," *Quarterly Journal of Economics* 133, no. 4 (2018): 1885–932.

12. John H. Blume & Rebecca K. Helm, "The unexonerated: Factually innocent defendants who plead guilty," *Cornell Law Review* 100, no. 1 (2014): 157–92; E. Leslie & N. G. Pope, "The unintended impact of pretrial detention on case outcomes: Evidence from New York City arraignments," *Journal of Law and Economics* 60, no. 3 (2017): 529–57.

13. M. Arvidson, "Time to bail on cash bail?" Council of State Courts, May 2, 2019, https://knowledgecenter.csg.org/kc/content/time-bail-cash-bail-growing-number-states-are-scrutinizing-current-systems-and-exploring.

14. M. Rempel & K. Rodriquez, "Bail reform revisited: The impact of New York's amended law," Center for Court Innovation, May 2020, https://www.courtinnovation.org/publications/bail-revisited-NYS.

15. L. Maruschak, M. Berzofsky, & J. Unangst, "Medical problems of state and federal prisoners and jail inmates, 2011–2012," Bureau of Justice Statistics, February 2015, https://bjs.ojp.gov/content/pub/pdf/mpsfpji1112.pdf.

16. D. James & L. Glaze, "Mental health problems of prison and jail inmates," Bureau of Justice Statistics, September 2006, https://bjs.ojp.gov/library/publications/mental-health-problems-prison-and-jail-inmates.

17. H. Steadman et al., "Prevalence of serious mental illness among jail inmates," *Psychiatric Services* 60, no. 6 (2009): 761–65.

18. B. Brasch, "Lawmakers tour crowded Fulton jail, hear about need for resources," *Atlanta Journal-Constitution*, December 10, 2019, https://www.ajc.com/news/local/lawmakers-tour-crowded-fulton-jail-hear-about-need-for-resources/Tyl0QpBBnCax8MrhmEoWFN/.

19. C. Trofatter, "Sheriffs say treatment lacking for mentally ill inmates," Capital News Service, March 8, 2021, https://news.jrn.msu.edu/2021/03/sheriffs-say-treatment-lacking-for-mentally-ill-inmates/.

20. K. Davis & J. McDonald, "Lapses in treatment, medical care spell horrific ends for mentally ill inmates," *San Diego Union-Tribune*, September 23, 2019, https://www.sandiegouniontribune.com/news/watchdog/story/2019-09-21/lapses-in-treatment-medical-care-spell-horrific-ends-for-mentally-ill-inmates.

21. E. Haas, "Mental illness revealed behind bars," KEPR, February 16, 2017, https://keprtv.com/news/local/mental-illness-revealed-behind-bars.

22. P. Tarr, "Homelessness and mental illness: A challenge to our society," Brain & Behavior Research Foundation, September 2018, https://www.bbrfoundation.org/blog/homelessness-and-mental-illness-challenge-our-society.

23. Tarr, "Homelessness and mental illness."

24. A. Ferrise, "Cuyahoga County Jail inmate accused of beating cellmate to death placed in general population despite history of attacking inmates, court records, sources say," Cleveland.com, November 10, 2020, https://www.cleveland.com/metro/2020/11/cuyahoga-county-jail-inmate-accused-of-beating-cellmate-to-death-placed-in-general-population-despite-history-of-attacking-inmates-court-records-sources-say.html.

25. J. Bronson et al., "Drug use, dependence, and abuse among state prisoners and jail inmates, 2007–2009," Bureau of Justice Statistics, June 2017, NCJ 250546, https://bjs.ojp.gov/content/pub/pdf/dudaspji0709.pdf.

26. J. Gramlich, "Four-in-ten U.S. drug arrests in 2018 were for marijuana offenses-mostly possession," PEW Research Center, January 22, 2020, https://www.pewresearch.org/fact-tank/2020/01/22/four-in-ten-u-s-drug-arrests-in-2018-were-for-marijuana-offenses-mostly-possession/.

27. E. Edwards et al., "A tale of two countries: Racially targeted arrests in the era of marijuana reform," ACLU, 2020, https://www.aclu.org/report/tale-two-countries-racially-targeted-arrests-era-marijuana-reform.

28. D. McVay, ed., Drug Policy Facts, last updated June 28, 2021, https://www.drugpolicyfacts.org/chapter/crime_arrests.

29. A. Buntin et al., "The impact of policy changes on heroin and nonmedical prescription opioid use among an incarcerated population in Kentucky, 2008–2016," *Criminal Justice Policy Review* 31, no. 5 (March 2019): 746–62.

30. N. Parker, "Georgia legislators seek scrutiny of jail deaths as new case emerges," Reuters, December 30, 2020, https://www.reuters.com/article/us-usa-jails-chatham -idUSKBN2941EQ.

31. A. Heymann, "Inmate who died at the Chesterfield County Jail Sunday identified," WFXR, September 27, 2020, https://www.wfxrtv.com/news/regional -news/virginia-news/inmate-dies-at-chesterfield-county-jail-sunday-morning/.

32. M. Mittelhammer, "Inmate dies after collapsing in Athens-Clarke County jail," *Red & Black*, September 25, 2020, https://www.redandblack.com/athensnews/inmate -dies-after-collapsing-in-athens-clarke-county-jail/article_60bd1f82-ff90-11ea-8eb9 -83b8f9c346ef.html.

33. B. Hailer, "Daniel Pastorek died in the Allegheny County Jail but he shouldn't have been there in the first place," *Pittsburgh Current*, December 16, 2020, https:// www.pittsburghcurrent.com/daniel-pastorek-died-in-the-allegheny-county-jail-but -he-shouldnt-have-been-there-in-the-first-place/.

34. J. Horowitz, "1 in 55 U.S. adults is on probation or parole," PEW Charitable Trusts, October 31, 2018, https://www.pewtrusts.org/en/research-and-analysis/ articles/2018/10/31/1-in-55-us-adults-is-on-probation-or-parole.

35. P. Launlus, "Murder suspect back in jail after allegedly failing drug test," KTLO, November, 20, 2020, https://www.ktlo.com/2020/11/20/murder-suspect-back-in-jail -after-allegedly-failing-drug-test/.

36. W. Sawyer & P. Wagner, "Mass incarceration: The whole pie 2020," Prison Policy Initiative, March 24, 2020, https://www.prisonpolicy.org/reports/pie2020.html; W. Sawyer, A. Jones, & M. Troilo, "Technical violations, immigration detainers, and other bad reasons to keep people in jail," Prison Policy Initiative, March 18, 2020, https://www.prisonpolicy.org/blog/2020/03/18/detainers/.

37. D. Kaeble, "Probation and parole in the United States, 2016," Bureau of Justice Statistics, April 2018, https://bjs.ojp.gov/library/publications/probation-and-parole -united-states-2016.

38. J. Heiss, "In our backyards: Ending mass incarceration where it begins," Vera Institute of Justice, September 14, 2017, https://www.vera.org/projects/in-our -backyards.

39. Heiss, "In our backyards."

CHAPTER 5

1. P. Eisler & J. Szep, "Congress presses DOJ to improve jail reporting system," Reuters, October 21, 2020, https://www.reuters.com/article/us-usa-jails-doj-idUS KBN2761L9.

2. A. Carson, "Mortality in local jails, 2000–2018—statistical tables." Bureau of Justice Statistics, April 2021, NCJ 256002, https://bjs.ojp.gov/library/publications/ mortality-local-jails-2000-2018-statistical-tables.

3. K. Fiscella et al., "Drug and alcohol associated deaths in U.S. jails," *Journal of Correctional Health Care* 26, no. 2 (April 2020).

4. S. Kajeepeta et al., "Association between county jail incarceration and cause-specific county mortality in the USA, 1987–2017: A retrospective, longitudinal study," *Lancet* online. February 23, 2021, https://www.thelancet.com/journals/ lanpub/article/PIIS2468-2667%2820%2930283-8/fulltext.

5. B. Knox, "Drug overdose leads to inmate's death," *Wise County Messenger*, December 9, 2020, https://www.wcmessenger.com/articles/drug-overdose-leads-to -inmates-death/.

6. N. Hegyi, "Indian Affairs promised to reform tribal jails," NPR, June 21, 2021, https://www.npr.org/2021/06/10/1002451637/bureau-of-indian-affairs-tribal -detention-centers-deaths-neglect.

7. C. Wilson, T. Schick, A. Jenkins, & S. Brownstone, "Booked and buried: Northwest jails' mounting death toll," April 1, 2019, https://www.opb.org/news/ article/jail-deaths-oregon-washington-data-tracking/.

8. G. Smith, "Jail deaths in America: Data and key findings of 'Dying Inside,'" Reuters Investigates, October 18, 2020, https://www.reuters.com/investigates/special -report/usa-jails-graphic/.

9. M. Sledge, "Louisiana doesn't count people who die behind bars," *Times-Picayune*, March 28, 2021, https://www.nola.com/news/courts/article_ae4490d4-8e4a -11eb-8968-e762f7d9234f.html.

10. J. Canicosa, "In five years, 786 people died in Louisiana's jails and prisons, a new report finds," *Louisiana Illuminator*, June 2, 2021, https://lailluminator.com/2021/ 06/02/in-five-years-786-people-died-in-louisianas-jails-and-prisons-a-new-report -finds/.

11. R. Grim, "Since Sandra Bland, there have been hundreds of suicides in American jails. It has to stop," *Huffington Post*, July 13, 2016, https://www.huffpost.com/entry/ sandra-bland-anniversary-suicide-in-jail_n_5786836fe4b0867123df4a20.

12. K. Davis & J. McDonald, "Some jail deaths are excluded from annual reports," *San Diego Union-Tribune*, September 20, 2019, https://www.sandiegouniontribune .com/news/watchdog/story/2019-09-19/dying-behind-bars-some-jail-deaths -excluded-from-reports.

13. K. Dayton, "Death behind bars: In Hawaii the death of a prisoner is often a closely held secret," *Honolulu Civil Beat*, March 3, 2021, https://www.civilbeat.org/ 2021/03/death-behind-bars-in-hawaii-the-death-of-a-prisoner-is-often-a-closely -held-secret/.

14. Smith, "Jail deaths in America."

15. C. Sheets, "Alabama's deadliest jail sees nine inmate deaths since 2019," AL.com, December 9, 2020, https://www.al.com/news/2020/12/alabamas-deadliest-jail-sees -nine-inmate-deaths-since-2019.html/; "Inmate dies at Madison County jail," News 19, Huntsville, Alabama, July 30, 2021, https://whnt.com/news/huntsville/inmate -dies-at-madison-county-jail-3/.

16. N. Manna, "Third death in one week being investigated at Tarrant County jail," *Fort Worth Star-Telegram*, June 25, 2020, https://www.star-telegram.com/news/local/ fort-worth/article243805552.html.; N. Manna, "Texas Rangers investigate 8th death at Tarrant County Jail this year," *Fort Worth Star-Telegram*, September 10, 2020, https://www.star-telegram.com/news/local/fort-worth/article245622650.html.; N. Manna, "Man dies in hospital ER after being transferred from Tarrant County Jail," *Fort Worth Star-Telegram*, September 15, 2020, https://www.msn.com/en-us/news/ crime/man-dies-in-hospital-er-after-being-transferred-from-tarrant-county-jail/ ar-BB19486E. N. Manna, "Second person dies after contracting COVID-19 in jail, Tarrant County sheriff says," *Fort Worth Star-Telegram*, November 10, 2020, https:// www.star-telegram.com/news/coronavirus/article247109317.html; E. Claridge, "Man, 60, is second Tarrant County jail inmate to die this week and 12th this year," *Fort Worth Star-Telegram*, November 11, 2020, https://www.star-telegram.com/news/ local/crime/article247136404.html.

17. L. Skene, "Baton Rouge jail inmate, locked up for failure to appear in court, dies in hospital," *Advocate*, December 8, 2020, https://www.theadvocate.com/baton_ rouge/news/crime_police/article_f5f8113c-38cb-11eb-966f-bfbb3d3978c3.html.

18. R. Lipsitz, "In Erie County, jail deaths continue despite high-profile tragedy," *The Appeal*, January 16, 2020, https://theappeal.org/erie-county-jail-deaths-continue/.

19. S. Nowlin, "Lost in lockup," *San Antonio Current*, March 23, 2021, https://www .sacurrent.com/sanantonio/lost-in-lockup-last-year-prisoners-in-bexar-county-and -across-texas-died-in-record-numbers/Content?oid=25836851.

20. U.S. Department of the Interior, Office of the Inspector General, "Neither safe nor secure, An assessment of Indian Detention Facilities," Report # 2004-I-0056, September 2004, https://www.ojp.gov/ncjrs/virtual-library/abstracts/neither-safe-nor -secure-assessment-indian-detention-facilities.

21. Hegyi, "Indian Affairs promised."

22. C. Byers, "Mother of man whose vomit resembled motor oil in jail before he died files lawsuit against St Louis County," KSDK, June 16, 2020, https://www.ksdk .com/article/news/local/st-louis-county-inmate-death-vomit-motor-oil-lawsuit/63 -76b40054-ecdc-43b1-a5f1-770928fd3916.

23. J. Ciavaglia, "Bucks County confirms opiate detox death of county prisoner," *Bucks County Courier Times*, December 20, 2018, https://journalismjo.blogspot .com/2019/01/bucks-county-confirms-opiate-detox.html.

24. C. Martin, "Tarrant County's Chief Medical Examiner announced retirement amid calls for investigation into the office," *Dallas Morning News*, April 30, 2021, https://www.dallasnews.com/news/2021/04/30/tarrant-countys-chief-medical -examiner-announces-retirement-amid-calls-for-investigations-into-the-office/.

25. D. Mash, "Excited delirium and sudden death," *Frontiers in Physiology* 7, no. 435 (October 13, 2016).

26. L. Voytko, "Daniel Prude's autopsy reports says 'Excited Delirium,' a controversial diagnosis, contributed to his death," *Forbes*, September 3, 2020, https://www.forbes.com/sites/lisettevoytko/2020/09/03/daniel-prudes-autopsy -report-says-excited-delirium-a-controversial-diagnosis-contributed-to-his-death/ ?sh=28beaf801784.

27. M. LaForgia & J. Valentino-DeVries, "How a genetic trait in Black people can give police cover," *New York Times*, May 15, 2021, https://www.nytimes.com/ 2021/05/15/us/african-americans-sickle-cell-police.html.

28. M. Hickman & K. Hughes, "Medical examiners and coroners' offices, 2004," Bureau of Justice Statistics, June 2007, NCJ-216756, https://bjs.ojp.gov/content/pub/ pdf/meco04.pdf.

29. K. Plog, "'A challenging way to practice medicine': Death investigation in Washington faces grim reality," KNKX, October 12, 2020, https://www.knkx.org/ other-news/2020-10-12/a-challenging-way-to-practice-medicine-death-investigation -in-washington-faces-grim-reality.

30. J. Donovan, "How are coroners and medical examiners different?" How Stuff Works, June 6, 2019, https://science.howstuffworks.com/coroners-medical -examiners.htm.

31. S. Michaels, "Why coroners often blame police killings on a made-up medical condition," *Mother Jones*, October 14, 2020, https://www.motherjones.com/crime-justice/2020/10/why-coroners-often-blame-police-killings-on-a-made-up-medical-condition/.

32. "Preventable deaths in Orange County jails, grand jury 2017–2018," County of Orange, California.

33. S. Cohen & N. Eckert, "AP Investigation: Many U.S. jails fail to stop inmate suicides," June 18, 2019, https://apnews.com/article/ap-top-news-ut-state-wire-ia-state-wire-ca-state-wire-us-news-5a61d556a0a14251bafbeff1c26d5f15.

34. "Washoe jail population down, potential suicides steady," KOLO, July 1, 2020, https://www.kolotv.com/2020/07/02/washoe-jail-population-down-potential-suicides-steady/.

35. HHS guide for clinicians on the appropriate dosage reduction or discontinuation of long-term opioid analgesics, October 2019, https://www.hhs.gov/opioids/sites/default/files/2019-10/Dosage_Reduction_Discontinuation.pdf.

36. C. Gallagher & A. Boring, "National study of jail suicide, 20 years later," National Center on Institutions and Alternatives, April 2010, https://s3.amazonaws.com/static.nicic.gov/Library/024308.pdf.

37. W. C. Bryson, J. Piel, & S. Thielke, "Associations between parole, probation, arrest, and self-reported suicide attempts," *Community Mental Health Journal* 57, no 4 (May 2021): 727–35.

38. M. Brannon, "Dying inside," *Redding Record Searchlight*, June 24, 2020, https://www.redding.com/in-depth/news/local/2020/06/24/shasta-county-jail-california-inmate-deaths-mental-health-services/5281201002/.

39. M. Brannon, "Man who spent an hour in custody is 1 of 5 deaths reported by Shasta County Jail in 2021," *Redding Record Searchlight*, May 3, 2021, https://www.redding.com/story/news/local/2021/05/03/shasta-county-jail-investigating-fifth-death-2021-one-hour-custody/7307791002/.

40. J. Hummel, "Jail death ruled suicide," KBND, June 19, 2020, https://kbnd.com/kbnd-news/local-news-feed/514360.

41. J. Veliz & J. Borges, "Bristol County House of Corrections internal review of completed suicides," Professional Psychiatric Services, January 12, 2018.

42. R. Furst, "Lawsuit: Sherburne County jail ignored inmate's warning signs before suicide," *Star Tribune*, April 2, 2020, https://www.startribune.com/lawsuit-sherburne-jail-ignored-inmate-s-warning-signs-before-suicide/569329772/.

43. B. Stahl, "KARE11 Investigates: Jail death results in $2.3 million payout," KARE11, February 3, 2021, https://www.kare11.com/article/news/investigations/ kare-11-investigates-jail-death-results-in-23-million-payout/89-bb7e639c-f669-4e7b -b44d-4255f7051dbd.

44. Cohen & Eckert, "AP Investigation: Many U.S. jails fail to stop inmate suicides."

45. S. Robbins, "Volusia County takes on high jail suicide rate," *Daytona Beach News-Journal*, August 25, 2018, https://www.news-journalonline.com/news/ 20180825/volusia-county-takes-on-high-jail-suicide-rate---too-late-for-some.

46. K. Anderson, "Vilas County annual jail inspection report finds two violations," WXPR, March 1, 2021, https://www.wxpr.org/news/2021-03-01/vilas-county-annual -jail-inspection-report-finds-two-violations.

47. Disability Rights Oregon, "Grave consequences: How the criminalization of disability leads to deaths in jail," Winter 2021, https://media.heartlandtv.com/ documents/DRO-Report-Grave+Consequences-2021-02-08+%28002%29.pdf.

48. Associated Press, "Texas law fails to slow jail suicides," Progressive Farmer, December 22, 2019, https://www.dtnpf.com/agriculture/web/ag/news/world-policy/ article/2019/12/22/texas-law-fails-slow-jail-suicides.

49. P. Ray, "Inmate's death spurs civil rights lawsuit," *Altoona Mirror*, March 17, 2021, https://www.altoonamirror.com/news/local-news/2021/03/inmates-death -spurs-civil-rights-lawsuit/.

50. G. Anderson, "Lake County District Attorney: 'No wrongdoings,'" *Press Democrat*, October 28, 2015; J. Johnson, "Lake County settles jail suicide case for $2 million," *Press Democrat*, June 18, 2018, https://www.pressdemocrat.com/article/ news/lake-county-district-attorney-no-wrongdoings-in-santa-rosa-womans-jail/.

51. A. Ferrise, "Attempted suicides at Cuyahoga County Jail tripled over three-year span," Cleveland.com, February 21, 2019, https://www.cleveland.com/metro/ 2019/02/attempted-suicides-at-cuyahoga-county-jail-tripled-over-three-year-span .html.

52. S. Bradbury, "Allegheny County jail spends $237K on 4,600 suicide prevention blankets," *Pittsburgh Post-Gazette*, May 12, 2019, https://www.post-gazette.com/ news/crime-courts/2019/05/13/Allegheny-County-Jail-Pittsburgh-suicide-prevention -thick-heavy-blankets-inmates/stories/201905100133.

53. C. Sokol, "Spokane County faces $5.25 million claim over 2018 jail death," *Spokesman-Review*, June 19, 2020, https://www.spokesman.com/stories/2020/jun/18/ spokane-county-faces-525-million-claim-over-2018-d/.

54. M. Gordon, "Lawsuit: Mecklenburg jail didn't help inmate despite 2 suicide tries. He killed himself hours later," *Charlotte Observer*, July 14, 2020, https://www .charlotteobserver.com/news/local/crime/article244188832.html.

55. City News Service, "Woman settles for $8.5 million in Pasadena attempted jail suicide," NBC Southern California, July 21, 2020, https://www.nbclosangeles.com/ news/local/pasadena-jail-suicide-settlement/2399912/.

56. D. Ibañez, "3 inmates attempt suicide at Bexar County Jail," KSAT, October 26, 2020, https://www.ksat.com/news/local/2020/10/26/3-inmates-attempt-suicide-at -bexar-county-jail-officials-say/.

57. M. Brannon, "With jail deaths on the rise, California counties look to improve," *Redding Record Searchlight*, October 7, 2020, https://www.redding.com/in-depth/ news/local/2020/10/07/shasta-county-jail-inmate-deaths-mental-health-california -reform-ideas/5621258002/.

58. J. de Biblana, T. Todd, & L. Pope, "Preventing suicide and self-harm in jail," Vera Institute of Justice, July 2019, https://www.vera.org/downloads/publications/ preventing-suicide-and-self-harm-in-jail.pdf.

59. J. Verdon, "Class action lawsuit filed against Missouri jail for intolerable living conditions," *Davis Vanguard*, December 29, 2020, https://www.davisvanguard .org/2020/12/class-action-lawsuit-filed-against-missouri-jail-for-intolerable-living -conditions/.

60. C. Shoup, "Sheriff seeking help as jail sees another suicide attempt," *Fremont News Messenger*, October 15, 2020, https://www.thenews-messenger.com/ story/news/local/2020/10/15/sheriff-seeking-hire-more-staff-jail-after-suicide -attempt/3662933001/.

61. World Health Organization, "Preventing suicide in jails and prisons," International Association for Suicide Prevention, 2007, https://apps.who.int/iris/ handle/10665/43678.

62. F. Kaba et al., "Solitary confinement and risk of self-harm among jail inmates," *American Journal of Public Health* 104, no. 3 (March 2014): 442–47.

63. L. Brinkley-Rubinstein et al., "Association of restrictive housing during incarceration with mortality after release," *Journal of American Medical Association* 2, no. 10 (2019).

64. Gallagher & Boring, "National study of jail suicide, 20 years later."

65. Disability Rights California, "Disability Rights California investigation find San Diego County Jail suicides far outpace other jail systems," April 25, 2018, https://

www.disabilityrightsca.org/press-release/disability-rights-california-investigation
-finds-san-diego-county-jail-suicides-far.

66. "Sheriff's office says death of inmate at Bradley County Jail was suicide by hanging," Chattanoogan.com, August 5, 2020, https://www.chattanoogan.com/2020/8/5/413110/Sheriff-s-Office-Says-Death-Of-Inmate.aspx.

67. Cohen & Eckert, "AP Investigation: Many U.S. jails fail to stop inmate suicides."

68. J. Feldman, "Some of the stories behind those involved in jail suicides," Capital News Service, June 19, 2019, https://apnews.com/257205c688714db2b76783d9c88 69c59.

69. M. Matray, "Hampton Roads Regional Jail facing a staffing shortage so severe it's moving 250 inmates," *Virginian-Pilot*, December 17, 2020, https://www .pilotonline.com/government/local/vp-nw-fz20-hrrj-staffing-20201217-a7iqkn2yiza jnohjeghwolcm6m-story.html.

70. E. Kaplan & M. Reisen, "'Tragic and horrible': Nine at MCD have died over past year," *Albuquerque Journal*, March 13, 2021, https://www.abqjournal.com/2369430/ tragic-and-horrible.html.

71. B. Hall, "Jail death sheds light on pay," NewsChannel5, Nashville, June 10, 2021, https://www.newschannel5.com/news/newschannel-5-investigates/jail-death-sheds -light-on-pay-some-sheriffs-forced-to-sue-their-own-county.

72. J. McDonald & K. Davis, "Mistakes, lack of oversight are not always fatal," *San Diego Union-Tribune*, September 23, 2019, https://www.sandiegouniontribune.com/ news/watchdog/story/2019-09-20/day-two-sidebar-mistakes-lack-of-oversight-are -not-always-fatal.

73. M. Baker et al., "Three words. 70 Cases. The Tragic History of 'I Can't Breathe,'" *New York Times*, June 29, 2020, https://www.nytimes.com/interactive/2020/06/28/ us/i-cant-breathe-police-arrest.html.

74. M. Reisen, "Jail official called dead inmate a loser," *Albuquerque Journal*, October 9, 2020, https://www.abqjournal.com/1505621/jail-official-called-dead -inmate-a-loser.html.

75. C. Allen, "MDC officers charged in death of inmate more than two years later," KRQE, May 20, 2021, https://www.krqe.com/news/crime/two-mdc-officers-charged -in-death-of-inmate-more-than-two-years-later/.

76. E. Means, "Accounts of 'cruelty' and 'indifference' at Salt Lake County Jail have some calling for reform," KUER, July 22, 2020, https://www.kuer.org/justice/2020-07 -22/accounts-of-cruelty-and-indifference-at-salt-lake-county-jail-have-some-calling -for-reform.

77. M. Powell, "Washington County Jail deputy charged with misconduct after allegations of racism," Oregon Public Radio, June 6, 2020, https://www.opb.org/news/article/washington-county-jail-deputy-misconduct-charge-racism-allegations/.

78. J. Griffith, "Georgia officer who called an inmate on suicide watch a 'crazy n-word' to be fired," NBC News, September 28, 2020, https://www.nbcnews.com/news/us-news/georgia-officer-who-called-inmate-suicide-watch-crazy-n-word-n1241283.

79. A. Hiruko, "Feces in a locker and other harassment," NPR, September 17, 2020, https://www.kuow.org/stories/feces-in-lockers-to-harassment-racism-is-rife-in-king-county-corrections-employees-say.

80. Hiruko, "Feces in a locker and other harassment."

81. C. Viglenzoni, "Vt. Defender general report outlines alleged racial bias behind inmate death," WCAX, July 22, 2020, https://www.wcax.com/2020/07/22/vt-defender-general-report-outlines-alleged-racial-bias-behind-inmate-death/.

82. L. Basye & A. Pierrotti, "'I can't breathe,' Man dies in custody after hours of begging for help," 11Alive, August 18, 2020, https://www.11alive.com/article/news/investigations/the-reveal/cobb-co-jail-death-of-kevil-wingo/85-846db820-3ffc-4fd9-957a-7c757bda38a2.

83. Basye & Pierrotti, "'I can't breathe,' Man dies in custody after hours of begging for help."

84. K. Dixon, "Family of man who died in Cobb County jail files lawsuit," Atlanta Journal-Constitution, September 10, 2020, https://www.ajc.com/news/atlanta-news/family-of-man-who-died-in-cobb-county-jail-files-lawsuit/NYX3472KDFDEHJFACJPNOGLTGI/.

85. R. Solomon, "Justice for Kevil Wingo: Mixed reactions to DA Holme's decision," Cobb County Courier, October 7, 2020, https://cobbcountycourier.com/2020/10/justice-kevil-wingo/.

86. J. Simerman, "$3 million in new payouts as Iberia Parish Sheriff's Office settles more abuse suits," Acadiana Advocate, March 2, 2019, https://www.theadvocate.com/acadiana/news/courts/article_6088cd64-3178-11e9-83dc-7fe2bd11b557.html.

87. J. Vaughn, "In a Louisiana parish, hundreds of cases may be tainted by sheriff's office misconduct," The Appeal, November 25, 2019, https://theappeal.org/iberia-parish-brady-letters/.

88. J. Rubin, "Ex-L.A. County Sheriff Lee Baca sentenced to three years in prison in jail corruption scandal," Los Angeles Times, May 12, 2017, https://www.latimes.com/local/lanow/la-me-baca-sentenced-jail-sheriff-corruption-20170512-story.html.

89. ACLU of Southern California, "ACLU report cites chaplains and other civilian witnesses to pervasive abuse of inmates by deputies at the L.A. County jails," September 28, 2011, https://www.aclusocal.org/en/news/aclu-report-cites-chaplains -and-other-civilian-witnesses-pervasive-abuse-inmates-deputies-la.

90. A. Tchekmedyian, "Deputies accused of being in secret societies cost L.A. County taxpayers $55 million," *Los Angeles Times*, August 4, 2020, https://www .latimes.com/california/story/2020-08-04/sheriff-deputy-clique-payouts.

91. K. Martin, "Lawsuit: Detainee's death 'terrifying, preventable and totally unnecessary,'" *Carolina Public Press*, June 18, 2020, https://carolinapublicpress .org/30667/lawsuit-detainees-death-terrifying-preventable-and-totally-unnecessary/.

92. K. Thornton, "Fired jail supervisor charged with assault," *Tahlequah Daily Press*, October 7, 2020, https://www.tahlequahdailypress.com/news/fired-jail-supervisor -charged-with-assault/article_0fd5e900-1582-5f6f-84ce-e69bcbd84be1.html.

93. J. Green, "GCSO denied claims of physical abuse in death of Tasha Thomas," *Triad City Beat*, February 3, 2021, https://triad-city-beat.com/gcso-denies-claims -physical-abuse-death-tasha-thomas/.

94. S. Allard, "Death at Cuyahoga County jail, second in two months, was trans woman," Cleveland.com, September 3, 2020, https://www.clevescene.com/scene-and -heard/archives/2020/09/03/death-at-cuyahoga-county-jail-second-in-two-months -was-trans-woman-lea-daye.

95. K. Sosin, "New video reveals Layleen Polanco's death at Rikers was preventable," NBC News Now, June 12, 2020, https://www.nbcnews.com/feature/nbc-out/new -video-reveals-layleen-polanco-s-death-rikers-was-preventable-n1230951.

96. A. Beck et al., "PREA data collection activities, 2015," Bureau of Justice Statistics, June 2015, NCJ 248824, https://bjs.ojp.gov/content/pub/pdf/pdca15.pdf.

97. "Inmate who died was subdued with Taser, locked in padded cell," CBSFW, June 23, 2020, https://dfw.cbslocal.com/2020/06/23/inmate-who-died-was-subdued-with -taser-locked-in-padded-cell/.

98. K. Rosenblatt, "'We want justice': Complaint seeks trial, $10m in case of Tenn. man who died in jail," NBC News, June 13, 2020, https://www.nbcnews.com/news/ us-news/we-want-justice-complaint-seeks-trial-10m-case-tenn-man-n1230681; T. Strickings, "Black man is 'gripped by neck with extreme pressure' by white cop," *Daily Mail*, June 19, 2020, https://www.dailymail.co.uk/news/article-8435275/Black -man-Sterling-Higgins-died-pinned-Tennessee-jail.html.

99. C. Byers, "'It's heinous and unforgivable,'" KSDK, August 13, 2020, https://www
.ksdk.com/article/news/local/family-of-man-who-died-at-st-francois-county-jail
-seek-reform/63-bfd710b9-f160-4fc7-89d9-f8406c8b2fd2.

100. J. Learn-Andes, "Statistics detail restraint chair use in Luzerne County prison,"
Times Leader, August 14, 2020, https://www.timesleader.com/news/796654/statistics
-detail-restraint-chair-use-in-luzerne-county-prison.

101. M. Chammah, "They went to jail. Then they say they were strapped to a
chair for days," Marshall Project, February 7, 2020, https://www.themarshallproject
.org/2020/02/07/they-went-to-jail-then-they-say-they-were-strapped-to-a-chair-for
-days.

102. A. Binion, "Investigation: Kitsap jail inmate who died improperly subdued in
restraint chair," *Kitsap Sun*, December 22, 2020, https://www.kitsapsun.com/story/
news/2020/12/22/investigation-kitsap-jail-inmate-who-died-improperly-subdued
-restraint-chair/3967083001/.

103. A. Binion, "Sheriff: 'Homicide' ruling in inmate's death needs context," *Kitsap
Sun*, September 11, 2020, https://www.kitsapsun.com/story/news/2020/09/11/sheriff
-homicide-ruling-kitsap-inmates-death-needs-context/3473165001/.

104. D. Battaglia, "Forsyth County detention officer received merit-based raise after
inmate's death," *News & Observer*, July 17, 2020, https://www.newsobserver.com/
news/state/north-carolina/article244275137.html.

105. U.S. Department of Justice, "Positional asphyxia—sudden death," National Law
Enforcement Technology Center, June 1995, https://www.ojp.gov/pdffiles/posasph
.pdf.

106. M. Hendricks, "FBI, Jackson County investigate injuries to inmates at hands
of jail guards," *Kansas City Star*, August 24, 2015, https://www.kansascity.com/news/
politics-government/article32213331.html.

107. R. McKetin et al., "Does methamphetamine use increase violent behaviour?"
Addiction 109, no. 5 (2014): 798–806.

108. J. Eble, "Everett Palmer, Jr. was hit twice with stun gun during scuffle with
York County Prison guards," WPMT-TV, York County, Pennsylvania, June 19, 2019,
https://www.fox43.com/article/news/local/contests/everett-palmer-jr-was-hit-twice
-with-stun-gun-during-scuffle-with-york-county-prison-guards-autopsy-report
-says/521-2e9b2656-3e35-4daa-a1a3-1625349be9c4.

109. L. Scolforo, "Grand jury report: Palmer had five contacts with police prior
to prison," *York Dispatch*, March 9, 2021, https://www.yorkdispatch.com/story/

news/crime/2021/03/09/grand-jury-report-palmer-had-five-contacts-police-prior -arrest/4592470001/.

110. P. Ward, "Inmates at Allegheny County Jail sue over dangers to their mental health," Trib Total Media, September 15, 2020, https://triblive.com/local/inmates-at -allegheny-county-jail-sue-over-dangers-to-their-mental-health/.

111. J. Rihl, "How transparent is Allegheny County Jail compared to other PA jails?" *Public Source*, March 16, 2021, https://www.publicsource.org/allegheny-county-jail -transparency-pa/.

112. W. Sawyer & P. Wagner, "Mass incarceration: The whole pie 2020," Prison Policy Initiative, March 24, 2020, https://www.prisonpolicy.org/reports/pie2020.html.

113. Columbia Legal Services, "Gone but not forgotten," May 2019, https://columbia legal.org/wp-content/uploads/2019/05/Gone-But-Not-Forgotten-May2019.pdf.

114. Substance Abuse and Mental Health Services Administration, "Treatment Episode Data Set (TEDS) 2016: Admissions to and discharges from publicly funded substance use treatment," 2018, table2.9a.

115. R. Cholodofsky, "Westmoreland inmates reach record detox level in February," Trib Total Media, March 18, 2019, https://triblive.com/local/westmoreland/ westmoreland-inmates-reach-record-detox-level-in-february/.

116. J. Bronson et al., "Drug use, dependence, and abuse among state prisoners and jail inmates, 2007–2009," Bureau of Justice Statistics, June 2017, NCJ 250546, https:// bjs.ojp.gov/content/pub/pdf/dudaspji0709.pdf.

117. J. Herrick, "Colorado lawmakers hope to end drug-addiction withdrawal in county jails," *Journal*, January 8, 2019, https://www.the-journal.com/articles/colorado -lawmakers-hope-to-end-drug-addiction-withdrawal-in-county-jails/.

118. J. Keller, "Using a wrench instead of a hammer for alcohol withdrawal," Jail Medicine, June 15, 2020, https://www.jailmedicine.com/using-a-wrench-instead-of -a-hammer-for-alcohol-withdrawal/.

119. J. Galloway, "U.S. Jails are killing people going through opioid withdrawals," Influence, December 6, 2017, https://www.huffpost.com/entry/us-jails-are-killing -people-opioid-withdrawals_b_9563940.

120. Substance Abuse and Mental Health Services Administration (SAMHSA), "Detoxification and substance abuse treatment, a treatment improvement protocol tip 45," October 2015, https://store.samhsa.gov/product/TIP-45-Detoxification-and -Substance-Abuse-Treatment/SMA15-4131.

121. J. D. Wines et al., "Suicidal behavior, drug use and depressive symptoms after detoxification: A 2-year prospective study," *Drug and Alcohol Dependence* 76, no. 7 (2004): S21–S29.

122. S. Long, Research Analyst, Curran-Fromhold Correctional facility, communication with author, November 18, 2020.

123. A. Ferrise, "Death of Cuyahoga County Jail inmate subject of criminal investigation," Cleveland.com, November 21, 2018, https://www.cleveland.com/news/erry-2018/11/12db721f324418/death-of-cuyahoga-county-jail.html.

124. C. Guyette, "Lawsuit targets billion-dollar company making life-and-death medical decisions in Michigan jails," *Detroit Metro Times*, March 12, 2020, https://www.metrotimes.com/news-hits/archives/2020/03/12/lawsuit-targets-billion-dollar-company-making-life-and-death-medical-decisions-in-michigan-jails.

125. K. Fiscella, "Guide to developing and revising alcohol and opioid detoxification protocols," National Commission on Correctional Health Care, 2015.

126. J. Miller, "Deaths at the Salt Lake County jail," *Salt Lake City Tribune*, June 6, 2020, https://www.sltrib.com/news/2020/06/07/deaths-salt-lake-county/.

127. D. Pratt, "Family's lawsuit details policies they say led to Whatcom County jail suicide," *Bellingham Herald*, August 2, 2020, https://www.bellinghamherald.com/news/local/article244649967.html.

128. E. Mieurem, "Wrongful death suit settled," *Jackson Hole News & Guide*, October 28, 2020, https://www.jhnewsandguide.com/news/cops_courts/wrongful-death-suit-settled-leads-to-medical-improvements-at-county-jail/article_c377cf45-f135-5705-a540-e516c1db3eb0.html.

129. C. Wilson, "Jefferson County Jail death raises questions of accountability," Oregon Public Broadcasting, December 30, 2019, https://www.opb.org/news/article/jefferson-county-jail-death-questions-accountability-james-whippel-case/.

130. 16 News Now, "Ruling comes in St. Joseph County Jail inmate death," WNDU, November 2, 2020, https://www.wndu.com/2020/11/02/ruling-comes-in-st-joseph-county-jail-inmate-death/.

131. T. Kless, "'She was screaming': Investigation reveals treatment Clay County mom received before dying in jail," *First Coast News*, January 31, 2020, https://www.firstcoastnews.com/article/news/crime/she-was-screaming-investigation-reveals-treatment-clay-county-mom-received-before-dying-in-jail/77-975ff54d-424a-471a-a28f-b7876de0efbf.

132. Kless, "'She was screaming.'"

133. Fiscella, "Guide to developing."

134. Herrick, "Colorado lawmakers."

135. C. Sokol, "New program to treat opioid withdrawal could prevent deaths at Spokane County Jail, officials say," *Spokesman-Review*, September 5, 2018, https://www.spokesman.com/stories/2018/sep/06/new-program-to-treat-opioid-withdrawal-could-preve/.

136. J. Ahmadi et al., "The effectiveness of different singly administered high doses of buprenorphine in reducing suicidal ideation in acutely depressed people with co-morbid opiate dependence: a randomized, double-blind, clinical trial," *Trials* 19, no. 1 (August 29, 2018): 416.

137. J. Russo et al., "Caring for those in custody," RAND Corporation, 2017. https://www.rand.org/pubs/research_reports/RR1967.html.

138. Advocates for Human Potential website for Justice Department RSAT Program, https://www.rsat-tta.com//Home.

139. A. Ferrise, "Disgraced ex-Cuyahoga County Jail warden tells FBI, Ohio AG, he was powerless to stop deaths," Cleveland.com, November 29, 2020, https://www.cleveland.com/metro/2020/11/disgraced-ex-cuyahoga-county-jail-wardens-tells-fbi-ohio-ag-he-was-powerless-to-stop-deaths-flow-of-drugs-in-troubled-jail.html.; C. Shaffer, "How Heartless Felons teamed up with Cuyahoga County Jail guards in jailhouse drug smuggling ring," Cleveland.com, November 27, 2020, https://www.cleveland.com/court-justice/2020/11/how-heartless-felons-teamed-up-with-cuyahoga-county-jail-guards-in-jailhouse-drug-smuggling-ring.html.

140. M. Regenstein & J. Christie-Maples, "Medicaid coverage for individuals in jail pending disposition," Health Policy Faculty Publications, Paper 1 (2012): 1–18.

141. F. S. Taxman, M. Thanner, & D. Weisburd, "Risk, need, and responsivity (RNR)," *Crime & Delinquency* 52, no. 1 (2016): 28–51; E. A. Wang et al., "Discharge planning and continuity of healthcare: Findings from the San Francisco County jail," *American Journal of Public Health* 98, no. 12 (December 2008): 2182–84.

142. L. Fernandez, "San Francisco jails had no coronavirus deaths, hospitalizations or outbreaks," KTVU, March 17, 2021, https://www.ktvu.com/news/san-francisco-jails-had-no-coronavirus-deaths-hospitalizations-or-outbreaks-sheriff-says.

143. B. Healy & C. Williamsen, "Rollins: Suffolk County Sheriff never alerted DA of inmate's death," WBUR, August 20, 2020, https://www.wbur.org/news/2020/08/20/suffolk-county-jail-death-sheriff-investigation.

144. A. Farish, "Lawsuit filed against Madison Co. Sheriff's Office, jail after 2018 death of Lanekia Brown," WJTV, Mary 24, 2021, https://www.wjtv.com/news/lawsuit -filed-against-madison-co-sheriffs-office-jail-after-2018-death-of-lanekia-brown/.

145. A. Brauer, "Data shows Marion County Jail's death rate is 2 to 3 times higher than the national average," WTTV, April 23, 2021, https://cbs4indy.com/news/ report-shows-the-marion-county-jails-death-rate-is-2-to-3-times-higher-than -the-national-average/; CoreCivic, "CoreCivic reports first quarter 2019 financial results," Global News Wire, May 8, 2019, https://www.globenewswire.com/news -release/2019/05/08/1819761/0/en/CoreCivic-Reports-First-Quarter-2019-Financial -Results.html.

146. J. Magdaleno, "Inmate dies of apparent suicide at Marion County Jail," *Indy Star*, July 27, 2021, https://www.indystar.com/story/news/local/marion-county/ 2021/07/27/marion-county-jail-inmate-dies-apparent-suicide-sheriff-says/ 5394043001/.

147. J. Allen, "Lawsuit: Naples Jail Center inmate did not receive proper treatment for diabetes before death," *Naples Daily News*, November 12, 2020, https://www.msn .com/en-us/news/crime/lawsuit-naples-jail-center-inmate-did-not-receive-proper -treatment-for-diabetes-before-death/ar-BB1aX2w5.

148. B. Shammas, "A Miami-based jail health-care company profits while patients die," *Miami New Times*, September 17, 2019, tps://www.miaminewtimes.com/news/ jail-health-care-company-armor-correctional-accused-of-multiple-inmate-deaths -11268351.

149. J. Szep, N. Parker, L. So, P. Eisler, & G. Smith, "Special Report: U.S. jails are outsourcing medical care-and the death toll is rising," Reuters, October 26, 2020, https://www.reuters.com/article/us-usa-jails-privatization-special-repor -idUSKBN27B1DH.

150. Szep et al., "Special Report."

151. M. Blau, "For sheriffs, health for inmates can be a burden," *Atlanta*, October 12, 2019, https://www.atlantamagazine.com/great-reads/for-sheriffs-healthcare -for-inmates-can-be-a-burden-for-one-doctor-it-has-been-the-opportunity-of-a -lifetime/.

152. M. Link, "Court testimony exposes Wellpath's jail medication policies," *Record Eagle*, July 16, 2021, https://www.record-eagle.com/news/court-testimony-exposes -wellpaths-jail-medication-policies/article_b23faf32-e5ae-11eb-aa5c-676d646444bc .html.

153. A. Leonard & A. May, "Arizona's privatized prison health care under fire after deaths," Aljazeera America, April 28, 2014, http://america.aljazeera.com/watch/ shows/america-tonight/america-tonight-blog/2013/12/2/arizona-s-privatizedprison healthcareunderfireafterdeaths.html.

154. Blau, "For sheriffs."

155. S. Coll, "The jail health care crisis," New Yorker, February 25, 2019, https://www .newyorker.com/magazine/2019/03/04/the-jail-health-care-crisis.

156. C. Ramirez, "Lawsuit: Inmate's in-custody death could have been prevented," KOB 4, June 11, 2021, https://www.kob.com/new-mexico-news/lawsuit-inmates-in -custody-death-could-have-been-prevented/6125143/.

157. Szep et al., "Special Report."

158. Link, "Court testimony."

159. Leonard & May, "Arizona's privatized prison health care."

160. Furst, "Lawsuit."

161. "$3 M lawsuit filed against Grainger County Sheriff's Office in connection to inmate death," WVLT8, August 5, 2020, https://www.wvlt.tv/2020/08/05/3m-lawsuit -filed-against-grainger-county-sheriffs-office-in-connection-to-inmates-death/.

162. Associated Press, "Virginia agency wants to shut down troubled regional jail," AP News, April 27, 2021, https://apnews.com/article/virginia -57382585da87625f029580d08d5e22da.

163. M. Bernstein, "Record $10 million judgment awarded in Washington County jail heroin withdrawal death," Oregonian, December 7, 2018, https://www.oregonlive .com/crime/2018/12/record-10-million-judgement-awarded-against-corizon-health -in-death-of-washington-county-jail-inmate.html.

164. R. Neate, "Welcome to Jail Inc: how private companies make money off U.S. prisons," Guardian, June 16, 2016, https://www.theguardian.com/us-news/2016/ jun/16/us-prisons-jail-private-healthcare-companies-profit.

165. Coll, "The jail health care crisis."

166. Blau, "For sheriffs."

CHAPTER 6

1. J. Pishko, "Jail deaths and the elected sheriff," The Appeal, March 21, 2019, https:// theappeal.org/politicalreport/jail-deaths-and-sheriffs/.

2. A. Jenkins, "'A black box.' It's not always easy getting answers when someone dies in jail," Northwest News Network, January 7, 2020, https://www.nwnewsnetwork.org/

crime-law-and-justice/2019-12-26/a-black-box-its-not-always-easy-getting-answers
-when-someone-dies-in-jail.

3. L. Fuller, "No charges will be filed in case of local jail inmate who died after
then-sheriff knelt on his neck," WPSD, February 26, 2021, https://www.wpsdlocal6
.com/news/no-charges-will-be-filed-in-case-of-local-jail-inmate-who-died-after
-then/article_949ea3a8-787a-11eb-9642-636ff7b6757d.html.

4. C. Guyette, "Lawsuit targets billion-dollar company making life-and-death
medical decisions in Michigan jails," *Detroit Metro Times*, March 12, 2020, https://
www.metrotimes.com/news-hits/archives/2020/03/12/lawsuit-targets-billion-dollar
-company-making-life-and-death-medical-decisions-in-michigan-jails.

5. R. King, "Sheriff investigates death in the county jail," KOEL, September 23,
2020, https://koel.com/sheriff-investigates-death-in-the-county-jail/.

6. WBSTV.com News Staff, "Gov. Kemp creates commission to look into possible
suspension of Clayton County Sheriff Victor Hill," WSBTV, May 19, 2021, https://
www.wsbtv.com/news/local/gov-kemp-creates-commission-look-into-possible
-suspension-clayton-county-sheriff-victor-hill/2ND3DD7TJRGOJLVBXVDF72K
CCQ/.

7. C. Parker, "Hamilton County investigates inmate death," WDEF, September 23,
2020, https://www.wdef.com/hamilton-county-investigates-inmate-death/.

8. *Monroe News* Staff, "Inmate dies after found hanging at jail," *Monroe News*,
October 7, 2020, https://www.monroenews.com/story/news/crime/2020/10/07/
inmate-dies-after-found-hanging-at-jail/42840599/.

9. A. Ferrise, "As Cuyahoga County Jail inmates died in record numbers, county
investigations into the deaths were minimal, records show," Cleveland.com, April 29,
2020, https://www.cleveland.com/metro/2020/04/as-cuyahoga-county-jail-inmates
-died-in-record-numbers-county-investigations-into-the-deaths-were-minimal
-records-show.html.

10. T. Sissom, "Washington County Sheriff's Office says procedures followed in
jail hanging incident," *Northwest Arkansas Democrat Gazette*, September 23, 2020,
https://www.nwaonline.com/news/2020/sep/23/washington-county-sheriffs-office
-says-procedures/.

11. C. Astolfi & A. Ferrise, "What's the story behind how the Cuyahoga County
jail became one of the worst in the nation?" Cleveland.com, November 23, 2018,
https://www.cleveland.com/metro/2018/11/whats-the-story-behind-how-the
-cuyahoga-county-jail-became-one-of-the-worst-in-the-nation-a-drive-for-money-a
-clevelandcom-investigation-finds.html.

12. K. Dixon, "Law firm to review Cobb County jail conditions," *Atlanta Journal-Constitution*, June 14, 2020, https://www.ajc.com/news/local/law-firm-review-cobb-county-jail-conditions/virAJo39jIoZ1SNcBeMrlN/.

13. M. Lutz, "Court: Cobb sheriff must turn over records of death in custody," *Atlanta Journal-Constitution*, April 23, 2020, https://www.ajc.com/news/local-govt--politics/court-cobb-sheriff-must-turn-over-records-death-custody/trrqFuNQ zhgGcDnWetjtfI/.

14. A. Robinson, "Broady criticized Republican officials' handling of jail deaths," *Cobb County Courier*, August 29, 2020, https://cobbcountycourier.com/2020/08/broady-criticizes-jail-deaths/.

15. A. McGlone, "Obscure sheriff's review board gets new scrutiny in court," KPBS, December 8, 2020, https://www.kpbs.org/podcasts/kpbs-midday-edition-segments/2020/dec/08/obscure-sheriffs-review-board-gets-new-scrutiny-co/.

16. J. McDonald, "Julian man choked to death on face mask in sheriff's custody," *San Diego Union-Tribune*, March 30, 2021, https://www.sandiegouniontribune.com/news/watchdog/story/2021-03-30/julian-man-choked-to-death-on-face-mask-in-sheriffs-custody-autopsy-finds.

17. A. Binion, "Investigation: Kitsap jail inmate who died improperly subdued in restraint chair," *Kitsap Sun*, December 22, 2020, https://www.kitsapsun.com/story/news/2020/12/22/investigation-kitsap-jail-inmate-who-died-improperly-subdued-restraint-chair/3967083001/.

18. M. DeFelice, "Training inadequate for use of restrain chair at Kitsap County Jail," *Kitsap Daily News*, January 7, 2021, https://www.kitsapdailynews.com/news/training-inadequate-for-use-of-restraint-chair-at-kitsap-county-jail/.

19. A. Binion, "No charges for Kitsap jail officers in death of mentally ill murder suspect," *Kitsap Sun*, June 21, 2021, https://www.kitsapsun.com/story/news/2021/06/21/no-charges-kitsap-jail-officers-death-mentally-ill-murder-suspect/7749538002/.

20. S. Acosta & B. Spicer, "BCSO deputy arrested in connection with inmate's suicide attempt at Bexar County Jail," KSAT, September 30, 2020, https://www.ksat.com/news/local/2020/09/30/bcso-deputy-arrested-in-connection-with-inmates-suicide-attempt-at-bexar-county-jail/.

21. J. Toberlin, "'Don't elect me': Sheriffs and the need for reform in county law enforcement," *Virginia Law Review* 194, no. 1 (March 2, 2018), https://papers.ssrn.com/sol3/papers.cfm?abstract_id=3135346.

22. J. Forbes, "Messenger: Ruling against $3 surcharge sends message to Missouri Legislature on court costs," *St. Louis Post-Dispatch*, June 3, 2021, https://www.stltoday .com/news/local/columns/tony-messenger/messenger-ruling-against-3-surcharge -sends-message-to-missouri-legislature-on-court-costs/article_381981a0-8ab5-5a60 -a55b-8368c6ec4c5f.html.

23. M. Johnston, "Will outrage over the Grand Traverse County jail be enough to topple incumbent sheriff?" IPR, October 22, 2020, https://www.interlochen publicradio.org/news/2020-10-22/will-outrage-over-the-grand-traverse-county-jail -be-enough-to-topple-an-incumbent-sheriff; M. Link, "At issue, Grand Traverse jail inmate health care," *Record Eagle*, November 13, 2020, https://www.record-eagle .com/news/at-issue-grand-traverse-jail-inmate-health-care/article_6c3d5f46-252b -11eb-a7bd-ff784b41da79.html.

24. T. Bartelme, "SC Sheriffs earn 2019 newsmaker of the year for scandalous behavior," *Post and Courier*, updated September 14, 2020, https://www.postand courier.com/news/sc-sheriffs-earn-2019-newsmaker-of-the-year-for-scandalous -behavior/article_3287a316-1847-11ea-bef3-673772ca16df.html.

25. M. Chammah, "Your local jail may be a house of horrors," Marshall Project, July 29, 2020, https://www.themarshallproject.org/2020/07/29/your-local-jail-may-be-a -house-of-horrors.

26. C. Byers, "'It's heinous and unforgivable,'" KSDK, August 13, 2020, https://www .ksdk.com/article/news/local/family-of-man-who-died-at-st-francois-county-jail -seek-reform/63-bfd710b9-f160-4fc7-89d9-f8406c8b2fd2.

27. K. Hyatt, "Ramsey County Board 'appalled and angered' by allegations of discrimination among jail staff," *Star Tribune*, June 23, 2020, https://www.startribune .com/ramsey-board-appalled-minority-officers-weren-t-allowed-to-guard-chauvin/ 571444672/.

28. T. Armus, "'Don't be a sheep': Sheriffs rebel against new statewide mask mandates," *Washington Post*, June 26, 2020, https://www.washingtonpost.com/ nation/2020/06/26/sheriffs-mask-covid/.

29. M. Silver, "Nearly $7 million settlement paid out in Terrill Thomas dehydration death civil rights case," WUWM, May 28, 2019, https://www.wuwm.com/news/2019 -05-28/nearly-7-million-settlement-paid-out-in-terrill-thomas-dehydration-death -civil-rights-case.

30. S. Yost, "Sheriff's department responds to protests over 2018 jail death," *Rhino Times*, June 26, 2020, https://www.rhinotimes.com/news/sheriffs-department -responds-to-protests-over-2018-jail-death/; J. Biggs, "Video of woman's death

at Greensboro jail to be released to her family to view," *News & Record*, August 25, 2020, https://greensboro.com/news/local_news/video-of-womans-death-at -greensboro-jail-to-be-released-to-her-family-to-view/article_3e9bd1e6-e6ea-11ea -8a38-f7010798b6fe.html.

31. S. Pickey, "District attorney says Ector Co. deputies used excessive force on prisoner who later died," CBS7, September 1, 2020, https://www.cbs7.com/2020/09/ 01/no-indictments-after-man-dies-in-custody-in-ector-county/.

32. J. Lipscomb, "Darren Rainey died in scalding prison shower eight years ago today," *Miami New Times*, June 23, 2020, https://www.miaminewtimes.com/news/ katherine-fernandez-rundle-criticized-for-darren-rainey-florida-prison-death -11657307.

33. S. Morris, "Lieutenant on leave after use of restraints leads to death in Santa Rita Jail," *East Bay Express*, August 7, 2019, https://eastbayexpress.com/lieutenant-on -leave-after-use-of-restraints-leads-to-death-in-santa-rita-jail-1/.

34. A. Ruggiero, "East Bay cops cleared in death of mentally ill man who died in custody," *Mercury News*, June 23, 2020, https://www.mercurynews.com/2020/06/22/ da-no-charges-in-death-of-mentally-ill-man-who-died-in-custody-chained-to-door/.

35. L. Fernandez, "Body cam footage in Santa Rita jail undercuts deputies' claims about 20-year-old inmate's death," KTVU, June 29, 2020, https://www.ktvu.com/ news/body-cam-footage-in-santa-rita-jail-undercuts-deputies-claims-about-20-year -old-inmates-death.

36. L. Fernandez, "Alameda County DA finds no criminal wrongdoing with Fremont man's suicide in Santa Rita," KTVU, June 22, 2020, https://www.ktvu.com/ news/alameda-county-da-finds-no-criminal-wrongdoing-with-fremont-mans -suicide-in-santa-rita.

37. A. Lee, "Parents grieve loss of son who died in chains at Santa Rita; sheriff's office moves to fire lieutenant," KTVU, July 1, 2020, https://www.ktvu.com/news/ parents-grieve-loss-of-son-who-died-in-chains-at-santa-rita-sheriffs-office-moves-to -fire-lieutenant.

38. L. Fernandez, "California auditor: Santa Rita Jail lacks information on inmate mental health, has surplus of $135M," KTVU, March 25, 2021, https://www.ktvu .com/news/california-auditor-santa-rita-jail-doesnt-screen-adequately-for-mental -health-has-excess-of-135m.

39. J. Ciavaglia, "DA: Pa. jail followed protocol in pepper spraying of mentally ill inmate," *Buck County Courier Times*, July 9, 2020, https://www.corrections1.com/ investigations/articles/da-pa-jail-followed-protocol-in-pepper-spraying-of-mentally

-ill-inmate-xYeqdgeH2DKGp9WU/; B. Sholtis, "'She's breaking down': Inmates at Bucks County jail decry treatment of suicidal woman with severe mental illness," WHYY, June 15, 2020, https://whyy.org/articles/shes-breaking-down-inmates-at -bucks-county-jail-decry-treatment-of-suicidal-woman-with-severe-mental-illness/.

40. E. Mark, "County council approves $3 million settlement in jail death lawsuit," *Citizens' Voice*, June 23, 2020, https://www.citizensvoice.com/news/county-council -approves-3-million-settlement-in-jail-death-lawsuit/article_28243c10-2f45-560f -a8b9-c762f748cff4.html.

41. "District attorney finds medical staff 'inadequate' but not criminal in prison death," WBRE/WYOU-TV, October 6, 2020, https://www.pahomepage.com/top -news/district-attorney-finds-medical-staff-inadequate-but-not-criminal-in-prison -death/.

42. S. Garrison & T. Novelly, "Solicitor will not charge deputies in Jamal Sutherland's jail death," *Post and Courier*, July 25, 2021, https://www.postandcourier.com/news/ solicitor-will-not-charge-deputies-in-jamal-sutherlands-jail-death/article_4c92a902 -ee2b-11eb-b89b-53ff6f11c14e.html.

43. B. Hicks, "Sutherland investigation exposed jail malpractice," *Post and Courier*, July 31, 2021, https://www.postandcourier.com/opinion/commentary/hicks -sutherland-investigation-exposed-jail-malpractice-graziano-agrees/article_9fcc2ede -f152-11eb-b8d3-bbedcfc0cfec.html.

44. S. Lieberman, "Rockland jail inmate death: Insufficient evidence of criminality by officers, AG says," *Rockland/Westchester Journal News*, January 29, 2021, https:// www.lohud.com/story/news/local/rockland/2021/01/29/rockland-jail-inmate-death -insufficient-evidence-criminality-ag/4311578001/.

45. A. Gardner, "DA: Use of force in Shasta County jail was justified," KRCR, August 31, 2020, https://krcrtv.com/news/local/da-use-of-force-in-shasta-county-jail-death -was-justified.

46. M. Brannon, "Dying inside," *Redding Record Searchlight*, June 25, 2020, https:// www.redding.com/in-depth/news/local/2020/06/24/shasta-county-jail-california -inmate-deaths-mental-health-services/5281201002/; M. Brannon, "Man who spent an hour in custody is 1 of 5 deaths reported by Shasta County Jail in 2021," *Redding Record Searchlight*, May 3, 2021, https://www.redding.com/story/news/ local/2021/05/03/shasta-county-jail-investigating-fifth-death-2021-one-hour -custody/7307791002/.

47. K. Sosin, "New video reveals Layleen Polanco's death at Rikers was preventable," NBC News Now, June 12, 2020, https://www.nbcnews.com/feature/nbc-out/new -video-reveals-layleen-polanco-s-death-rikers-was-preventable-n1230951.

48. K. McMahon, "The death of Layleen Xtravaganza Cubilette-Polanco, 1991– 2019," New York City Board of Correction, June 23, 2020, https://www1.nyc.gov/ assets/boc/downloads/pdf/Reports/BOC-Reports/2020.06_Polanco/Final_Polanco_ Public_Report_1.pdf; A. Branigin, "New report on Layleen Xtravaganza Polanco's death highlights the cruelty of NYC jails' policies toward trans people," *Root*, June 25, 2020, https://www.theroot.com/new-report-on-layleen-xtravaganza-polancos-death -highli-1844162814.

49. J. Anuta, "City slaps jail staffers with charges over death of Layleen Polanco," *Politico*, June 26, 2020, https://www.politico.com/states/new-york/city-hall/story/ 2020/06/26/city-slaps-jail-staffers-with-charges-over-death-of-layleen-polanco -1295312.

50. K. Sison, "N.Y.C. to end solitary confinement after trans woman's Riker Island death," NBC News, June 30, 2020, https://news.yahoo.com/n-y-c-end-solitary -165050676.html.

51. T. Prohaska, "Niagara corrections officer pleads guilty to records tampering," *Buffalo News*, February 11, 2020, https://buffalonews.com/news/local/crime-and -courts/niagara-corrections-officer-pleads-guilty-to-records-tampering/article_ d7d5cf58-e4c2-51de-87cf-0ae362a57c92.html.

52. T. Saccente, "Charges ruled out in jail death," *Arkansas Democrat Gazette*, November 8, 2020, https://www.arkansasonline.com/news/2020/nov/08/charges -ruled-out-in-jail-death/.

53. P. Eisler, L. So, J. Szep, G. Smith, & N. Parker, "Dying inside, part 1," Reuter Investigates, October 16, 2020, https://www.reuters.com/investigates/special-report/ usa-jails-deaths/.

54. J. Rihl, "Mixed-up meds & long waits: How understaffing hurts medical treatment at Allegheny County Jail," *Public Source*, January 7, 2021, https://www .publicsource.org/allegheny-county-jail-inmate-medical-wait-times-understaffing/.

55. K. Ross, "Oklahoma's jail mortality rate second in nation," Oklahoma Watch, February 9, 2021, https://oklahomawatch.org/2021/02/09/oklahomas-jail-mortality -rate-ranks-second-in-nation/.

56. J. Pohl & R. Gabrielson, "A jail increased extreme isolation to stop suicides. More people killed themselves," ProPublica, November 5, 2019, https://www.propublica

.org/article/a-jail-increased-extreme-isolation-to-stop-suicides-more-people-killed
-themselves.

57. A. Lagoe, B. Stahl, & S. Eckert, "KARE 11 Investigates: Flawed—often
toothless—jail death investigations," KARE 11, September 29, 2020, https://www
.kare11.com/article/news/investigations/kare-11-investigates-flawed-often-toothless
-jail-death-investigations/89-0255d498-8679-4961-959a-6f19c4a9e040.

58. P. Blume, "DOC finds numerous jail violations in death of inmates in Bemidji,
Minnesota," Fox 9, May 20, 2020, https://www.fox9.com/news/doc-finds-numerous
-jail-violations-in-death-of-inmate-in-bemidji-minnesota.

59. M. McKinney, "Beltrami County sued for black man's death while in custody,"
Minnesota Spokesman-Recorder, July 2, 2020, https://spokesman-recorder
.com/2020/07/02/beltrami-county-sued-for-black-mans-death-while-in-custody/.

60. "Minnesota DOC wants independent law enforcement agency to investigate
possible criminal charges in jail death," Fox 9, July 12, 2020, https://www.fox9.com/
news/minnesota-doc-wants-independent-law-enforcement-agency-to-investigate
-possible-criminal-charges-in-jail-death.

61. Lagoe, Stahl, & Eckert, "KARE 11 Investigates: Flawed—often toothless—jail
death investigations."

62. A. Aguilar, "WTOC Investigates: Wrongful death lawsuit filed after inmate dies
in Appling Co. Jail," WTOC, August 27, 2020, https://www.wtoc.com/2020/08/27/
wtoc-investigates-wrongful-death-lawsuit-filed-after-inmate-dies-appling-co-jail/.

63. T. Kless, "Family says medical attention wasn't given to Southeast Georgia man
who died in jail," *First Coast News*, July 30, 2020, https://www.firstcoastnews.com/
article/news/local/family-says-medical-attention-wasnt-given-to-southeast-georgia
-man-who-died-while-in-jail/77-5200aff9-0523-4ecd-83f1-158e3b71fe6e.

64. Kless, "Family says medical attention wasn't given to Southeast Georgia man
who died in jail."

65. J. Gerritt, "Death without conviction: Texas needs access to jail videos," *Palestine
Herald-Press*, August 15, 2019, https://www.palestineherald.com/news/php-editorial
-death-without-conviction-texas-needs-access-to-jail-videos/article_e33b8600-bfcd
-11e9-8134-531ecbee318f.html.

66. F. Romero, "Five indicted in connection to inmate's death at Midland County
Jail," KMID, August 1, 2020, https://www.yourbasin.com/news/five-indicted-in
-connection-to-inmates-death-at-midland-county-jail/.

67. L. LaRowe, "Jail surveillance recordings still being disputed," *Texarkana Gazette*, August 21, 2021, https://texarkanagazette.com/news/2021/aug/22/jail-surveillance-recordings-still-being-disputed-/.

68. A. Sundaram, "How Texas jails avoid investigations of inmate deaths," *Texas Observer*, October 29, 2020, https://www.texasobserver.org/how-texas-jails-avoid-investigations-of-inmate-deaths/.

69. E. Conrad, "Investigates: Former Washington Co. Jail administrator alleges jail unsafe, files suit," KJRH, November 13, 2020, https://www.kjrh.com/news/local-news/investigates-former-washington-co-jail-administrator-files-lawsuit-alleges-jail-unsafe.

70. D. Wright, "Inmate families speak about jail concerns," *Gallipolis Daily Tribune*, November 20, 2019, https://www.mydailyregister.com/top-stories/48257/inmate-families-speak-about-jail-concerns-county-answers.

71. S. Trafton, "State: Inmate death investigation 'inadequate,'" *Hudson Valley 360*, August 10, 2020, https://www.hudsonvalley360.com/top_story/state-inmate-death-investigation-inadequate-jail-deaths-not-reported/article_cae57d9f-6ed2-5674-8316-18e42a65c7f7.html.

72. E. Waldon, "Montcalm County Jail inmate cried, 'Help me, Mommy,'" *Daily News*, August 26, 2020, https://www.thedailynews.cc/articles/montcalm-county-jail-inmate-cried-help-me-mommy-help-me-im-sick-before-dying/.

73. J. Harrison, "Penobscot jail board's 1st report didn't address inmates," *Bangor Daily News*, February 1, 2021, https://bangordailynews.com/2021/02/01/news/penobscot/penobscot-jail-boards-1st-report-didnt-address-inmates-mental-health-as-law-requires/.

74. P. Tollefson, "Judge drops family's lawsuit over 2015 jail suicide due to statute of limitations," *Billings Gazette*, August 19, 2020, https://billingsgazette.com/news/state-and-regional/crime-and-courts/judge-drops-familys-lawsuit-over-2015-jail-suicide-due-to-statute-of-limitations/article_9edd0b66-d9dc-5fbe-a835-58843a2027db.html.

75. Associated Press, "Family of man who died by suicide in jail awarded $156k," AP News, January 15, 2021, https://apnews.com/article/billings-montana-88b9676d3c1b16e649fb93db56cf1dc8.

76. Lagoe, Stahl, & Eckert, "KARE 11 Investigates: Flawed—often toothless—jail death investigations."

77. F. Hatton, "Rolette County jail reopens under new classification, requirements," KFYR, September 17, 2020, https://www.msn.com/en-us/news/crime/rolette-county-jail-reopens-under-new-classification-requirements/ar-BB199P6C.

78. Jenkins, "'A black box.'"

79. L. Basye & A. Pierrotti, "'How can somebody investigate themselves?' Ga. lawmaker drafts bill for jail death investigation oversight," 11Alive, October 28, 2020, https://www.11alive.com/article/news/investigations/the-reveal/ga-lawmaker-plans -to-create-jail-death-oversight/85-bd90936f-fdf7-4da6-8909-adbf458fadc5.

80. M. Balsamo, "Justice Department: Virginia jail officials must improve medical treatment for inmates," Associated Press, August 6, 2020, https://wjla.com/news/ local/virginia-jail-medical-treatment-inmates-justice-department.

81. G. Harki, "Deaths continue at Hampton Roads Jail," *Virginian-Pilot*, May 31, 2019, https://www.pilotonline.com/government/virginia/article_88f85c36-82f6-11e9 -be70-ffbb08602899.html.

82. S. Jenkins, "Hampton Roads Regional Jail is investigating an inmate's death," *Virginian-Pilot*, February 22, 2021, https://www.pilotonline.com/news/crime/vp -nw-hampton-roads-regional-jail-investigating-inmate-death-monday-20210222 -pyxnaxkigbfknhtk5gupalp7sa-story.html.

83. J. MacDonald & K. Davis, "Vista suicide is county's second jail death this year," *San Diego Union-Tribune*, May 24, 2020, https://www.sandiegouniontribune.com/ news/watchdog/story/2020-05-24/vista-suicide-is-countys-second-jail-death-this -year.

84. J. McDonald, "Fifth inmate dies this year in San Diego County Jail," *San Diego Union-Tribune*, October 13, 2020, https://www.msn.com/en-us/news/crime/fifth -inmate-dies-this-year-in-san-diego-county-jail/ar-BB19ZLBI.

85. J. McDonald & K. Davis, "Widow kept in the dark about husband's death in San Diego County jail," *San Diego Union-Tribune*, March 19, 2021, https://www .sandiegouniontribune.com/news/watchdog/story/2021-03-19/widow-kept-in-the -dark-about-husbands-death-in-san-diego-county-jail.

86. L. Schroeder, K. Davis, & J. McDonald, "County sheriff's department questions national standard when counting jail suicide rates," *San Diego Union-Tribune*, September 20, 2019, https://www.sandiegouniontribune.com/news/watchdog/ story/2019-09-19/sheriffs-department-avoids-national-standard-for-calculating -mortality-rates.

87. J. McDonald, "Vista jail worker says she warned sheriff's officials before jail suicide," *San Diego Union-Tribune*, September 9, 2020, https://www.sandiegounion tribune.com/news/watchdog/story/2020-09-09/vista-jail-worker-says-she-warned -sheriffs-officials-before-inmate-suicide.

88. J. McDonald & K. Davis, "Three more inmates die in Sheriff's Department custody," *San Diego Union-Tribune*, December 11, 2020, https://www.sandiegounion tribune.com/news/watchdog/story/2020-12-11/three-more-inmates-die-in-sheriffs -department-custody.

89. N. Parker, J. Szep, & L. So, "Death and politics roil a Georgia jail," Reuters, September 4, 2019, https://www.reuters.com/investigates/special-report/usa-jails -monitor/.

90. M. Congedo, "Friend of inmates who died in the CCDC speaks out," WTOC, September 13, 2020, https://www.wtoc.com/2020/09/13/friend-inmate-who-died -ccdc-says-he-has-received-conflicting-stories-cause-death/.

91. A. Jennerjahn, "Chatham Co. Jail uses new guardian system to monitor inmates," WTGS, March 1, 2021, https://www.msn.com/en-us/news/crime/chatham-co-jail -uses-new-guardian-system-to-monitor-inmates/ar-BB1e8pni.

92. L. Sherman, "Public records in death investigations would be limited through legislation passed by North Carolina General Assembly," *News & Observer*, June 27, 2020, https://www.newsobserver.com/news/politics-government/article243837792 .html.

93. M. Hewlett, "Jail officers, nurse charged in John Neville's death," *News & Record*, July 8, 2020, https://greensboro.com/news/crime/jail-officers-nurse-charged-in-john -nevilles-death-greensboro-man-was-restrained-choked-while-in/article_8db969c9 -0012-5fc8-9dab-c7ede27590f9.html.

94. D. Kane & D. Battaglia, "NC jails have known this position is deadly. So why was it used again?" *News & Observer*, August 12, 2020, https://www.newsobserver.com/ news/state/north-carolina/article244777867.html.

95. M. Hewlett, "Federal judge approves confidential settlement in lawsuit over Winston-Salem man's death at the Forsyth County Jail," *Winston-Salem Journal*, July 19, 2020, https://greensboro.com/news/local_news/federal-judge-approves -confidential-settlement-in-lawsuit-over-winston-salem-mans-death-at-the-forsyth/ article_de994923-3502-50a0-aac9-1ab6d8814d68.html.

96. P. Jackson, "'The scores are abysmal': ACLU alleges failures at Baltimore jail led to 12 preventable deaths," *Baltimore Sun*, December 2, 2020, https://www .baltimoresun.com/news/crime/bs-md-ci-cr-aclu-medical-professionals-filing -inmate-deaths-20201202-shidmiw4lzbb7n6b5tncndpafi-story.html.

CHAPTER 7

1. H. Elattar, "OC Jail deaths count highest in 2020 of the last 4 years," *Voice of OC*, September 24, 2020, https://voiceofoc.org/2020/09/oc-jail-deaths-count-highest-in -2020-of-the-last-4-years-none-from-covid-19/.

2. B. Stahl, "KARE 11 Investigates: Minnesota jail failures costing taxpayers millions," KARE 11, October 29, 2020, https://www.kare11.com/article/news/ investigations/jail-failures-costing-millions/89-519c65ec-0b35-4912-8966-b764e 8bd2b5c.

3. B. Williams, "Wrongful death lawsuit involving Roanoke City Jail settled," WFXR, November 9, 2020, https://www.wfxrtv.com/news/local-news/roanoke-valley -news/wrongful-death-lawsuit-involving-roanoke-city-jail-staff-settled/.

4. *Jody Lombardo, Bryan Gilbert vs City of St Louis et al.*, No. 19-1469, April 20, 2020.

5. M. Shenefelt, "Weber County prevails in jail death lawsuit, family weighs appeal," *Standard-Examiner*, June 11, 2020, https://www.standard.net/news/2020/ jun/11/weber-county-prevails-in-jail-death-lawsuit-family-weighs-appeal/.

6. D. E. Smoot, "Appeals court affirms dismissal of claim brought by inmate's estate," *Muskogee Phoenix*, August 25, 2020, https://www.muskogeephoenix.com/ news/appeals-court-affirms-dismissal-of-claim-brought-by-inmates-estate/article_ aa41cc92-5853-5c5d-ac0e-8934208aaca3.html.

7. *Estate of Johnson v. Miller*, No. 2:11-CV-00067, U.S. Dist. LEXIS 95322 at 11 (S.D. Ohio Aug. 25, 2011).

8. *Keeling, Administrator of Estate of Davageah K. Jones v. Correction Care Solutions, LLC*, No. 2:19-cv-225 (AWA-DEM) and 2:20-cv-245 (AWA-DEM), U.S. District Court for Eastern District of Virginia, October 10, 2020.

9. M. Shenefelt, "Expert witnesses dominate Utah jail death civil court cases, but who pays for them?" *Standard-Examiner*, February 23, 2020, https://www.standard .net/police-fire/2020/feb/23/expert-witnesses-dominate-utah-jail-death-civil-court -cases-but-who-pays-for-them/.

10. M. Shenefelt, "Judge won't absolve Davis County in Miller jail death case," *Standard-Examiner*, October 1, 2020, https://www.standard.net/police-fire/2020/ oct/01/judge-wont-absolve-davis-county-in-miller-jail-death-case/.

11. L. Appleman, "Cashing in on convicts: Privatization, punishment, and the people," *Utah Law Review* 2018, no. 3 (2018): 579–637.

12. T. Juranovich, "Family, sheriff's department reach settlement over jailed man's death," *Kokomo Tribune*, September 9, 2020, https://www.kokomotribune.com/news/local_news/family-sheriffs-department-reach-settlement-over-jailed-mans-death/article_b5870d50-f209-11ea-bd20-879d0015ce9f.html.

13. *Borum v. Swisher County*, 2015 WL 327508 (N.D. Tx. 2015).

14. T. W. Anderson, "Duchesne County nurse charged with negligent homicide nine months after 21-year-old inmate died from dehydration," *Salt Lake Tribune*, September 25, 2017, https://www.sltrib.com/news/politics/2017/09/25/duchesne-county-nurse-charged-with-negligent-homicide-nine-months-after-21-year-old-inmate-died-from-dehydration/.

15. M. Walsh, "Lawsuit: Inmate died after being held in solitary for drug withdrawal," *Seven Days*, February 20, 2019, https://www.sevendaysvt.com/OffMessage/archives/2019/02/20/lawsuit-inmate-died-after-being-held-in-solitary-for-drug-withdrawal.

16. J. Lurie, "Go to jail. Die from drug withdrawal. Welcome to the criminal justice system," *Mother Jones*, February 5, 2017, https://www.motherjones.com/politics/2017/02/opioid-withdrawal-jail-deaths/; R. G. Dunlop, "Lawsuit over 2013 Montgomery County jail death settled," Kentucky Center for Investigative Reporting, February 9, 2017, https://kycir.org/2017/02/09/lawsuits-over-2013-montgomery-county-jail-death-settled/; *King v. Kramer*, 680 F. Supp. 3d 1013 (7 Cir. 2014).

17. *Finn v. Warren County, Kentucky*, 768 F. Supp. 3d 441 (6 Cir. 2014); *McConnell v. Butler County, Ohio*, 2013 WL 4482411 (S.D. Oh. 2013).

18. *Thornhill v. Aylor*, 2016 WL 8737358 (W.D. Wv. 2016); A. Mitchell, "Family members get $1 million of $1.75 million settlement in lawsuit over Kalamazoo County Jail inmate death," MLive, October 31, 2013, https://www.mlive.com/news/kalamazoo/2013/10/see_breakdown_of_175_million_s.html.

19. K. Davis, "$3M verdict upheld in jail death," *San Diego Union-Tribune*, January 22, 2015, https://www.sandiegouniontribune.com/sdut-sisson-verdict-jail-death-motion-denied-2015jan22-story.html.

CHAPTER 8

1. K. Quandt, "America's rural-jail-death problem," *Atlantic*, March 29, 2021, https://www.theatlantic.com/politics/archive/2021/03/americas-rural-jail-death-problem/618292/.

2. A. Ferrise, "Cuyahoga County Jail inmates dies, first death at troubled jail in 14 months," *Cleveland Plain-Dealer*, July 8, 2020, https://www.cleveland.com/

metro/2020/07/cuyahoga-county-jail-inmate-dies-first-death-at-troubled-jail-in-14
-months.html.

3. S. Trafton, "New era for sheriff's office," *Hudson Valley 360*, January 1, 2020, https://www.hudsonvalley360.com/news/greenecounty/new-era-for-sheriff-s-office/article_58be4b3c-f472-59b1-ab56-7c408045fea3.html.

4. O. Brand-Williams, "Fieger alleges coverup in woman's Harper Woods jail death," *Detroit News*, August 20, 2020, https://www.detroitnews.com/story/news/local/wayne-county/2020/08/20/fieger-alleges-coverup-womans-harper-woods-jail-death/5616907002/.

5. G. Hunter, "Ex-officer sues over firing in Harper Woods jail death," *Detroit News*, September 9, 2020, https://www.detroitnews.com/story/news/local/wayne-county/2020/09/09/harper-woods-jail-death-fired-officer-sues/5761761002/.

6. B. Addison, "Man who died in Collin County jail was having 'mental health crisis,' attorney says," *Dallas Morning News*, March 17, 2021, https://www.dallasnews.com/news/2021/03/17/man-who-died-in-collin-county-jail-was-having-mental-health-crisis-attorney-says/.

7. C. Martin, "Family of man who died in Collin County jail calls for arrest of officers present during his death," *Dallas Morning News*, March 19, 2021, https://www.dallasnews.com/news/courts/2021/03/19/family-of-man-who-died-in-collin-county-jail-calls-for-arrest-of-officers-present-during-his-death/.

8. M. Yeomans, "Protestors gather outside Collin County Jail after death of Marvin Scott III," NBC5 Dallas-Fort Worth, March 19, 2021, https://www.msn.com/en-us/news/crime/protestors-gather-outside-collin-county-jail-after-death-of-marvin-scott-iii/ar-BB1eJUSN; S. House, "7 detention officers fired after investigation into death of Marvin Scott at Collin County jail," *Dallas Morning News*, April 1, 2021, https://www.dallasnews.com/news/2021/04/01/7-detention-officers-fired-after-investigation-into-death-of-marvin-scott-at-collin-county-jail/.

9. D. Laferney, "A story of two deaths at the Collins County Jail," *D Magazine*, August 2, 2021, https://www.dmagazine.com/frontburner/2021/08/a-story-of-two-deaths-at-the-collin-county-jail/.

10. H. Beedle, "Former El Paso County Sheriff's deputy loses POST certification under new law," *Colorado Springs Indy*, January 6, 2021, https://www.csindy.com/news/local/former-el-paso-county-sheriff-s-deputy-loses-post-certification-under-new-law/article_7528c808-4ed8-11eb-94d9-df42008c2e58.html.

11. R. Franklin, M. Hickman, & M. Hiller, "2009 survey of POST agencies regarding certification practices," International Association of Directors of Law Enforcement Standards and Training, July 2009, https://www.ojp.gov/pdffiles1/nij/227927.pdf.

12. E. Williams, "Fourth Circuit rules against Virginia sheriff's deputies in jail death case," Courthouse News Service, March 30, 2021, https://www.courthousenews.com/fourth-circuit-rules-against-virginia-sheriffs-deputies-in-jail-death-case/.

13. B. Stahl, "KARE 11 Investigates: Message from the grave reveals another needless jail death," KARE 11, November 12, 2020, https://www.kare11.com/article/news/investigations/message-from-the-grave-jail-death/89-16b5b10b-8335-4a2a-9581-d53053d01e11.

14. D. Smith, "Man awaiting sentencing dies at Pima County Jail over weekend," *Tucson Sentinel*, June 23, 2020, https://www.tucsonsentinel.com/local/report/062320_jail_death/man-awaiting-sentencing-dies-pima-county-jail-over-weekend/; D. Smith, "Inmate found dead in Pima County jail cell," *Tucson Sentinel*, September 6, 2020, https://www.tucsonsentinel.com/local/report/090620_pima_jail_death/inmate-found-dead-pima-county-jail-cell/.

15. M. Hewlett & W. Young, "Will jail video in John Neville's death be made public? A judge in Winston-Salem will decide Friday," *Winston-Salem Journal*, July 29, 2020, https://journalnow.com/news/local/will-jail-video-in-john-nevilles-death-be-made-public-a-judge-in-winston-salem/article_344403fc-f05f-571b-a733-c8c78a96239a.html.

16. T. Foreman Jr., "Judge orders partial release of video in man's jail death," Associated Press, August 2, 2020, https://apnews.com/article/winston-salem-north-carolina-u-s-news-d4781857fda9a3f9081d9b186467f65c.

17. L. Basye & A. Pierrotti, "Judge orders Cobb County sheriff to turn over files on jail deaths," 11Alive, October 15, 2020, https://www.11alive.com/article/news/investigations/the-reveal/judge-orders-cobb-sheriff-to-turn-over-documents/85-b647208d-b7f7-42a2-b198-183dc755645d.

18. A. Pierrotti, "GBI and DA decline to investigate suspicious jail death, family claims promises were broken," 11Alive, February 24, 2021, https://www.11alive.com/article/news/investigations/the-reveal/wingo-cobb-jail-death-investigation-update/85-31583d64-1d95-4557-83cf-00869a07369c.

19. *Mercury News* Editorial Board, "Editorial: Santa Clara County Sheriff must stop stalling on oversight plan," *Mercury News*, November 12, 2020, https://www.mercurynews.com/2020/11/12/editorial-sheriff-must-stop-stalling-on-oversight-plan/.

20. T. Kaplan, "Santa Clara County, inmate-rights group agree to settle suit over deplorable jail conditions," *Mercury News*, October 23, 2018, https://www.mercurynews.com/2018/10/23/settlement-reached-over-lousy-jail-conditions/.

21. E. Rogers, "Brevard Sheriff's Office changed restraint chair and spit hood policy after vet's death," *Florida Today*, November 12, 2020, https://www.floridatoday.com/story/news/2020/11/12/brevard-sheriffs-office-changed-policies-after-army-vets-jail-death/6263005002/.

22. C. Clark, "We cannot become numb to San Diego jail deaths," *San Diego Union-Tribune*, February 11, 2021, https://www.sandiegouniontribune.com/columnists/story/2021-02-11/column-we-cannot-become-numb-to-san-diego-jail-deaths-we-have-to-demand-better.

23. A. Damon, "Death behind bars: Washoe County Jail inmates are dying from suicide, accidents and homicides," *Reno Gazette-Journal*, April 5, 2017, updated December 8, 2020, https://www.rgj.com/story/news/2017/04/05/washoe-county-jail-inmates-dying-suicide-accidents-and-homicide/98972810/.

24. A. Damon, "Washoe County Jail audit finds serious health care deficiencies in wake of inmate deaths," *Reno Gazette-Journal*, April 5, 2017, https://www.rgj.com/story/news/2017/04/05/washoe-county-jail-audit-finds-serious-health-care-deficiencies-wake-inmate-deaths/99545012/.

25. M. Corona, "General election 2018 guide: Get to know the Washoe County sheriff race candidates," *Reno Gazette-Journal*, October 3, 2018, https://www.rgj.com/story/news/2018/10/03/candidates-washoe-sheriff-general-election-2018/1454587002/.

26. D. Goodyear, "After years of protests every Wednesday, L.A. activists welcome a new D.A.," *New Yorker*, November 16, 2020, https://www.newyorker.com/magazine/2020/11/16/after-years-of-protests-every-wednesday-la-activists-welcome-a-new-da.

27. CBSLA Staff, "LA County DA Gascon to eliminate cash bail, will re-sentence death penalty inmates," KCAL, December 8, 2020, https://losangeles.cbslocal.com/2020/12/08/la-county-da-gascon-cash-bail-death-penalty/.

28. K. Fernelius, "New D.A. commits to fixing Georgia's 'backdoor to incarceration,'" *The Appeal*, January 11, 2021, https://theappeal.org/politicalreport/athens-georgia-probation-reform/.

29. B. Metrick, "Dauphin County prison board OKs investigations into suspended director of corrections, inmates' death," *Patriot-News*, September 9, 2020, https://

www.pennlive.com/news/2020/09/independent-investigations-approved-for-dauphin
-county-prison-by-board.html.

30. M. Lutz, "Democrat declares victory in Cobb sheriff's race," *Atlanta Journal-
Constitution*, November 4, 2020, https://www.ajc.com/news/atlanta-news/owens
-declares-victory-in-cobb-sheriffs-race/QZYTYGWTCRB7TPKLY7CG2KWGOQ/.

31. O. Diaz, "Charleston County sheriff implements 8 policies to change mental
health response at jail," *Post and Courier*, July 24, 2021, https://www.postandcourier
.com/news/charleston-county-sheriff-implements-8-policies-to-change-mental
-health-response-at-jail/article_0dbeb104-ecd1-11eb-b9f4-cbf1fd730723.html.

32. L. Zheng, "Tarrant County leaders eyeing 'jail diversion' center aimed at
providing mental health services," NBC5 Dallas-Fort Worth, May 12, 2021, https://
www.nbcdfw.com/news/local/tarrant-county-leaders-eying-jail-diversion-center
-aimed-at-providing-mental-health-services-instead/2630990/.

33. S. Kaplan, "U.S. DOJ continues investigating Palmer York Co. Prison death
despite grand jury findings," ABC27, March 9, 2021, https://www.abc27.com/news/
local/york/u-s-doj-continues-investigating-palmer-york-co-prison-death-despite
-grand-jury-findings/.

34. J. Smith, "Justice Department slams Cumberland jail over suicides, orders
immediate corrective steps," *Vineland Daily Journal*, January 15, 2021, https://www
.thedailyjournal.com/story/news/2021/01/15/nj-cumberland-jail-suicides-federal
-civil-rights-violations-opiate-treatment-lawsuit/4175278001/.

35. L. Crimaldi, "Biden administration terminates ICE contract with Bristol
sheriff Thomas Hodgson," *Boston Globe*, May 21, 2021, https://www.bostonglobe
.com/2021/05/20/metro/biden-administration-terminates-ice-contract-bristol-sheriff
-thomas-hodgson/.

36. Office of Public Affairs, "Former Rapides Parish correctional officer sentenced
for violating civil rights of three inmates," Department of Justice, May 17, 2021,
https://www.justice.gov/opa/pr/former-rapides-parish-correctional-officer-sentenced
-violating-civil-rights-three-inmates.

37. U.S. Department of Justice, Civil Rights Division, "Notice regarding investigation
of Alameda County, John George Psychiatric Hospital, and Santa Rita Jail," April 22,
2021.

38. L. Fowler, "WA state Senate passes bill to ban private, for-profit prisons," KNKX,
March 30, 2021, https://www.knkx.org/politics/2021-03-30/wa-state-senate-passes
-bill-to-ban-private-for-profit-prisons.

39. K. Carey, "County prison helps more than 40 inmates kick substance abuse," *Daily Times*, January 13, 2021, https://www.delcotimes.com/2021/01/12/county -prison-helps-more-than-40-inmates-kick-substance-abuse/.

40. O. Paschal & E. Brown, "How Alabama organizers blocked Gov. Ivey's Prison lease plan," *Facing South*, June 17, 2021, https://www.facingsouth.org/2021/06/ how-alabama-organizers-blocked-gov-iveys-prison-lease-plan; M. Simon, "Toxic Alabama private prison deal falling apart with Barclays exit," *Forbes*, April 21, 2021, https://www.forbes.com/sites/morgansimon/2021/04/21/toxic-alabama-private -prison-deal-falling-apart-with-barclays-exit/?sh=4467879952f0.

41. J. Aere, "County Board set to discuss outsourcing proposal for jail health care," KPBS, August 3, 2020, https://www.kpbs.org/news/2020/aug/03/county-board-set -discuss-outsourcing-proposal-jail/.

42. E. Kaplan, "Jail health care provider terminates contract," *Albuquerque Journal*, April 26, 2021, https://www.abqjournal.com/2383953/jail-health-care-provider -terminates-contract.html.

43. Kaplan, "Jail health care provider terminates contract."

44. R. Treisman, "Maryland to probe cases handled by ex-medical examiner who testified in Chauvin trial," NPR, April 24, 2021, https://www.npr .org/2021/04/24/990536193/maryland-to-probe-cases-handled-by-ex-medical -examiner-who-testified-in-chauvin-.

45. M. Holcombe & C. Mossburg, "Los Angeles coroner orders inquest in Andres Guardado's death," CNN, November 11, 2020, https://www.msn.com/en-us/news/ crime/los-angeles-coroner-orders-inquest-in-andres-guardados-death-the-first-in -3-decades/ar-BB1aTWnK.

46. C. Vanderveen, "PRONE: Facedown and handcuffed is no way to die," 9News, November 9, 2020, https://www.9news.com/article/news/investigations/prone -restraint-police-brutality-cases/73-18ad62df-b66a-45c9-af93-53b15afc5b7c; A. Lagoe & S. Eckert, "KARE 11 Investigates: Prone restraint banned in MN jails and prisons," KARE 11, June 30, 2021, https://www.kare11.com/article/news/ investigations/prone-restraint-banned-in-mn-jails-and-prisons/89-f9314130-f9db -4cfb-b3de-15c92cda6cbf.

CHAPTER 9

1. K. Vlamis, "Baltimore will no longer prosecute for drug possession, prostitution, or other low-level crimes after pandemic experiment 'success,'" Yahoo News, March

27, 2021, https://www.yahoo.com/news/baltimore-no-longer-prosecute-drug
-024836435.html.

2. C. Wolfson, "Allegheny County wants to cut its jail capacity, but advocates
see deeper problems," Public Source, July 29, 2021, https://www.publicsource.org/
allegheny-county-wants-to-cut-its-jail-capacity-but-advocates-see-deeper-problems/.

3. E. Kaplan, "Jail health care provider terminates contract," *Albuquerque Journal*,
April 25, 2021, https://www.abqjournal.com/2383953/jail-health-care-provider
-terminates-contract.html.

4. K. Lyons, "DOC emails show officials were aware of prison health care problems
years before taking over from UConn," *CT Mirror*, November 13, 2020, https://
ctmirror.org/2020/11/13/doc-emails-show-officials-were-aware-of-prison-health
-care-problems-years-before-taking-over-from-uconn/.

5. Duke University Research Funding, Jail Administration for New Sheriffs,
deadline August 25, 2019.

6. W. Culverwell & K. Kraemer, "Benton sheriff refuses to commission jail officers
after takeover. Kennewick cops called in," *Tri-City Herald*, December 12, 2019,
https://www.tri-cityherald.com/news/local/article236747228.html.

7. D. Demwalt, "DA: Oklahoma County Jail Trust's 'incompetent administration'
made jail dangerous," *Oklahoman*, March 28, 2021, https://www.oklahoman.com/
story/news/2021/03/28/oklahoma-county-jail-trust-hostage-inmate/7037050002/.

8. Associated Press, "Virginia agency wants to shut down troubled regional jail,"
AP News, April 27, 2021, https://apnews.com/article/virginia-57382585da87625
f029580d08d5e22da.

9. J. Wilkie, "Proposed legislation would let sheriffs challenge state findings in
jail inspections," *Carolina Public Press*, April 16, 2021, https://carolinapublicpress
.org/44333/proposed-legislation-would-let-sheriffs-challenge-state-findings-in-jail
-investigations/.

10. Editorial Board, "Dragging state prisons into the 21st century," *Boston Globe*,
March 22, 2021, https://www.bostonglobe.com/2021/03/22/opinion/dragging-state
-prisons-into-21st-century/.

11. N. Parker, "Georgia legislators seek scrutiny of jail deaths as new case emerges,"
Reuters, December 30, 2020, https://www.reuters.com/article/us-usa-jails-chatham
-idUSKBN2941EQ.

12. N. Parker, "Georgia legislators, citing Reuters report, want every jail death
investigated," Reuters, January 25, 2021, https://www.reuters.com/article/us-usa-jails
-hearing-idUSKBN29U2B7; 11Alive Staff, "Cobb County Sheriff's Office will no

longer investigate jail deaths," 11Alive, January 26, 2021, https://www.11alive.com/
article/news/local/cobb-county-sheriffs-office-no-longer-investigating-detainee
-deaths/85-d00c2832-3daa-4ce9-a82e-23d7591a8e6c.

13. B. Stahl, "KARE 11 Investigates: Sweeping reforms proposed to protect jail
inmates," KARE 11, February 22, 2021, https://www.kare11.com/video/news/
investigations/kare-11-investigates-sweeping-reforms-proposed-to-protect-jail
-inmates/89-4a14bbac-d53f-43ab-8aa3-8ca169c843f4.

14. M. Weir & J. Pierce, "What's going on with the Santa Cruz County Jail?" *Good
Times*, December 8, 2020, https://goodtimes.sc/cover-stories/santa-cruz-county-jail/.

15. L. So, "West Virginia lawmakers push jail reform in response to Reuters data on
inmate deaths," KFGO, December 17, 2020. https://www.reuters.com/article/us-usa
-jails-westvirginia-idUSKBN28R36Z.

16. P. Smith, "6 key reforms in the massive criminal justice bill Illinois lawmakers
passed last week," WBEZ, January 20, 2021, https://www.wbez.org/stories/6-key
-reforms-in-the-massive-criminal-justice-bill-illinois-lawmakers-passed-last
-week/5f526342-9f19-40e6-8563-d8e0bbfe1138.

17. T. Closson, "New York will end long-term solitary confinement in prisons
and jails," *New York Times*, April 1, 2021, https://www.nytimes.com/2021/04/01/
nyregion/solitary-confinement-restricted.html.

18. D. Telvock, "Erie County Sheriff's Office addresses state allegations for first
time," WIVB, May 6, 2021, https://www.wivb.com/news/investigates/erie-county
-sheriffs-office-addresses-state-allegations-for-first-time/.

19. L. O'Conner, "Detaining people who can't afford bail is unconstitutional,
California high court rules," *Huffington Post*, March 25, 2021, https://www.huffpost
.com/entry/california-court-bail-unconstitutional_n_605d03dcc5b67593e056fbc9.

CONCLUSION

1. J. McDonald & K. Davis, "Woman left alone to die after striking her head in jail,
independent review finds," *San Diego Union-Tribune*, February 7, 2021, https://www
.sandiegouniontribune.com/news/watchdog/story/2021-02-07/woman-left-alone-to
-die-after-striking-her-head-while-collapsing-in-jail-independent-review-finds.

2. S. Pascoe, "State auditor to investigate deaths at San Diego County jails," *San
Diego Union-Tribune*, July 1, 2021, https://www.sandiegouniontribune.com/news/
public-safety/story/2021-07-01/state-legislators-consider-audit-of-san-diego-county
-sheriffs-department.

3. G. Jones-Wright, "Opinion: San Diego County's DA must prosecute the sheriff's deputies for their role in jailhouse deaths," *San Diego Union-Tribune*, July 12, 2021, https://www.sandiegouniontribune.com/community-voices-project/story/2021-07 -12/opinion-san-diego-jail-deaths-bill-gore-summer-stephan.

Bibliography

"$3 M lawsuit filed against Grainger County Sheriff's Office in connection to inmate death." WVLT8, August 5, 2020. https://www.wvlt.tv/2020/08/05/3m-lawsuit-filed -against-grainger-county-sheriffs-office-in-connection-to-inmates-death/.

"$10 million settlement approved in death of inmate at South Carolina jail." NBC 10 Philadelphia, May 26, 2021. https://www.nbcphiladelphia.com/news/national -international/10-million-settlement-approved-in-death-of-inmate-at-south -carolina-jail/2827156/.

11Alive Staff. "Cobb County Sheriff's Office will no longer investigate jail deaths." 11Alive, January 26, 2021. https://www.11alive.com/article/news/local/cobb -county-sheriffs-office-no-longer-investigating-detainee-deaths/85-d00c2832-3daa -4ce9-a82e-23d7591a8e6c.

16 News Now. "Ruling comes in St. Joseph County Jail inmate death." WNDU, November 2, 2020. https://www.wndu.com/2020/11/02/ruling-comes-in-st-joseph -county-jail-inmate-death/.

Abusaid, S. "Rockdale inmate dies of apparent suicide, officials say; GBI investigating." *Atlanta Journal-Constitution*, August 14, 2020. https://www.ajc.com/ news/rockdale-inmate-dies-of-apparent-suicide-officials-say-gbi-investigating/ DVAD7O3UNRECJCFUVMF2S6MLNY/.

ACLU of Southern California. "ACLU report cites chaplains and other civilian witnesses to pervasive abuse of inmates by deputies at the L.A. County jails." September 28, 2011. https://www.aclusocal.org/en/news/aclu-report-cites -chaplains-and-other-civilian-witnesses-pervasive-abuse-inmates-deputies-la.

Acosta, S., & B. Spicer. "BCSO deputy arrested in connection with inmate's suicide attempt at Bexar County Jail." KSAT, September 30, 2020. https://www.ksat.com/news/local/2020/09/30/bcso-deputy-arrested-in-connection-with-inmates-suicide-attempt-at-bexar-county-jail/.

Addison, B. "Man who died in Collin County jail was having 'mental health crisis,' attorney says." *Dallas Morning News*, March 17, 2021. https://www.dallasnews.com/news/2021/03/17/man-who-died-in-collin-county-jail-was-having-mental-health-crisis-attorney-says/.

Adger, P. "Court documents outline investigation into death at Oklahoma County Jail." KOCO, January 11, 2021. https://www.koco.com/article/court-documents-outline-investigation-into-death-at-oklahoma-county-jail-uncover-problems-at-jail/35182691.

Advocates for Human Potential website for Justice Department RSAT Program. https://www.rsat-tta.com//Home.

Aere, J. "County Board set to discuss outsourcing proposal for jail health care." KPBS, August 3, 2020. https://www.kpbs.org/news/2020/aug/03/county-board-set-discuss-outsourcing-proposal-jail/.

Aguilar, A. "WTOC Investigates: Wrongful death lawsuit filed after inmate dies in Appling Co. Jail." WTOC, August 27, 2020. https://www.wtoc.com/2020/08/27/wtoc-investigates-wrongful-death-lawsuit-filed-after-inmate-dies-appling-co-jail/.

Ahmadi, J., et al. "The effectiveness of different singly administered high doses of buprenorphine in reducing suicidal ideation in acutely depressed people with co-morbid opiate dependence: a randomized, double-blind, clinical trial." *Trials* 19, no. 1 (August 29, 2018): 416.

Allard, S. "Death at Cuyahoga County jail, second in two months, was trans woman." *Cleveland Scene*, September 3, 2020. https://www.clevescene.com/scene-and-heard/archives/2020/09/03/death-at-cuyahoga-county-jail-second-in-two-months-was-trans-woman-lea-daye.

Allen, C. "MDC officers charged in death of inmate more than two years later." KRQE, May 20, 2021. https://www.krqe.com/news/crime/two-mdc-officers-charged-in-death-of-inmate-more-than-two-years-later/.

Allen, J. "Lawsuit: Naples Jail Center inmate did not receive proper treatment for diabetes before death." *Naples Daily News*, November 12, 2020. https://www.msn.com/en-us/news/crime/lawsuit-naples-jail-center-inmate-did-not-receive-proper-treatment-for-diabetes-before-death/ar-BB1aX2w5.

Alves, I. "Father files wrongful death lawsuit on behalf of his late daughter." *Albuquerque Journal*, March 1, 2021. https://www.abqjournal.com/2364809/father-files-wrongful-death-lawsuit-on-behalf-of-his-late-daughter-ex-carmela-devargas-allegedly-became-ill-and-died-while-incarcerated-in-the-santa-fe-county-jail.html.

Anderson, G. "Lake County District Attorney: 'No wrongdoings.'" *Press Democrat*, October 28, 2015. https://www.pressdemocrat.com/article/news/lake-county-district-attorney-no-wrongdoings-in-santa-rosa-womans-jail/.

Anderson, K. "Vilas County annual jail inspection report finds two violations." WXPR, March 1, 2021. https://www.wxpr.org/news/2021-03-01/vilas-county-annual-jail-inspection-report-finds-two-violations.

Anderson, T. W. "Duchesne County nurse charged with negligent homicide nine months after 21-year-old inmate died from dehydration." *Salt Lake Tribune*, September 25, 2017. https://www.sltrib.com/news/politics/2017/09/25/duchesne-county-nurse-charged-with-negligent-homicide-nine-months-after-21-year-old-inmate-died-from-dehydration/.

Anuta, J. "City slaps jail staffers with charges over death of Layleen Polanco." *Politico*, June 26, 2020. https://www.politico.com/states/new-york/city-hall/story/2020/06/26/city-slaps-jail-staffers-with-charges-over-death-of-layleen-polanco-1295312.

Appleman, L. "Cashing in on convicts: Privatization, punishment, and the people." *Utah Law Review* 2018, no. 3 (2018): 579–637.

"Arlington NAACP calls for independent investigation into inmate death." ARLnow.com, October 5, 2020. https://www.arlnow.com/2020/10/05/arlington-naacp-calls-for-investigation-into-inmate-death/.

Armus, T. "'Don't be a sheep': Sheriffs rebel against new statewide mask mandates." *Washington Post*, June 26, 2020. https://www.washingtonpost.com/nation/2020/06/26/sheriffs-mask-covid/.

Arnold, D., W. Dobbie, & C. Yang. "Racial bias in bail decisions." *Quarterly Journal of Economics* 133, no. 4 (2018): 1885–932.

Arvidson, M. "Time to bail on cash bail?" Council of State Courts, May 2, 2019, https://knowledgecenter.csg.org/kc/content/time-bail-cash-bail-growing-number-states-are-scrutinizing-current-systems-and-exploring.

Associated Press. "Family of Black man who died in Missouri jail offered $2.5 million." AP News, April 29, 2021. https://apnews.com/article/tennessee-michael-brown-crime-lawsuits-23ef061df841215cf0f85bbeb9eb7a76.

Associated Press. "Family of man who died by suicide in jail awarded $156k." AP News, January 15, 2021. https://apnews.com/article/billings-montana -88b9676d3c1b16e649fb93db56cf1dc8.

Associated Press. "Texas law fails to slow jail suicides." Progressive Farmer, December 22, 2019. https://www.dtnpf.com/agriculture/web/ag/news/world -policy/article/2019/12/22/texas-law-fails-slow-jail-suicides.

Associated Press. "Virginia agency wants to shut down troubled regional jail." AP News, April 27, 2021. https://apnews.com/article/virginia-57382585da87625f 029580d08d5e22da.

Astolfi, C., & A. Ferrise. "What's the story behind how the Cuyahoga County jail became one of the worst in the nation?" Cleveland.com, November 23, 2018. https://www.cleveland.com/metro/2018/11/whats-the-story-behind-how-the -cuyahoga-county-jail-became-one-of-the-worst-in-the-nation-a-drive-for-money -a-clevelandcom-investigation-finds.html.

Baker, M., et al. "Three words. 70 Cases. The Tragic History of 'I Can't Breathe.'" *New York Times*, June 29, 2020. https://www.nytimes.com/interactive/2020/06/28/us/i -cant-breathe-police-arrest.html.

Balsamo, M. "Justice Department: Virginia jail officials must improve medical treatment for inmates." Associated Press, August 6, 2020. https://wjla.com/news/ local/virginia-jail-medical-treatment-inmates-justice-department.

Bartelme, T. "SC Sheriffs earn 2019 newsmaker of the year for scandalous behavior." *Post and Courier*, updated September 14, 2020. https://www.postandcourier.com/ news/sc-sheriffs-earn-2019-newsmaker-of-the-year-for-scandalous-behavior/ article_3287a316-1847-11ea-bef3-673772ca16df.html.

Basye, L., & A. Pierrotti. "'How can somebody investigate themselves?' Ga. lawmaker drafts bill for jail death investigation oversight." 11Alive, October 28, 2020. https:// www.11alive.com/article/news/investigations/the-reveal/ga-lawmaker-plans-to -create-jail-death-oversight/85-bd90936f-fdf7-4da6-8909-adbf458fadc5.

Basye, L., & A. Pierrotti. "'I can't breathe,' Man dies in custody after hours of begging for help." 11Alive, August 18, 2020. https://www.11alive.com/article/news/ investigations/the-reveal/cobb-co-jail-death-of-kevil-wingo/85-846db820-3ffc -4fd9-957a-7c757bda38a2.

Basye, L., & A. Pierrotti. "Judge orders Cobb County sheriff to turn over files on jail deaths." 11Alive, October 15, 2020. https://www.11alive.com/article/news/ investigations/the-reveal/judge-orders-cobb-sheriff-to-turn-over-documents/85 -b647208d-b7f7-42a2-b198-183dc755645d.

Battaglia, D. "Forsyth County detention officer received merit-based raise after inmate's death." *News & Observer*, July 17, 2020. https://www.newsobserver.com/news/state/north-carolina/article244275137.html.

Beauge, J. "Inadequate medical care was factor in Lycoming prison inmate's death, suit claims." PennLive, September 30, 2020. https://www.pennlive.com/news/2020/09/inadequate-medical-care-was-factor-in-lycoming-prison-inmates-death-suit-claims.html.

Beck, A., et al. "PREA data collection activities, 2015." Bureau of Justice Statistics, June 2015, NCJ 248824. https://bjs.ojp.gov/content/pub/pdf/pdca15.pdf.

Beedle, H. "Former El Paso County Sheriff's deputy loses POST certification under new law." *Colorado Springs Indy*, January 6, 2021. https://www.csindy.com/news/local/former-el-paso-county-sheriff-s-deputy-loses-post-certification-under-new-law/article_7528c808-4ed8-11eb-94d9-df42008c2e58.html.

Benchaabane, N. "St. Louis County Council backs call for outside investigation." *Post-Dispatch*, January 26, 2021. https://www.stltoday.com/news/local/govt-and-politics/st-louis-county-council-backs-call-for-outside-investigation-of-jail/article_3de86d07-939e-5dc7-a91e-d1c3ceeb4894.html.

Berg, K. "'I can't breathe': Wrongful death lawsuit filed against Lansing Police Department officers." *Lansing State Journal*, October 27, 2020. https://www.lansingstatejournal.com/story/news/2020/10/28/lansing-police-officers-jail-wrongful-death-lawsuit-back-work/3745749001/.

Bernstein, M. "Record $10 million judgment awarded in Washington County jail heroin withdrawal death." *Oregonian*, December 7, 2018. https://www.oregonlive.com/crime/2018/12/record-10-million-judgement-awarded-against-corizon-health-in-death-of-washington-county-jail-inmate.html.

Betancourt, S. "Healy: Civil rights of ICE detainees violated." *CommonWealth*, December 15, 2020. https://commonwealthmagazine.org/immigration/healey-civil-rights-of-ice-detainees-violated/.

Biggs, J. "Video of woman's death at Greensboro jail to be released to her family to view." *News & Record*, August 25, 2020. https://greensboro.com/news/local_news/video-of-womans-death-at-greensboro-jail-to-be-released-to-her-family-to-view/article_3e9bd1e6-e6ea-11ea-8a38-f7010798b6fe.html.

Binion, A. "Investigation: Kitsap jail inmate who died improperly subdued in restraint chair." *Kitsap Sun*, December 22, 2020. https://www.kitsapsun.com/story/news/2020/12/22/investigation-kitsap-jail-inmate-who-died-improperly-subdued-restraint-chair/3967083001/.

Binion, A. "Kitsap jail inmate restrained by officers died of homicide from 'restraint asphyxia.'" *Kitsap Sun*, September 10, 2020. https://www.kitsapsun .com/story/news/2020/09/10/kitsap-jail-inmate-restrained-officers-died -homicide/3460421001/.

Binion, A. "No charges for Kitsap jail officers in death of mentally ill murder suspect." *Kitsap Sun*, June 21, 2021. https://www.kitsapsun.com/story/ news/2021/06/21/no-charges-kitsap-jail-officers-death-mentally-ill-murder -suspect/7749538002/.

Binion, A. "Sheriff: 'Homicide' ruling in inmate's death needs context." *Kitsap Sun*, September 11, 2020. https://www.kitsapsun.com/story/news/2020/09/11/sheriff -homicide-ruling-kitsap-inmates-death-needs-context/3473165001/.

Blackmon, D. *Slavery by Another Name: The Re-Enslavement of Black Americans from the Civil War to World War II*. New York: Anchor Books, 2009.

Blau, M. "For sheriffs, healthcare for inmates can be a burden." *Atlanta*, October 12, 2019. https://www.atlantamagazine.com/great-reads/for-sheriffs-healthcare -for-inmates-can-be-a-burden-for-one-doctor-it-has-been-the-opportunity-of-a- lifetime/.

Blume, J. H., & R. K. Helm. "The unexonerated: Factually innocent defendants who plead guilty." *Cornell Law Review* 100, no. 1 (2014): 157–92.

Blume, P. "DOC finds numerous jail violations in death of inmates in Bemidji, Minnesota." Fox 9, May 20, 2020. https://www.fox9.com/news/doc-finds -numerous-jail-violations-in-death-of-inmate-in-bemidji-minnesota.

Boldrey, R. "Man charged with arson in Kalamazoo hospital fire found dead in county jail." MLive, December 24, 2020. https://www.mlive.com/news/ kalamazoo/2020/12/man-charged-with-arson-in-kalamazoo-hospital-fire-found -dead-in-county-jail.html.

Borrelli, A. "How Broome County responded to a negligence lawsuit after man died in jail." *Binghamton Press & Sun-Bulletin*, October 24, 2020. https://www.msn .com/en-us/news/crime/how-broome-county-responded-to-a-negligence-lawsuit -after-man-died-in-jail/ar-BB1alTwC.

Boyle, J. "Buncombe County reaches $2M settlement in jail death." *Asheville Citizen Times*, December 18, 2019. https://www.citizen-times.com/story/ news/local/2019/12/18/buncombe-county-reaches-2-m-settlement-jail -death/2678255001/.

Bradbury, B. "Allegheny County jail spends $237K on 4,600 suicide prevention blankets." *Pittsburgh Post-Gazette*, May 12, 2019. https://www.post-gazette

.com/news/crime-courts/2019/05/13/Allegheny-County-Jail-Pittsburgh-suicide -prevention-thick-heavy-blankets-inmates/stories/201905100133.

Brand-Williams, O. "Fieger alleges coverup in woman's Harper Woods jail death." *Detroit News*, August 20, 2020. https://www.detroitnews.com/story/news/local/ wayne-county/2020/08/20/fieger-alleges-coverup-womans-harper-woods-jail -death/5616907002/.

Branigin, A. "New report on Layleen Xtravaganza Polanco's death highlights the cruelty of NYC jails' policies toward trans people." *Root*, June 25, 2020. https:// www.theroot.com/new-report-on-layleen-xtravaganza-polancos-death-highli -1844162814.

Brannon, M. "Dying inside." *Redding Record Searchlight*, June 24, 2020. https:// www.redding.com/in-depth/news/local/2020/06/24/shasta-county-jail-california -inmate-deaths-mental-health-services/5281201002/.

Brannon, M. "Man who spent an hour in custody is 1 of 5 deaths reported by Shasta County Jail in 2021." *Redding Record Searchlight*, May 3, 2021. https://www .redding.com/story/news/local/2021/05/03/shasta-county-jail-investigating-fifth -death-2021-one-hour-custody/7307791002/.

Brannon, M. "With jail deaths on the rise, California counties look to improve." *Redding Record Searchlight*, October 7, 2020. https://www.redding.com/in-depth/ news/local/2020/10/07/shasta-county-jail-inmate-deaths-mental-health-california -reform-ideas/5621258002/.

Brasch, B. "Lawmakers tour crowded Fulton jail, hear about need for resources." *Atlanta Journal-Constitution*, December 10, 2019. https://www.ajc.com/news/ local/lawmakers-tour-crowded-fulton-jail-hear-about-need-for-resources/ Tyl0QpBBnCax8MrhmEoWFN/.

Brauer, A. "Data shows Marion County Jail's death rate is 2 to 3 times higher than the national average." WTTV, April 23, 2021, https://cbs4indy.com/news/report -shows-the-marion-county-jails-death-rate-is-2-to-3-times-higher-than-the -national-average/.

Brinkley-Rubinstein, L., et al. "Association of restrictive housing during incarceration with mortality after release." *Journal of American Medical Association* 2, no. 10 (2019).

Bronson, J., et al. "Drug use, dependence, and abuse among state prisoners and jail inmates, 2007–2009." Bureau of Justice Statistics, June 2017, NCJ 250546. https:// bjs.ojp.gov/content/pub/pdf/dudaspji0709.pdf.

Bryson, A. "Third Charlotte County Jail suicide within two months." *Sun Port Charlotte*, December 28, 2020. https://www.yoursun.com/charlotte/third-charlotte -county-jail-suicide-within-two-months/article_cacac566-4863-11eb-8a45 -c7bf22e25633.html.

Bryson, W. C., J. Piel, & S. Thielke. "Associations between parole, probation, arrest, and self-reported suicide attempts." *Community Mental Health Journal* 57, no 4 (May 2021): 727–35.

Buntin, A., et al. "The impact of policy changes on heroin and nonmedical prescription opioid use among an incarcerated population in Kentucky, 2008– 2016." *Criminal Justice Policy Review* 31, no. 5 (March 2019): 746–62.

Byers, C. "'It's heinous and unforgivable.'" KSDK, August 13, 2020. https://www.ksdk .com/article/news/local/family-of-man-who-died-at-st-francois-county-jail-seek -reform/63-bfd710b9-f160-4fc7-89d9-f8406c8b2fd2.

Byers, C. "Mother of man whose vomit resembled motor oil in jail before he died files lawsuit against St Louis County." KSDK, June 16, 2020. https://www.ksdk .com/article/news/local/st-louis-county-inmate-death-vomit-motor-oil-lawsuit/63 -76b40054-ecdc-43b1-a5f1-770928fd3916.

Cain, J. "Fears of more COVID-19 spread as thousands of L.A. County inmates await transfer to state prisons." *Los Angeles Daily News*, December 2, 2020. https://www .dailynews.com/2020/12/02/fears-of-more-covid-19-spread-as-thousands-of-l-a -county-inmates-await-transfer-to-state-prisons/.

Canicosa, J. "In five years, 786 people died in Louisiana's jails and prisons, a new report finds." *Louisiana Illuminator*, June 2, 2021. https://lailluminator .com/2021/06/02/in-five-years-786-people-died-in-louisianas-jails-and-prisons-a- new-report-finds/.

Carey, K. "County prison helps more than 40 inmates kick substance abuse." *Daily Times*, January 13, 2021. https://www.delcotimes.com/2021/01/12/county-prison -helps-more-than-40-inmates-kick-substance-abuse/.

Carlisle, M. & J. Bates. "With over 275,000 infections and 700 deaths, COVID-19 has devastated the U.S. prison and jail population." *Time*, December 28, 2020. https:// www.msn.com/en-us/news/crime/with-over-275000-infections-and-1700-deaths -covid-19-has-devastated-the-us-prison-and-jail-population/ar-BB1ciyY1.

Carson, A. "Mortality in local jails, 2000–2018—statistical tables." Bureau of Justice Statistics, April 2021, NCJ 256002. https://bjs.ojp.gov/library/publications/ mortality-local-jails-2000-2018-statistical-tables.

CBSLA Staff. "LA County DA Gascon to eliminate cash bail, will re-sentence death penalty inmates." KCAL, December 8, 2020. https://losangeles.cbslocal .com/2020/12/08/la-county-da-gascon-cash-bail-death-penalty/.

Chammah, M. "They went to jail. Then they say they were strapped to a chair for days." Marshall Project, February 7, 2020. https://www.themarshallproject .org/2020/02/07/they-went-to-jail-then-they-say-they-were-strapped-to-a-chair -for-days.

Chammah, M. "Your local jail may be a house of horrors." Marshall Project, July 29, 2020. https://www.themarshallproject.org/2020/07/29/your-local-jail-may-be-a- house-of-horrors.

Cholodofsky, R. "Westmoreland inmates reach record detox level in February." Trib Total Media, March 18, 2019. https://triblive.com/local/westmoreland/ westmoreland-inmates-reach-record-detox-level-in-february/.

Churchwell, B. "Federal lawsuit filed against Nueces County Jail in connection with 2018 inmate death." KIIITV.com, December 3, 2020. https://www.kiiitv.com/ article/news/local/federal-lawsuit-filed-against-nueces-county-jail-in-connection -with-2018-inmate-death/503-118c462b-07a2-4902-a06b-22d9272a335f.

Ciavaglia, J. "Bucks County confirms opiate detox death of county prisoner." Buck County Courier Times, December 20, 2018. https://journalismjo.blogspot .com/2019/01/bucks-county-confirms-opiate-detox.html.

Ciavaglia, J. "DA: Pa. jail followed protocol in pepper spraying of mentally ill inmate." Buck County Courier Times, July 9, 2020. https://www.corrections1 .com/investigations/articles/da-pa-jail-followed-protocol-in-pepper-spraying-of -mentally-ill-inmate-xYeqdgeH2DKGp9WU/.

City News Service. "Autopsy: Inmate died of accidental drug overdose." Fox5, January 12, 2021. https://fox5sandiego.com/news/local-news/autopsy-inmate-died -of-accidental-drug-overdose/.

City News Service. "Family of man who committed suicide at Vista Jail files wrongful death lawsuit." Times of San Diego, August 10, 2021. https://timesofsandiego .com/crime/2021/08/10/family-of-man-who-committed-suicide-at-vista-jail-files -wrongful-death-lawsuit/.

City News Service. "Jail inmate who died in January suffered from Asphysiation, with Meth use a factor." Times of San Diego, March 25, 2021. https:// timesofsandiego.com/crime/2021/03/25/jail-inmate-who-died-in-january-suffered -from-asphyxiation-with-meth-use-a-factor/.

City News Service. "Woman settles for $8.5 million in Pasadena attempted jail suicide." NBC Southern California, July 21, 2020. https://www.nbclosangeles.com/news/local/pasadena-jail-suicide-settlement/2399912/.

Claridge, E. "Man, 60, is second Tarrant County jail inmate to die this week and 12th this year." *Fort Worth Star-Telegram*, November 11, 2020. https://www.star-telegram.com/news/local/crime/article247136404.html.

Clark, C. "We cannot become numb to San Diego jail deaths." *San Diego Union-Tribune*, February 11, 2021. https://www.sandiegouniontribune.com/columnists/story/2021-02-11/column-we-cannot-become-numb-to-san-diego-jail-deaths-we-have-to-demand-better.

Closson, T. "New York will end long-term solitary confinement in prisons and jails." *New York Times*, April 1, 2021. https://www.nytimes.com/2021/04/01/nyregion/solitary-confinement-restricted.html.

Closson, T., & J. Bromwich. "'A ticking time bomb': City jails are crowded again, stoking Covid fears." *New York Times*, March 10, 2021. https://www.nytimes.com/2021/03/10/nyregion/nyc-jail-covid.html.

Cohen, L. "Corrections officer allegedly smuggled drugs, cell phones into Atlantic County jail." *Breaking AC*, October 16, 2020. https://breakingac.com/2020/10/corrections-officer-allegedly-smuggled-drugs-cell-phones-into-atlantic-county-jail/.

Cohen, S., & N. Eckert. "AP investigation: Many U.S. jails fail to stop inmate suicides." AP News, June 18, 2019. https://apnews.com/article/ap-top-news-ut-state-wire-ia-state-wire-ca-state-wire-us-news-5a61d556a0a14251bafbeff1c26d5f15.

Cohen, S., & N. Eckert. "Pennsylvania inmate threatened to choke herself." *Morning Call*, June 18, 2019. https://www.mcall.com/news/pennsylvania/mc-nws-pa-jail-suicide-20190618-gcjwi77erzdabecu4757eendz4-story.html.

Coll, S. "The jail health care crisis." *New Yorker*, February 25, 2019. https://www.newyorker.com/magazine/2019/03/04/the-jail-health-care-crisis.

Columbia Legal Services. "Gone but not forgotten." May 2019. https://columbialegal.org/wp-content/uploads/2019/05/Gone-But-Not-Forgotten-May2019.pdf.

Congedo, M. "Friend of inmates who died in the CCDC speaks out." WTOC, September 13, 2020. https://www.wtoc.com/2020/09/13/friend-inmate-who-died-ccdc-says-he-has-received-conflicting-stories-cause-death/.

Conrad, E. "Investigates: Former Washington Co. Jail administrator alleges jail unsafe, files suit." KJRH, November 13, 2020. https://www.kjrh.com/news/local

-news/investigates-former-washington-co-jail-administrator-files-lawsuit-alleges
-jail-unsafe.

CoreCivic. "CoreCivic reports first quarter 2019 financial results." Global
News Wire, May 8, 2019. https://www.globenewswire.com/news
-release/2019/05/08/1819761/0/en/CoreCivic-Reports-First-Quarter-2019
-Financial-Results.html.

Corona, M. "General election 2018 guide: Get to know the Washoe County
sheriff race candidates." *Reno Gazette-Journal*, October 3, 2018. https://www
.rgj.com/story/news/2018/10/03/candidates-washoe-sheriff-general-election
-2018/1454587002/.

Crimaldi, L. "Biden administration terminates ICE contract with Bristol sheriff
Thomas Hodgson." *Boston Globe*, May 21, 2021. https://www.bostonglobe
.com/2021/05/20/metro/biden-administration-terminates-ice-contract-bristol
-sheriff-thomas-hodgson/.

Criminal Justice System Assessment, Cuyahoga County, Criminal Justice Center
Master Plan. August 7, 2019. Presentation PowerPoints. PMC & DLR Group.

Critchfield, H. "North Carolina jail suicides reached record high last year, amid
calls for reform." North Carolina Health News, June 4, 2020. https://www
.northcarolinahealthnews.org/2020/06/04/north-carolina-jail-suicides-reached
-record-high-last-year-amid-calls-for-reform/.

Culverwell, W., & K. Kraemer. "Benton sheriff refuses to commission jail officers
after takeover. Kennewick cops called in." *Tri-City Herald*, December 12, 2019,
https://www.tri-cityherald.com/news/local/article236747228.html.

Damon, A. "Death behind bars: Washoe County Jail inmates are dying from suicide,
accidents and homicides." *Reno Gazette-Journal*, April 5, 2017, updated December
8, 2020. https://www.rgj.com/story/news/2017/04/05/washoe-county-jail-inmates
-dying-suicide-accidents-and-homicide/98972810/.

Damon, A. "Washoe County Jail audit finds serious health care deficiencies in wake
of inmate deaths." *Reno Gazette-Journal*, April 5, 2017. https://www.rgj.com/story/
news/2017/04/05/washoe-county-jail-audit-finds-serious-health-care-deficiencies
-wake-inmate-deaths/99545012/.

Davis, K. "$3M verdict upheld in jail death." *San Diego Union-Tribune*, January
22, 2015. https://www.sandiegouniontribune.com/sdut-sisson-verdict-jail-death
-motion-denied-2015jan22-story.html.

Davis, K., & J. McDonald. "Investigators said San Diego deputy neglected to check
inmate found dead in 2020." *San Diego Union-Tribune*, July 12, 2021. https://www

.sandiegouniontribune.com/news/watchdog/story/2021-07-12/investigators-said
-san-diego-deputy-neglected-to-check-inmate-found-dead-in-2020.

Davis, K., & J. McDonald. "Lapses in treatment, medical care spell horrific ends for
mentally ill inmates." *San Diego Union-Tribune*, September 23, 2019. https://www
.sandiegouniontribune.com/news/watchdog/story/2019-09-21/lapses-in-treatment
-medical-care-spell-horrific-ends-for-mentally-ill-inmates.

Davis, K., & J. McDonald. "Some jail deaths are excluded from annual reports." *San
Diego Union-Tribune*, September 20, 2019. https://www.sandiegouniontribune
.com/news/watchdog/story/2019-09-19/dying-behind-bars-some-jail-deaths
-excluded-from-reports.

Dayton, K. "Death behind bars: In Hawaii, the death of a prisoner is often a
closely held secret." *Honolulu Civil Beat*, March 3, 2021. https://www.civilbeat
.org/2021/03/death-behind-bars-in-hawaii-the-death-of-a-prisoner-is-often-a-
closely-held-secret/.

de Biblana, J., T. Todd, & L. Pope. "Preventing suicide and self-harm in jail." Vera
Institute of Justice, July 2019. https://www.vera.org/downloads/publications/
preventing-suicide-and-self-harm-in-jail.pdf.

DeFelice, M. "Training inadequate for use of restrain chair at Kitsap County Jail."
Kitsap Daily News, January 7, 2021. https://www.kitsapdailynews.com/news/
training-inadequate-for-use-of-restraint-chair-at-kitsap-county-jail/.

Demwalt, D. "DA: Oklahoma County Jail Trust's 'incompetent administration' made
jail dangerous." *Oklahoman*, March 28, 2021, https://www.oklahoman.com/story/
news/2021/03/28/oklahoma-county-jail-trust-hostage-inmate/7037050002/.

Diaz, O. "Charleston County sheriff implements 8 policies to change mental health
response at jail." *Post and Courier*, July 24, 2021. https://www.postandcourier.com/
news/charleston-county-sheriff-implements-8-policies-to-change-mental-health
-response-at-jail/article_0dbeb104-ecd1-11eb-b9f4-cbf1fd730723.html.

Disability Rights California. "Disability Rights California investigation finds San
Diego County Jail suicides far outpace other jail systems." April 25, 2018. https://
www.disabilityrightsca.org/press-release/disability-rights-california-investigation
-finds-san-diego-county-jail-suicides-far.

Disability Rights North Carolina. "Suicide in North Carolina jails, 2019 jail suicide
report." June 2020. https://disabilityrightsnc.org/wp-content/uploads/2020/06/
Report_Suicide-in-NC-Jails_June-2020.pdf.

Disability Rights Oregon. "Grave consequences: How the criminalization of disability leads to deaths in jail." Winter 2021. https://media.heartlandtv.com/documents/DRO-Report-Grave+Consequences-2021-02-08+%28002%29.pdf.

"District attorney finds medical staff 'inadequate' but not criminal in prison death." WBRE/WYOU-TV, October 6, 2020. https://www.pahomepage.com/top-news/district-attorney-finds-medical-staff-inadequate-but-not-criminal-in-prison-death/.

Dixon, K. "Family of man who died in Cobb County jail files lawsuit." *Atlanta Journal-Constitution*, September 10, 2020. https://www.ajc.com/news/atlanta-news/family-of-man-who-died-in-cobb-county-jail-files-lawsuit/NYX3472KDFDEHJFACJPNOGLTGI/.

Dixon, K. "Law firm to review Cobb County jail conditions." *Atlanta Journal-Constitution*, June 14, 2020. https://www.ajc.com/news/local/law-firm-review-cobb-county-jail-conditions/virAJo39jIoZ1SNcBeMrlN/.

Dixon, K. "TV news station sues Cobb sheriff over alleged open records violation." *Atlanta Journal-Constitution*, September 24, 2020. https://www.ajc.com/news/atlanta-news/tv-news-station-sues-cobb-sheriff-over-alleged-open-records-violation/WGTAMA3UTNDUTOUTOBBAXWO67Q/.

Dobruck, J. "Police repeatedly Tased a man and left him on the jail floor." *Long Beach Post*, May 6, 2021. https://lbpost.com/news/taser-death-alan-ramos-jail-long-beach-police-heart-disease.

Donovan, J. "How are coroners and medical examiners different?" How Stuff Works, June 6, 2019. https://science.howstuffworks.com/coroners-medical-examiners.htm.

Duke University Research Funding. "Jail Administration for New Sheriffs." Deadline August 25, 2019.

Dunlop, R. G. "Lawsuit over 2013 Montgomery County jail death settled." Kentucky Center for Investigative Reporting, February 9, 2017. https://kycir.org/2017/02/09/lawsuits-over-2013-montgomery-county-jail-death-settled/.

DuVernay, A. dir. *The 13th*. Los Gatos, CA: Netflix, 2016.

Dys, A. "Lancaster S.C. detention officer arrested in plot to smuggle drugs to inmate." *Herald*, November 14, 2020. https://www.msn.com/en-us/news/crime/lancaster-sc-detention-officer-arrested-in-plot-to-smuggle-drugs-to-inmate-cops-say/ar-BB1b0355.

Eble, J. "Everett Palmer, Jr. was hit twice with stun gun during scuffle with York County Prison guards." WPMT-TV, York County, Pennsylvania, June 19, 2019.

https://www.fox43.com/article/news/local/contests/everett-palmer-jr-was-hit
-twice-with-stun-gun-during-scuffle-with-york-county-prison-guards-autopsy
-report-says/521-2e9b2656-3e35-4daa-a1a3-1625349be9c4.

Editorial Board. "Dragging state prisons into the 21st century." *Boston Globe*, March
22, 2021. https://www.bostonglobe.com/2021/03/22/opinion/dragging-state
-prisons-into-21st-century/.

Edwards, E., et al. "A tale of two countries: Racially targeted arrests in the era of
marijuana reform." ACLU, 2020. https://www.aclu.org/report/tale-two-countries
-racially-targeted-arrests-era-marijuana-reform.

Eisler, P., & J. Szep. "Congress presses DOJ to improve jail reporting system."
Reuters, October 21, 2020. https://www.reuters.com/article/us-usa-jails-doj
-idUSKBN2761L9.

Eisler, P., L. So, J. Szep, & G. Smith. "As more women fill America's jails, medical
tragedies mount." Reuters, December 16, 2020. https://www.reuters.com/
investigates/special-report/usa-jails-women/.

Eisler, P., L. So, J. Szep, G. Smith, & N. Parker. "Dying inside, part 1." Reuter
Investigates, October 16, 2020. https://www.reuters.com/investigates/special
-report/usa-jails-deaths/.

Elattar, H. "OC Jail deaths count highest in 2020 of the last 4 years." *Voice of OC*,
September 24, 2020. https://voiceofoc.org/2020/09/oc-jail-deaths-count-highest-in
-2020-of-the-last-4-years-none-from-covid-19/.

Enfinger, E. "Lawsuit settled over Tuscaloosa jail inmate's 2015 death." *Tuscaloosa
News*, February 17, 2021. https://www.tuscaloosanews.com/story/news/
local/2021/02/18/lawsuit-over-death-phillip-david-anderson-settled/6718767002/.

Farish, A. "Lawsuit filed against Madison Co. Sheriff's Office, jail after 2018 death of
Lanekia Brown." WJTV, Mary 24, 2021. https://www.wjtv.com/news/lawsuit-filed
-against-madison-co-sheriffs-office-jail-after-2018-death-of-lanekia-brown/.

Feldman, J. "Some of the stories behind those involved in jail suicides." Capital News
Service, June 19, 2019. https://apnews.com/257205c688714db2b76783d9c8869c59.

Fennell, N., & M. Prescott. "Risk, not resources: Improving the pretrial release
process in Texas." Lyndon Baines Johnson School of Public Affairs, June 2016.
https://lbj.utexas.edu/sites/default/files/file/Risk,%20Not%20Resources-%20
Improving%20the%20Pretrial%20Release%20Process%20in%20Texas--FINAL.pdf.

Fernandez, L. "Alameda County DA finds no criminal wrongdoing with Fremont man's
suicide in Santa Rita." KTVU, June 22, 2020. https://www.ktvu.com/news/alameda
-county-da-finds-no-criminal-wrongdoing-with-fremont-mans-suicide-in-santa-rita.

Fernandez, L. "Body cam footage in Santa Rita jail undercuts deputies' claims about 20-year-old inmate's death." KTVU, June 29, 2020. https://www.ktvu.com/news/body-cam-footage-in-santa-rita-jail-undercuts-deputies-claims-about-20-year-old-inmates-death.

Fernandez, L. "California auditor: Santa Rita Jail lacks information on inmate mental health, has surplus of $135M." KTVU, March 25, 2021. https://www.ktvu.com/news/california-auditor-santa-rita-jail-doesnt-screen-adequately-for-mental-health-has-excess-of-135m.

Fernandez, L. "Father blames son's fatal drug overdose on Santa Rita jail guards' negligence." KTVU, September 13, 2020. https://www.ktvu.com/news/father-blames-sons-fatal-drug-overdose-on-santa-rita-jail-guards-negligence.

Fernandez, L. "San Francisco jails had no coronavirus deaths, hospitalizations or outbreaks." KTVU, March 17, 2021. https://www.ktvu.com/news/san-francisco-jails-had-no-coronavirus-deaths-hospitalizations-or-outbreaks-sheriff-says.

Fernelius, K. "New D.A. commits to fixing Georgia's 'backdoor to incarceration.'" *The Appeal*, January 11, 2021. https://theappeal.org/politicalreport/athens-georgia-probation-reform/.

Ferrise, A. "As Cuyahoga County Jail inmates died in record numbers, county investigations into the deaths were minimal, records show." Cleveland.com, April 29, 2020. https://www.cleveland.com/metro/2020/04/as-cuyahoga-county-jail-inmates-died-in-record-numbers-county-investigations-into-the-deaths-were-minimal-records-show.html.

Ferrise, A. "Attempted suicides at Cuyahoga County Jail tripled over three-year span." Cleveland.com, February 21, 2019. https://www.cleveland.com/metro/2019/02/attempted-suicides-at-cuyahoga-county-jail-tripled-over-three-year-span.html.

Ferrise, A. "Cuyahoga County Jail inmate accused of beating cellmate to death placed in general population despite history of attacking inmates, court records, sources say." Cleveland.com, November 10, 2020. https://www.cleveland.com/metro/2020/11/cuyahoga-county-jail-inmate-accused-of-beating-cellmate-to-death-placed-in-general-population-despite-history-of-attacking-inmates-court-records-sources-say.html.

Ferrise, A. "Cuyahoga County Jail inmate dies, first death at troubled jail in 14 months." *Cleveland Plain-Dealer*, July 8, 2020, https://www.cleveland.com/metro/2020/07/cuyahoga-county-jail-inmate-dies-first-death-at-troubled-jail-in-14-months.html.

Ferrise, A. "Death of Cuyahoga County Jail inmate subject of criminal investigation." Cleveland.com, November 21, 2018. https://www.cleveland.com/news/erry -2018/11/12db721f324418/death-of-cuyahoga-county-jail.html.

Ferrise, A. "Disgraced ex-Cuyahoga County Jail warden tells FBI, Ohio AG, he was powerless to stop deaths." Cleveland.com, November 29, 2020. https://www .cleveland.com/metro/2020/11/disgraced-ex-cuyahoga-county-jail-wardens-tells -fbi-ohio-ag-he-was-powerless-to-stop-deaths-flow-of-drugs-in-troubled-jail.html.

Ferrise, A. "Family of man who died of suicide in Cuyahoga County Jail after repeatedly warning jail staff sues county." Cleveland.com, December 21, 2020. https://www.cleveland.com/metro/2020/12/family-of-man-who-died-of-suicide-in -cuyahoga-county-jail-after-repeatedly-warning-jail-staff-sues-county.html.

Ferrise, A. "Mother of man who died of suicide in Cuyahoga County Jail: 'They failed him.'" *Plain Dealer*, August 15, 2019. https://www.cleveland.com/metro/ 2019/08/mother-of-man-who-died-of-suicide-in-cuyahoga-county-jail-they-failed -him.html.

Ferrise, A. "U.S. Marshals: Cuyahoga County deprives inmates of food, water, and Constitutional Rights among string of seven deaths." *Plain Dealer*, November 21, 2018. https://www.cleveland.com/news/erry-2018/11/9b3d3f3cc89150/us-marshals -cuyahoga-county-de.html.

First Coast News Staff. "Jacksonville corrections officers arrested." *First Coast News*, November 2020. https://www.firstcoastnews.com/article/news/crime/ jacksonville-corrections-officer-arrested-charged-with-smuggling-meth-marijuana -contraband-into-jail/77-0130cf28-5573-4935-997c-43751b75157c.

First Coast News Staff. "Wrongful death lawsuit filed in 2018 death of woman in JSO custody." *First Coast News*, October 16, 2020. https://www.firstcoastnews.com/ article/news/crime/wrongful-death-lawsuit-filed-in-2018-death-of-duval-county -inmate/77-aedc4c34-c52a-46c5-8f81-f8f4829fdaad.

Fiscella, K. "Guide to developing and revising alcohol and opioid detoxification protocols." National Commission on Correctional Health Care, 2015.

Fiscella, K., et al. "Drug and alcohol associated deaths in U.S. jails." *Journal of Correctional Health Care* 26, no. 2 (April 2020).

Fitzhugh, J. "Fatal 2006 beating of inmate by Coast jailers brought denials, then justice." *Sun Herald*, September 10, 2018. https://www.sunherald.com/news/local/ crime/article218153040.html.

Forbes, J. "Messenger: Ruling against $3 surcharge sends message to Missouri Legislature on court costs." *St. Louis Post-Dispatch*, June 3, 2021. https://

www.stltoday.com/news/local/columns/tony-messenger/messenger-ruling
-against-3-surcharge-sends-message-to-missouri-legislature-on-court-costs/
article_381981a0-8ab5-5a60-a55b-8368c6ec4c5f.html.

Foreman, T., Jr. "Judge orders partial release of video in man's jail death." Associated
Press, August 2, 2020. https://apnews.com/article/winston-salem-north-carolina
-u-s-news-d4781857fda9a3f9081d9b186467f65c.

Forman, B. "Corrections data raise big questions." *Commonwealth Magazine*, March
4, 2020. https://commonwealthmagazine.org/opinion/corrections-data-raise-big
-questions/.

Fowler, L. "WA state Senate passes bill to ban private, for-profit prisons." KNKX,
March 30, 2021. https://www.knkx.org/politics/2021-03-30/wa-state-senate-passes
-bill-to-ban-private-for-profit-prisons.

Franklin, R., M. Hickman, & M. Hiller. "2009 survey of POST agencies regarding
certification practices." International Association of Directors of Law Enforcement
Standards and Training, July 2009. https://www.ojp.gov/pdffiles1/nij/227927.pdf.

Frye, C. "Cuyahoga County sued by family claiming improper medical care
in death of former inmate." WOIO, June 25, 2020. https://www.cleveland19
.com/2020/06/25/cuyahoga-county-sued-by-family-claiming-improper-medical
-care-death-former-inmate/.

Fuller, L. "No charges will be filed in case of local jail inmate who died after then-
sheriff knelt on his neck." WPSD, February 26, 2021. https://www.wpsdlocal6
.com/news/no-charges-will-be-filed-in-case-of-local-jail-inmate-who-died-after
-then/article_949ea3a8-787a-11eb-9642-636ff7b6757d.html.

Furst, R. "Lawsuit: Sherburne County jail ignored inmate's warning signs before
suicide." *Star Tribune*, April 2, 2020. https://www.startribune.com/lawsuit
-sherburne-jail-ignored-inmate-s-warning-signs-before-suicide/569329772/.

Gallagher, C., & A. Boring. "National study of jail suicide, 20 years later." National
Center on Institutions and Alternatives, April 2010. https://s3.amazonaws.com/
static.nicic.gov/Library/024308.pdf.

Galloway, J. "U.S. Jails are killing people going through opioid withdrawals."
Influence, December 6, 2017. https://www.huffpost.com/entry/us-jails-are-killing
-people-opioid-withdrawals_b_9563940.

Gandsey, J. "Mother sues after 2017 inmate death." *Bemidji Pioneer*, July 6, 2020.
https://www.bemidjipioneer.com/news/crime-and-courts/6563614-Mother-sues
-after-2017-inmate-death-3rd-lawsuit-filed-against-Beltrami-County.

Garcia, M. "Family files federal lawsuit of man who committed suicide in 2019." KKYR, February 5, 2021. https://kkyr.com/family-files-federal-lawsuit-on-man -who-committed-suicide-in-2019/.

Gardner, A. "DA: Use of force in Shasta County jail was justified." KRCR, August 31, 2020. https://krcrtv.com/news/local/da-use-of-force-in-shasta-county-jail-death -was-justified.

Garrison, S., & T. Novelly. "Solicitor will not charge deputies in Jamal Sutherland's jail death." *Post and Courier*, July 25, 2021. https://www.postandcourier.com/ news/solicitor-will-not-charge-deputies-in-jamal-sutherlands-jail-death/ article_4c92a902-ee2b-11eb-b89b-53ff6f11c14e.html.

Gartrell, N. "Man died of drug overdose in Contra Costa jail." *Mercury News*, September 23, 2020. https://www.mercurynews.com/2020/09/23/man-died-of -drug-overdose-in-contra-costa-jail-days-after-he-was-arrested-and-briefly -hospitalized/.

Gentzler, S. "28-year-old deemed homicide victim in latest probe of inmate death at Nisqually jail." *Olympian*, September 16, 2020. https://www.theolympian.com/ news/local/article245722615.html.

Gerritt, J. "Death without conviction: Texas needs access to jail videos." *Palestine Herald-Press*, August 15, 2019. https://www.palestineherald.com/news/php -editorial-death-without-conviction-texas-needs-access-to-jail-videos/article_ e33b8600-bfcd-11e9-8134-531ecbee318f.html.

Goggin, K. "Georgia sheriff argues against order requiring better jail conditions." Courthouse News Service, December, 16, 2020. https://www.courthousenews .com/georgia-sheriff-urges-panel-to-toss-order-requiring-better-jail-conditions/.

Goodyear, D. "After years of protests every Wednesday, L.A. activists welcome a new D.A." *New Yorker*, November 16, 2020. https://www.newyorker.com/ magazine/2020/11/16/after-years-of-protests-every-wednesday-la-activists -welcome-a-new-da.

Gordon, M. "Lawsuit: Mecklenburg jail didn't help inmate despite 2 suicide tries. He killed himself hours later." *Charlotte Observer*, July 14, 2020. https://www .charlotteobserver.com/news/local/crime/article244188832.html.

Gramlich, J. "Four-in-ten U.S. drug arrests in 2018 were for marijuana offenses- mostly possession." PEW Research Center, January 22, 2020. https://www.pew research.org/fact-tank/2020/01/22/four-in-ten-u-s-drug-arrests-in-2018-were-for -marijuana-offenses-mostly-possession/.

Green, J. "GCSO denied claims of physical abuse in death of Tasha Thomas." *Triad City Beat*, February 3, 2021. https://triad-city-beat.com/gcso-denies-claims -physical-abuse-death-tasha-thomas/.

Griffith, J. "Georgia officer who called an inmate on suicide watch a 'crazy n-word' to be fired." NBC News, September 28, 2020. https://www.nbcnews.com/news/us -news/georgia-officer-who-called-inmate-suicide-watch-crazy-n-word-n1241283.

Grim, R. "Since Sandra Bland, there have been hundreds of suicides in American jails. It has to stop." *Huffington Post*, July 13, 2016. https://www.huffpost.com/ entry/sandra-bland-anniversary-suicide-in-jail_n_5786836fe4b0867123df4a20.

Guyette, C. "Lawsuit targets billion-dollar company making life-and-death medical decisions in Michigan jails." *Detroit Metro Times*, March 12, 2020. https://www .metrotimes.com/news-hits/archives/2020/03/12/lawsuit-targets-billion-dollar -company-making-life-and-death-medical-decisions-in-michigan-jails.

Gyee, G. "Questions emerge in death of inmate at Charleston County jail, family's attorney says." *Post and Courier*, January 12, 2021. https://www.postandcourier .com/news/questions-emerge-in-death-of-inmate-at-charleston-county-jail -familys-attorney-says/article_91222bea-54e0-11eb-8493-8ba238b4ea94.html.

Haas, E. "Mental illness revealed behind bars." KEPR, February 16, 2017. https:// keprtv.com/news/local/mental-illness-revealed-behind-bars.

Hailer, B. "Daniel Pastorek died in the Allegheny County Jail but he shouldn't have been there in the first place." *Pittsburgh Current*, December 16, 2020. https://www .pittsburghcurrent.com/daniel-pastorek-died-in-the-allegheny-county-jail-but-he -shouldnt-have-been-there-in-the-first-place/.

Hall, B. "Jail death sheds light on pay." NewsChannel5, Nashville, June 10, 2021. https://www.newschannel5.com/news/newschannel-5-investigates/jail-death-sheds -light-on-pay-some-sheriffs-forced-to-sue-their-own-county.

Hall, K. "Grand jury declines to indict correctional officer, nurse in Travis County inmate's death." *Austin-American-Statesman*, August 13, 2021. https:// www.statesman.com/story/news/2021/08/13/travis-county-inmate-death-jail -correctional-officer-nurse-not-indicted/8105853002/.

Harki, G. "Deaths continue at Hampton Roads Jail." *Virginian-Pilot*, May 31, 2019. https://www.pilotonline.com/government/virginia/article_88f85c36-82f6-11e9 -be70-ffbb08602899.html.

Harris County, Texas. "Jail population statistics." https://charts.hctx.net/jailpop/App/ JailPopCurrent, downloaded December 6 and 7, 2020.

Harris, S. "Idaho AG now involved in investigation of local jail inmate Lance Quick's 2018 death." *Idaho State Journal*, October 28, 2020. https://www.idahostatejournal .com/news/local/idaho-ag-now-involved-in-investigation-of-local-jail-inmate -lance-quicks-2018-death/article_0728bc0b-0507-522c-9245-bcca43e9669a.html.

Harrison, J. "Penobscot jail board's 1st report didn't address inmates." *Bangor Daily News*, February 1, 2021. https://bangordailynews.com/2021/02/01/news/ penobscot/penobscot-jail-boards-1st-report-didnt-address-inmates-mental-health -as-law-requires/.

Hatton, F. "Rolette County jail reopens under new classification, requirements." KFYR, September 17, 2020. https://www.msn.com/en-us/news/crime/rolette -county-jail-reopens-under-new-classification-requirements/ar-BB199P6C.

Healy, B., & C. Williamsen. "Rollins: Suffolk County Sheriff never alerted DA of inmate's death." WBUR, August 20, 2020. https://www.wbur.org/news/2020/08/20/ suffolk-county-jail-death-sheriff-investigation.

Heaton, P., et al. "The downstream consequences of misdemeanor pretrial detention." *Stanford Law Review* 69, no. 3 (2017): 711–94.

Hegyi, N. "Indian Affairs promised to reform tribal jails." NPR, June 21, 2021. https://www.npr.org/2021/06/10/1002451637/bureau-of-indian-affairs-tribal -detention-centers-deaths-neglect.

Heidelberg, K. "Suit over inmate's 2015 death ends in dismissal." *Montrose Press*, November 17, 2020. https://www.montrosepress.com/news/suit-over-inmate-s -2015-death-ends-in-dismissal/article_68252b88-2859-11eb-8586-5fa6c60d2e5e .html.

Heiss, J. "In our backyards: Ending mass incarceration where it begins." Vera Institute of Justice, September 14, 2017. https://www.vera.org/projects/in-our -backyards.

Hendricks, M. "FBI, Jackson County investigate injuries to inmates at hands of jail guards." *Kansas City Star*, August 24, 2015. https://www.kansascity.com/news/ politics-government/article32213331.html.

Hendrickson, M. "Cook County Jail was one of the nation's largest COVID-19 hotspots last spring, It's worse now." *Chicago Sun Times*, December 15, 2020. https://chicago.suntimes.com/coronavirus/2020/12/15/22165917/cook-county-jail -covid-19-coronavirus-bond-release-reform-judge-kim-foxx-tom-dart.

Herrick, J. "Colorado lawmakers hope to end drug-addiction withdrawal in county jails." *Journal*, January 8, 2019. https://www.the-journal.com/articles/colorado -lawmakers-hope-to-end-drug-addiction-withdrawal-in-county-jails/.

Herring, T. "Jail incarceration rates vary widely, but inexplicably, across U.S. cities." *Prison Policy Initiative*, May 4, 2021. https://www.prisonpolicy.org/blog/2021/05/04/city-jail-rates/.

Hewlett, M. "Federal judge approves confidential settlement in lawsuit over Winston-Salem man's death at the Forsyth County Jail." *Winston-Salem Journal*, July 19, 2020. https://greensboro.com/news/local_news/federal-judge-approves -confidential-settlement-in-lawsuit-over-winston-salem-mans-death-at-the -forsyth/article_de994923-3502-50a0-aac9-1ab6d8814d68.html.

Hewlett, M. "Jail officers, nurse charged in John Neville's death." *News & Record*, July 8, 2020. https://greensboro.com/news/crime/jail-officers-nurse-charged -in-john-nevilles-death-greensboro-man-was-restrained-choked-while-in/ article_8db969c9-0012-5fc8-9dab-c7ede27590f9.html.

Hewlett, M., & W. Young. "Will jail video in John Neville's death be made public? A judge in Winston-Salem will decide Friday." *Winston-Salem Journal*, July 29, 2020. https://journalnow.com/news/local/will-jail-video-in-john-nevilles-death-be-made -public-a-judge-in-winston-salem/article_344403fc-f05f-571b-a733-c8c78a96239a .html.

Heymann, A. "Inmate who died at the Chesterfield County Jail Sunday identified." WFXR, September 27, 2020. https://www.wfxrtv.com/news/regional-news/virginia -news/inmate-dies-at-chesterfield-county-jail-sunday-morning/.

HHS guide for clinicians on the appropriate dosage reduction or discontinuation of long-term opioid analgesics, October 2019. https://www.hhs.gov/opioids/sites/ default/files/2019-10/Dosage_Reduction_Discontinuation.pdf.

Hickman, M., & K. Hughes. "Medical examiners and coroners' offices, 2004." Bureau of Justice Statistics, June 2007, NCJ-216756. https://bjs.ojp.gov/content/pub/pdf/ meco04.pdf.

Hicks, B. "Hicks: Video of Charleston County jail death is coming, and it's not good." *Post and Courier*, May 11, 2021. https://www.postandcourier.com/columnists/ hicks-video-of-charleston-county-jail-death-is-coming-and-it-s-not-good/ article_294732fe-b25f-11eb-843b-3f3d586e5260.html.

Hicks, B. "Sutherland investigation exposed jail malpractice." *Post and Courier*, July 31, 2021. https://www.postandcourier.com/opinion/commentary/hicks-sutherland -investigation-exposed-jail-malpractice-graziano-agrees/article_9fcc2ede-f152 -11eb-b8d3-bbedcfc0cfec.html.

Hiruko, A. "Feces in a locker and other harassment." NPR, September 17, 2020. https://www.kuow.org/stories/feces-in-lockers-to-harassment-racism-is-rife-in -king-county-corrections-employees-say.

Holcombe, M., & C. Mossburg. "Los Angeles coroner orders inquest in Andres Guardado's death." CNN, November 11, 2020. https://www.msn.com/en-us/news/ crime/los-angeles-coroner-orders-inquest-in-andres-guardados-death-the-first-in -3-decades/ar-BB1aTWnK.

Horowitz, J. "1 in 55 U.S. adults is on probation or parole." PEW Charitable Trusts, October 31, 2018. https://www.pewtrusts.org/en/research-and-analysis/ articles/2018/10/31/1-in-55-us-adults-is-on-probation-or-parole.

House, S. "7 detention officers fired after investigation into death of Marvin Scott at Collin County jail." *Dallas Morning News*, April 1, 2021. https://www.dallasnews .com/news/2021/04/01/7-detention-officers-fired-after-investigation-into-death-of -marvin-scott-at-collin-county-jail/.

Hummel, J. "Jail death ruled suicide." KBND, June 19, 2020. https://kbnd.com/kbnd -news/local-news-feed/514360.

Hunter, G. "Ex-officer sues over firing in Harper Woods jail death." *Detroit News*, September 9, 2020. https://www.detroitnews.com/story/news/local/wayne -county/2020/09/09/harper-woods-jail-death-fired-officer-sues/5761761002/.

Hyatt, K. "Ramsey County Board 'appalled and angered' by allegations of discrimination among jail staff." *Star Tribune*, June 23, 2020. https://www .startribune.com/ramsey-board-appalled-minority-officers-weren-t-allowed-to -guard-chauvin/571444672/.

Iannelli, J. "Family of man who died at California jail after shouting 'I can't breathe' demands answers from sheriff." *The Appeal*, June 19, 2020. https://theappeal.org/ california-jail-death-sheriff/.

Iannelli, J. "Rundle won't charge prison guards who allegedly boiled schizophrenic Black man to death." *Miami New Times*, March 17, 2017. https://www .miaminewtimes.com/news/florida-wont-charge-prison-guards-who-boiled -schizophrenic-black-man-darren-rainey-to-death-9213190.

Ibañez, D. "3 inmates attempt suicide at Bexar County Jail." KSAT, October 26, 2020. https://www.ksat.com/news/local/2020/10/26/3-inmates-attempt-suicide-at-bexar -county-jail-officials-say/.

"Inmate dies at Madison County jail." News 19, Huntsville, Alabama, July 30, 2021. https://whnt.com/news/huntsville/inmate-dies-at-madison-county-jail-3/.

"Inmate who died was subdued with Taser, locked in padded cell." CBSFW, June 23, 2020. https://dfw.cbslocal.com/2020/06/23/inmate-who-died-was-subdued-with -taser-locked-in-padded-cell/.

Jackson, P. "'The scores are abysmal': ACLU alleges failures at Baltimore jail led to 12 preventable deaths." *Baltimore Sun*, December 2, 2020. https://www.baltimoresun .com/news/crime/bs-md-ci-cr-aclu-medical-professionals-filing-inmate-deaths -20201202-shidmiw4lzbb7n6b5tncndpafi-story.html.

"Jail inmate hangs himself inside jail cell with bed sheets." Charlotte Alerts, May 23, 2021. https://newsmaven.io/charlottealerts/news/jail-inmate-hangs-himself-inside -jail-cell.

James, D., & L. Glaze. "Mental health problems of prison and jail inmates." Bureau of Justice Statistics, September 2006. https://bjs.ojp.gov/library/publications/mental -health-problems-prison-and-jail-inmates.

Jenkins, A. "'A black box.' It's not always easy getting answers when someone dies in jail." Northwest News Network, January 7, 2020. https://www.nwnewsnetwork .org/crime-law-and-justice/2019-12-26/a-black-box-its-not-always-easy-getting -answers-when-someone-dies-in-jail.

Jenkins, S. "Hampton Roads Regional Jail is investigating an inmate's death." *Virginian-Pilot*, February 22, 2021. https://www.pilotonline.com/news/crime/vp -nw-hampton-roads-regional-jail-investigating-inmate-death-monday-20210222 -pyxnaxkigbfknhtk5gupalp7sa-story.html.

Jennerjahn, A. "Chatham Co. Jail uses new guardian system to monitor inmates." WTGS, March 1, 2021. https://www.msn.com/en-us/news/crime/chatham-co-jail -uses-new-guardian-system-to-monitor-inmates/ar-BB1e8pni.

Johnson, J. "Lake County settles jail suicide case for $2 million." *Press Democrat*, June 18, 2018.

Johnston, M. "Will outrage over the Grand Traverse County jail be enough to topple incumbent sheriff?" IPR, October 22, 2020. https://www.interlochenpublicradio .org/news/2020-10-22/will-outrage-over-the-grand-traverse-county-jail-be -enough-to-topple-an-incumbent-sheriff.

Jones-Wright, G. "Opinion: San Diego County's DA must prosecute the sheriff's deputies for their role in jailhouse deaths." *San Diego Union-Tribune*, July 12, 2021. https://www.sandiegouniontribune.com/community-voices-project/story/2021-07 -12/opinion-san-diego-jail-deaths-bill-gore-summer-stephan.

Juranovich, T. "Family, sheriff's department reach settlement over jailed man's death." *Kokomo Tribune*, September 9, 2020. https://www.kokomotribune.com/news/

local_news/family-sheriffs-department-reach-settlement-over-jailed-mans-death/
article_b5870d50-f209-11ea-bd20-879d0015ce9f.html.

Kaba, F., et al. "Solitary confinement and risk of self-harm among jail inmates."
American Journal of Public Health 104, no. 3 (March 2014): 442–47.

Kaeble, D. "Probation and parole in the United States, 2016." Bureau of Justice
Statistics, April 2018. https://bjs.ojp.gov/library/publications/probation-and-parole
-united-states-2016.

Kaeble, D. "Time served in state prison, 2016." Bureau of Justice Statistics, November
2018, NCJ 252205. https://bjs.ojp.gov/library/publications/time-served-state
-prison-2016.

Kaffer, N. "Expert poses new theory on what really killed woman in Harper Woods
jail." *Detroit Free Press*, November 12, 2020. https://www.freep.com/story/
news/local/michigan/wayne/2020/11/12/priscilla-slater-autopsy-jail-harper
-woods/6251487002/.

Kaffer, N. "Wayne County: No charges in Harper Woods jail death." *Detroit
Free Press*, May 20, 2021. https://www.freep.com/story/news/local/michigan/
wayne/2021/05/20/priscilla-slater-harper-woods-jail-death/5185358001/.

Kajeepeta, S., et al. "Association between county jail incarceration and cause-specific
county mortality in the USA, 1987–2017: A retrospective, longitudinal study."
Lancet online, February 23, 2021. https://www.thelancet.com/journals/lanpub/
article/PIIS2468-2667%2820%2930283-8/fulltext.

Kamp, L. "An Eastern Washington teen went to a mental health clinic for help. Eight
days later, he was dead in a jail cell." *Seattle Times*, November 1, 2020. https://www
.seattletimes.com/seattle-news/an-eastern-washington-teen-went-to-a-mental
-health-clinic-for-help-eight-days-later-he-died-in-a-jail-cell/.

Kane, A. "Coroner wants to appeal juvenile autopsy release, despite court order."
Las Vegas Review-Journal, November 20, 2020. https://www.reviewjournal.com/
investigations/coroner-wants-to-appeal-juvenile-autopsy-release-despite-court
-order-2187415/.

Kane, D., & D. Battaglia. "NC jails have known this position is deadly. So why was it
used again?" *News & Observer*, August 12, 2020. https://www.newsobserver.com/
news/state/north-carolina/article244777867.html.

Kaplan, E. "APD officer violated policies in inmate's suicide." *Albuquerque Journal*,
October 6, 2020. https://www.abqjournal.com/1504426/apd-officer-violated
-policies-in-inmates-suicide.html.

Kaplan, E. "Jail health care provider terminates contract." *Albuquerque Journal*, April 26, 2021, https://www.abqjournal.com/2383953/jail-health-care-provider -terminates-contract.html.

Kaplan, E., & M. Reisen. "'Tragic and horrible': Nine at MCD have died over past year." *Albuquerque Journal*, March 13, 2021. https://www.abqjournal .com/2369430/tragic-and-horrible.html.

Kaplan, S. "U.S. DOJ continues investigating Palmer York Co. Prison death despite grand jury findings." ABC27, March 9, 2021. https://www.abc27.com/news/local/ york/u-s-doj-continues-investigating-palmer-york-co-prison-death-despite-grand -jury-findings/.

Kaplan, T. "Santa Clara County, inmate-rights group agree to settle suit over deplorable jail conditions." *Mercury News*, October 23, 2018. https://www .mercurynews.com/2018/10/23/settlement-reached-over-lousy-jail-conditions/.

Karlik, M. "Federal court dismisses lawsuit over 2017 suicide in Jeffco jail." *Colorado Politics*, January 22, 2021. https://www.coloradopolitics.com/news/federal-court -dismisses-lawsuit-over-2017-suicide-in-jeffco-jail/article_b3c58b58-5ce5-11eb -9151-8bc42ed25165.html.

Kelety, J. "Inmate deaths in Maricopa County decrease under Sheriff Paul Penzone." *Phoenix New Times*, December 3, 2020. https://www.phoenixnewtimes.com/news/ inmate-deaths-maricopa-county-sheriff-paul-penzone-arpaio-lawsuits-11517648.

Keller, J. "Using a wrench instead of a hammer for alcohol withdrawal." Jail Medicine, June 15, 2020. https://www.jailmedicine.com/using-a-wrench-instead-of -a-hammer-for-alcohol-withdrawal/.

KENS 5 Staff. "Bexar Co. deputies' union says poor staffing is having a negative impact." KENS 5, December 9, 2020. https://www.kens5.com/article/news/local/ law-enforcement/deputy-sheriffs-association-of-bexar-county-says-poor-staffing -at-jail-is-resulting-in-negative-consequences/273-e3206f2b-644d-4f25-be64 -d54b2c18fb43.

Killion, A. "WDSU Investigates: Videos show final hours of St. Bernard woman who died in jail without medication." WDSU, February 10, 2021. https://www.wdsu .com/article/wdsu-investigates-videos-show-final-hours-of-st-bernard-woman -who-died-in-jail-without-her-medication/35470942.

King, R. "Sheriff investigates death in the county jail." KOEL, September 23, 2020. https://koel.com/sheriff-investigates-death-in-the-county-jail/.

Kless, T. "Family says medical attention wasn't given to Southeast Georgia man who died in jail." *First Coast News*, July 30, 2020. https://www.firstcoastnews.com/

article/news/local/family-says-medical-attention-wasnt-given-to-southeast-georgia -man-who-died-while-in-jail/77-5200aff9-0523-4ecd-83f1-158e3b71fe6e.

Kless. T. "'She was screaming': Investigation reveals treatment Clay County mom received before dying in jail." *First Coast News*, January 31, 2020. https://www .firstcoastnews.com/article/news/crime/she-was-screaming-investigation-reveals -treatment-clay-county-mom-received-before-dying-in-jail/77-975ff54d-424a -471a-a28f-b7876de0efbf.

Knopf, T. "NC jail suicide and overdose deaths on the rise." North Carolina Health News, October 31, 2019. https://www.northcarolinahealthnews.org/2019/10/31/nc -jail-suicide-overdose-deaths-on-the-rise/.

Knox, B. "Drug overdose leads to inmate's death." *Wise County Messenger*, December 9, 2020. https://www.wcmessenger.com/articles/drug-overdose-leads-to-inmates -death/.

Komarla, A. "Guest Commentary: Another suicide at Santa Rita Jail sparks cry for sheriff oversight in Alameda County." *Davis Vanguard*, April 21, 2021. https:// www.davisvanguard.org/2021/04/another-suicide-at-santa-rita-jail-sparks-cry-for -sheriff-oversight-in-alameda-county/.

Kraemer, K. "Benton's ex-healthcare company destroyed evidence in teen's death." *Tri-City Herald*, June 7, 2020. https://www.wenatcheeworld.com/news/northwest/ benton-jails-ex-healthcare-company-destroyed-evidence-in-teens-death/ article_68fd8e0c-a9aa-11ea-afbb-6b5e472bfa42.html.

Krafcik, M. "Family plans legal action after son dies in Kalamazoo County Jail." WWMT TV, April 8, 2021. https://wwmt.com/news/i-team/family-plans-legal -action-after-son-dies-in-kalamazoo-county-jail.

KUSI Newsroom. "Sheriff: Jail inmate's death was due to drug overdose." KUSI, December 8, 2020. https://www.kusi.com/sheriff-jail-inmates-death-was-due-to -drug-overdose/.

Laferney, D. "A story of two deaths at the Collins County Jail." *D Magazine*, August 2, 2021. https://www.dmagazine.com/frontburner/2021/08/a-story-of-two-deaths-at -the-collin-county-jail/.

LaForgia, M. & J. Valentino-DeVries. "How a genetic trait in Black people can give police cover." *New York Times*, May 15, 2021. https://www.nytimes .com/2021/05/15/us/african-americans-sickle-cell-police.html.

Lagoe, A., & S. Eckert. "KARE 11 Investigates: Prone restraint banned in MN jails and prisons." KARE 11, June 30, 2021. https://www.kare11.com/article/news/

investigations/prone-restraint-banned-in-mn-jails-and-prisons/89-f9314130-f9db
-4cfb-b3de-15c92cda6cbf.

Lagoe, A., B. Stahl, & S. Eckert. "KARE 11 Investigates: Flawed—often toothless—jail
death investigations." KARE 11, September 29, 2020. https://www.kare11.com/
article/news/investigations/kare-11-investigates-flawed-often-toothless-jail-death
-investigations/89-0255d498-8679-4961-959a-6f19c4a9e040.

LaRowe, L. "Jail surveillance recordings still being disputed." *Texarkana Gazette*,
August 21, 2021. https://texarkanagazette.com/news/2021/aug/22/jail-surveillance
-recordings-still-being-disputed-/.

Launlus, P. "Murder suspect back in jail after allegedly failing drug test." KTLO,
November, 20, 2020. https://www.ktlo.com/2020/11/20/murder-suspect-back-in
-jail-after-allegedly-failing-drug-test/.

Lazarus, J. "Federal lawsuit filed over tear-gassing of inmates at Richmond Justice
Center." *Richmond Free Press*, December 3, 2020. http://richmondfreepress.com/
news/2020/dec/03/federal-lawsuit-filed-over-tear-gassing-inmates-ri/.

Leader News Staff. "Jefferson County commissioners approve settlement in
public records case." *Leader*, September 10, 2020. https://www.ptleader.com/
stories/jefferson-county-commissioners-approve-settlement-in-public-records
-case,71136.

Learn-Andes, J. "Statistics detail restraint chair use in Luzerne County prison." *Times
Leader*, August 14, 2020. https://www.timesleader.com/news/796654/statistics
-detail-restraint-chair-use-in-luzerne-county-prison.

Lee, A. "Parents grieve loss of son who died in chains at Santa Rita; sheriff's office
moves to fire lieutenant." KTVU, July 1, 2020. https://www.ktvu.com/news/parents
-grieve-loss-of-son-who-died-in-chains-at-santa-rita-sheriffs-office-moves-to-fire
-lieutenant.

Leonard, A., & A. May. "Arizona's privatized prison health care under fire after
deaths." Aljazeera America, April 28, 2014. http://america.aljazeera.com/watch/
shows/america-tonight/america-tonight-blog/2013/12/2/arizona-s-privatizedpriso
nhealthcareunderfireafterdeaths.html.

Leslie, E., & N. G. Pope. "The unintended impact of pretrial detention on case
outcomes: Evidence from New York City arraignments." *Journal of Law and
Economics* 60, no. 3 (2017): 529–57.

Lewis, R. "Waiting for justice." Cal Matters, March 31, 2021. https://calmatters.org/
justice/2021/03/waiting-for-justice/.

Lieberman, S. "Rockland jail inmate death: Insufficient evidence of criminality by officers, AG says." *Rockland/Westchester Journal News*, January 29, 2021. https://www.lohud.com/story/news/local/rockland/2021/01/29/rockland-jail-inmate-death-insufficient-evidence-criminality-ag/4311578001/.

Link, M. "At issue, Grand Traverse jail inmate health care." *Record Eagle*, November 13, 2020. https://www.record-eagle.com/news/at-issue-grand-traverse-jail-inmate-health-care/article_6c3d5f46-252b-11eb-a7bd-ff784b41da79.html.

Link, M. "Court testimony exposes Wellpath's jail medication policies." *Record Eagle*, July 16, 2021. https://www.record-eagle.com/news/court-testimony-exposes-wellpaths-jail-medication-policies/article_b23faf32-e5ae-11eb-aa5c-676d646444bc.html.

Lipscomb, J. "Darren Rainey died in scalding prison shower eight years ago today." *Miami New Times*, June 23, 2020. https://www.miaminewtimes.com/news/katherine-fernandez-rundle-criticized-for-darren-rainey-florida-prison-death-11657307.

Lipsitz, R. "In Erie County, jail deaths continue despite high-profile tragedy." *The Appeal*, January 16, 2020. https://theappeal.org/erie-county-jail-deaths-continue/.

Liu, P., R. Nunn, & J. Shambaugh. "The economics of bail and pretrial detention." Brookings Institute, December 2018. https://www.brookings.edu/research/the-economics-of-bail-and-pretrial-detention/.

LoBianco, T. "Report: Aide says Nixon's war on drugs targeted blacks, hippies." CNN, March 24, 2016. https://www.cnn.com/2016/03/23/politics/john-ehrlichman-richard-nixon-drug-war-blacks-hippie/index.html.

Lofstrom, M., & B. Martin. "California's county jails." Public Policy Institute of California, February 2021. https://www.ppic.org/publication/californias-county-jails/.

Long. S. Research Analyst, Curran-Fromhold Correctional facility, communication with author, November 18, 2020.

Lopez, T. "Mother wants answers after son found dead in New Mexico jail." KOB4 Eyewitness News, December 10, 2020, https://www.kob.com/new-mexico-news/mother-wants-answers-after-son-found-dead-in-new-mexico-jail/5948457/.

Lurie, J. "Go to jail. Die from drug withdrawal. Welcome to the criminal justice system." *Mother Jones*, February 5, 2017. https://www.motherjones.com/politics/2017/02/opioid-withdrawal-jail-deaths/.

Lutz, M. "Court: Cobb sheriff must turn over records of death in custody." *Atlanta Journal-Constitution*, April 23, 2020. https://www.ajc.com/news/local

-govt--politics/court-cobb-sheriff-must-turn-over-records-death-custody/
trrqFuNQzhgGcDnWetjtfI/.

Lutz, M. "Democrat declares victory in Cobb sheriff's race." *Atlanta Journal-Constitution*, November 4, 2020. https://www.ajc.com/news/atlanta-news/
owens-declares-victory-in-cobb-sheriffs-race/QZYTYGWTCRB7TPKLY
7CG2KWGOQ/.

Lyons, K. "DOC emails show officials were aware of prison health care problems
years before taking over from UConn." *CT Mirror*, November 13, 2020. https://
ctmirror.org/2020/11/13/doc-emails-show-officials-were-aware-of-prison-health
-care-problems-years-before-taking-over-from-uconn/.

Magdaleno, J. "Inmate dies of apparent suicide at Marion County Jail." *Indy Star*, July
27, 2021. https://www.indystar.com/story/news/local/marion-county/2021/07/27/
marion-county-jail-inmate-dies-apparent-suicide-sheriff-says/5394043001/.

Mangold, B. "Oklahoma district attorney says he will ask OSBI to reopen
investigation into 2019 jail death." News 9, August 16, 2021. https://www.news9
.com/story/61173882cb160e0c0778fcd5/oklahoma-district-attorney-says-he-will
-ask-osbi-to-reopen-investigation-into-2019-jail-death-.

Manna, N. "Man dies in hospital ER after being transferred from Tarrant County
Jail." *Fort Worth Star-Telegram*, September 15, 2020. https://www.msn.com/en-us/
news/crime/man-dies-in-hospital-er-after-being-transferred-from-tarrant-county
-jail/ar-BB19486E.

Manna, N. "Second person dies after contracting COVID-19 in jail, Tarrant County
sheriff says." *Fort Worth Star-Telegram*, November 10, 2020, https://www.star
-telegram.com/news/coronavirus/article247109317.html.

Manna, N. "Texas Rangers investigate 8th death at Tarrant County Jail this year." *Fort
Worth Star-Telegram*, September 10, 2020. https://www.star-telegram.com/news/
local/fort-worth/article245622650.html.

Manna, N. "Third death in one week being investigated at Tarrant County jail." *Fort
Worth Star-Telegram*, June 25, 2020. https://www.star-telegram.com/news/local/
fort-worth/article243805552.html.

Marcius, C. "Rikers Island correction officers, inmates charged in drug smuggling
scheme." *New York Daily News*, January 14, 2020. https://www.nydailynews.com/
new-york/ny-rikers-island-officers-inmates-charged-narcotics-bribes-contraband
-20200115-geohurt4n5acrdkdazqygk7rve-story.html.

Mark, E. "County council approves $3 million settlement in jail death lawsuit."
Citizens' Voice, June 23, 2020. https://www.citizensvoice.com/news/county-council

-approves-3-million-settlement-in-jail-death-lawsuit/article_28243c10-2f45-560f
-a8b9-c762f748cff4.html.

Martin, C. "Family of man who died in Collin County jail calls for arrest of officers
present during his death." *Dallas Morning News*, March 19, 2021. https://www
.dallasnews.com/news/courts/2021/03/19/family-of-man-who-died-in-collin
-county-jail-calls-for-arrest-of-officers-present-during-his-death/.

Martin, C. "Tarrant County's Chief Medical Examiner announced retirement amid
calls for investigation into the office." *Dallas Morning News*, April 30, 2021. https://
www.dallasnews.com/news/2021/04/30/tarrant-countys-chief-medical-examiner
-announces-retirement-amid-calls-for-investigations-into-the-office/.

Martin, K. "Lawsuit: Detainee's death 'terrifying, preventable and totally
unnecessary.'" *Carolina Public Press*, June 18, 2020. https://carolinapublicpress
.org/30667/lawsuit-detainees-death-terrifying-preventable-and-totally
-unnecessary/.

Martinez, C. & S. Lehr. "Attorney General: No charges against officers in Lansing
Lockup." *Lansing State Journal*, April 9, 2021. https://www.msn.com/en-us/news/
crime/attorney-general-no-charges-in-anthony-hulon-death-in-lansing-lockup/ar
-BB1ftA9i.

Maruschak, L., M. Berzofsky, & J. Unangst. "Medical problems of state and federal
prisoners and jail inmates, 2011–2012." Bureau of Justice Statistics, February 2015.
https://bjs.ojp.gov/content/pub/pdf/mpsfpji1112.pdf.

Maruschak, L. & T. Minton, "Correctional populations in the United States, 2017–
2018." Bureau of Justice Statistics, August 2020, NCJ 252157. https://bjs.ojp.gov/
content/pub/pdf/cpus1718.pdf.

Mash, D. "Excited delirium and sudden death." *Frontiers in Physiology* 7, no. 435
(October 13, 2016).

Mathews, J., II, & F. Curiel. "Criminal justice debt problems." American Bar
Association, November 30, 2019, https://www.americanbar.org/groups/crsj/
publications/human_rights_magazine_home/economic-justice/criminal-justice
-debt-problems/.

Matray, M. "Hampton Roads Regional Jail facing a staffing shortage so severe
it's moving 250 inmates." *Virginian-Pilot*, December 17, 2020. https://www
.pilotonline.com/government/local/vp-nw-fz20-hrrj-staffing-20201217
-a7iqkn2yizajnohjeghwolcm6m-story.html.

McCullough, J. "With a stalled court system, some Texas jails are dangerously
overcrowded in the pandemic." *Texas Tribune*, January 28, 2021. https://www

.msn.com/en-us/news/crime/with-a-stalled-court-system-some-texas-jails-are
-dangerously-overcrowded-in-the-pandemic/ar-BB1dbSnc.

McDonald, J. "Broken cameras, lack of evidence limit inquiring into Vista jail
suicide, review board finds." *San Diego Union-Tribune*, August 9, 2021. https://
www.sandiegouniontribune.com/news/watchdog/story/2021-08-09/lack-of
-evidence-limits-investigation-into-vista-jail-suicide-last-year.

McDonald, J. "Fifth inmate dies this year in San Diego County Jail." *San Diego
Union-Tribune*, October 13, 2020. https://www.msn.com/en-us/news/crime/fifth
-inmate-dies-this-year-in-san-diego-county-jail/ar-BB19ZLBI.

McDonald, J. "Julian man choked to death on face mask in sheriff's custody." *San
Diego Union-Tribune*, March 30, 2021. https://www.sandiegouniontribune.com/
news/watchdog/story/2021-03-30/julian-man-choked-to-death-on-face-mask-in
-sheriffs-custody-autopsy-finds.

McDonald, J. "Vista jail worker says she warned sheriff's officials before jail suicide."
San Diego Union-Tribune, September 9, 2020. https://www.sandiegouniontribune
.com/news/watchdog/story/2020-09-09/vista-jail-worker-says-she-warned-sheriffs
-officials-before-inmate-suicide.

McDonald, J., & K. Davis. "Mistakes, lack of oversight are not always fatal." *San
Diego Union-Tribune*, September 23, 2019. https://www.sandiegouniontribune
.com/news/watchdog/story/2019-09-20/day-two-sidebar-mistakes-lack-of
-oversight-are-not-always-fatal.

McDonald, J., & K. Davis. "Three more inmates die in Sheriff's Department custody."
San Diego Union-Tribune, December 11, 2020. https://www.sandiegouniontribune
.com/news/watchdog/story/2020-12-11/three-more-inmates-die-in-sheriffs
-department-custody.

McDonald, J. & K. Davis. "Woman left alone to die after striking her head in jail,
independent review finds." *San Diego Union-Tribune*, February 7, 2021. https://
www.sandiegouniontribune.com/news/watchdog/story/2021-02-07/woman-left
-alone-to-die-after-striking-her-head-while-collapsing-in-jail-independent-review
-finds.

McDonald, J., & K. Davis. "Widow kept in the dark about husband's death in San
Diego County jail." *San Diego Union-Tribune*, March 19, 2021. https://www
.sandiegouniontribune.com/news/watchdog/story/2021-03-19/widow-kept-in-the
-dark-about-husbands-death-in-san-diego-county-jail.

McDonald, T. "Family members of inmates who died allege negligence at Johnston County Jail." *Indy Week*, February 1, 2021. https://indyweek.com/news/family -members-of-inmates-who-died-allege-negligence-at-john/.

McGlone, A. "Obscure sheriff's review board gets new scrutiny in court." KPBS, December 8, 2020. https://www.kpbs.org/podcasts/kpbs-midday-edition -segments/2020/dec/08/obscure-sheriffs-review-board-gets-new-scrutiny-co/.

McKetin, R., et al. "Does methamphetamine use increase violent behavior?" *Addiction* 109, no. (2014): 798–806.

McKinney, M. "Beltrami County sued for black man's death while in custody." *Minnesota Spokesman-Recorder*, July 2, 2020. https://spokesman-recorder .com/2020/07/02/beltrami-county-sued-for-black-mans-death-while-in-custody/.

McMahon, K. "The death of Layleen Xtravaganza Cubilette-Polanco, 1991–2019." New York City Board of Correction, June 23, 2020. https://www1.nyc.gov/assets/ boc/downloads/pdf/Reports/BOC-Reports/2020.06_Polanco/Final_Polanco_ Public_Report_1.pdf.

McNeil, H. "Attorney general finds no one criminally culpable in death of India Cummings." *Buffalo News*, October 2, 2020. https://buffalonews.com/news/local/ attorney-general-finds-no-one-criminally-culpable-in-death-of-india-cummings/ article_dde72c90-04f0-11eb-a77a-b31610125251.html.

McVay, D., ed. Drug Policy Facts, last updated June 28, 2021. https://www .drugpolicyfacts.org/chapter/crime_arrests.

Means, E. "Accounts of 'cruelty' and 'indifference' at Salt Lake County Jail have some calling for reform." KUER, July 22, 2020. https://www.kuer.org/justice/2020-07-22/ accounts-of-cruelty-and-indifference-at-salt-lake-county-jail-have-some-calling -for-reform.

Mental Health Rights Project. "Report: 9 of 10 people who died in Oregon jails in 2020 had a disability." Disability Rights Oregon, February 8, 2021. https://www .droregon.org/advocacy/report-9-of-the-10-people-who-died-in-oregon-jails-in -2020-had-a-disability?rq=jails.

Mercury News Editorial Board. "Editorial: Santa Clara County Sheriff must stop stalling on oversight plan." *Mercury News*, November 12, 2020. https://www .mercurynews.com/2020/11/12/editorial-sheriff-must-stop-stalling-on-oversight -plan/.

Metrick, B. "Dauphin County prison board OKs investigations into suspended director of corrections, inmates' death." *Patriot-News*, September 9, 2020. https://

www.pennlive.com/news/2020/09/independent-investigations-approved-for -dauphin-county-prison-by-board.html.

Michaels, S. "Why coroners often blame police killings on a made-up medical condition." *Mother Jones*, October 14, 2020. https://www.motherjones.com/ crime-justice/2020/10/why-coroners-often-blame-police-killings-on-a-made-up -medical-condition/.

Mieurem, E. "Wrongful death suit settled." *Jackson Hole News & Guide*, October 28, 2020. https://www.jhnewsandguide.com/news/cops_courts/wrongful-death-suit -settled-leads-to-medical-improvements-at-county-jail/article_c377cf45-f135-5705 -a540-e516c1db3eb0.html.

Miller, J. "A Utah jail nurse will once again face a criminal charge in dehydration death of an inmate." *Salt Lake City Tribune*, June 14, 2019. https://www.sltrib.com/ news/2019/06/14/utah-jail-nurse-will/.

Miller, J. "Deaths at the Salt Lake County jail." *Salt Lake City Tribune*, June 6, 2020. https://www.sltrib.com/news/2020/06/07/deaths-salt-lake-county/.

"Minnesota DOC wants independent law enforcement agency to investigate possible criminal charges in jail death." Fox 9, July 12, 2020. https://www.fox9.com/news/ minnesota-doc-wants-independent-law-enforcement-agency-to-investigate -possible-criminal-charges-in-jail-death.

Minton, T., Z. Zeng, & L. Maruschak. "Impact of COVID-19 on the local jail population, January–June 2020." Bureau of Justice Statistics, March 2021. https:// bjs.ojp.gov/content/pub/pdf/icljpjj20.pdf.

Mitchell, A. "Family members get $1 million of $1.75 million settlement in lawsuit over Kalamazoo County Jail inmate death." MLive, October 31, 2013. https://www .mlive.com/news/kalamazoo/2013/10/see_breakdown_of_175_million_s.html.

Mittelhammer, M. "Inmate dies after collapsing in Athens-Clarke County jail." *Red & Black*, September 25, 2020. https://www.redandblack.com/athensnews/inmate-dies -after-collapsing-in-athens-clarke-county-jail/article_60bd1f82-ff90-11ea-8eb9 -83b8f9c346ef.html.

Monroe News Staff. "Inmate dies after found hanging at jail." *Monroe News*, October 7, 2020. https://www.monroenews.com/story/news/crime/2020/10/07/inmate-dies -after-found-hanging-at-jail/42840599/.

Morehead, B. "Medical examiner rules jail death a suicide." *Barberton Herald*, August 12, 2020. https://www.barbertonherald.com/2020/08/12/medical-examiner-rules -jail-death-suicide/.

Morris, S. "Lieutenant on Leave after use of restraints leads to death in Santa Rita Jail." *East Bay Express*, August 7, 2019. https://eastbayexpress.com/lieutenant-on-leave-after-use-of-restraints-leads-to-death-in-santa-rita-jail-1/.

Murphy, D. "'They're trying to kill me,' Tory Sanders told mother before fatal collapse in rural Missouri jail." *Riverfront Times*, May 10, 2017. https://www.riverfronttimes.com/newsblog/2017/05/10/theyre-trying-to-kill-me-tory-sanders-told-mother-before-fatal-collapse-in-rural-missouri-jail.

Narciso, D. "Morrow County: COVID, escapes, suicide called 'run of bad luck' at understaffed jail." *Columbus Dispatch*, September 13, 2020. https://www.dispatch.com/story/news/local/2020/09/13/morrow-county-covid-escapes-suicide-called-lsquorun-of-bad-luckrsquo-at-understaffed-jail/114006270/.

Neate, R. "Welcome to Jail Inc: How private companies make money off U.S. prisons." *Guardian*, June 16, 2016. https://www.theguardian.com/us-news/2016/jun/16/us-prisons-jail-private-healthcare-companies-profit.

Nowlin, S. "Lost in lockup." *San Antonio Current*, March 23, 2021. https://www.sacurrent.com/sanantonio/lost-in-lockup-last-year-prisoners-in-bexar-county-and-across-texas-died-in-record-numbers/Content?oid=25836851.

O'Conner, L. "Detaining people who can't afford bail is unconstitutional, California high court rules." *Huffington Post*, March 25, 2021. https://www.huffpost.com/entry/california-court-bail-unconstitutional_n_605d03dcc5b67593e056fbc9.

O'Donnell, B. "Wilkinson County to pay $420,000 settlement in woman's jail death." WMAZ, January 2, 2020. https://www.13wmaz.com/article/news/local/wilkinson-settlement-lawsuit-woman-jail-death/93-7f9a63bc-4298-4f81-a575-2a1bc2628200.

Office of Public Affairs. "Former Rapides Parish correctional officer sentenced for violating civil rights of three inmates." Department of Justice, May 17, 2021. https://www.justice.gov/opa/pr/former-rapides-parish-correctional-officer-sentenced-violating-civil-rights-three-inmates.

Parker, C. "Hamilton County investigates inmate death." WDEF, September 23, 2020. https://www.wdef.com/hamilton-county-investigates-inmate-death/.

Parker, N. "Georgia legislators seek scrutiny of jail deaths as new case emerges." Reuters, December 30, 2020. https://www.reuters.com/article/us-usa-jails-chatham-idUSKBN2941EQ.

Parker, N. "Georgia legislators, citing Reuters report, want every jail death investigated." Reuters, January 25, 2021. https://www.reuters.com/article/us-usa-jails-hearing-idUSKBN29U2B7.

Parker, N., J. Szep & L. So. "Death and politics roil a Georgia jail." Reuters, September 4, 2019. https://www.reuters.com/investigates/special-report/usa-jails -monitor/.

Paschal, O., & E. Brown. "How Alabama organizers blocked Gov. Ivey's Prison lease plan." *Facing South*, June 17, 2021. https://www.facingsouth.org/2021/06/how -alabama-organizers-blocked-gov-iveys-prison-lease-plan.

Pascoe, S. "County authorities say jail inmate died from fentanyl overdose." *San Diego Union-Tribune*, August 5, 2021. https://www.sandiegouniontribune.com/ news/public-safety/story/2021-08-05/county-authorities-say-jail-inmate-died -from-fentanyl-overdose.

Pascoe, S. "State auditor to investigate deaths at San Diego County jails." *San Diego Union-Tribune*, July 1, 2021. https://www.sandiegouniontribune.com/news/public -safety/story/2021-07-01/state-legislators-consider-audit-of-san-diego-county -sheriffs-department.

Pickey, S. "District attorney says Ector Co. deputies used excessive force on prisoner who later died." CBS7, September 1, 2020. https://www.cbs7.com/2020/09/01/no -indictments-after-man-dies-in-custody-in-ector-county/.

Pierrotti, A. "GBI and DA decline to investigate suspicious jail death, family claims promises were broken." 11Alive, February 24, 2021. https://www.11alive.com/ article/news/investigations/the-reveal/wingo-cobb-jail-death-investigation -update/85-31583d64-1d95-4557-83cf-00869a07369c.

Pilger, L. "Grand jury review recent deaths at prison, county jail." *Lincoln Journal Star*, August 19, 2021. https://journalstar.com/news/local/crime-and-courts/grand -jury-reviews-recent-deaths-at-prison-county-jail/article_0dd3b040-e20d-5474 -9938-edffa5a17a83.html.

Pishko, J. "Jail deaths and the elected sheriff." *The Appeal*, March 21, 2019. https:// theappeal.org/politicalreport/jail-deaths-and-sheriffs/.

Plog, K. "'A challenging way to practice medicine': Death investigation in Washington faces grim reality." KNKX, October 12, 2020. https://www.knkx .org/other-news/2020-10-12/a-challenging-way-to-practice-medicine-death -investigation-in-washington-faces-grim-reality.

Pohl, J. "People are dying in Sacramento County jails. The sheriff isn't telling the public." *Sacramento Bee*, August 17, 2021. https://www.msn.com/en-us/news/ crime/people-are-dying-in-sacramento-county-jails-the-sheriff-isnt-telling-the -public/ar-AANqdW1.

Pohl, J., & R. Gabrielson. "A jail increased extreme isolation to stop suicides. More people killed themselves." ProPublica, November 5, 2019. https://www.propublica .org/article/a-jail-increased-extreme-isolation-to-stop-suicides-more-people-killed -themselves.

Popp, A. "Teen's death in Dawson county Jail ruled accidental by GBI." *Dawson County News*, July 24, 2020. https://www.dawsonnews.com/local/crimecourts/ teens-death-dawson-county-jail-ruled-accidental-gbi/.

Powell, M. "Washington County Jail deputy charged with misconduct after allegations of racism." Oregon Public Radio, June 6, 2020. https://www.opb .org/news/article/washington-county-jail-deputy-misconduct-charge-racism -allegations/.

Powers, A. "The renegade sheriffs." *New Yorker*, April 23, 2018. https://www .newyorker.com/magazine/2018/04/30/the-renegade-sheriffs.

Pratt, D. "Family's lawsuit details policies they say led to Whatcom County jail suicide." *Bellingham Herald*, August 2, 2020. https://www.bellinghamherald.com/ news/local/article244649967.html.

Press, E. "Dying behind bars." *New Yorker*, August 23, 2021. https://www.newyorker .com/magazine/2021/08/23/a-fight-to-expose-the-hidden-human-costs-of -incarceration.

"Preventable deaths in Orange County jails, grand jury 2017–2018." County of Orange, California.

Prohaska, T. "Niagara corrections officer pleads guilty to records tampering." *Buffalo News*, February 11, 2020. https://buffalonews.com/news/local/crime-and-courts/ niagara-corrections-officer-pleads-guilty-to-records-tampering/article_d7d5cf58 -e4c2-51de-87cf-0ae362a57c92.html.

Puente, N. "Inmate dies in custody at Starr County jail." KGBT-TV, August 20, 2020. https://www.valleycentral.com/news/local-news/inmate-dies-in-custody-at-starr -county-jail/.

Quandt, K. "America's rural-jail-death problem." *Atlantic*, March 29, 2021, https:// www.theatlantic.com/politics/archive/2021/03/americas-rural-jail-death -problem/618292/.

Ramirez, C. "Lawsuit: Inmate's in-custody death could have been prevented." KOB 4, June 11, 2021. https://www.kob.com/new-mexico-news/lawsuit-inmates-in -custody-death-could-have-been-prevented/6125143/.

Randle, C. "Employees not indicted in death at Ector County jail." *Midland Reporter-Telegram*, September 1, 2020. https://www.mrt.com/news/article/Employees-not -indicted-in-death-at-Ector-County-15533309.php.

Ray, P. "Inmate's death spurs civil rights lawsuit." *Altoona Mirror*, March 17, 2021. https://www.altoonamirror.com/news/local-news/2021/03/inmates-death-spurs -civil-rights-lawsuit/.

Rayman, G. "NYC mom who learned on Facebook of son's Rikers suicide demands answers from city." *Daily News*, August 17, 2021. https://www.nydailynews.com/ new-york/nyc-crime/ny-brandon-rodriguez-suicide-rikers-mother-20210817 -4oqqvrtemzd7zgoecj3ju3ywki-story.html.

Reaves, B., & A. Goldberg. "Local police departments 1997." Bureau of Justice Statistics, February 2000, NCJ 173429. https://bjs.ojp.gov/content/pub/pdf/lpd97 .pdf.

Regenstein, M., & J. Christie-Maples. "Medicaid coverage for individuals in jail pending disposition." Health Policy Faculty Publications, Paper 1 (2012): 1–18.

Reisen, M. "Jail official called dead inmate a loser." *Albuquerque Journal*, October 9, 2020. https://www.abqjournal.com/1505621/jail-official-called-dead-inmate-a-loser.html.

Reisman, N. "Advocates: Reduce jail population to halt COVID spread." Spectrum News, December 7, 2020. https://spectrumlocalnews.com/nys/central-ny/ny-state -of-politics/2020/12/07/advocates--release-jail-inmates-to-halt-covid-spread.

Rempel, M., & K. Rodriquez. "Bail reform revisited: The impact of New York's amended law." Center for Court Innovation, May 2020, https://www .courtinnovation.org/publications/bail-revisited-NYS.

Rihl, J. "How transparent is Allegheny County Jail compared to other PA jails?" *Public Source*, March 16, 2021. https://www.publicsource.org/allegheny-county-jail -transparency-pa/.

Rihl, J. "Mixed-up meds & long waits: How understaffing hurts medical treatment at Allegheny County Jail." *Public Source*, January 7, 2021. https://www.publicsource .org/allegheny-county-jail-inmate-medical-wait-times-understaffing/.

Riordan, K. "Family of man who died by suicide in Spokane County Jail files wrongful death suit." KREM2, December 30, 2020. https://www.krem.com/article/ news/crime/family-of-man-who-died-by-suicide-in-spokane-jail-files-wrongful -death-suit/293-a91b947e-21b6-430f-9418-df342891b669.

Robbins, S. "Volusia County takes on high jail suicide rate—too late for some." *Daytona Beach News-Journal*, August 25, 2018. https://www.news-journalonline

.com/news/20180825/volusia-county-takes-on-high-jail-suicide-rate---too-late-for
-some.

Robinson, A. "Broady criticized Republican officials' handling of jail deaths." *Cobb
County Courier*, August 29, 2020. https://cobbcountycourier.com/2020/08/broady
-criticizes-jail-deaths/.

Robinson, A. "Justice can't wait: An indictment of Louisiana's pretrial system." ACLU
Louisiana, undated, https://www.laaclu.org/en/justice-cant-wait-indictment
-louisianas-pretrial-system.

Robinson, A. "Lawsuit filed against Shasta County Jail." KRCR, April 30, 2021.
https://www.msn.com/en-us/news/crime/lawsuit-filed-against-shasta-county-jail
-claims-beatings-lead-to-inmates-death/ar-BB1gcBVH.

Rogers, E. "Brevard Sheriff's Office changed restraint chair and spit hood policy after
vet's death." *Florida Today*, November 12, 2020. https://www.floridatoday.com/
story/news/2020/11/12/brevard-sheriffs-office-changed-policies-after-army-vets
-jail-death/6263005002/.

Romero, F. "Five indicted in connection to inmate's death at Midland County
Jail." KMID, August 1, 2020. https://www.yourbasin.com/news/five-indicted-in
-connection-to-inmates-death-at-midland-county-jail/.

Rosenblatt, K. "'We want justice': Complaint seeks trial, $10m in case of Tenn. man
who died in jail." NBC News, June 13, 2020. https://www.nbcnews.com/news/us
-news/we-want-justice-complaint-seeks-trial-10m-case-tenn-man-n1230681.

Ross, K. "Oklahoma's jail mortality rate second in nation." Oklahoma Watch,
February 9, 2021. https://oklahomawatch.org/2021/02/09/oklahomas-jail
-mortality-rate-ranks-second-in-nation/.

Rubin, J. "Ex-L.A. County Sheriff Lee Baca sentenced to three years in prison in jail
corruption scandal." *Los Angeles Times*, May 12, 2017. https://www.latimes.com/
local/lanow/la-me-baca-sentenced-jail-sheriff-corruption-20170512-story.html.

Ruggiero, A. "East Bay cops cleared in death of mentally ill man who died in
custody." *Mercury News*, June 23, 2020. https://www.mercurynews.com/2020/06/
22/da-no-charges-in-death-of-mentally-ill-man-who-died-in-custody-chained-to
-door/.

Ruggiero, A. "Ex-Alameda County deputies avoid jail time for inmate feces-
throwing." *Mercury News*, January 21, 2020. https://www.mercurynews.com/2020/
01/21/ex-alameda-county-deputies-avoid-jail-time-for-inmate-feces-throwing/.

Russo, J., et al. "Caring for those in custody." Rand Corporation, 2017. https://www
.rand.org/pubs/research_reports/RR1967.html.

Sabino, P. "8th detainee dies from Coronavirus as Cook County Jail population swells again." Block Club Chicago, November 18, 2020. https://blockclubchicago .org/2020/11/18/8th-detainee-dies-from-coronavirus-as-cook-county-jail -population-swells-again-causing-concern-another-outbreak-coming/.

Saccente, T. "Charges ruled out in jail death." *Arkansas Democrat Gazette*, November 8, 2020. https://www.arkansasonline.com/news/2020/nov/08/charges-ruled-out-in -jail-death/.

Sawyer, W., & P. Wagner. "Mass incarceration: The whole pie 2020." Prison Policy Initiative, March 24, 2020. https://www.prisonpolicy.org/reports/pie2020.html.

Sawyer, W., A. Jones, & M. Troilo. "Technical violations, immigration detainers, and other bad reasons to keep people in jail." Prison Policy Initiative, March 18, 2020. https://www.prisonpolicy.org/blog/2020/03/18/detainers/.

Schmelzer, E. "Colorado jail deputies failed to check on inmate after he made suicidal comments." *Denver Post*, March 4, 2021. https://www.denverpost .com/2021/03/04/colorado-jail-suicide-jackson-maes/.

Schroeder, L., K. Davis, & J. McDonald. "County sheriff's department questions national standard when counting jail suicide rates." *San Diego Union-Tribune*, September 20, 2019. https://www.sandiegouniontribune.com/news/watchdog/ story/2019-09-19/sheriffs-department-avoids-national-standard-for-calculating -mortality-rates.

Scolforo, L. "Grand jury report: Palmer had five contacts with police prior to prison." *York Dispatch*, March 9, 2021. https://www.yorkdispatch.com/story/ news/crime/2021/03/09/grand-jury-report-palmer-had-five-contacts-police-prior -arrest/4592470001/.

Scolforo, L. "Police: York prison guard accused in drug-smuggling plot still being actively investigated." *York Dispatch*, August 5, 2020. https://www.yorkdispatch .com/story/news/crime/2020/08/05/police-york-prison-guard-accused-drug -smuggling-plot-still-being-actively-investigated/3297790001/.

Shaffer, C. "How Heartless Felons teamed up with Cuyahoga County Jail guards in jailhouse drug smuggling ring." Cleveland.com, November 27, 2020. https:// www.cleveland.com/court-justice/2020/11/how-heartless-felons-teamed-up-with -cuyahoga-county-jail-guards-in-jailhouse-drug-smuggling-ring.html.

Shammas, B. "A Miami-based jail health-care company profits while patients die." *Miami New Times*, September 17, 2019. https://www.miaminewtimes.com/news/ jail-health-care-company-armor-correctional-accused-of-multiple-inmate-deaths -11268351.

Sheets, C. "Alabama's deadliest jail sees nine inmate deaths since 2019." AL.com, December 9, 2020. https://www.al.com/news/2020/12/alabamas-deadliest-jail-sees -nine-inmate-deaths-since-2019.html/.

Shenefelt, M. "Expert witnesses dominate Utah jail death civil court cases, but who pays for them?" *Standard-Examiner*, February 23, 2020. https://www.standard.net/ police-fire/2020/feb/23/expert-witnesses-dominate-utah-jail-death-civil-court -cases-but-who-pays-for-them/.

Shenefelt, M. "Judge won't absolve Davis County in Miller jail death case." *Standard-Examiner*, October 1, 2020. https://www.standard.net/police-fire/2020/oct/01/ judge-wont-absolve-davis-county-in-miller-jail-death-case/.

Shenefelt, M. "Weber County prevails in jail death lawsuit, family weighs appeal." *Standard-Examiner*, June 11, 2020. https://www.standard.net/news/2020/jun/11/ weber-county-prevails-in-jail-death-lawsuit-family-weighs-appeal/.

"Sheriff's office says death of inmate at Bradley County Jail was suicide by hanging." Chattanoogan.com, August 5, 2020. https://www.chattanoogan .com/2020/8/5/413110/Sheriff-s-Office-Says-Death-Of-Inmate.aspx.

Sherman, L. "Public records in death investigations would be limited through legislation passed by North Carolina General Assembly." *News & Observer*, June 27, 2020. https://www.newsobserver.com/news/politics-government/ article243837792.html.

Sholtis, B. "'She's breaking down': Inmates at Bucks County jail decry treatment of suicidal woman with severe mental illness." WHYY, June 15, 2020. https://whyy .org/articles/shes-breaking-down-inmates-at-bucks-county-jail-decry-treatment -of-suicidal-woman-with-severe-mental-illness/.

Shoup, C. "Sheriff seeking help as jail sees another suicide attempt." *Fremont News Messenger*, October 15, 2020. https://www.thenews-messenger.com/ story/news/local/2020/10/15/sheriff-seeking-hire-more-staff-jail-after-suicide -attempt/3662933001/.

Silver, M. "Nearly $7 million settlement paid out in Terrill Thomas dehydration death civil rights case." WUWM, May 28, 2019. https://www.wuwm.com/ news/2019-05-28/nearly-7-million-settlement-paid-out-in-terrill-thomas -dehydration-death-civil-rights-case.

Simerman, J. "$3 million in new payouts as Iberia Parish Sheriff's Office settles more abuse suits." *Acadiana Advocate*, March 2, 2019. https://www.theadvocate.com/ acadiana/news/courts/article_6088cd64-3178-11e9-83dc-7fe2bd11b557.html.

Simon, M. "Toxic Alabama private prison deal falling apart with Barclays exit." *Forbes*, April 21, 2021. https://www.forbes.com/sites/morgansimon/2021/04/21/toxic-alabama-private-prison-deal-falling-apart-with-barclays-exit/?sh=4467879952f0.

Simone, A. "KBI probes inmate death." *Marion County Record*, December 10, 2020. http://www.marionrecord.com/direct/kbi_probes_inmate_death+5212death+4b42 492070726f62657320696e6d617465206465617468.

Simpson, T. "Protestors want ASO to take accountability, for a baby that died as her mom gave birth in jail." WCJB, August 21, 2021. https://www.msn.com/en-us/news/crime/protesters-want-aso-to-take-accountability-for-a-baby-that-died-as-her-mom-gave-birth-in-jail/ar-AANAiFr.

Sison, K. "N.Y.C. to end solitary confinement after trans woman's Riker Island death." NBC News, June 30, 2020. https://news.yahoo.com/n-y-c-end-solitary-165050676.html.

Sissom, T. "Washington County Sheriff's Office says procedures followed in jail hanging incident." *Northwest Arkansas Democrat Gazette*, September 23, 2020. https://www.nwaonline.com/news/2020/sep/23/washington-county-sheriffs-office-says-procedures/.

Six, C. "Sheriff shares what led to the death of a Wright County inmate." KOLR, February 16, 2021. https://www.ozarksfirst.com/local-news/local-news-local-news/sheriff-shares-what-led-to-the-death-of-a-wright-county-inmate/.

Skene, L. "Baton Rouge jail inmate, locked up for failure to appear in court, dies in hospital." *Advocate*, December 8, 2020, https://www.theadvocate.com/baton_rouge/news/crime_police/article_f5f8113c-38cb-11eb-966f-bfbb3d3978c3.html.

Sledge, M. "Louisiana doesn't count people who die behind bars." *Times-Picayune*, March 28, 2021. https://www.nola.com/news/courts/article_ae4490d4-8e4a-11eb-8968-e762f7d9234f.html.

Smith, D. "Inmate found dead in Pima County jail cell." *Tucson Sentinel*, September 6, 2020. https://www.tucsonsentinel.com/local/report/090620_pima_jail_death/inmate-found-dead-pima-county-jail-cell/.

Smith, D. "Man awaiting sentencing dies at Pima County Jail over weekend." *Tucson Sentinel*, June 23, 2020. https://www.tucsonsentinel.com/local/report/062320_jail_death/man-awaiting-sentencing-dies-pima-county-jail-over-weekend/.

Smith, D. "Man found hanging Feb. 9 at Kenosha County Jail has died." *Kenosha News*, February 17, 2021. https://www.kenoshanews.com/news/local/man-found

-hanging-feb-9-at-kenosha-county-jail-has-died/article_42721274-da49-5739
-93c7-773eb180fa49.html.

Smith, G. "Jail deaths in America: Data and key findings of 'Dying Inside.'" Reuters
Investigates, October 18, 2020. https://www.reuters.com/investigates/special
-report/usa-jails-graphic/.

Smith, J. "Justice Department slams Cumberland jail over suicides, orders immediate
corrective steps." *Vineland Daily Journal*, January 15, 2021. https://www
.thedailyjournal.com/story/news/2021/01/15/nj-cumberland-jail-suicides-federal
-civil-rights-violations-opiate-treatment-lawsuit/4175278001/.

Smith, P. "6 key reforms in the massive criminal justice bill Illinois lawmakers
passed last week." WBEZ, January 20, 2021. https://www.wbez.org/stories/6-key
-reforms-in-the-massive-criminal-justice-bill-illinois-lawmakers-passed-last
-week/5f526342-9f19-40e6-8563-d8e0bbfe1138.

Smoot, D. E. "Appeals court affirms dismissal of claim brought by inmate's estate."
Muskogee Phoenix, August 25, 2020. https://www.muskogeephoenix.com/news/
appeals-court-affirms-dismissal-of-claim-brought-by-inmates-estate/article_
aa41cc92-5853-5c5d-ac0e-8934208aaca3.html.

Smoot, D. E. "Officer's testimony sought in lawsuit stemming from inmate's
death." *Muskogee Phoenix*, January 5, 2021. https://www.muskogeephoenix.com/
news/officers-testimony-sought-in-lawsuit-stemming-from-inmates-death/
article_767831c2-c947-5623-a8d7-710f7d788fd0.html.

So, L. "Mississippi state, federal lawmakers seek inquiry after Reuters report of jail
beating death." Reuters, November 2, 2020. https://www.reuters.com/article/us-usa
-jails-mississippi-idUSKBN27I2OP.

So, L. "West Virginia lawmakers push jail reform in response to Reuters data on
inmate deaths." KFGO, December 17, 2020. https://www.reuters.com/article/us
-usa-jails-westvirginia-idUSKBN28R36Z.

Sokol, C. "New program to treat opioid withdrawal could prevent deaths at Spokane
County Jail, officials say." *Spokesman-Review*, September 5, 2018. https://www
.spokesman.com/stories/2018/sep/06/new-program-to-treat-opioid-withdrawal
-could-preve/.

Sokol, C. "Spokane County faces $5.25 million claim over 2018 jail death."
Spokesman-Review, June 19, 2020. https://www.spokesman.com/stories/2020/
jun/18/spokane-county-faces-525-million-claim-over-2018-d/.

Solomon, R. "Justice for Kevil Wingo: Mixed reactions to DA Holme's decision." *Cobb County Courier*, October 7, 2020. https://cobbcountycourier.com/2020/10/justice-kevil-wingo/.

Sosin, K. "New video reveals Layleen Polanco's death at Rikers was preventable." NBC News Now, June 12, 2020. https://www.nbcnews.com/feature/nbc-out/new-video-reveals-layleen-polanco-s-death-rikers-was-preventable-n1230951.

Staff Reports. "Jail inmate died of fentanyl overdose." *Republic*, August 18, 2021. http://www.therepublic.com/2021/08/19/jail_inmate_died_of_fentanyl_overdose/.

Stahl, B. "KARE11 Investigates: Jail death results in $2.3 million payout." KARE11, February 3, 2021. https://www.kare11.com/article/news/investigations/kare-11-investigates-jail-death-results-in-23-million-payout/89-bb7e639c-f669-4e7b-b44d-4255f7051dbd.

Stahl, B. "KARE 11 Investigates: Message from the grave reveals another needless jail death." KARE 11, November 12, 2020. https://www.kare11.com/article/news/investigations/message-from-the-grave-jail-death/89-16b5b10b-8335-4a2a-9581-d53053d01e11.

Stahl, B. "KARE 11 Investigates: Sweeping reforms proposed to protect jail inmates." KARE 11, February 22, 2021. https://www.kare11.com/video/news/investigations/kare-11-investigates-sweeping-reforms-proposed-to-protect-jail-inmates/89-4a14bbac-d53f-43ab-8aa3-8ca169c843f4.

Stahl, B. "KARE 11 Investigates: With his license on the line, doctor at center of jail deaths faces judge." KARE 11, July 12, 2021. https://www.kare11.com/video/news/investigations/kare-11-investigates-with-his-license-on-the-line-doctor-at-center-of-jail-deaths-faces-judge/89-85b61e38-79f2-45f6-b272-38aadbb77f0d.

Stahl, B., A. Lagoe, & S. Eckert. "KARE 11 Investigates: Minnesota jail failures costing taxpayers millions." Kare 11, October 29, 2020. https://www.kare11.com/article/news/investigations/jail-failures-costing-millions/89-519c65ec-0b35-4912-8966-b764e8bd2b5c.

Stahl, B. A. Lagoe, & S. Eckert. "KARE11 Investigates: Mother sues Hennepin County following son's jail death." KARE 11, March 4, 2021. https://www.kare11.com/article/news/investigations/kare-11-investigates-mother-sues-hennepin-co-following-sons-jail-death/89-e6609d63-4122-4a34-893f-031fafe2118b.

Steadman, H., et al. "Prevalence of serious mental illness among jail inmates." *Psychiatric Services* 60, no. 6 (2009): 761–65.

Strickings, T. "Black man is 'gripped by neck with extreme pressure' by white cop." *Daily Mail*, June 19, 2020. https://www.dailymail.co.uk/news/article-8435275/ Black-man-Sterling-Higgins-died-pinned-Tennessee-jail.html.

Strub, C. "Video shows incident before inmate Shaheen Mackey's death." WNEP, August 5, 2020. https://www.wnep.com/article/news/local/luzerne-county/ shaheen-mackey-luzerne-county-prison-video/523-470b3307-4822-4f7c-b0a1 -874e5c963a0e.

Substance Abuse and Mental Health Services Administration. "Detoxification and substance abuse treatment, a treatment improvement protocol tip 45." October 2015. https://store.samhsa.gov/product/TIP-45-Detoxification-and-Substance -Abuse-Treatment/SMA15-4131.

Substance Abuse and Mental Health Services Administration. "Treatment Episode Data Set (TEDS) 2016: Admissions to and discharges from publicly funded substance use treatment." 2018, table 2.9a.

Sundaram, A. "How Texas jails avoid investigations of inmate deaths." *Texas Observer*, October 29, 2020. https://www.texasobserver.org/how-texas-jails-avoid -investigations-of-inmate-deaths/.

Szep, J., N. Parker, L. So, P. Eisler, & G. Smith. "Special Report: U.S. jails are outsourcing medical care-and the death toll is rising." Reuters, October 26, 2020. https://www.reuters.com/article/us-usa-jails-privatization-special-repor -idUSKBN27B1DH.

Tarr, P. "Homelessness and mental illness: A challenge to our society." Brain & Behavior Research Foundation, September 2018. ttps://www.bbrfoundation.org/ blog/homelessness-and-mental-illness-challenge-our-society.

Taxman, F. S., M. Thanner, & D. Weisburd. "Risk, need, and responsivity (RNR)." *Crime & Delinquency* 52, no. 1 (2016): 28–51.

Tchekmedyian, A. "Deputies accused of being in secret societies cost L.A. County taxpayers $55 million." *Los Angeles Times*, August 4, 2020. https://www.latimes .com/california/story/2020-08-04/sheriff-deputy-clique-payouts.

Telvock, D. "Erie County Sheriff's Office addresses state allegations for first time." WIVB, May 6, 2021. https://www.wivb.com/news/investigates/erie-county-sheriffs -office-addresses-state-allegations-for-first-time/.

Thornton, K. "Fired jail supervisor charged with assault." *Tahlequah Daily Press*, October 7, 2020. https://www.tahlequahdailypress.com/news/fired-jail-supervisor -charged-with-assault/article_0fd5e900-1582-5f6f-84ce-e69bcbd84be1.html.

Toberlin, J. "'Don't elect me': Sheriffs and the need for reform in county law enforcement." *Virginia Law Review* 194, no 1 (March 2, 2018). https://papers.ssrn .com/sol3/papers.cfm?abstract_id=3135346.

Tollefson, P. "Judge drops family's lawsuit over 2015 jail suicide due to statute of limitations." *Billings Gazette*, August 19, 2020. https://billingsgazette.com/news/ state-and-regional/crime-and-courts/judge-drops-familys-lawsuit-over-2015 -jail-suicide-due-to-statute-of-limitations/article_9edd0b66-d9dc-5fbe-a835 -58843a2027db.html.

Trafton, S. "New era for sheriff's office." *Hudson Valley 360*, January 1, 2020, https:// www.hudsonvalley360.com/news/greenecounty/new-era-for-sheriff-s-office/ article_58be4b3c-f472-59b1-ab56-7c408045fea3.html.

Trafton, S. "State: Inmate death investigation 'inadequate.'" *Hudson Valley 360*, August 10, 2020. https://www.hudsonvalley360.com/top_story/state-inmate-death -investigation-inadequate-jail-deaths-not-reported/article_cae57d9f-6ed2-5674 -8316-18e42a65c7f7.html.

Treanor, J. "Vegas Lost: Starved to death." KSNV, July 23, 2020. https://news3lv.com/ features/vegas-lost/vegas-lost-starved-to-death-the-story-of-stephen-burrell.

Treisman, R. "Maryland to probe cases handled by ex-medical examiner who testified in Chauvin trial." NPR, April 24, 2021. https://www.npr .org/2021/04/24/990536193/maryland-to-probe-cases-handled-by-ex-medical -examiner-who-testified-in-chauvin-.

Trofatter, C. "Sheriffs say treatment lacking for mentally ill inmates." Capital News Service, March 8, 2021. https://news.jrn.msu.edu/2021/03/sheriffs-say-treatment -lacking-for-mentally-ill-inmates/.

U.S. Department of the Interior, Office of the Inspector General. "Neither safe nor secure, An assessment of Indian Detention Facilities." Report # 2004-I-0056, September 2004. https://www.ojp.gov/ncjrs/virtual-library/abstracts/neither-safe -nor-secure-assessment-indian-detention-facilities.

U.S. Department of Justice. "Positional asphyxia—sudden death." National Law Enforcement Technology Center, June 1995. https://www.ojp.gov/pdffiles/posasph .pdf.

U.S. Department of Justice, Civil Rights Division. "Notice regarding investigation of Alameda County, John George Psychiatric Hospital, and Santa Rita Jail." April 22, 2021.

Vanderveen, C. "PRONE: Facedown and handcuffed is no way to die." 9News, November 9, 2020. https://www.9news.com/article/news/investigations/prone -restraint-police-brutality-cases/73-18ad62df-b66a-45c9-af93-53b15afc5b7c.

Vaughn, J. "In a Louisiana parish, hundreds of cases may be tainted by sheriff's office misconduct." *The Appeal*, November 25, 2019. https://theappeal.org/iberia-parish -brady-letters/.

Vela, S. "Former police sergeant sues Westland, says he was a scapegoat in prisoner death." Hometownlife.com, May 29, 2020. https://www.hometownlife.com/story/ news/local/westland/2020/05/29/police-sergeant-sues-westland-after-prisoner -death-triggers-his-firing/5273233002/.

Veliz, J., & J. Borges. "Bristol County House of Corrections internal review of completed suicides." Professional Psychiatric Services, January 12, 2018.

Vendel, C. "Dauphin County Prison guards start wearing body cameras." *Patriot- News*, January 18, 2021. https://www.pennlive.com/news/2021/01/dauphin-county -prison-guards-start-wearing-body-cameras.html.

Vendel, C. "Family files $35M suit, claims Harrisburg police took overdosing man to jail, not hospital." *Real-Time News*, July 10, 2020. https://www.pennlive.com/ news/2020/07/family-files-35m-suit-claims-harrisburg-police-took-overdosing -man-to-jail-not-hospital.html.

Vendel, C. "Harrisburg police took man who swallowed crack to jail but he 'should have received urgent medical care': mayor." *Real-Time News*, January 17, 2020. https://www.pennlive.com/news/2020/01/harrisburg-police-took-man-who -swallowed-crack-to-jail-but-he-should-have-received-urgent-medical-care-mayor .html.

Verdon. J. "Class action lawsuit filed against Missouri jail for intolerable living conditions." Davis Vanguard, December 29, 2020. https://www.davisvanguard .org/2020/12/class-action-lawsuit-filed-against-missouri-jail-for-intolerable-living -conditions/.

Viglenzoni, C. "Vt. Defender general report outlines alleged racial bias behind inmate death." WCAX, July 22, 2020. https://www.wcax.com/2020/07/22/vt -defender-general-report-outlines-alleged-racial-bias-behind-inmate-death/.

Vlamis, K. "Baltimore will no longer prosecute for drug possession, prostitution, or other low-level crimes after pandemic experiment 'success.'" Yahoo News, March 27, 2021, https://www.yahoo.com/news/baltimore-no-longer-prosecute-drug -024836435.html.

Voytko, L. "Daniel Prude's autopsy reports says 'Excited Delirium,' a controversial diagnosis, contributed to his death." *Forbes*, September 3, 2020. https://www.forbes.com/sites/lisettevoytko/2020/09/03/daniel-prudes-autopsy-report-says-excited-delirium-a-controversial-diagnosis-contributed-to-his-death/?sh=28beaf801784.

Wagner, P., & W. Sawyer. "States of incarceration: The global context 2018." Prison Policy Initiative, June 2018. https://www.prisonpolicy.org/global/appendix_2018.html.

Waldon, E. "Montcalm County Jail inmate cried, 'Help me, Mommy.'" *Daily News*, August 26, 2020. https://www.thedailynews.cc/articles/montcalm-county-jail-inmate-cried-help-me-mommy-help-me-im-sick-before-dying/.

Walker, T. "As LA moves toward closing Men's Central Jail, county supes vote to move toward building a Restorative Justice Village." WitnessLA, January 26, 2021. https://witnessla.com/moving-toward-the-closure-of-mens-central-jail-la-county-supes-to-consider-plan-for-restorative-justice-village/.

Walsh. J. "Judge: Jury can hear lawsuit over Cumberland County Jail suicide." *Courier Post*, December 22, 2020. https://www.courierpostonline.com/story/news/2020/12/22/cumberland-county-jail-suicide-lawsuit-david-conroy/4008867001/.

Walsh, M. "Lawsuit: Inmate died after being held in solitary for drug withdrawal." *Seven Days*, February 20, 2019. https://www.sevendaysvt.com/OffMessage/archives/2019/02/20/lawsuit-inmate-died-after-being-held-in-solitary-for-drug-withdrawal.

Wang, E. A., et al. "Discharge planning and continuity of healthcare: Findings from the San Francisco County jail." *American Journal of Public Health* 98, no. 12 (December 2008): 2182–84.

Ward, P. "Inmates at Allegheny County Jail sue over dangers to their mental health." Trib Total Media, September 15, 2020. https://triblive.com/local/inmates-at-allegheny-county-jail-sue-over-dangers-to-their-mental-health/.

"Washoe jail population down, potential suicides steady." KOLO, July 1, 2020. https://www.kolotv.com/2020/07/02/washoe-jail-population-down-potential-suicides-steady/.

WBSTV.com News Staff. "Gov. Kemp creates commission to look into possible suspension of Clayton County Sheriff Victor Hill." WSBTV, May 19, 2021. https://www.wsbtv.com/news/local/gov-kemp-creates-commission-look-into-possible-suspension-clayton-county-sheriff-victor-hill/2ND3DD7TJRGOJLVBXVDF72KCCQ/.

Webb, R. "Milwaukee County is suing right-wing sheriff David Clarke." *Milwaukee Journal Sentinel*, April 2017.

Weir, M., & J. Pierce. "What's going on with the Santa Cruz County Jail?" *Good Times*, December 8, 2020. https://goodtimes.sc/cover-stories/santa-cruz-county-jail/.

Whitmire, L. "'He's turning blue.' Family demands answers in Richland death after video surfaces." *Mansfield News Journal*, January 10, 2021. https://www.mansfieldnewsjournal.com/story/news/2021/01/10/ohio-richland-county-jail-death-video-alexander-rios-family/4128410001/.

Wilcox, T. "Managing Opiate Withdrawal." Cited in J. Miller. "Deaths at the Salt Lake County Jail." *Salt Lake Tribune*, June 7, 2020. https://www.sltrib.com/news/2020/06/07/deaths-salt-lake-county/.

Wilkie, J. "Proposed legislation would let sheriffs challenge state findings in jail inspections." *Carolina Public Press*, April 16, 2021. https://carolinapublicpress.org/44333/proposed-legislation-would-let-sheriffs-challenge-state-findings-in-jail-investigations/.

Williams, B. "Wrongful death lawsuit involving Roanoke City Jail settled." WFXR, November 9, 2020. https://www.wfxrtv.com/news/local-news/roanoke-valley-news/wrongful-death-lawsuit-involving-roanoke-city-jail-staff-settled/.

Williams, E. "Fourth Circuit rules against Virginia sheriff's deputies in jail death case." Courthouse News Service, March 30, 2021. https://www.courthousenews.com/fourth-circuit-rules-against-virginia-sheriffs-deputies-in-jail-death-case/.

Willmsen, C., & B. Healy. "When inmates die of poor medical care, jails often keep it secret." WBUR, March 23, 2020. https://www.wbur.org/news/2020/03/23/county-jail-deaths-sheriffs-watch.

Wilson, C. "Jefferson County Jail death raises questions of accountability." Oregon Public Broadcasting, December 30, 2019. https://www.opb.org/news/article/jefferson-county-jail-death-questions-accountability-james-whippel-case/.

Wilson, C. "Lawsuit reveals details about Josephine County jail death uncovered in OPB investigation." Oregon Public Broadcasting, May 15, 2020. https://www.opb.org/news/article/josephine-county-jail-lawsuit-death-investigation/.

Wilson, C., T. Schick. A. Jenkins, & S. Brownstone. "Booked and buried: Northwest jails' mounting death toll." April, 1, 2019. https://www.opb.org/news/article/jail-deaths-oregon-washington-data-tracking/.

Wines, J. D., et al. "Suicidal behavior, drug use and depressive symptoms after detoxification: A 2-year prospective study." *Drug and Alcohol Dependence* 76, no. 7 (2004): S21–S29.

WNEP Web Staff. "Council votes against further investigation into inmate death." WNEP, September 8, 2020. https://www.wnep.com/article/news/local/luzerne-county/council-votes-not-to-investigate-inmate-death-any-further/523-062e29db-2ac8-475e-ac32-f3a1a5c4d1b6.

Wolfson, C. "Allegheny County wants to cut its jail capacity, but advocates see deeper problems." Public Source, July 29, 2021, https://www.publicsource.org/allegheny-county-wants-to-cut-its-jail-capacity-but-advocates-see-deeper-problems/.

World Health Organization. "Preventing suicide in jails and prisons." International Association for Suicide Prevention, 2007. https://apps.who.int/iris/handle/10665/43678.

Wright, D. "Inmate families speak about jail concerns." *Gallipolis Daily Tribune*, November 20, 2019. https://www.mydailyregister.com/top-stories/48257/inmate-families-speak-about-jail-concerns-county-answers.

Yeomans. M. "Protestors gather outside Collin County Jail after death of Marvin Scott III." NBC5 Dallas-Fort Worth, March 19, 2021. https://www.msn.com/en-us/news/crime/protestors-gather-outside-collin-county-jail-after-death-of-marvin-scott-iii/ar-BB1eJUSN.

Yost, S. "Sheriff's department responds to protests over 2018 jail death." *Rhino Times*, June 26, 2020. https://www.rhinotimes.com/news/sheriffs-department-responds-to-protests-over-2018-jail-death/.

Zeng, Z. "Jail inmates in 2018." Bureau of Justice Statistics, March 2020, NCJ 253044. https://bjs.ojp.gov/library/publications/jail-inmates-2018.

Zheng, L. "Tarrant County leaders eyeing 'jail diversion' center aimed at providing mental health services." NBC5 Dallas-Fort Worth, May 12, 2021. https://www.nbcdfw.com/news/local/tarrant-county-leaders-eying-jail-diversion-center-aimed-at-providing-mental-health-services-instead/2630990/.

Index

About the Authors

Andrew R. Klein is a senior scientist for criminal justice for Advocates Human Potential, Inc. (AHP). His areas of expertise include substance abuse, criminal justice, domestic violence, court administration, and institutional and community corrections. For the past decade, he has directed training and technical assistance for prison and jail substance use disorder treatment programs throughout the United States and U.S. territories. In this position, he has championed medication-assisted treatment and the use of Medicaid expansion resources for aftercare. Before joining AHP, Klein served as a Massachusetts chief probation officer in an adult and juvenile court, creating the first domestic violence court in the county, as well as model restitution programming. He is the author of *Alternative Sentencing, Intermediate Sanctions, and Probation*; *The Criminal Justice Response to Domestic Violence*; and *Abetting Abusers: What Police, Prosecutors, and Courts Aren't Doing to Protect America's Women*, also from Rowman & Littlefield. Klein obtained a PhD in law, policy, and society from Northeastern University and a BA from Harvard University.

Jessica L. Klein is a rape crisis and domestic violence victim advocate for Beth Israel Hospital, New York, providing advocacy, counseling, safety planning, and service referrals to patients admitted to Emergency Department after experiencing sexual assault or intimate partner violence. She is also a rape crisis counselor on a hotline for the Anti-Violence Project, a New York–based organization that services LGBTQ and HIV-affected people across New York City. She has provided training at the Judicial Domestic Violence Training for Hawaiian Judges, training judges on the basic warning signs/components of intimate partner violence. She is also a contributor for Thomson-West's *National Bulletin on Domestic Violence Prevention.*